MINDFULNESS

Ted Sadler is Adviser to the Athlone Contemporary European Thinkers series on the translations of works by Martin Heidegger.

Also available from Continuum

Heidegger, *Towards the Definition of Philosophy*
Heidegger, *The Essence of Truth*
Heidegger, *The Essence of Human Freedom*

MINDFULNESS

Martin Heidegger

Translated by Parvis Emad and Thomas Kalary

continuum

Continuum International Publishing Group

The Tower Building	80 Maiden Lane
11 York Road	Suite 704
London SE1 7NX	New York, NY 10038

www.continuumbooks.com

This English translation © Continuum 2006

This edition first published 2006
Reprinted 2006, 2008

Originally published as *Besinnug* © Vittorio Klostermann GmbH, Frankfurt am Main, 1997.

British Library Cataloguing-in-Publication Data
A catalogue record for this book is available from the British Library.

ISBN-10: HB 0-8264-8081-0
         PB 0-8264-8082-9
ISBN-13: HB 978-0-8264-8081-1
         PB 978-0-8264-8082-8

Library of Congress Cataloging-in-Publication Data
Heidegger, Martin, 1889–1976.
    [Besinnung. English]
    Mindfulness / Martin Heidegger; translated by Parvis Emad and Thomas Kalary.
        p. cm. – (Athlone contemporary European thinkers)
    ISBN 0–8264–8081–0 (hardcover) – ISBN 0–8264–8082–9 (pbk.)
    1. Ontology. 2. Consciousness. I. Emad, Parvis. II. Kalary, Thomas. III. Title. IV. Series.
    B3279.H48B4713 2006
    193–dc22   2005024745

Typeset by RefineCatch Limited, Bungay, Suffolk
Printed and bound in Great Britain by Biddles Ltd, King's Lynn, Norfolk

Table of Contents

CONTENTS

Translators' Foreword

With the publication of Martin Heidegger's *Mindfulness*, written in 1938/39 right after the completion of *Contributions to Philosophy (From Enowning)*,[1] his second major being-historical treatise becomes available in English for the first time. Published in 1997 as volume 66 of Heidegger's *Gesamtausgabe* under the title *Besinnung*, this work – much like other being-historical treatises that Heidegger wrote between 1936 and 1941 – has a significant thematic proximity to *Contributions to Philosophy*. In *Mindfulness* Heidegger returns to and elaborates in detail many of the individual dimensions – first laid out in *Contributions* – of the historically self-showing and transforming allotments of be-ing. In this work, Heidegger returns to and elaborates further that decisive hermeneutic-phenomenological perspective that experiences, thinks and projects-open the truth of be-ing as enowning. It is under the purview of this perspective that Heidegger's thinking of the 1950s and 60s falls.

In addition to the text entitled *Besinnung*, volume 66 of the *Gesamtausgabe* also includes as an *Appendix* two further important texts. The first one, written in 1937/38, is entitled *"A Retrospective Look at the Pathway"*, and the second one, written in the same period, is entitled "The Wish and the Will (On Preserving What is Attempted)". In this text Heidegger surveys his unpublished works and, in addition to reflecting on his life's path, gives a number of instructions for the publication of these works in the future.

In what follows we shall take a quick look at the text of *Besinnung* and the two appended texts, discuss the dynamics involved in translating the keywords of *Mindfulness*, address the philosophical significance of

Heidegger's hyphenations and the philosophical role that he assigns to the prefixes that emerge from his hyphenations. We shall also discuss how we came to terms with a problem in the text of *Mindfulness* that is created by Heidegger's penchant to quote certain words and phrases from the works of a few historical figures without interpreting the words or phrases that he quotes, and conclude this foreword by addressing the technical aspects of this translation and its relevance to contemporary realities of Heidegger-research.

I. The Texts

The texts that appear in *Mindfulness* have been edited by Friedrich-Wilhelm von Herrmann, who was appointed by Heidegger chief contributing editor of his *Gesamtausgabe*. In his "Epilogue", von Herrmann gives a clear account of the materials that were at his disposal: besides the manuscript, he worked with a typescript of *Besinnung* that Heidegger's brother Fritz had prepared at the request of the philosopher. What we have as the German original of *Mindfulness* is the result of the editorial work, which included frequent collating of Heidegger's manuscript with this typescript, as well as a systematic arrangement of the cross references and footnotes. It is important in this context to note that Heidegger drew von Herrmann's attention to the thematic proximity of *Mindfulness* to *Contributions* as he discussed with the latter the plan for the publication of his *Gesamtausgabe*.[2] It is to this proximity that von Herrmann alludes in his "Epilogue" when he says: "Thus *Mindfulness* is the first of the . . . treatises that, following the *Contributions to Philosophy*, takes up the task of opening up, via questioning the whole domain of being-historical thinking".[3]

This proximity becomes more clear when we take into account Heidegger's characterization of the table of contents of *Mindfulness* as a "Listing of Leaps".[4] By using the word "leap", which is a central keyword of *Contributions* and is the title of its third "Joining", Heidegger directly and unambiguously points to the thematic proximity of the two works, *Contributions to Philosophy* and *Mindfulness*. Furthermore, in a preliminary remark on *Mindfulness*, Heidegger makes clear how he appraised *Mindfulness*, and how he wanted this work to be understood: *not as a system, not as a doctrine, not as a series of aphorisms* but as *"a series of short and long leaps of inquiring into the preparedness for the enowning of be-ing"*.[5] Thus, to fully grasp and appreciate the editorial procedure whose outcome is the existing original German text of *Mindfulness*, we have to bear in mind the three factors mentioned so far: the collating of the manuscript with the typescript, the characterization of the table of contents and Heidegger's own appraisal and understanding of this work. Considering these factors and after a careful examination of the entire edited text of *Besinnung*, we understand why the original German text of *Mindfulness* is edited the way it has been edited: von Herrmann offers the text as it was originally written by Heidegger *without the least* editorial intervention in and adjustment of the original text. This makes clear why the German original of *Mindfulness* is not free from occasional grammatical ambiguities which would have easily been remediable had von Herrmann decided to copy-edit the text in addition to merely editing it.

As mentioned earlier, in addition to the original German text of *Mindfulness* volume 66 of the *Gesamtausgabe* also includes an appendix which presents two highly significant and revealing texts. In the first one of these texts Heidegger thinks over the development of his thought from the PhD dissertation of 1913 to the completion of *Contributions to Philosophy* of 1936–38. In the second text he surveys his unpublished works by dividing them into seven parts, gives a number of instructions concerning their future publication, reflects on his life's path, and addresses his relationship to Christianity. He alerts the reader to the 'historical' and 'genetic' misconstrual and misrepresentation that would ensue if his lecture course texts were confused with and treated like historical surveys, in short if they were to be historicized. He says in this text:

> Whoever *without hesitation* reads and hears the lecture courses only as a 'historical' presentation of some work and whoever then compares and reckons up the interpretation [*Auffassung*] with the already existing views or exploits the interpretation in order to "correct" the existing views, *he has not grasped anything at all.* (*Mindfulness*, 372)

Indeed, a prophetic insight considering what is happening to his work today!

If we take a close look at the last section of *Mindfulness*, numbered 135, and entitled "Steps", we understand why von Herrmann was prompted to include in this volume these two texts. For, with section 135 Heidegger brings *Mindfulness* to a close in that he lists a series of "steps" which include his doctoral and qualifying dissertations, *Sein und Zeit, Vom Wesen des*

Grundes and *Contributions to Philosophy* (the latter referred to with the word "crossing".) And by including these two texts as an appendix in *Mindfulness*, von Herrmann helps the reader not only to grasp section 135 in spite of its brevity but also to realize that the *raison d'être* of the two appended texts is purely philosophical.

In order to see the present translation in its proper light, the reader should keep in mind the following: (a) the point we made concerning the grammatical ambiguities of the original German text of *Mindfulness*; (b) the inner dynamism involved in the keywords of *Besinnung* that calls for the evolvement of an appropriate vocabulary when rendered into English as employed by this translation; and (c) the significance of Heidegger's hyphenations of some of these keywords, and the resulting prefixes. This translation considers its responsibility to account for and deal with each of these dimensions.

II. Keywords of *Besinnung* in Translation, Heidegger's Hyphenations and the Philosophical Significance of the Prefixes

The real challenge before us was to present a translation that remains as close to the original as possible in order to retain and to reflect the integrity of the original German text of *Mindfulness*, without at the same time compromising the English readability. As can be seen from the text of this translation, these two concerns mutually condition and foster each other. Only by grasping this closeness can a reader see this translation in its own rights.

(1) The first factor that shaped this translation of *Besinnung* and played a major role in retaining and reflecting the integrity of the original German text is the thematic proximity of *Mindfulness* to the six "Joinings" of *Contributions to Philosophy*. The being-historical thinking that unfolds in *Contributions* takes the shape of six "Joinings" – not to be confused with "chapters" – that are called "Echo", "Playing-Forth", "Leap", "Grounding", "The Ones to Come", and "The Last God", each of which attempts "to say the same of the same, but in each case from within another essential domain of that which enowning names" (*Contributions*, 57).[6] This "saying of the same in six "Joinings" is what sustains the thematic proximity of *Mindfulness* to *Contributions*, necessitating the reappearance of the latter's keywords in the text of *Mindfulness*. It goes without saying then that this thematic proximity and consequent appearance of the keywords of

Contributions in *Mindfulness* by necessity require that, except for those words that Heidegger introduces for the first time in *Mindfulness* which demand their own translation, the English renditions of the keywords of *Contributions* be retained in translating *Mindfulness*. Only by holding on to those renditions was it possible for the present translation to reflect in *Mindfulness* the active character of be-ing-historical thinking, which in *Contributions* Heidegger explicitly calls mindfulness.[7]

(2) The second factor that shaped this translation of *Mindfulness* is directly related to the grammatical ambiguities of the original German text and to the fact that this text is presented in volume 66 of the *Gesamtausgabe* exactly as Heidegger wrote this text, without the least editorial intervention and adjustment. The grammatical ambiguities of the German original did not prove to be a serious obstacle in retaining and reflecting the integrity of the German original in the text of *Mindfulness*. In order to take these ambiguities into account, we have occasionally inserted into the text a word or two that we have placed in square brackets. These words are directly drawn from the context and, while they facilitate a fuller understanding of the text, they also meet the needs dictated by English readability.

(3) The third factor that contributed to the shaping of *Mindfulness* and that had to be taken into account in this translation in order to retain and reflect the integrity of the German original was the need to address the dialogues that Heidegger carries out with certain historical figures in this volume without indicating which of their works he has in mind, and how he interprets those works. On the one hand, these dialogues are certainly confusing to the English-speaking reader who is not familiar with the works of Heidegger's dialogue partners, and, on the other hand, these dialogues are important components of the original German text of *Mindfulness*. Unless specifically addressed, these dialogues hamper an easy accessibility to certain segments of *Mindfulness*. To remedy this problem and thus to make the text of *Mindfulness* more accessible, we have put together a short list of those words and concepts (see below) which become more graspable once they are read in the light of what Heidegger says about these very same words in other volumes of the *Gesamtausgabe*. Just to give one example: in *Mindfulness* Heidegger often uses the words "organic construction" without indicating that hereby he refers to Ernst Jünger's work *Der Arbeiter*. What Heidegger says in *Mindfulness* about "organic construction" is important for grasping his views on modernity, technicity and calculative thinking. As mentioned in the listing that we

have prepared, "organic construction" becomes more graspable in the light of what Heidegger says about Jünger in volume 90 of the *Gesamtausgabe* entitled *Zur Ernst Jünger*.

(4) The fourth factor that shaped this translation in our attempt to retain and reflect the integrity of the German original is the clear realization on our part that in *Mindfulness* no English rendition of the keywords should aspire to replace and substitute the German original keywords of *Besinnung*. As translators, we abandoned as *unobtainable* the 'ideal' of an absolute transfer of Heidegger's original German words into English.[8] Rather than succumbing to the widespread naïveté that manifests itself in the search for absolute replaceability of the German original keywords of Heidegger's with their translated counterparts, we have aimed at an approximation of these keywords in their original usage by Heidegger in German. In short, the translation of *Mindfulness*, precisely like the translation of *Contributions to Philosophy*, considers unobtainable the 'ideal' of an absolute transfer and absolute replaceability of the original German keywords. Instead of striving for an absolute transfer and absolute replaceability, this translation is guided by the *obtainable* 'ideal' of approximation.

(5) The fifth factor that has shaped this translation in its attempt to retain and reflect the integrity of the original German text is the seriousness with which we have attended to Heidegger's hyphenations, and the resultant prefixes. As in *Contributions to Philosophy*, we recognized that these hyphenations are philosophical means for Heidegger to express certain hermeneutic-phenomenological insights. By hyphenating certain keywords of *Mindfulness*, Heidegger radically *transforms* a number of familiar German words and invests them with *entirely* new meanings.

On account of the importance of this last and fifth factor, we shall first address in what follows the impact on this translation of the hyphenations of two keywords, *Abgrund* and *Ereignis*, and then proceed to deal with our renditions of other keywords of *Mindfulness*.

As indicated earlier, hyphenation is not just a lexicographical device that Heidegger used in order to interrupt the flow of words such as *Ab-grund* and *Er-eignis* but a means for articulating a hermeneutic-phenomenological insight. (One wonders why the hyphenation should be necessary if it fulfills no philosophical function.) The corollary of hyphenating words such as *Ab-grund*, *Er-eignis* and *Er-eignung* (to name only a few) is the saying power that emanates from the prefixes "*Ab-*", and "*Er-*", which endow these prefixes the status of independent words. And the translation of these keywords into English must take this independent status into account and try to reflect it in *Mindfulness* by finding prefixes in English that fulfill the same function and have similar saying power. (The same holds for other equally important prefixes such as "*Ver-*", and "*Ent-*", which will occupy us later.) Let us first take a look at the prefix "*Ab-*".

The first word in which the prefix "*Ab-*" assumes the status of an independent word, is the word *Ab-grund*. This word plays as much a decisive role in *Mindfulness* as it does in *Contributions*. In the original German text of *Contributions* Heidegger drew attention to the hermeneutic-phenomenological significance of the prefix "*Ab-*" for grasping what he means by *Abgrund*, when he hyphenated this word and alternatively italicized the prefix "*Ab-*" and the word "*grund*": "Der *Ab*-grund ist Ab-*grund*".[9] With this hyphenation Heidegger introduced a new word in the syntax of *Mindfulness* (and earlier in the syntax of *Contributions*) which is intended to articulate a ground that prevails while it *stays away* and, strictly speaking, is the hesitating refusal of ground. In other words, the hyphenation of *Abgrund* aims at *a very specific* hermeneutic-phenomenological insight and is thus to be carefully differentiated from a basically ignorable lexicographical device, which perhaps like a hiccup might serve only to interrupt the flow of the word *Abgrund*.

This thematically crucial alternating italicization of the prefix "*Ab-*", and the noun "grund" will lose its real meaning if "*Ab-*", and "grund" are not treated as independent words and translated distinctly. If this hyphenation is merely conceived as a hiccup which interrupts the flow of a word, then one fails to grasp the hermeneutic-phenomenological insight that Heidegger captures by hyphenating the word. Only by blindly over-looking this factor one can proceed to translate *Abgrund* with "abyss" and for good measure to hyphenate this word. But this hyphenation accomplishes nothing. For hyphenation of the "abyss" ends up with "*ab-*", and "*yss*", the latter of which (i.e., "yss") is not a word and is thus totally unfit for accounting for the ground that as *Ab-grund* is a ground that stays away as well as prevails as a hesitating refusal of ground. Even after subjecting the word "abyss" to the lexicographical device of hyphenation, it can still never reach the dimension of what Heidegger has in mind when he hyphenates *Abgrund*. While the word "grund" in *Abgrund* is a perfectly legitimate German word, the letters "yss" which result from the hyphenation of "abyss" do not make up a word in English.

The realization that a hyphenation of "abyss" comes nowhere near what Heidegger captures with his hyphenation of *Ab-grund* should be enough of a deterrent to translate *Abgrund* with "abyss". Understood along these lines the conclusion is inevitable that the German *Abgrund* cannot be translated with a word such as "abyss". As indicated already, *Ab-grund* is the hesitating refusal of ground: it is a ground that prevails while it *stays away*. The dimension of prevailing in staying away is of paramount importance for bringing this word *Abgrund* into English. And renditions of *Ab-grund* with "abyss" or with "non-ground" totally fail to reflect this dimension. Moreover, Heidegger is quite aware of the difference between *Ab-grund* and *Kluft* (i.e., abyss) when he points out in *Mindfulness* that "Question and question recognize each other across the unbridgeable abyss wherein they are suspended . . ." (*Mindfulness*, 321).

Thus, given the necessity of translating the prefix "*Ab-*", there emerges the question as to how to translate the word *Ab-grund*. As earlier in *Contributions*, we opted for translating *Ab-grund* with the word *Ab-ground*. There are several advantages in this choice of word: (a) the English prefix "*ab-*" meaning "away from" has a similar saying power as the German prefix "*Ab-*"; (b) the English word "ground" comes as close as possible to the German "grund" and approximates this word; (c) the word "abground" easily lends itself to hyphenation with the result that, in stark contrast to the contrived "yss" of the "abyss", the word "ground" is a perfectly legitimate English word; (d) considered within the interaction of "ab-", and "ground" the word "ab-ground" reflects the movement of staying-away that is inherent to *Ab-grund* and also reflects the tension that is peculiar to this word – a tension to which Heidegger explicitly alludes when he characterizes the *Ab-grund* as the hesitating refusal of ground; (e) the rendition of *Ab-grund* with *ab-ground* opens the possibility of bringing into English other words that are related to the German "*Grund*", such as "*Ungrund*", ("unground") and "*Urgrund*" ("urground"); and finally (f) the rendition of *Ab-grund* with *ab-ground* and the intact presence of "ground" in this rendition also allow for thinking through the being-historical verb *gründen* which speaks of a ground that is simultaneously urground, abground, and unground.

In the context of dealing with the prefix "*Ab-*", we must also deal with the word *das Abhafte*. In this word the prefix "*Ab-*" assumes such an independence that it allows Heidegger to coin this word as a whole. It goes without saying that unless the prefix "*Ab-*" is treated as an independent word and translated as such, the expression *das Abhafte* cannot be brought into English meaningfully at all. When Heidegger attends to the inter-connection of 'ab-ground', 'clearing' and 'refusal', he speaks explicitly of "*das Abhafte des Grundes*" (G. 312). If we were to overlook the phenomeno-logical-hermeneutic meaning of the prefix "*Ab-*" and translate *Ab-grund* with abyss, then we would totally have to ignore the meaning and sig-nificance of this *Abhafte*. When the German prefix "*Ab-*" is recognized in its independent nature but as related to "*grund*", there emerges a meaningful rendition of "*das Abhafte des Grundes*" as "what in the ground is of the nature of 'ab'" (*Mindfulness*, 277), i.e., in the nature of staying away. It was by taking our bearings from the saying power that is peculiar to *das Abhafte* that we translated *Abgründigkeit* either as "holding unto abground" or as "abground-dimension", depending on the context, and *das Abgründigste* as "most of all holding to ab-ground".

Turning our attention to the prefix "*Er-*", we note that in words such as *erdenken, ersagen, eröffnen, erfragen, erfügen, Eröffnung, Erschweigung, Erwesung, Erzitterung*, to name the most important ones, the prefix "*Er-*" fulfills a variety of functions depending on the infinitive to which this prefix is attached. In the customary German usage, when the prefix "*er-*" is attached to an infinitive, the infinitive enjoys a priority over the prefix. For instance, when "*er-*" is attached to *klingen* (sounding) it forms *erklingen*, which means "resounding". Similarly, when "*er-*" is attached to *tragen* (carrying) it forms *ertragen*, which means "bearing up". Here the prefix either achieves or enhances something or carries forth what is indicated by the infinitive. In being-historical words, on the other hand, the infinitive has not only no such priority over the prefix "*er-*", but is in fact unified with the prefix to form a unique word. In fact, this prefix "determines what goes on in the infinitive and *not the other way around*" (*Contributions*, xxxviii). The prefix "*er-*" in such words as *erdenken, ersagen, ersehen, eröffnen, erbringen* and so forth has such an impact on the infinitives that it indicates a direction that these infinitives have to take. By using these verbs Heidegger shows that as being-historical words they say much more than what the infinitives alone say or imply.

In the context of translating *Mindfulness*, the being-historical word "*er-sagen*" assumes paramount significance, because Heidegger differentiates this "*Sagen*" – this 'saying' – from assertion or *Aussage* when he points out that

this saying does not describe or explain, does not proclaim or teach. This saying does not stand over against what is to be said. Rather, the saying itself *is* the 'to be said', . . . (*Contributions*, 4).

In *er-sagen* the prefix "*er-*" indicates the being-historical dimension of enabling and enowning, which point to the openness to the allotments of be-ing. We translated *er-sagen* with 'en-saying', that is, with a word that retains and reflects the enabling power that is inherent in *er-sagen* and points to the swaying of being as enowning.

Turning now to the problems that pertain to the translation of *Ereignis*, the most crucial being-historical word, we should point out that in bringing this word into English we took our bearings from Heidegger's own stance toward this "guiding word". (He articulates this stance when he points out that *Ereignis* is as untranslatable as the Greek λόγος or the Chinese *Tao*.[10]) First, we considered the possibility of leaving this word untranslated. But we realized that leaving this word untranslated in the text requires an explanation which cannot be given without interpreting *Ereignis*, and such an interpretation *ipso facto* requires translating this word. Besides, leaving *Ereignis* untranslated leads to other problems that concern the family of words closely related to *Ereignis*, such as *Ereignung, Eignung, Zueignung, Übereignung, Eigentum ereignen, zueignen, Übereignen, eignen*. Thus, as earlier in *Contributions*, we translated the word *Ereignis* with enowning – a word "that approximates the richness of the German word *without pretending to replace it*" (*Contributions*, xx).

The English prefix "en-" in enowning adequately takes over the same function as the German prefix "*Er-*" in *Ereignis*. The English prefix "en-", with its varied meanings of "enabling something", "bringing it into a certain condition", and "carrying thoroughly through" unifies into one the threefold meanings of the German prefix "*Er-*", i.e., of achieving, enhancing and carrying forth. Here the first thing to be kept in mind is that the prefix "*Er-*" and the syllable "*eignis*" have independent status that calls for distinct translations of both "*Er-*" and "*eignis*" if the translation is to be hermeneutically truthful to what Heidegger says with the word *Er-eignis*. In *Er-eignis* the prefix "*Er-*" has an active character, which places an unmistakable emphasis on, and highlights the dynamism and the movement that are inherent in the verb "*eignen*" in "*eignis*". Besides, "*eignis*" opens the way to the being-historical word *Eigentum* or ownhood. The English prefix "en-", with its meanings such as "enabling" and "bringing into condition of", provides the possibility of capturing the movement character implied in "*Er-*" of *Ereignis*. When enjoined with "owning" this prefix "en-" puts across a different meaning of owning: an un-possessive owning with no appropriatable content, as differentiated from an owning of something. At the same time, the prefix "en-" preserves the active, dynamic character of *Ereignis*.

The rendition of *Ereignis* with enowning has several advantages: (a) unlike words such as *"event"*, *"appropriation"* and *"event of appropriation"*, the word enowning lends itself readily to hyphenation and thus functions as an approximate rendition of the *"Er-"*, and *"eignis"* of *Er-eignis*; (b) unlike words such as *"event"*, *"appropriation"*, *"event of appropriation"*, and *"befitting"* the word enowning is not tied to any appropriatable, fittable content whose appropriation or fitting would be an 'event'; (c) unlike words such as *"event"*, *"appropriation"*, *"event of appropriation"*, and *"befitting"* the word enowning speaks of an "owning" that has nothing in common with a seizing that seizes without negotiation; (d) unlike words such as *"event"*, *"appropriation"*, *"event of appropriation"* and *"befitting"* that are hard put to reflect the hermeneutic-phenomenological kinship of *Ereignis* to words such as *Ereignung, Eignung, Zueignung* and *Übereignung*, the word enowning readily reflects this kinship and allows for an approximate rendition of the following words: *Ereignung* with *enownment, Eignung* with *owning, Eigentum* with *ownhood, Eigenheit* with *ownness, Zueignung* with *owning-to, Übereignung* with *owning-over-to, Eigentümliche* with *what is of ownhood*.

Having addressed the renditions of the keywords *Abgrund* and *Ereignis*, we now turn our attention to the word *mindfulness* itself, which appears in the title as well as throughout this translation as the English rendition of Heidegger's word *Besinnung*. Right from its onset, be-ing-historical thinking unfolds itself as *Besinnung* and not as reflection since the latter belongs to the domain of a thinking that is not being-historical. Accordingly, it is of paramount importance in translating the word *Besinnung* to hone in on the foundational difference between *reflection* and *Besinnung*. In this context it would serve well to note the intimate hermeneutic-phenomenological connection between *Sinn* and *Besinnung* to which Heidegger pays especial attention both in *Being and Time* and *Contributions to Philosophy*. To obtain a rendition of the word *Besinnung* that approximates in English to what Heidegger regards as the very unfolding of being-historical thinking, we have to bear in mind that *Besinnung* is nothing but an inquiry into the self-disclosure of being — self-disclosure that in *Being and Time* Heidegger calls the meaning or *'der Sinn'* of being and that in *Contributions to Philosophy* he calls the truth of being. What is of utmost significance here is that philosophy as *Besinnung* unfolds this inquiry. This inquiry is not merely a human enterprise of reflecting on the data of consciousness, on the peculiarities of perception or on the states of mind.

It differs from reflection in that, as *Besinnung*, this inquiry is not entirely and exhaustively in human discretion. What distinguishes this inquiry as *Besinnung* is that it is basically determined and shaped by the truth of being. Thus there is an intimate interconnection between this inquiry, as *Besinnung*, and being. As *Besinnung*, this inquiry is already enowned by being. As enowned, it stands at the service of being by projecting-opening being's enowning sway or being's conferments, its 'enowning throw'. Thus, what distinguishes this inquiry is that it is *mindful* of – does not, via reflection, lay siege on being's conferments — its 'enowning throw'. This 'being mindful of being's enowning throw' cannot even be classified as a particular kind of reflection, or even as a mode of conscious awareness. Two factors are important here: on the one hand there is "the inexhaustibility of being's enowning-throw" and on the other hand "the inconclusiveness of its projecting-opening".[11] As a result, 'being mindful of being's enowning-throw' is not an *addendum* to this inquiry but "originates from within the inexhaustibility of being's enowning-throw . . .".[12]

One way of grasping the distinction that Heidegger draws between *Besinnung* and reflection is to consider their bearings upon the issue called 'self.' Reflection on the 'self', which sustains all psychology and psychiatry, attends to the empirical states of the 'self' in order to render these states accessible to objectification. By contrast, in *Besinnung* on the 'self' these states are bracketed out and what is at stake is the grounding of the 'self' via 'temporality', 'linguisticality', 'historicality', 'mortality', and so forth. Heidegger alludes to the distinction between *Besinnung* on the 'self', as its grounding, and reflection on the 'self' by first questioning whether the 'self' is accessible to reflection at all and then by alluding to the necessity of grounding the 'self'. He says:

> [*Besinnung*] is . . . so originary that it above all asks how the *self* is to be grounded . . . Thus it is questionable whether through *reflection* on 'ourselves' we ever find our *self* . . . (*Contributions*, xxxii)

Here we see that while Heidegger endorses a grounding of the 'self' via mindfulness of the 'self' he questions the very possibility of accessibility of the 'self' to reflection.

In order to obtain in English an approximate rendition of the word *Besinnung*, we took our bearing from the distinction that Heidegger draws between reflection on the 'self', and being mindful of the 'self', and rendered the word *Besinnung* with *mindfulness*. The unique advantage of this rendition consists in the fact that the word mindfulness has a pliability that is denied to reflection — a pliability that does not let mindfulness become rigid and unyielding and end up in doctrines, systems, and so forth. In section 11 of *Mindfulness*, which comes right after the "Introduction", Heidegger brings to mind this pliability of mindfulness when he says:

> Coming from the overcoming of "metaphysics", mindfulness must nevertheless touch upon the hitherto and cannot become inflexible as the finished product of a usable presentation either in a "doctrine" or in a "system", or as "exhortation" or "edification". (*Mindfulness*, 17)

The next keyword of *Mindfulness* to be addressed in this foreword is the word *Auseinandersetzung* that appears sometimes hyphenated as *Auseinander-setzung*. Assuming a broader and more fundamental role in *Mindfulness* than it did in *Contributions*, this word requires special attention in order to be brought into English and approximate a keyword of *Mindfulness*. A careful reading of part III of *Mindfulness*, and the sections in which Heidegger brings his being-historical inquiry to bear upon Parmenides, Heraclitus, Plato, Aristotle, Hegel and Nietzsche, soon convinced us that in *Mindfulness* the word *Auseinandersetzung* can no longer be taken exclusively to mean 'debate', 'confrontation' and 'coming to terms with'. Taking our bearings from the components of this word, namely *"Auseinander"* — apart, dissociated — and *"setzung"* — setting, positioning — we decided to bring this word into English with the expression "dissociating exposition".

This decision is based on a precise grasping of what transpires hermeneutically-phenomenologically when Heidegger places and positions side by side the metaphysical question of being and the being-historical question of being in order to dissociate the metaphysical and being-historical *responses* to these questions. It is his insight that the metaphysical response to the metaphysical question of being (i.e., determination of the beingness of beings the general, κοινόν) relates in a subtle way to the being-historical response (i.e., the non-metaphysical determination of be-ing as enowning). In *Mindfulness* Heidegger takes great pain to highlight this relatedness by distinguishing his dissociating exposition of the metaphysical responses (such as those given in terms of ἰδέα, ἐντελέχεια, *ego cogito, monas*, reason, absolute idea and will to power) from *rejection* and *refutation* of the metaphysical doctrines within which these responses are housed. Central to a dissociating exposition of these responses is the fundamental difference between the being-historical insight into a given metaphysical position and that position itself. Based on such a difference, a dissociating exposition of any one of these responses is never the same as *rejection* or *refutation* of a metaphysical doctrine. Often functioning as the hidden motivating forces behind historical discussions in philosophy, rejection and refutation never accomplish what the dissociating exposition of a given metaphysical response or a metaphysical doctrine accomplishes, namely the overcoming of the metaphysical responses to the question of being by the being-historical response to this question.

The next word to be discussed in this foreword is *Vermenschung*, which is Heidegger's counter-concept of *animal rationale*. He uses this word for the first time in *Mindfulness* and gives it an unparalleled importance in those sections of this work in which he addresses the themes of modernity and gods. *Vermenschung* is derived from the verb *vermenschen*, which has meanings such as 'to humanize', 'to become human' and 'to assume human shape'.[13] In these meanings *vermenschen* is the exact opposite of *entmenschen*, that is, 'to dehumanize'. However, as used in *Mindfulness* the words *vermenschen* and *Vermenschung* have none of these meanings. How to bring this word *Vermenschung* as a keyword of *Mindfulness* into English?

Considering the context of the sections in *Mindfulness* in which Heidegger addresses the themes of modernity and gods, and taking our bearings from the prefix "*Ver-*" in the word *Vermenschung*, we rendered this word with 'dis-humanization'. This rendition is based on the realization that the contexts of the discussions devoted to the themes of modernity and gods free the word *Vermenschung*, not only from the usual connotations of 'humanization', 'assuming human shape', and 'becoming human' but also from what is exactly the opposite of *Vermenschung*, that is, *Entmenschung*, or dehumanization. Those contexts in conjunction with the saying power that emanates from the German prefix "*Ver-*" accomplished for us this realization. Whereas in ordinary usage of the word *Vermenschung* this prefix "*Ver-*" is so mute as to be almost un-hearable (how else could this word mean humanization?), in Heidegger's usage of *Vermenschung* in *Mindfulness* it is precisely the silent ringing of this prefix that qualifies the word *Vermenschung* to become a being-historical word. We found that in bringing *Vermenschung* into English, we have to take our bearings from the prefix "*Ver-*". Now, since the English counterpart of the German prefix "*Ver-*" is the prefix "dis-", and insofar as hyphenation of "*Ver-menschung*" does not eliminate the sense of 'humanization', we arrived at the approximate rendition of the being-historical keyword *Vermenschung* with 'dis-humanization'.

Closely related to *Vermenschung* and central to grasping the treatment of the themes of 'godding', 'godhood' and the 'last god' is the word *Vergötterung*. In the context of the being-historical treatment of 'godding', *Vergötterung* alludes to the 'dis-enowning' process that is inherent in 'godding' – a process that in conjunction with 'dis-humanization' sustains the flight of gods. We found a good approximate rendition of *Vergötterung* in the English word divinization, which we use in the strict technical sense of raising a being — nature, man, a historical figure — to divinity. Although this word divinization does not clearly reflect the thrust of the German prefix "*Ver-*" that is in play in *Vergötterung*, given the strict technical sense in which divinization is used here it fits the above mentioned 'dis-enowning' process.

Next to be addressed here are two keywords of *Mindfulness*, namely *Machbarkeit* and *Machsamkeit*. These keywords are of central importance for grasping those sections in *Mindfulness* that attend to the themes of 'machination' in conjunction with technicity — a theme that Heidegger already introduced and dealt with in *Contributions* (see *Contributions*, 88). The two keywords *Machbarkeit* and *Machsamkeit* have a proximity to each other that makes their rendition into English rather difficult. Heidegger alludes to this proximity and tries to elucidate it by using a parallelism no less difficult to bring into English. Right at the outset of section 9 of *Mindfulness* he writes:

> Machination here means the makability of beings which produces as well as makes up everything, such that only in this makability the beingness of beings that are abandoned by be-ing (and by the grounding of its truth) determines itself. (Here makable is thought as "watchable" = *watchful*. And hence makability is thought in the sense of *producibility*). *Machination* means the accordance of everything with producibility, indeed in such a way that the unceasing, unconditioned reckoning of everything is pre directed. (*Mindfulness*, 12)

Alluding to the 'makable' and using 'watchable' as a parallel, he suggests that 'makable' be thought of as 'producible'. This opens the way for an additional determination of machination – additional insofar as machination is still fundamentally a manner of the swaying of being – but now machination means also the accordance of everything with 'producibility'. In this connection the reader should bear in mind that both words, *'makability'* and *'producibility'*, refer to that clearing which, as machination, houses the making and producing that are hallmarks of instrumentally anthropologically conceived technology that should be carefully distinguished from what Heidegger calls technicity. Accordingly, 'makability' and 'producibility' as used in this translation are not to be confused with descriptive terms that pertain to the technological, instrumental 'making', and 'producing'.

The next keyword of *Mindfulness* to be addressed in this foreword is *Inständigkeit*. We translate this word with *inabiding*. This rendition has the following advantages: (a) the component "in" in "inabiding" is a good approximation of the German prefix *"In-"* in *Inständigkeit*; (b) the component "abiding" is a good approximation of the German *"-ständigkeit"*; and (c) *"inabiding"* as a rendition of *Inständigkeit* reflects Heidegger's intention to rethink the earlier concept of *Existenz* within the being-historical horizon. The corollary of rethinking *Existenz* being-historically is the differentiation of this concept not only from Karl Jaspers' existential philosophy but from existentialism in general.

The often attempted rendering of *Inständigkeit* with "insistence" is not only inappropriate, it is also totally wrong, for "insistence" does not at all reflect the hermeneutic-phenomenological insight into man's relationship to the truth of being which is what *Inständigkeit* is all about. What distinguishes this relationship is man's inabiding the truth of being. Even if we consider the word "insistence" etymologically, the "standing" to which this word refers is not the same as inabiding the truth of being, since that "standing" means insisting on an already adopted position or a preferred opinion. But the truth of being is neither a position nor an opinion. To see how misleading the rendition of *Inständigkeit* with "insistence" is, all we need to do is to grasp that the "standing in" of which *Inständigkeit* speaks is a "standing in" the clearing of being's enowning "forth-throw" and in the latter's projecting-opening. It is the sway of being as an enowning "forth-throw" that lets man as Dasein "abide in" the truth of being in the manner of an enowned projecting-opening.

The next word to be addressed here is *be-ing* as a rendition of *Seyn*. In translating this word we took our bearings from the distinction that Heidegger draws in sections 98 and 97 of *Mindfulness* between the metaphysical question of being and the being-historical question of be-ing. The former question asks "What are beings?" and the latter "How does be-ing sway?" The metaphysical question of being winds up with grasping being as the beingness of beings while the being-historical question of being realizes that it is enowned by be-ing and as enowned it thinks be-ing as enowning. It is important to realize that parallel to the differentiation between the metaphysical question of being and the being-historical question of be-ing is the differentiation between being (*Sein*) and be-ing (*Seyn*). It is also important to realize that the differentiation between be-ing (*Seyn*) and being (*Sein*) is already at work in the differentiation between the metaphysical and being-historical questions of being.

Heidegger uses the word *Seyn* in its eighteenth-century orthography as what historically enowns thinking, and so initiates a thinking that is no longer metaphysical but is being-historical. Insofar as being-historical thinking of being does not oppose but complement the metaphysical thinking of being, Heidegger's differentiation between be-ing and being should not be mistaken as a setting up of an opposition between the two. In other words, differentiation between being (*Sein*) and be-ing (*Seyn*) is just that: a differentiation and not an opposition. Any English rendition that on the basis of the orthography of *Seyn* is oriented to, or establishes an opposition between *Sein* and *Seyn* (like the rendition "being" and "beon") pushes "too far a simple orthographic device" (*Contributions*, xxii). What speaks further against a rendition that suggests an opposition between *Sein* and *Seyn* is the fact that these German words, like their English counterparts being and be-ing, are pronounced exactly the same way, whereas the alternative rendition with "beon" uses a word that is not pronounced the same way as "being".

However, it should be pointed out that in spite of the philosophical importance of the differentiation between *Sein* and *Seyn*, Heidegger has not been consistent throughout *Mindfulness* in maintaining the different spellings of *Sein* and *Seyn*: sometimes he writes *Sein* but means *Seyn* and sometimes he writes *Seyn* and means *Sein*. However, the clue for grasping what he means in each case lies in the differentiation between the metaphysical and being-historical question of being that Heidegger elaborates upon in sections 98 and 99 of *Mindfulness*.

The next word to be addressed is *Geschichte*, as differentiated from *Historie*. As the scientific-erudite recording and analysis of, and the debate about, past events, *Historie* has no inkling of a past that still is in sway and is 'on-coming'. *Geschichte*, on the other hand, is nothing but the gatheredness of that still swaying 'on-coming' past. What drives *Historie* forth is the finality and irretrievability of the past events with which

Historie is preoccupied. What distinguishes *Geschichte* is the suddenness and the coming to presence of that past that, strictly speaking, has not passed away since it is still in sway and 'on-coming'. To allude to *Geschichte* with the brevity that is required in this foreword, we should mention Heidegger's accounts of the temple of Athena in the two trips he made to Greece in 1962 and 1967. In stark contrast to an erudite historical-archeological account of that temple, Heidegger's account is *geschichtlich*.[14] He bespeaks of the suddenness and the coming to presence of a past-ness of which the erudite historical archeology has no inkling; that is, of the pastness that *is* the temple of Athena wherein the goddess is gathered and comes to presence in the midst of the technological hubbub and technologically organized and maintained tourism of the twentieth century.

For us as translators the question became one of how to bring *Historie* and *Geschichte* into English. Given the fact that English has no word that would approximate *Geschichte*, we decided to use the same word history for both *Historie* and *Geschichte* but place this word between inverted comas – single quotation marks – when it stands for *Historie*. Here again it should be borne in mind that in *very* few cases Heidegger does not main-tain the difference between *Historie* and *Geschichte*. However, the context usually helps to understand those isolated cases in which he uses the word *Geschichte* when what he actually has in mind is *Historie*.

The next word to be addressed here is the word *Untergang*, usually translated as decline, downfall and going under. First used in *Contributions* in the verbal form of *untergehen* (see *Contributions*, 6), *Untergang* plays a significant role in *Mindfulness*, especially in those passages in which Heidegger directly speaks of be-ing as ab-ground. The word *Untergang* assumed philosophical prominence in Nietzsche's *Thus Spoke Zarathustra* where he proclaimed the necessity for man to 'go under' so that the 'overman' may arise. Thereafter, this word *Untergang* was taken over by such diverse but related thinkers as Oswald Spengler and Ernst Jünger. But as Heidegger's extended discussion of φύσις in *Mindfulness* as well as elsewhere in his writings (such as his lecture course texts on Heraclitus) shows, he understands *Untergang* in the context of *Aufgang* or "rising". Thus, in his parlance, words such as *untergehen*, and *Untergang* do not have the connotations of decline and degeneration that they have, for example, in Spengler's *Untergang des Abendlandes*, which is translated into English under the title *The Decline of the West*. We rendered *Untergang* with 'going under' and in order to allude to the technical nature of this word — that is, to its close connection to φύσις and 'rising' — we placed it throughout *Mindfulness* between inverted comas: 'going under'.

The next two keywords to be addressed in this foreword are *Wesen* and *Wesung*. In translating these being-historical words we took our bearings from the differentiation in sections 98 and 99 of *Mindfulness* between the metaphysical and being-historical question of being and the concomitant differentiation between metaphysical and being-historical thinking. We realized that if the English rendition of these words did not respect these differentiations, it would fail to retain and reflect the integrity of the original German of *Mindfulness*. If we were to name the center toward which that integrity gravitates, we would have to say that what concerns Heidegger's non-metaphysical thinking above all is to articulate what is *fundamentally denied* to metaphysical thinking. And he reaches the single most important locus of this fundamental denial with the word *Wesen*, respectively *Wesung*.

Accordingly, we realized that translating *Wesen* and *Wesung* must take its bearings from this fundamental denial instead of taking the easy way and accepting the dictionary as the ultimate authority. Having considered every statement that Heidegger has made on *essentia* (from the early pages of *Sein und Zeit* to the texts of his Nietzsche lectures and beyond), we found that *Wesen* and *Wesung* cannot be brought into English with the cognates of *essentia* because the latter is a word that blocks the hermeneutic-phenomenological viewing of what is fundamentally denied to metaphysical thinking. Having also taken into account Heidegger's own repeated stricture that *Wesen* in his texts is used in the verbal sense of 'swaying', 'enduring', 'abiding', 'whiling', and so forth we found that this word should be brought into English with a word that in approximating to the original German reflects its verbal character. In short, in translating *Wesen* and *Wesung* we found ourselves committed to three criteria: (a) the word in question must not be a cognate of *essentia*; (b) it should have a verbal meaning; and (c) it should be an approximation and not aspire unrealistically to replace the original German word. These criteria guided us not only in our efforts to translate *Wesen* and *Wesung* but also in facing the task of rendering into English crucial phrases such as *Wesen des Seins* and *Wesung des Seyns*.

In the English words "sway" and "swaying" we found a good approximation to *Wesen* and *Wesung*. Translating *Wesen* and *Wesung* with "sway", and "swaying" has several advantages: (a) these words are not cognates of *essentia* and thus do not block the hermeneutic-phenomenological viewing of what is fundamentally denied to metaphysical thinking; (b) untouched by that denial these words cannot assume the universality of a concept to which being or be-ing could be subsumed – *essentia* and its cognates are such universal concepts; (c) the words "sway" and "swaying" have a distinct verbal meaning that indicates dynamism and movement, both of which are denied to *essentia* and its cognates; (d) by being removed from the domain of *essentia*, these words stand at the service of the thinking that unfolds in the 'other beginning', and Heidegger calls being-historical thinking; (e) in stark contrast to *essentia* and its cognates, which are shaped by the power and the preeminence that thinking already assumes in the first Greek beginning vis-à-vis φύσις, the words "sway" and "swaying" *do not in the least* reflect that power and preeminence; and (f) in stark contrast to *essentia* and its cognates, the words "sway" and "swaying" fit into the futural task which consists not only of 'saying' ἀλήθεια (as the first Greek beginning did) but also of thinking ἀλήθεια.

However, in translating *Wesen* in relation to man, we took our bearings from Heidegger's own remarks about this word to the effect that *Wesen* also means what is ownmost to something.[15] Accordingly, we translated the phrase "*das Wesen des Menschen*" with "what is ownmost to man", or sometimes with "man's ownmost". Here again we should point out that in *Mindfulness* Heidegger is not consistent in his use of the words *Wesen* and *Wesung*, but the context often makes clear the specific sense that he has in mind in using these words.

The next keyword, "saying", is a rendition of both "*Sagen*" and "*Spruch*". Placed between single quotation marks 'saying' brings into English Heidegger's word "*Spruch*". Placed between double quotation marks, it is our rendition of the original German "*Sagen*".

Finally, we conclude this discussion of the keywords of *Mindfulness* with a brief remark on the differentiation between *Beständigung* and *Beständigkeit*. In most cases we translated the former with "making presencing constant", and the latter with "constancy of presencing". But there are exceptions. In some cases we translate *Beständigung* simply with "constancy", and *Beständigkeit* with "constantness".

III. Two Phrases of *Besinnung* in Translation

In the very first sentence of the prose section of the "Introduction" to *Mindfulness* there is a phrase that places special demands on translation and reads: *"eines einzigen im Seienden"*. This usage of the word *"das Seiende"* poses some problems for an accurate rendition in English. Because of this underlying difficulty, the rendition of *"eines einzigen im Seienden"* as *"that which is sole and unique in beings"* is unavoidable but precarious. If philosophical precision were to be the only criterion, then *"das Seiende"* has to be uniformly translated as *"a being"*, and consequently the phrase *"eines einzigen im Seienden"* as *"that which is sole and unique in *a being*"*. But what Heidegger wants to say with this phrase has nothing to do with a single being as such, nor with a chain of beings, nor with their inherent hierarchy. With this in mind, we have rendered *"das Seiende"* with the plural form "beings", except for those contexts where the reference is specifically to the singular (in which case we have opted for "a being"). We did this in the interest of articulating what Heidegger has in mind as well as to enhance readability.

In order to grasp the justification of translating *"das Seiende"* in the plural, we need to bear in mind (a) that what Heidegger calls *das Einzige* is *Seyn* (be-ing), which is identical neither with a being nor with beings, nor does it reside (come to pass) beyond a being or beings; (b) hence his use of the preposition *"im"* in *"eines einzigen im* Seienden". This preposition plays a significant role at crucial junctures of Heidegger's thought, for instance when he speaks of *"in*-der-Welt-sein", ("being-*in*-the world") or when he uses the phrase "das Seiende *im* Ganzen" in order to allude to the situatedness of beings *within* a whole. Considering (a) and (b), our translation of the phrase *"eines einzigen im Seienden"* with *"that which is sole and unique in beings"* should not be misconstrued as implying that be-ing is a singular and unique being, or is something that mysteriously prevails amongst beings, or is something hidden deep within beings. The uniqueness (*Einzigkeit*) of be-ing comes from the incomparability of be-ing with *a being* or with *beings*, since both *a being* as well as *beings* owe their beingness to be-ing. It is to reflect this incomparability of be-ing that we say for *"eines einzigen im Seienden"* *"that which is sole and unique in beings"*.

The other phrase that plays a significant role throughout *Mindfulness* and must be brought into English with a great deal of care, is the phrase *"das Seiende im Ganzen"*. With one single exception (see below), this phrase has not so far received an appropriate rendition in the English translations of Heidegger's works. Indeed, the prevailing rendition of this phase with "beings as a whole" is so misleading that it blocks an adequate understanding of Heidegger's thought in general. Considering Heidegger's hermeneutic-phenomenological finding that beings are always already situated within a whole (see his "being-in the world" as a case in point), the phrase *"das Seiende im Ganzen"* should be brought into English with "beings *in* a whole" and *not* with "beings *as* a whole". Accordingly, we translated this phrase with "beings in a whole" and in order to point to the technical nature of this phrase we placed it between inverted commas.

The first and the last translator who correctly grasped the significance of the preposition *"im"* in the phrase *"das Seiende im Ganzen"* was William J. Richardson, who in his *Heidegger Through Phenomenology to Thought* accounted for this *"im"* by translating the phrase *"das Seiende im Ganzen"* with "beings-in-the-ensemble".[16] The advantage that Richardson's rendition has over the prevailing rendition, namely "beings as a whole", is the fact that he clearly sees that at stake in this phrase is the situatedness of beings – *any* being, be it a tool, a human being or a god – within a whole. It is with the phrase "being-in-the world", that Heidegger for the first time makes a decisive allusion to this situatedness. Being aware of the fact that this situatedness is what counts, Richardson rendered the German preposition *"im"* with the English preposition "in" and brought *"das Seiende im Ganzen"* into English with "beings-in-the ensemble". Even though Richardson's choice of "ensemble" for *"Ganzes"* is a poor choice because ensemble implies a human contrivance of putting something together and assembling it, his choice of *"in"* as a rendition of Heidegger's *"im"* is an excellent choice since it precisely reflects the hermeneutic-phenomenological insight into the situatedness of beings within a pre-given whole. Is it perhaps the epistemology of analytic philosophy that hinders other translators of Heidegger from "seeing" the situatedness of beings within a whole and blinds them to the insight that there are no beings in isolation from a whole? How else is one to understand and assess the mistranslation of the *"im"* – how else is one to grasp the fact that "beings as a whole" translates *"das Seiende als Ganzes"* and not Heidegger's *"das Seiende im Ganzen"* – other than look in the direction of that epistemology?

IV. Unnamed Sources in *Mindfulness*

In *Mindfulness* every detail counts, particularly those that concern the dialogue that Heidegger carries out with a number of named or unnamed historical figures. Often a proper grasping of what Heidegger says – about modernity for example – depends on knowing how certain words or phrases are to be understood in relation to the historical figures to which those words and phrases refer. A case in point is the phrase "organic construction" that first appears near the end of section 10, and then in other sections of *Mindfulness* such as section 64. Near the end of section 10 Heidegger points out that Ernst Jünger

> thinks planetarily (not economically, not societally, not "politically") the gestalt of the "worker" in whom the modern humanity becomes a permanent member of the "organic construction" of "beings in the whole". (*Mindfulness*, 21)

The reader unfamiliar with Ernst Jünger's *Der Arbeiter* [The Worker] will probably be in a better position to understand why Heidegger can say that Jünger thinks the "worker" planetarily as the gestalt in whom modern humanity becomes a permanent member of the "organic construction" of "beings in a whole" if the reader takes into account what Heidegger says about "organic construction" in volume 90 of his *Gesamtausgabe* entitled *Zur Ernst Jünger*.

As a response to such a need, in what follows we list the number of the volumes of the *Gesamtausgabe* in which the reader may find a more elaborate treatment of certain words, concepts and phrase that appear in *Mindfulness*. This list does not claim to be complete; it is offered here only as a help in need.

For "organic", "organic construction", "heroism", "heroic realism": GA 90.
For "life", "all life", "chaos", "values", "becoming": GA 43, GA 44, GA 46, GA 47, GA 48, GA 50, and GA 87.
For "real ontology", "realistic ontology", "critical ontology": GA 2.
For "encompassing": GA 9, GA 65.
For "sacrifice": GA 65.
For "the new awakening": GA 16.
For "love of wisdom": GA 9.

Moreover, a few passages in *Mindfulness* become more graspable in the light of the fact that in those passages Heidegger has some of his contemporaries and their works in mind, although none is mentioned explicitly in *Mindfulness*. A case in point is what Heidegger says in the following passage:

> The subsequent scholarly exploitation of this Nietzschean thought that originates in Nietzsche's reversal of Platonism, for the purpose of playing certain "categorial" games with the "layers of being" and the like is meaningless and can never render the deciding question discernible. (*Mindfulness*, 167)

Unless the reader is aware of the fact that words and phrases such as "categorial" and "layers of being" refer to Nicolai Hartmann's *Aufbau der realen Welt*, the reader will be hard put to fully grasp this passage. In similar vein, only when the reader knows that Nicolai Hartmann in his *Zur Grundlegung der Ontologie* refers to the question of being and criticizes this question, will the reader understand the passage in which Heidegger alludes to those who ascribe to this question their own preconceived ideas. The passage in question is the following:

> Therefore, it is only an illusion when out of "one's" heedless opinion "one" ascribes "one's" own meaning to the phrase, the "question of being". (*Mindfulness*, 301)

Furthermore, the phrase "enlargement of the stock of categories" would probably be incomprehensible to the reader unless in reading the following passage he bears in mind that it was Nicolai Hartmann who, with his *Metaphysik der Erkenntnis*, fostered a metaphysical critique of "understanding of being" which ended up with rejecting this "understanding" on the ground that it does not contribute to the "enlargement of the stock of categories". The passage in question reads:

> Thus addressing the "*understanding* of being" would mean returning to the "anthropological" and so to the one-sidedly grasped conditions for the enactment of thinking – roughly put, would amount to a "psychology" of metaphysics and so would prove to be anything but a contribution to the enlargement of the stock of categories." (*Mindfulness*, 187)

V. Technical Aspects of the Translation

(1) Layout

In each of its pages this translation reproduces the layout of the original German. All paragraphs, all indentations and spacings are exactly the same as they appear in the original German text. It should be noted that the layout of the original German text had to be retained because the diction of the original text requires this layout.

(2) Double Quotation Marks and Single Quotation Marks:

Except when placed around "saying", double quotation marks in this translation are Heidegger's own. All single quotation marks – the so-called inverted commas – are translators'. Thus we place between single quotation marks words and phases that because of their technical nature need to be singled out. Just to give a few examples we should mention 'in-between', 't/here', 'history', 'historical' (as differentiated from *Geschichte*, see above), 'the ones to come', 'beings in a whole', 'going under', 'un-ownmost'.

(3) Italics

With a few exceptions all italics are Heidegger's. However, being part of the translation process, we have on occasion used a few italics of our own.

(4) Parentheses and Square Brackets

All parentheses are Heidegger's, while all square brackets are translators'. To avoid confusing translators' additions to the text with editor's foot-notes (which in the original German text are also placed between square brackets) editor's footnotes are placed between braces { }. In this foreword as well as throughout *Mindfulness* the abbreviation G followed by a page number and placed within a square bracket indicates the pagination of the original German text.

(5) Footnotes

All footnotes and cross-references in this translation are identical to those in the original German text. There are no translators' footnotes.

(6) Works Cited

Except for *Contributions to Philosophy (From Enowning)*, the titles of all Heidegger's works are given as they appear in the original German text of *Mindfulness*. The thematic proximity of *Mindfulness* to *Contributions* and the necessity of retaining the keywords of the latter in the text of the former required that we use the title *Contributions to Philosophy (From Enowning)* in the footnotes. However, including bibliographical information of the existing English translations in the footnotes proved to be impractical for two reasons. First, to include such information meant acting as if Heidegger refers to these translations – which in fact he does not. To give one example, Heidegger often refers to his first major work in a general sort of way by mentioning the title *Sein und Zeit*, and sometimes he mentions this title not so much as the title of a book but as an achievement. Mentioning *Being and Time* instead seemed to us to obfuscate this distinction. Secondly, in some cases there is more than one English translation of the same work, and in some cases even the titles in English are not identical. (Cases in point are the existing English translations of *Vom Wesen des Grundes* and *Kant und das Problem der Metaphysik*, not to mention the translations of the lecture *"Was ist Metaphysik?"*) Given this state of affairs, the reader who needs bibliographical information concerning the English translations of the volumes of the *Gesamtausgabe* should use "Update on the *Gesamtausgabe*", *Heidegger Studies* 21/ 2005, pp. 207–18.

(7) Retaining the Word *Gesamtausgabe*

The word *Gesamtausgabe* is left untranslated in this text and abbreviated with GA since the term is now accepted as a standard technical term. All references in the footnotes are to the volumes of this edition and use the abbreviation GA. (It should be mentioned in passing that the rendition of the word *Gesamtausgabe* with "collected edition" is not a correct translation since *Gesamtausgabe* is to be distinguished from *Gesammelte Werke*, that is, a collected edition. If we were to translate the word *Gesamtausgabe* we would have to say "complete edition".)

VI. *Mindfulness* and Contemporary Realities of Heidegger Research

In reading *Contributions* and *Mindfulness*, the reader should consider the following dimensions: (1) Heidegger understands these works as originating from the 'non-representational apophantic' character of be-ing-historical thinking. It is the unique nature of *Contributions* and *Mindfulness* as philosophical statements that they emerge from and return to that which shows and manifests itself as it is in itself. Failing to grasp this will lead to the mischaracterization of these works as "working notes", "aphorisms", "mystical expressions", and so forth. (2) Heidegger does not understand these works as absolute statements *about* be-ing, but rather as formal indications of the historical sway of being – formal indications that await fulfillment. (3) Be-ing-historical thinking has an unusual syntax because of the referential dependence of this syntax on the already-mentioned fulfillment. Seen in this light the syntax of being-historical thinking is not a deficient one. The singularity of the syntax of be-ing-historical thinking follows from the fact that this thinking is not a thinking *about* being but is one that is enowned by being. And insofar as this thinking itself is enowned by being, the translation of the syntax of this thinking must take its bearings from this enownment. Thus the goal of translating the syntax of being-historical thinking is not to make the translation more intelligible than the original, but to let this thinking come alive once again:

> The key for entering into be-ing-historical thinking of *Contributions* and [*Mindfulness*] does not lie in "translating" Heidegger's language of thinking into another "more" intelligible language but precisely in dwelling in Heidegger's language of thinking itself.[17]

Once these three dimensions are attended to, the possibility opens up of taking a brief look at *Mindfulness* in the light of contemporary realities of Heidegger research.

In the context of appropriation and co-enactment of Heidegger's thought, *Mindfulness*, besides being the second major being-historical treatise, is significant in two other respects. The first pertains to the question concerning Heidegger's political error of the 1930s. Any one who is still interested in this question would do well to take a close look at those passages and sections of *Mindfulness* that shed considerable light on the political situation in the Germany of the 1930s and, by extension, on Heidegger's political error. More than *Contributions* before it, *Mindfulness* contains passages that have unmistakable bearing on politics in general and on German politics of the 1930s in particular. While in the "Joining" entitled "Grounding" *Contributions* addressed the being-historical act of founding the political state and, in this sense, implicitly criticized Germany's National Socialist state, *Mindfulness* makes explicit statements on Hitlerism by critically evaluating one of the speeches that Hitler gave to the *Reichstag*. The being-historical questions to which Heidegger subjects this speech, and what he says about the role of youth in the arena of politics, are clear evidence that he disagreed with the politics of Hitler and National Socialism. Given the fact that this treatment of Hitler's speech was not intended for immediate publication, one can still see, by thinking through Heidegger's treatment of this speech in *Mindfulness*, how being-historical questioning demonstrates the baselessness of Hitler's assertions.

In the 1930s Heidegger, like the majority of German people, did not know anything of the horrors that later came to be known as the Holocaust. Yet, with brief remarks here and there in the text of *Mindfulness*, Heidegger deeply expresses a critique and disapproval of the ruling clique. So, for instance, when he says:

> That is why all dictators eagerly exploit the "youth" that suits them because "youth" brings along the required ignorance which guarantees that lack of respect and that incapability for admiration that are necessary for carrying out, under the guise of a new awakening, the planned destruction and thereby evading all decisions. (*Mindfulness*, 14)

Here Heidegger shows how clearly he is aware of the Nazi's capability to exploit "youth" for planning and executing destruction under the guise of 'the new awakening' [*der neue Aufbruch*, a slogan at the time]. Who can read this passage and not notice that Heidegger is alluding here to the Party organization known as "*Hitlerjugend*"?

With the availability of *Mindfulness* and other texts that are now published in GA 16, the whole question concerning Heidegger's political error of the 1930s needs to be reexamined in a manner that is no longer prosecutorial and journalistic but fully considers his being-historical stance toward politics. Such a reexamination is likely to prove that much of the furore of the 1980s that surrounded Heidegger's political error was irrelevant and prejudicial.

The second aspect in which *Mindfulness* becomes significant in the light of contemporary realities is the message this work conveys with respect to those who are at the present time engaged in historicizing Heidegger's thought. In one of the texts that appears in this volume as an appendix, Heidegger asks "what would happen if the pack of the curious once throws itself at the 'posthumous works'!" (*Mindfulness*, 378). With a prophetic look into the future, he warns against historicization of his life's work and says:

> Whoever *without hesitation* reads . . . the lecture-courses only as a 'historical' presentation of some work and whoever then compares and reckons up the interpretation [*Auffassung*] with the already existing views or exploits the

interpretation in order to "correct" the existing views, *he has not grasped anything at all. (Mindfulness, 372)*

While in the 1980s the pack of the curious threw itself upon the *Gesamtausgabe* and tried to diminish its philosophical significance on the ground that this edition has not gone through Heidegger's own editorial "cutting board", the present members of the pack are relentlessly busy with historicizing Heidegger's thought. They take his work as a 'historical' presentation, and compare it with the already existing views for the purpose of either disproving or endorsing it. They thus totally overlook the distinction between history (*Geschichte*) and 'history' (*Historie*). However, an unhurried reading of the text of *Mindfulness* in the light of this distinction will show the futility of both present and past historicizing of Heidegger's thought. It is to this end that the present translation of *Mindfulness* hopes to be able to make a contribution.[18]

Parvis Emad
Thomas Kalary

Notes

1 M. Heidegger, *Contributions to Philosophy (From Enowning)*, trans. Parvis Emad and Kenneth Maly (Bloomington: Indiana University Press, 1999). All references to this work will be made in the body of the text with *"Contributions"* followed by page number.

2 See *Mindfulness*, pp. 382–383.

3 *Ibid.*, p. 383.

4 *Ibid.*

5 *Ibid.*

6 Regarding these "Joinings" see Friedrich-Wilhelm von Herrmann, *"Contributions to Philosophy* and Enowning-Historical Thinking*"*, in *Companion to Heidegger's Contributions to Philosophy*, ed. Charles E. Scott, *et al* (Indiana: Indiana University Press, 2001), pp. 105–26; Parvis Emad, "On 'Be-ing': The Last Part of *Contributions to Philosophy"*, *ibid.*, pp. 229–45; Thomas Kalary, "Hermeneutic Pre-conditions for Interpreting Heidegger: A Look at Recent Literature (Part Two) – Focusing on, and Thinking *after Beiträge"*, in *Heidegger Studies*, 19 (2003), 129–57.

7 See *Contributions*, pp. xv–xvi.

8 For more on the question of an absolute transfer of Heideggerian ter-

minology, see Parvis Emad, "Translating Heidegger's *Beiträge zur Philosophie* as an Hermeneutic Responsibility", in *Studia Phaenomenologica*, vol. V, (2006).

9 M. Heidegger, *Beiträge zur Philosophie (Vom Ereignis)*, ed. Friedrich-Wilhelm von Herrmann (Frankfurt am Main: Klostermann Verlag, 1994) p. 379.

10 M. Heidegger, *Identität und Differenz* (Pfullingen: Neske Verlag, 1982), p. 25.

11 Parvis Emad, "On the Inception of Being-Historical Thinking and Its Unfolding as Mindfulness", in *Heidegger Studies*, XVI (2000), pp. 66 ff.

12 *Ibid.*, 66.

13 See the entry "*Vermenschen*" in *Deutsches Wörterbuch von Jacob und Wilhelm Grimm*, (Leipzig: Verlag von S. Hirzel, 1956), vol. 12, p. 860. There, the brothers Grimm use the following quote: "*Adam ain vermenschter teuffel, Christus ain vermenschter gott.*" [Adam a humanized devil, Christ a humanized god.] From this quote the primary meaning of *Vermenschen* proves to be 'to humanize', 'to take human shape'.

14 See M. Heidegger, *Zu Hölderlin – Griechenlandreisen* (Frankfurt am Main: Klostermann Verlag, 2000), GA 75, pp. 213–73.

15 See M. Heidegger, *Wegmarken* (Frankfurt am Main: Klostermann Verlag, 1976), p. 141.

16 William J. Richardson, *Heidegger Through Phenomenology to Thought* (The Hague: Martinus Nijhoff, 1977), p. 197, *passim*.

17 Parvis Emad, 'On the Inception', p. 71.

18 For a general discussion of *Mindfulness*, see Parvis Emad, "A Conversation with Friedrich-Wilhelm von Herrmann on *Mindfulness*", in *The New Yearbook for Phenomenology and Phenomenological Philosophy*, (2006), vol. VI, pp. 1–20.

Acknowledgments

We would like to express our gratitude to those who assisted us in this translation in a variety of ways. First, our thanks go to Herr Dr Hermann Heidegger, the literary executor of Martin Heidegger's *Nachlaß*, for granting us permission to write an extended "Foreword" to this translation. Next our thanks are due to Professor Friedrich-Wilhelm von Herrmann, chief contributing editor of Heidegger's *Gesamtausagbe*, for his generosity in devoting a considerable amount of time to a private seminar with Parvis Emad in order to discuss the difficulties of the syntax of *Mindfulness*. While the final responsibility for this translation rests with us, its indebtedness to Professor von Herrmann should be duly acknowledged. Finally, we would like to extend our thanks to Gertrude Emad for her help in so many ways during the course of completing this translation.

[G1]

I
INTRODUCTION

[G3]   1. Prelude from Periander and Aeschylus

μελέτα τὸ πᾶν
Periander.[1]
Take into care 'beings in the whole'.

ἅπαντ᾽ ἐπαχθῆ πλὴν θεοῖσι κοιρανεῖν.
Aeschylus, Prometheus v. 49.[2]
Often everything is a load to bear, except the mastery over gods.

[G4]   2. The other Thinking

At first take the last glow of blessing
from the dark hearth of be-ing
that it may kindle the countering:
godship – humankind in one.

Throw the distress of bold clearing
between the world and the earth as song

---

[1] H. Diels, *Die Fragmente der Vorsokratiker, Griechisch u. Deutsch*, fifth edition, ed. W. Kranz. vol. I, chapter 10, *"Die Sieben Weisen"* (Berlin: 1934).
[2] Aeschyli Tragoediae, Recensuit G. Hermannus. Editio altera., Tomus primus. Berolini 1859.

3

to inaugurate all things
in joyful thanks to accord and rank.

Shelter in word the silent message
of a leap over the large and small
and lose the empty findings
of a sudden semblance on the way to be-ing.

Summer 1938

[G5]   3. The Leap

Take, throw and shelter
and be the leap
from the most remote memory
into an ungrounded realm:

Carry before you
the one 'Who'?
Who is man?

Say without fail
the one 'What'?
What is be-ing?

Never disregard
the one 'How'?
How is their concord?

Man, truth, be-ing
respond out of heightening of man's ownmost; of the sway of
truth and be-ing
unto refusal,
wherein they are granted to themselves.

[G6]   ## 4. The Guardians

Away rolls the subterranean storm,
inaudible to all the many,
into spaces above worldly –
remote thrust of be-ing.

The world and the earth blended long since
disturbed in their law of strife
withdraw from things any destiny.
Number raves into empty quantity
no longer bestows bond and likeness.
What counts as a "being" is what "lives",
but "living" lives only by the uproar
of a noisy presumption,
which is already late to the ones that follow.

But they guard –
the secret guardians
of an unrisen transformation:
remote thrust of be-ing
between the turbulent making and contrivance.

[G7]   ## 5. The Knowing-awareness

But we know the beginning,
the other one, we know it by questioning,
we stay in the leap ahead of any yes and no.
Certainly we *are* never the knowing ones,
yet in knowing-awareness we are those who *are*,
we leave ourselves behind
in questioning the clearing of be-ing.
Decision is still be-ing's,
whether be-ing – crushing power and powerlessness
calls to the earth
the world into strife,
whether be-ing brings god to distress
and en-owns the expansive stillness
to Da-sein, to man.

[G8]   6. The Word

Nothing, nowhere, never
before every "something", before all "then" and "there"
towers the word
out of the ab-ground, which granted,
what every ground failed to grant,
since only the bond
with what is said
fits out every thing as a thing
and scatters in a maze
the hunted senses.

[G9]   6a. We do not know goals

We do not know goals
and are only a pathway.

We do not need many,
that are long since intertwined

the mania for contrivances –
that one would only bring

the heart for the tune
of stillness in be-ing,

which thrashes the wild
in the grounding shrine,

            is our courage.

[G10]   6b. Da-sein

that Da-sein be, to say be-ing,
to carry out of it the distress

into the span
of an upward glance filled with bids.

That Da-sein be, to take be-ing back
into the awakened ear
of the one, who chooses
stillness as his work.

That Da-sein be, to sing be-ing,
out of a distant song
to bring be-ing where it is at home,
what as power avoided be-ing's sway for long.

[G11]   7. ΑΛΗΘΕΙΑ

Ἀρχὰ μεγάλας ἀρετᾶς
  ὤνασσ' Ἀλά –
  θεια, μὴ πταίσῃς ἐμάν
σύνθεσιν τραχεῖ ποτὶ ψεύδει . . .
        Pindar, Fragment 205 (Schroeder)[1]

Beginning of a worthiness to greatness
  Lady, godly, sheltering-unconcealing,
  that thou do not ever upset my
inabiding thou through wild-hard (crude) reversal . . .

                    *

In a free thinking-interpretation:

The truth (clearing) of be-ing is
the being of errancy –
the sphere of error (just like the sphere of riches) is first
placed in this abode. But how about the reversal?
Clearing is the ab-ground as distress of grounding.

---

[1] Pindari Carmina cum Fragmentis Selectis. Interum edidit O. Schroeder. In aedibus B. G. Teubneri Lipsiae, 1914.

[G12] The inceptuality of that which is sole and unique in beings rises out of the clearing of be-ing, which uncomparably has already outlasted every "eternity" – the eternity which we always calculate additionally as empty duration and clinging to it, ascertain it as groundless consolation. The inceptuality of that which is sole and unique is that greatness, which protected out of be-ing has its beginning in freedom but whose sway is the mastery as sacrifice of gifting the highest distress from out of the jubilation of preserving the non-coercive transmission into the domain of the nearness and remoteness of god.

This clearing of be-ing is at the same time the be-ing of errancy; the site of the origin of distortion into which we are easily thrust and into which we easily fall and as we fall, we fall prey to mere beings and their exclusive predominance, powerful and powerless in alternation of things and circumstances – this clearing calculates for us in advance causes (drives and inclinations, desires and pleasures) for everything and twists everything into what is merely extant, easily possessed, familiar and used by everyone.

The true enowns itself only in the truth, so that we belong to its swaying, know the danger of distortion as something rooted in that swaying, and do not let in and do not fear the distorted and its unleashed power – abide in the venture of be-ing, belong to the unique service of the not yet appeared but proclaimed god.

II

LEAPING AHEAD UNTO THE UNIQUENESS OF BE-ING[*]

---

[*] *"On Mindfulness"* (Machination – truth of be-ing). *The Completion of Modernity*: 1. Nietzsche's metaphysics and its unfolding by O. Spengler and E. Jünger. 2. Art and the epoch (history of art and sciences).

8. On Mindfulness

Only by coming from far away from the remote beginning of the history "of" be-ing, free from every "history", can *thinking* prepare the readiness for the grounding of the *one decision* (cf. below G 45, and for the more detailed account of decision see *Überlegungen* XII, 29*) and only this: whether machination of beings would make man exceedingly powerful and transpose him into an unbridled being of power, or whether be-ing would gift the grounding of its truth as distress from out of which the *countering* of god and man cross with the strife of the earth and the world. Such a criss-crossing is the struggle of struggles: the en-owning wherein beings are 'owned over' again to the belongingness to be-ing. War is only the uncontrolled machination of beings, peace only the seeming suspension of that uncontrolledness. *Struggle* is but the mirroring of the gifting of the sway from out of the mildness of the pride of refusal. "Struggle" is thought here from out of the stillness of the swaying. "Struggle" is the all too human name for the "en-owning" that is withdrawn from man. Be-ing is en-owning, [it is] *the settleable* en-owning: *settlement* (cf. below G 84). The futural thinking (the en-owned saying in imageless word) is en-thinking of the preparedness for the history of the crossing (the overcoming of metaphysics).

* See *Überlegungen* C. GA 96.

[G16]
9. Machination[*]
(Coercive Force, Power, Mastery)[a]

Machination here means the makability of beings which produces as well as makes up everything, such that only in this makability the being-ness of beings that are abandoned by be-ing (and by the grounding of its truth) determines itself. (Here makable is thought as "watchable" = *watchful*. And hence makability is thought in the sense of *producibility*). *Machination* means the accordance of everything with producibility, indeed in such a way that the unceasing, unconditioned reckoning of everything is pre-directed. Such things allow "progress" only marginally, because progress seems, or intends to be able to surmount destruction as the indicator of "retrogression". But then machination adjoins beings as such to the space of a play that continually plays into machination as an ongoing *annihilation*. Already constantly annihilating in the very threat of annihilation, machination expands its sway as coercive force. By securing power, this coercive force develops as the immediately eruptible and always transformable capability for subjugation that knows no discretion, and supersedes itself as it spreads. The coercive force that is released within the sway of machination is always subordinated only to power and never grounds mastery, because machination reaches ahead of everything makable, blocks and finally undermines all decision. Mastery, however, arises out of the grounding capability for decision. It not only possesses dignity, but is also the free capability of originarily honouring, not [G17] a being, but be-ing itself. Mastery is the dignity of be-ing as be-ing. All mastery is inceptual and belongs to the beginning. Under all kinds of disguises of manifold coercive forces machination fosters in advance the completely surveyable calculability of the subjugating empowering of beings to an accessible arrangement. Modern technicity arises out of this foundational but at the same time concealed fostering. Modern technicity releases man into the urge towards structuring his massive way of being

---

[*] See 65. Be-ing and Power, also cf., *the basic words*, machination and power.
[a] Be-ing (rising – enowning)
Machination
Power
Coercive Force
Force
{Two words are illegible} Mastery.

through which every human particularity is overpowered because each particularity must enjoin the makable as the co-enacting subject who only *seemingly* steers and leads. To the extent that in the epoch of machination that is empowered to its unbounded coercive force man also grasps himself as animal (*living*-being), the only thing that still remains for man himself (equally for "we" and for "I") is the *"lived-experience"* as that arrangement of his comportment and attitude which in the sphere of machination confers upon him the *appearance* of self-assertion vis-à-vis beings. The heightening of the expanse and quickness, of affordability and publicness of "live-experience" is an indication that the last barriers to the coercive force of machination have fallen away. The foundational consequence of the epoch of the completion of modernity (cf. 10. Completion of Modernity) is already the power of technicity over beings and its powerlessness vis-à-vis be-ing – this epoch can never posit technicity as its ground. The characterizations that are subsumed under the titles "civilization" and "culture" are no longer adequate for this epoch. Both "civilization" and "culture" certainly belong to modernity but only to the epoch of its preparation which has come to an end. The sway of technicity is still held back in both "civilization" and "culture" and hence counts only as a special domain and above all as the limited form of dominating things as well as man's massive way of being (cf. 63. Technicity).

As the ownmost of beings, as the manner in which beings as such generally *are*, machination impels all the forces capable of power and of transforming power to total unleashing into self-overpowering of power. [G18] True to the basic sway of power, power has always continued by furthering and heightening of power such that its superseding should count only as something unessential and exclusively conspicuous in external process. This self-overpowering of power that continues in this way shows itself in manifold phenomena which – as they are experienced – fall prey to an interpretation with the help of a stock of metaphysical concepts which have been handed down.

Without determining the sway of force closely or in general, one speaks of the *"dynamic"* and means propulsiveness of power that is launched and let loose and overflows itself.

One names the *"total"* and thinks of the peculiarity of the being of power that it can tolerate nothing outside its arena of effectiveness which could still be addressed as "actual".

One points at the *"imperial"* and touches upon the commanding character of power which loathes to request, to negotiate or to await the accidental, since its own overpowering of itself necessarily includes commanding everything to subjugation that finds itself in the sphere of disposal of power.

One mentions the "*rational*" and strikes upon that calculating character in everything of the nature of command as it surrounds the closed circle of the distribution and the steering of forces.

One points at the "*planetary*" and wants to say not only that each instance of the empowering of power is always "total" in itself (in relation to a country, a people), but also that each sets its limits only at the boundaries of the inhabited globe and its domain of disposability (the atmosphere and stratosphere) which says right away that the planet as a whole is "used" as a product of power and that therefore detecting a planetary opponent becomes unavoidable.

However, all these and other characterizations of the sway of power [G19] are never sufficient, because they are fundamentally inadequate for recognizing machination as such and for grasping it being-historically as a form of mastery of the self-refusing be-ing and its ungrounded truth. For such a grasping can take place only in a deciding, through which one side of machination as such and, along with it, machination in its unconcealed sway in general, first comes to a halt. However, every sway of power and every power-possessing being is in itself an evasion of such decisions – decisions which simply remain hidden to the foundational trait of power because the commanding character of that trait occupies the forefront at the same time as the command nevertheless exhibits at least the transmission and forming of a decidedness. And yet not every decidedness arises from out of a decision – if ever this were to be the case, then the decision need not be a foundational one in which the sway of be-ing itself is put at risk. (That is why all dictators eagerly exploit the "youth" that suits them because "youth" brings along the required ignorance which guarantees that lack of respect and that incapability for admiration that are necessary for carrying out, under the guise of a new awakening, the planned destruction and thereby evading all decisions.)

Out of an only superficially experienced and interpreted machination as indicated in the above-mentioned characterizations an attitude arises that believes to be able to identify and to recognize – by a simple affirmation of the overpowering of power that is unleashed in the heightening of coercion – that which "is". One interprets this acceptance of the "actual" as "heroism". But this so-called "heroism" has all the markings of "capitulating" before the extant as such, that is, before the machinationally determined beings that are abandoned by being. Where only the inevitable is accepted, the necessary need not have been experienced in advance. And the necessary can be experienced only out of the knowing-awareness of a *distress* that thoroughly prevails in beings and challenges the sway of beingness. The "heroic realism" – seemingly the highest form of knowing of, and [G20] attitude towards beings – amounts only to the most covert way of evading being. But by pretending that it has the sharpest insight into what "is", this "realism" explicitly seals off the forgottenness of being: it thus proves publicly how up to date it is in the epoch of the beginning of the completion of modernity.

And yet, all the attempts made at the service of "world-view" to interpret the unrecognizable entanglement in the concealed history of the epoch are always superficial and a fruitless supplement that does not prepare any origin for decisions. By contrast, what is important to mindfulness is the growing knowing-awareness of the sway of power and of what is fundamentally effective in the self-overpowering of power.

On the one hand, the self-overpowering that distinguishes all power always leaves behind the already attained stage of power and extent of power (the annihilation that belongs to power as the preform of the devastation that is fundamental to the unconditionality of power). On the other hand, this self-surrendering of the attained phase of power includes and pursues that self-seeking that belongs to power and absolutely sticks to itself. That is why only such a being of power that, as it were, is sent ahead by machination grants that swaying of being that is suitable to sustaining man metaphysically as "subject" and continually to confirm his "right" vis-à-vis himself. For, where power overpowers itself through coercive force, the appeal to "right"[b] accumulates – the appeal to a word, which reaches ahead into the self-overpowering and names only what has to be posited as the claim on expansion of power and on effectiveness of coercive force.

On the basis of the unconditionality of power, the constant search for the new and suitable opponents – peculiar to every unfolding of power – leads at the end to the utmost phase of devastation of the circle of the limitlessly subjugated power. With this phase of devastation, [G21] which more obtrusive than ever before still looks like construction,

---

[b] What the justification of power here means.

achievement, deed, "engagement", and which, when understood in the light of the coercive force, also "is", a "point" will be reached in which destruction becomes impossible. Here destruction means bringing about a final disturbance of the hitherto out of the decision that has already been enacted in favour of another beginning. Devastation, on the other hand, is the undermining of every possibility of a beginning on the basis of a com- pletely bedazzled self-seeking that lacks all measures and has become absolute. Such a self-seeking has to admit mindfulness as its unassailable opponent in the form in which coercive force makes admissions: coercive force casts out what it admits into the supposed nothingness of the "ridiculous" and the feeble. But even this self-rescuing of the sway of power is a foundational consequence of machination, in which all beings and "subject" are specially abandoned to the ungroundedness of the truth of the forgotten be-ing.

The predominance of machination shows itself most intensely in cases in which machination also takes possession of thinking and arranges machinationally the thinking of the beingness of beings, such that being itself is made into something that makes itself, arranges and erects itself. Its precondition primarily is interpretation of being as "objectivity" of "objects", as "objectness" of objects. The "objectness" is "constituted" and this "constitution" in turn is relegated into a self-constitution of the "subject" as the "subject" of "thinking". Thus "being" will be grasped "constitutively" as "becoming". But because "time" is the form of "becoming", on these machinational pathways of interpreting being there arises an obvious interconnection between "being" and "time". But these trains of thought could have *nothing in common* with that which is inceptually inquired under the title "being and time". Moreover, these trains of thought could not have an inkling of what has taken possession of them, namely being which as machination compels the thinking [G22] of the sway of machination to be of the same kind as machination, and this leads to a situation that does not allow this thinking, that is, metaphysics, ever to come across the truth of be-ing as inquirable.

Likewise, the seemingly "natural" and ordinary thinking that is rooted in metaphysics lacks every possibility for thinking unto the question of being, because this "natural" and ordinary thinking – in a more coarse manner – renders machination at home in beings. In the unbounded field of machination within the daily care, only "purpose" and "means" expand as cohesive powers. And this in such a way that all purposes and everything ostensibly represented as purpose are levelled off as means.

Obviously, the means find their only law in the process-like mediation. They mediate only the mediation as such, that is, the pure empowering of power which drags itself down into the form of a mere empowering. Under the pressure of the effectiveness of the pure process of empowering of power, goals become superfluous.

The struggle between countering and strife is the en-owning that lights up – the clearing – wherein god overshadows the earth in its closure and man erects the world so that the world awaits god and the earth receives man. This clearing frees all the swaying of the en-owned unto the ab-ground of en-owning. But this en-owning is that within which thinking names be-ing. En-owning does not sit enthroned over the en-owned as from the beyond, nor does it encompass merely the totality of beings as the purposeless emptiness. Rather, enowning is the "in-between", which in advance unfolds within the stretches of "that which removes itself unto" (the stretches of the "free play of time-space") that has to be grounded by "man" as the "t/here" – a grounding wherein for the first time man finds his other ownmost out of which he receives accord and rank: Da-*sein*.

Da-sein means taking over the distress of the grounding of the truth of be-ing – it is the beginning of a history that has no 'history'. From the perspective of *thinking*, mindfulness means preparing the preparedness for such a takeover in the form of a knowing-awareness of be-ing, because thinking inquires into the truth of be-ing [G23] in imageless saying of the word. But the *word* is the tune of the struggle between countering and strife – the word is attuned out of en-owning, is thoroughly tuning the clearing and is tuned-in to the ab-ground of be-ing. In accordance with the mirroring of en-ownment, every foundational word (every 'saying') is ambiguous. But such ambiguity does not know the arbitrariness of the unbridled, it remains enveloped within the richness of the uniqueness of be-ing. Because be-ing sways in and as the word, all "dialectic" of "propositions" and "concepts" moves constantly within objects and blocks every step towards mindfulness.

Coming from the overcoming of "metaphysics", mindfulness must nevertheless touch upon the hitherto and cannot become inflexible as the finished product of a usable presentation either in a "doctrine" or in a "system", or as "exhortation" or "edification". The fittingness and the rigour of this thinking vis-à-vis all the unfittingness of opinions and the casualness of mere talking, have their rooting and branching in the sway of the truth of be-ing, which, exempt from all the power of the effective and not compelled by the powerlessness of the mere represented, must ground itself in the "nowhere" and "never" of beings, ground itself unto the siteless place and the hourless time of the struggle of en-ownment wherein those en-owned call each other unto their sway, which foundational call of be-ing attunes itself as the word and determines the thinking "of" be-ing as saying.

The preparation for that unique decision can be enacted only by leaping ahead unto an appropriate decidedness, which reckoned 'historically', is not yet "actual", discernible or effective, and has nonetheless taken over the history of the other beginning as the history of the swaying of the truth of be-ing.

That decision is, therefore, never a 'historical' critique which always would have to remain within its epoch. The decision prepares itself as mindfulness of what is ownmost to the epoch that consists of the *completion of modernity*. This completion is the "either" to the "or" of the other beginning. [G24] The preparation for decision is in the crossing and yet it is not affected by that piecemealness that marks undecidedness. The crossing is sustained and retained clearly by the knowing-awareness of the sway of the completion of the metaphysical epoch and by the unique inquiry that is denied to any metaphysics, namely the inquiry into the truth of be-ing. Necessitated and held within decision itself, mindfulness, as the originary onefold of that historical knowing-awareness and this inquiry, only prepares the decision. Beyond the machinational wars and organizations of peace, and in accord with the en-ownment of that struggle, this decision itself is not only historical, but is also the ground of the fundamental transformation of that history which is free from all 'history'. This decision is not made as an "act" of an individual man; it is the thrust of be-ing itself, by which machination of beings and man as a 'historical' animal are separated vis-à-vis the ab-ground of be-ing and are left to their own lack of origin. That is why preparation for decision does not mean paving the way for it as if decision is a contrivance of man, or possibly *still* could be such a contrivance. Only the 'free-play of the time-space' is prepared wherein the *fundamental* transformation (not a mere higher breeding or a re-breeding) of the *animal rationale* has to enown historically. Thinking mindfulness must recognize itself as only *one* action – perhaps the one which thinks ahead the furthest – for this preparation and therefore it should engage itself in the most intensive mindfulness as *inceptual* self-mindfulness of philosophy. But thinking saying cannot become the word that actually sways – this needs a poet, who must grow out of that stock whose lineage Hölderlin erected (*"Wie wenn am Feiertage . . ."*).

Specifically, thinking mindfulness should grasp the sway of the completion of modernity and leave behind all thinking that acquiesces to metaphysics, even in cases in which such thinking seemingly rejects metaphysics on the assumption that by no longer questioning it, metaphysics has been mastered. But "metaphysics" [G25] – and this always means domination of being that is determined by thinking as representing, a domination whose truth is ungrounded – can be overcome only by a more inceptual questioning of metaphysics's ownmost question and by relegating metaphysics to its full historical necessity.

Questioning more inceptually means, on the one hand, to raise to what is most question-worthy that which remained fundamentally unquestioned (the truth of be-ing, not of beings), that is, the be-ing of truth. Questioning more inceptually means, on the other hand, to leap into the hitherto hidden history of be-ing and thereby to grasp history itself in the whole more foundationally than any kind of 'history'. That is why mindfulness requires a knowing-awareness of the sway of "its" epoch – the epoch that mindfulness has already abandoned and has to abandon at the moment when the completion of this epoch begins (cf. 10. Completion of Modernity).

Cf. the inquiry into the truth of be-ing, which as questioning never leads up to an answer but wholly entrusts *itself* to the tune of stillness – to the answer that is attuned to be-ing as its swaying.

10. Completion of Modernity*

Completion of modernity is simultaneously completion of the metaphysical history of the Occident – the history which explicitly or implicitly is sustained by metaphysics. More precisely put, completion of metaphysics determines and sustains the beginning of the completion of modernity.

Here completion means the unbounded and therefore untangled simple empowering of the sway of the epoch. Completion thus neither

---

* Cf., "Die Begründung des neuzeitlichen Weltbildes durch die Metaphysik", of July 1938 published under the title "Die Zeit des Weltbildes", in *Holzwege*, GA 5, ed. F.-W. von Herrmann (Frankfurt am Main: 1977) pp. 75–113.

indicates a mere attaching of a still [G26] missing period, nor the coming to an end of what is basically already known. Rather, completion heralds what is lastly and mostly *disconcerting* within the epoch, and does not cease with the completion, but *begins* the foundational domination. The completion of the metaphysical epoch raises being in the sense of machination to such a "domination", that within machination being is indeed forgotten, and yet the beings of such nature are pursued as the only unconditionally secured representing and producing. Such arrangeable representedness and producedness decides upon what should be admitted as being and discarded as non-being. The producibility of beings that produces and makes up everything is machination, which predetermines also the nature of the effectiveness of beings and provides actuality with its unique meaning. What is effective as such is not calculated according to the short-term "purposes" of a being. Rather it consists solely in the manner of the effectiveness of *machination* itself (of being). Machination prevails at the same time as the ground of interpreting the actual as "the will to power" – the ground that is not known in its sway and is also unrecognizable by all metaphysics. Its sway consists in the necessary and therefore unceasing overpowering of all power, an overpowering whose sway fosters in advance – but does not cause – the makability of machination. Planning, calculating, arranging and breeding foster a being that has come to power in this way and thereby fosters the affirmation of "becoming", but not with the intention of progressing towards a goal and an "ideal", rather for the sake of "becoming itself". For "becoming" pursues the overpowering, since any kind of power can maintain itself only in overpowering. However, "becoming" is fundamentally fostered beforehand by machination itself *because* machination arises out of the sway of being as presencing and constancy. "Being is becoming" – this is not a denial of being. On the contrary, with "being is becoming" being's inceptual sway (φύσις – ἰδέα – οὐσία) is foundationally fulfilled through beingness as machination that is marked in advance by the staying away of the grounding of truth [G27] (cf. below G92 f., G110 f.). The seeming priority of "becoming" over "being" indicates only the self-empowering of producibility for rendering its unconditioned presencing constant and thus for the completed empowering of becoming to being. When thinking insists on the seeming oppositionality of becoming to being, thinking does not know what it thinks. This insistence is an indication that thinking has failed to come to terms with metaphysics. Hegel's and Nietzsche's metaphysics – belonging together within the completion of Occidental metaphysics like left and right – enact that interpretation of 'beings as such in the whole', which can no longer be surpassed and undermined within metaphysics, not even considering what constitutes the position of each thinker, namely "absolute reason" in Hegel and "body" in Nietzsche; in short in both *the absolute rational animal*. The completion of the metaphysical epoch "frees" being unto the sway of machination, but man (the unrecognized guardian of the truth of being) completes himself initially as the despiser of this truth with a contempt that indeed has to know nothing of that which it overlooks. The rational animal has become subject and has developed reason into 'history', whose sway coincides with the sway of technicity. The man of the completed modernity is the 'historical' animal, who out of his drivenness raises his own "doings" as "lived-experience" to a desideratum and to whom 'beings in the whole' appear as "life".

The only two *developments* of the final Occidental metaphysics in Nietzsche that struggle toward the completion of modernity and are worthy of attention are O. Spengler's Caesarist's metaphysics of history and E. Jünger's metaphysics of "the worker". The former thinks in the perspective of man as a "predator" and sees the ongoing completion and the end in the domination of "Caesars" to whom the masses have become serviceable through economy, technicity and World Wars. The latter thinks planetarily [G28] (not economically, not societally, not "politically") the gestalt of the "worker" in whom the modern humanity becomes a permanent member of the "organic construction" of 'beings in the whole'. However, neither Spengler's nor Jünger's thought should be confined to words like "Caesar" and "the worker" – words with which Spengler and Jünger having great *individuals* in mind, seek to capture the ownmost of the overman, that is, the henceforth determined animal.

(However, such stereotyped allusions to the actually enacted trains of thought shorten and postpone things continually. These allusions only suggest that here a struggle is going on for positions and standpoints, which unfolds its disclosive power exclusively through an unpublic encounter with that struggle. Although Spengler and Jünger grow out of the same metaphysical root, their thinking is different from the ground up. It is not important how as the upshot of a latter-day 'historical' psychology both Spengler and Jünger "become effective" publicly, are rejected, used and rendered harmless. Spengler's pure pessimism of doom and Jünger's pure dynamism in each case only make up the foregrounds in the domain of publicly necessitated thoughtless labelling.)

On both Spengler's and Jünger's ways of unfolding Nietzsche's metaphysics, 'beings in the whole' are machinationally thought, and due to man's fundamental entanglement in machination he is determined as executor of machination. As organized mass and as individual member of such organization, man is thus simultaneously always the powerful and the indifferent, the leader and the melted down. Therefore, the final word wherein 'beings in the whole' and being human cross is called "destiny". As the highest will to power of the predator, the military thinking that comes from the World War and the unconditionality of armament always indicate the completion of the metaphysical epoch. World War as well as World Peace (in the Judeo-Christian ambiguity) mean machinational organizations that correspond to each other. [G29] War and peace in this epoch can no longer be a means for any purpose and goal, nor can they be purposes and goals in themselves. Rather, World War as well as World Peace are only that in which the actual and beings have to be completed – beings whose strength and distinction consists in the abandonment by being (cf. VII. Be-ing and Man; cf. 63. Technicity).

The appeal to "destiny" means arming being's abandonment of beings vis-à-vis beings. This appeal is at the same time the empty victory of the heroism of man as "subject", which lacks decision. The appeal to "destiny" is only the reverse side of the '*historical*' conception of history – is its thoroughgoing "explanation" out of what always *is a being* – an "explanation" out of causes and purposes that are wished to be.

The "affirmation" of destiny is the exit into the metaphysics that has no exit – into the metaphysics which exhausts itself in all its possible expressions and reversals and thereby has become totally entangled in itself. Where out of an honesty of attitude the appeal to an 'existing' [*seienden*] being, "*God*" (the appeal to the Judeo-Christian [God] and his rational derivations into "providence" and the like) is abandoned; where the retreat both to "*man*" and his "creative" glory has lost its magic; where only the "doings" of the "*world*" in its controllability still *offer* a course of action but cannot *afford* it and nonetheless seek help from both "man" and his "mania for lived-experience" and from "God" and his "consolations", there god, world and man – the threefold structured 'beings in the whole' – as metaphysics' domain of flight err groundlessly in the ungrounded truth of be-ing: a staggering of man between threat and security or the absolute indifference.

[G30]   11. Art in the Epoch of Completion of Modernity*

In the epoch of the completion of modernity what is hitherto metaphysically ownmost to art becomes complete. The sign of this is the disappearance of the *work* of art but not art itself. Art becomes a manner in
which machination completes itself in a thorough construction of beings
unto the unconditioned, secure disposability of the organized. As the form
of the fundamental effectiveness of their machination, the created beings
(highways, aircraft hangars at airports, giant ski-jumps, power stations
and reservoirs, manufacturing plants and fortifications) are, in a different
way than up to now, fully eased into what is not their component, that is,
into "what is", into "nature" and into the public "world". "Nature" transforms itself according to these "installations", plants itself entirely into
them and comes to light only in them and is held in their purview. With
and through these installations and according to their style, nature
becomes "beautiful". According to the metaphysical character of art which
is totally fulfilled in the completion, beauty even now remains the basic
determination. Beauty is what pleases and must please the being of the
power of man, the predator. But already hidden behind the basic
determination is that which within the 'crossing' is ownmost to this
determination insofar as with the disappearance of the work of art in
favour of sheer machination, being's complete abandonment of beings
consolidates itself. Therefore, every possibility of looking for a "meaning"
of this art that could still prevail "behind" or "above" its "creations" fades.
Indeed, in the gestalt of modern technicity and "history" art becomes
τέχνη again – not by simply relapsing unto τέχνη but by completing itself.
In the gestalt of its fittingness into machination, i.e., in its pleasantness,
art is an unconditionally organized delivery of makability of beings unto
machination.

[G31] The hitherto existing classes of art dissolve and continue only by
name or as isolated, unreal fields of occupation for those latecomer
"romantics" who lack a future; the hitherto existing classes of art continue
by name, for example in the forging of "poems", "dramas" and corresponding works of music, "painting" and "sculpture". What art brings forth
is not *such* works, and particularly not works in being-historical sense that
inaugurate a clearing of be-ing – the be-ing in which beings would first

---

* Cf. *Überlegungen* VIII, 64 ff., 89 f., to appear in *Überlegungen* B. GA 95.

have to be grounded. What art brings forth are "installations" (forms of *organizing* beings): "poems" are "declarations"; they are "appeals" in the sense of *calling out* what already exists in the domain of the all-deciding and all-securing public. Word, sound and image are means for structuring, stirring, rousing and assembling of masses, in short, they are means of organizing. "Photography" and "cinema" should not be compared with and measured by the 'historically' known "works of art"; both have their own norm in the ownmost of the metaphysically completed "art" as the organization of the all-producing and all-constituting makability of beings. "Motion picture" is the public installation of the "new" societal comportments, fashion, gestures and "live-experience" of "actual" "lived-experiences". It is not films that are trashy, but what they offer as the consequence of machination of lived-experience and what they disseminate as worthy of live-experience. Stemming from imitating works of art, and losing its prop through the machinationally necessitated disappearance of what is hitherto ownmost to the works of art, kitsch becomes autonomous and no longer experienceable as kitsch. "Kitsch" is not the "inferior" art but the very best skill that is devoted to what is empty and is not fundamental, which in order still to secure itself a significance seeks support in the public advertising of its symbolic character.

Not only is the 'historical' *comparison* of kitsch with the stock [of art work] that is 'historically' preserved up to now inappropriate, but also inappropriate is the very orientation to the "values" of what is [G32] 'historically' handed down. As material for learning and provocation, what is 'historically' handed down can count in the same way only as "perfect" art – "perfect" in the sense of an indiscriminate, uncommitted "historicism". That today all of what is gone by is found again in the "products of art" is not due to the fact that *this* epoch lacks its own style. Rather, the machinational epoch has its own style which consists precisely in the uncommitted adoption of everything that fits into organizing the public life of the masses, which like every other community, has *its* own "individuals" and "personalities". Hence, the growing "affability" of the "profession of art" which coincides with the secure rhythm that originates from within the predominance of technicity and shapes everything that is installable and organizable. Unlike its preceding form in the nineteenth century, historicism now no longer means a thoroughgoing savouring of random possibilities of objectified history that squanders itself and has no commitment. Rather, historicism is tied beforehand to the machinationality of all beings from which it obtains above all its own already committed completion. "Museum" now is no longer the place for storing what is past but the place for exhibiting what is planned that appeals, educates and thereby commits. In the broad sense of organizing the "earth", what is planned is not simply planned and executed piecemeal and in stages and at different places. Rather, what is planned is planned in prior accord with the sway of planning from out of the whole; what is planned is made accessible and exhibited beforehand and immediately: proclamation of power, the parade of numbers, of length, of width and of height extension. Exhibition means that what is shown is already principally rendered stable.

Productions of art generally have the character of "*installation*" which is already guided by a pre-ordained direction of a surpassing that plans and produces the beings that are to be controlled – a pre-ordained direction which is never to become explicit but should "organically" "fit" into the "landscape", into the public needs and measures. [G33] However, in the light of that which machinationally sways in these productions, *that into which*, for instance, the "landscape" fits will be seen[a] in advance "technologically" [*technisch*] so that the "technological" products also conform *to the landscape*.

(*Appendix*: land, and populated valleys, mountains and rivers are not seen "technologically" as if only what otherwise remains a landscape should additionally be made useful in terms of technicity. A being is no longer primarily admitted as landscape, nor does mere technicity dominate it. Rather, what is created is determined in advance as *installation* by the machinational securing and ordering of 'beings in the whole', that is, by an installation which installs itself on beings and in beings, thus installing them unto the securing of organizing as an organization of securing. The grounding-attunement of organizing *installation* is the grounding-attunement of the heightening of power through a playful unobtrusiveness of calculation. [For] the origin of installation within *producibility*, cf. above G 16.)

The manner of representing the productions corresponds to the installation character of productions and to the way of dealing with them: control and embracement. And this as "lived-experience"; as "*training-in-lived-experience*", which means honing in on everything by taking and assessing everything entirely according to what machinationally sways in beings

---

[a] Rigorously thought, there *is* neither one visible landscape – nor a self "shaping" "technicity".

(itself hidden and ungraspable). This means: no longer searching "behind" or "above" beings, not even feeling "emptiness", but searching and finding, exclusively and maximally, what in the enactment of the machinational is 'liveable', [*Er-lebbare*] and as such can be incorporated into one's "own" "life" – which is shaped by the masses – and thus to foster this as what is solely valid and assuring.

Installation and training-in-lived-experience belong to the sway of the machinational security of 'beings in the whole' and to man's securing that is herein incorporated. But what is metaphysically ownmost to art and completes itself [G34] need not be grasped immediately at all. On the contrary! Following being's abandonment of beings that is organized along with art, man's forgottenness of being becomes boundless. When grasped according to be-ing, that is, being-historically, what in the epoch of completion "actually" happens must be not only hidden, but also disguised. The explicit regard for art, and the preoccupation with art (all the way to the industry called art-history) are animated by entirely different "categories" of thinking, namely by those that are required by the pre-eminence of man as subject, that is, by the interpretation of "beings in the whole" and of man in terms of "life". "Art" counts as an "expression" of "life" and is valued depending on the extent it succeeds in being such an expression, whereby what "life" is, is simultaneously laid out along with the type of "artistic" productions (e.g. masculinity of man is laid out along with huge muscles and genitals, blank faces that are tense with brutality). But interpretation of "art" as "expression" indicates at the same time that art (although still interpreted 'historically' according to "work"-character and according to how art makes pleasure possible) must be adequate to the sway of installation whose appropriation simply can be effected only by training in lived-experience. Thus 'history' as a science has received – not created – a "new" "horizon" of interpretation, which beyond a corresponding span of time guarantees 'history' the hitherto unused possibilities for new "knowledge" and likewise secures fellow travellers the means for proving their "superiority" and a "new" "awakening" and thus the occasion for securing their indispensability.

(But with this indispensability science has become something entirely different than what it was meant to be and once might have been: neither the grounding nor the pathway of grounding that belongs to a foundational *knowing-awareness*, rather a "technical" organization of training for the security of lived-experience vis-à-vis [G35] the machinational. Therefore, the operational forms of the modern and perfected sciences are developed forthwith most purely there, where they are allowed to operate with the unlimited means of organizing and 'representing,' i.e., within the "universities". These are in all respects nothing but the mandated forms of training as distinguished from research institutes and research establishments and all kinds of higher schools of learning.)

In this way, art becomes the development that is germane to modes of representing and producing of machinational beings. Art becomes so germane to the very development of the modes of producing which remain entirely in serviceability that this development delimits the relevant matter [*das Sachhafte*] and only admits as "relevant" [*sachlich*] what can be machinationally planned. Art means organizing the installations of producibility of all beings: hence it lacks decision in advance. Sharing the sway of technicity and 'history', art undertakes the organizing of beings whose being is decided upon in advance as machination. That is why art is not at all entitled to a free play of decision, and a decidability. It is difficult to see the ownmost of art in the perspective of 'historical' comparison of art-history and still more difficult to behold in that comparison the completion of what metaphysically sways in art.

(By contrast, determining the sway of art as 'setting the truth of be-ing unto work' means leaping ahead into another history. And only by misusing this history can one interpret the 'history' of metaphysical art. Insofar as in this art, too, being of beings takes shape, one can initially interpret what being-historically sways in art from out of the historical remembrance, whereby this interpretation already no longer thinks metaphysically, but being-historically.) (Cf. lectures on the origin of the work of art.[*])

[G36] Nietzsche's concept of art as "stimulant of life" takes a peculiar position between aesthetic, metaphysical artwork and the art that completes and consolidates its ownmost in the mode of organizing machination. Thus this concept remains entirely in the metaphysical domain, of course, according to *Nietzsche's* way of reversing Platonism. Today Nietzsche's interpretation of art is also crudely and subtly effective in a designing of art that concerns the massive character of "life".

The *genuine modern art*, which had to grow beyond what Hegel was able to see as art and beyond what the nineteenth century attempted, is distinguished by "creativity's" own covert installation-character that

---

[*] See "*Der Ursprung des Kunstwerkes*", in *Holzwege*. GA 5, 1–74.

interpenetrates all beings. Next to this and in part desired and fostered by the same spirit, there is a 'historical' continuation of the "art-industry" of the nineteenth century which is now assessed in terms of cultural politics, but remains unreal and only indicates the historicism that shimmers in all its possible colors. Besides, parallel or lingering next to this historicism there is a cultivation and an enjoyment of the 'historical' traditions of Occidental art that are aesthetically sure of their taste and mostly supported and guided by the educationally motivated dissemination of historical research into art.

On the other hand, no mindfulness of art can be pursued in all of this, because such a mindfulness should no longer discuss the direction and kind of the art heretofore and *its* possibilities, but must put to decision a transformation of *what is ownmost* to art, and this, moreover, only out of a grounding decision on the domination of machinational beings and on the grounding of the truth of be-ing.

Such a mindfulness of art that is charged with decision lies outside all theories of art. That is why the overcoming of aesthetics remains a con-current task, and what is more, easily misinterpretable as it could suggest that aesthetics is to be exchanged with, and replaced by, another way of observing art. [G37] This mindfulness has nothing to do with emphasizing the "work in itself" over against the artist, over against the recipients of art, and over against the historical circumstances and historically effective interconnections that condition both the artist and the recipient, because even such an emphasis need not step out of the metaphysically experienced art. In all this the artwork is grasped only as an "object".

However, as soon as the ownmost of the artwork is seen together with be-ing itself and with the grounding of its truth, the being-historical question concerning the work of art will be seen as having a completely different meaning. Now the artwork itself meets the foundational task of unfolding itself as the decision unto be-ing.

[Such a] work of art is neither a symbolic object, nor the installation that organizes beings, but is the clearing of be-ing as such which holds the decision for man's other way of being. Now art has the character of *Da-sein*, and moves out of all striving concerned with "culture". Taking the enactment of art, or its appropriation as measure, either way the work of art does not belong to man. Art is now the sites of decision of the 'rare ones'. "Artwork" now is the gathering of purest solitude unto the ab-ground of be-ing. Such creative prowess will not be affected by "fame" or by "disregard". According to its ownmost, the work of art remains withdrawn from the "public" and "private" adventure and belongs solely to inabiding the 'going under', which alone can become the foundationally proper history that leaves behind a clearing of be-ing. Artwork's complete lack of relation to beings and to their familiar organization guarantees in itself a belongingness to the creator, which does not "biographically" connect the creator to the work, but casts creator's Da-sein as "sacrifice" unto the ab-ground. But this "sacrifice" too can no longer become an "object" of mourning and revering, because remembrance of such a "sacrifice" would still revert to a spiritualized cultural operation and deteriorate into the 'dis-humanization' of art. What is ownmost to "sacrifice" – a word all too easily misinterpretable in the context of the heretofore – consists in reticently inabiding in an awaiting that is bequeathed [to us] for the truth of be-ing [G38], the truth which as such has the struggle between countering and strife as its ownmost.[+] Therefore, it *is* only work that within the mutual calling forth of the sway of the earth and the sway of the world puts to decision the sway of gods and the ownmost of man. Whatever does *not* let the sphere of such a preparation for decision prevail all around itself, may still serve as entertainment (banishing boredom), stand out as proclamation and confirmation of the extant, distinguish itself as the focus of a group of admirers – it is nowhere and never a "work of art". The criteria of the future "art" cannot at all be gleaned from the metaphysical art hitherto, even if one would look for these criteria in some kind of "classical" art and would enhance the latter beyond itself.

(Therefore all decision is already withdrawn from all '*historical*' instructions about the art heretofore and about the contemporary art, if prior to each transmission of knowledge, and in each transmission of knowledge these instructions do not venture to pave ways for mindfulness. Since within the 'science-industry' something like this paving of the way remains impossible insofar as here the *knowing-awareness* of the foundational has become unfamiliar, no impetus to mindfulness can possibly come from the 'historical' humanistic disciplines.)

But wherever the semblance of mindfulness surfaces, what is strived for becomes immediately transparent. On the one hand, an *analysis of the circumstances* ("situations") becomes public, on the other, *planning for* the futural attempts at providing a security. Analysis ("the analytic") and planning ("construction") mutually foster each other – the former not only

[+] {sic}

mostly introduces the latter, but also guides it, and the latter already determines the course of the former. With its determinedness, [*Entschiedenheit*] analytic-constructive "thinking" corresponds fully to the unbounded power of machination. In all spheres of human striving and acting this determinedness shows the same uniformity and [G39] defines the style of the semblance of decidedness, [*Entschiedenheit*] which is entirely fed by the lack of decision. But this lack of decision increasingly consolidates itself as that "presupposition" which expands the unbounded overpowering of power as the pure actuality of what is effective. What resistance thereby still arises from the realms of the "liberal" cultural optimism is not fundamental, even if it could occasionally score a "success". As resistance and mere resistance it is bogged down in the heretofore, entangles itself increasingly in the dependence on historical necessities which it even tries – fundamentally in vain – to evade. (True to its nature, the *Judeo-Christian* domination is engaged in a double dealing and sides at the same time with the "dictatorship" of the proletariat and with the liberal-democratic zeal for culture. For a long time this double dealing disguises even the already existing uprootedness and the asthenia for foundational decisions.)

Initially, of course, the illusion that here a mindfulness or perhaps only a "rescue" takes place may sporadically achieve "effects" even if only in the direction of misconstruing the ownmost of the genuine historical mindfulness of the Occident – or if intimating this mindfulness, distorting and misguiding it.

That the completion of modernity is "actually" the completion of the metaphysical history of the Occident and that this completion prepares at the same time the highest decision (cf. 8. On Mindfulness) – which alone has the binding historical strength for mindfulness – reveals itself quite simply in the historical movement of the epoch that begins. This completion is grounded in the differentiation between beings and being that in various formations is already formed by metaphysics. Machination takes hold of beings and absolutely legitimizes the forgottenness of being. The heretofore "cultural"-pursuits (the Judeo-Christian, classically formed, democratic-Occidental, and American kinds) entrust themselves to being (ideals and values) [G40]. With utmost exaggeration, machination and the culture-industry juxtapose beings and being as measure and take along in each case the differentiated ones into the claim of attention and care. Machination of beings incorporates the culture-industry into its planning as a means of power. Similarly, democratic cultural optimism presumes to recover and liberate the masses and uses and fosters technicity in all its "achievements". Historically, the incipient epoch becomes the unlimited overpowering of what is metaphysically differentiated, namely beings and being which mutually play into each other. And foundational to this overpowering is that it needs a lack of mindfulness of itself in order to unfold its own sway, and thus to enact all interpretations and proclamations of its sway in opposition to its counter players which in each case are counter players only seemingly and only in the foreground.

What is uncanniest and already a sign of the ab-ground of being is that in this process beings cast aside being and become increasingly and irresistibly attractive. And the more beings succeed in this casting aside and in this becoming irresistibly attractive, the more unrelenting the pursuit of culture and of its ideals have to remain pure evasion and benumbing—have to remain powerless means of an empty resistance. Thus a historical situation arises in which be-ing no longer even looks like the evanescence of the palest shadow of an empty dream. Be-ing – a fading last echo of a mere hollow word – and the questioning of it? Not even an error – only a matter of indifference.

12. Inceptual Thinking, the one Readiness . . .

Removed already out of the epoch that just begins its completion, inceptual thinking that prepares a readiness for the decision between grounding the truth of be-ing and unleashedness of machination of beings [G41] stands under its own conditions.

No success or failure should lure and intimidate such thinking; neither hope nor hopelessness can motivate or suppress such mindfulness. The necessity of what is undecided since the first beginning is alone the ground for thinking-mindfulness. This necessity has nothing in common with the mere unavoidability of "fate": it is the accepted liberation unto a distress of be-ing so that be-ing may sway as the necessitating.

However, this ground unfolds its power of grounding only if that thinking-mindfulness arises from out of the knowing-awareness "of" (the "of" is the be-ing-historical genitive) Da-sein: to think in long drafts, to think unto the *truth of be-ing* and seldom to interrupt this course of thought with a brief and casually made statement about the *be-ing of truth*.

Only whoever is capable of traversing again and again such reticent and prolonged paths is fit to be a thinker that comes. Whoever has never advanced into such paths, and has not withstood for a short while the powerful tremors of all foundational 'time-spaces' at the threshold of the transformation of man into Da-sein, does not know what *thinking* is.

For a while and at irrevocable junctures the pathways unto engrounding the truth of be-ing touch upon the limits of human capability and in this capacity possess the warrant for lighting up be-ing's 'free-play of time-space' which can never be propped up by a being.

Only when that history of surrendering the foundational thinkers of this beginning to ruination enters the knowing-awareness is philosophy removed from trivialization and degradation done to it by 'history', because philosophy has then gained access to the ground which alone is appropriate to philosophy, that is, attained its own necessity as leaping ahead into the uniqueness of be-ing. In the 'free-play of the time-space' of be-ing, philosophy risks the truth of be-ing. Thus philosophy neither belongs to gods nor to man, it is neither something that [G42] grows out of the earth nor is it a product of the world: It is the midpoint in the intersection of all beings in the sense of an ab-grounding surge of preserving all simple question-worthiness.

Philosophy is the knowing-awareness that is charged with *the* decision which itself will be decided by be-ing. Thus, as this thinking easily loses itself in a conflict, the pathway of inceptual thinking becomes clear in stretches: should not first man be transformed, so that be-ing may receive the grounding of its truth through him, or is this the first that be-ing itself en-owns truth and necessitates man unto a decision, or does neither the one nor the other count?

If one wanted first to breed the strong type of man, who would be fit for bringing about the grounding of being, this would still mean to think of man as the subject of beings so that only another pursuit of beings would be bred, a pursuit that would have to subscribe soon to continuation of the heretofore.

But if one wanted to hope for a clearing of be-ing like a revelation, then even thus man would be permanently driven into his heretofore.

Neither calculation nor empty hope can sustain the crossing, rather only the inquiry into the utmost decision – an inquiry that originarily thinks unto what is to come and thereby remains prepared for the word of be-ing.

Because now any foundational thinking solely thinks for the sake of *be-ing*, everywhere the pathways of this thinking are like accidental approaches and advances, that is, movements unto Da-sein with being as measure, i.e., they are of enowning. These approaches and advances are neither a description of beings nor a symbolic interpretation, rather the leaping-forth of en-ownment.

III

PHILOSOPHY

(Self-mindfulness: Historical Contention;
Being-historical Thinking — Metaphysics)

13. Philosophy

What is in play in the play which in the future has to be played with the "entry" of be-ing itself, is what has never been in play in the history of thinking, namely that the truth of be-ing be inquired into, that a ground be grounded for this truth, and that man – transforming himself – becomes ab-grounded in this ground: the tremor not only of the "earth" and of "people" but also of 'beings as such in the whole'. The only decision ahead is this: whether be-ing is inquired into in terms of the sway of its truth or whether beings retain their machination and pursue a lack of decision that prevents that which is sole and unique from ever again coming forth and be a beginning.

Nowadays all speaking of "decision" (cf. 16. Be-ing; 39. Clearing of Be-ing and Man) must fall easily prey to the perils of this insidious "slogan", because much of what is loudly and frequently passed off as "decisive" is merely the foreground of what is decided long ago and its offshoots that evade decision. Nevertheless in defiance of every misuse, a word must be said about decision in terms of the one question: whether decision[a] is to be between "being" and "non-being", that is, between preserving the extant and what continues to go on, and cessation of such prospects and ways, *or* whether the decision is to be more originary [Ursprünglich], that is, to be a decision on be-ing and beings (cf. 39. Clearing of Be-ing and Man). For, that decision never decides about

---

[a] What does de-cision mean? Why this and from where?

"being", rather only about rescuing or losing *beings* which are nevertheless questionless in their being – beings that belong to the modern procuring of culture and power in terms of an omnipresent life.

It is all the same and unworthy of decision, whether we—people and individuals of this epoch—*"are"* or *"are not"*, whether we possess the securing of this "life" or fall prey to the mere flow of the epoch and its inner decay in the illusion of unfolding of power and of the unbounded "art" of inventing and organizing. [G46] What is de-ciding above all is enopening the decision and casting it unto the future: what is de-ciding is whether in advance be-ing itself (be-ing of possible 'beings in the whole') arrives at its grounded truth or whether be-ing is overshadowed and eclipsed by the mere actuality and effectivity of beings.

Decision is not decision between "being" or "non-being" of man but between the truth of being of any possible being and the machination of 'beings in the whole' that are abandoned by being.

Decision belongs to the sway of be-ing itself and it is not a contrivance of man because he always receives from this de-cision and its refusal what is for his way of being either inherently grounding or operational and fleeting. Be-ing de-cides. In its swaying, and as such, be-ing dis-engages itself unto en-ownment. (Here decision is not what gets added to a discriminating attitude.) As refusal, be-ing extricates itself from every differentiation [*Scheidung*] à la discriminated beings; whether posited equal to a being or only placed ahead or even behind a being, be-ing no longer lets itself be "metaphysically" called being "of" a being.

Be-ing is the de-cision unto itself as unto the ab-ground and is thus the ungroundable distress of the necessity of all grounding; in this way, be-ing is the hidden exuberance of Da-sein, and therefore the swaying sites of a possible history of man since be-ing is of yore the ab-ground of gods – ab-ground as the chaos (the gaping opening) of gods (cf. below G83).

What philosophy has to know in the future – what is primary and comes from long ago – is that be-ing has to be grounded from out of *its* truth.

Therefore, as decidedly as never before philosophy's mindfulness of itself – that means mindfulness of what is to be en-thought in philosophy – must be a mindfulness of its "time". Philosophy's mindfulness of itself must know what is of today, not for purposes of practical enhancement and alteration of the status of a "historical situation", but [G47] by taking what is of today as fundamental hints at that which being-historically sways in the epoch of modernity. Moreover, this mindfulness is not at the service of a mere extended calculation of "epochs" or even their classification: it solely serves the echo of being itself, which as machination has relinquished 'beings in the whole' to their own contrivance and their own onward rend as "life" so that the utmost distress of the concealed lack of distress prepares de-cision in the quietest stillness. To the extent that philosophy, as en-thinking of be-ing (cf. below G357) obtains its genuine ownmost, it is enowned by *this* de-cision – by be-ing itself – and belongs to the ab-ground of be-ing and remains a stranger in every "culture". And yet, if *this* decision "of" be-ing between being and beings is in play, and if be-ing calls humanness to the *thinking* of be-ing for the grounding of its truth so that be-ing as such might sway in the open again, then in the history of being philosophy must once again become for being a beginning. Towards such a beginning, philosophy needs to have an inkling of possessing, in strict accordance with its ownmost, its own necessity. Philosophy obtains this possessing only through a *mindfulness of itself.*

Philosophy should not evade the demeaning impression that surrounds every mindfulness, namely that it is a hesitation and a cover-up for the incapability for acting.

In our estimations we still know little about the *acting*-character of thoughtful thinking; still we do not appraise the enigma, namely that philosophy often and readily determines itself in the light of what is alien to philosophy (erudition, wisdom) – a determination that philosophy itself has probably brought about and conditioned in its continuance. Through mindfulness philosophy ventures unto the mandate of what is set ahead of philosophy – a venturing unto what is to be en-thought and to be grounded in Da-sein by virtue of this thinking, so that the mystery of man's being will be *saved* rather than abolished.

However, from where does this thinking receive directions for *its style*? From where, if not from that which is to be en-thought [G48] itself? But before that which is to be en-thought is interrogated, how can it already beforehand grant directive for the style of this thinking? Does the old saying, "τοῖς ὁμοίοις τὰ ὅμοια γιγνώσκεσθαι"[a] – "only through the like the like will be known" – primarily apply here, and, if yes, why?

Prior to thinking and always the most question-worthy is be-ing, is *that* de-ciding [*Ent-scheidende*]. That which is 'like' be-ing can only be the highest honouring, it is the capability to project-open greatness still

---

[a] Cf. Aristoteles, *De anima* (Biehl / Apelt, Leipzig: Teubner, 1911), A 2, 405 b 15.

greater, so that what is great might be engrossed in its greatness. But only what is great possesses the strength to be greater, whereas what is small betrays its ownmost by always becoming smaller – even if it is "only" so that from time to time it claims greatness as its own. The sheerest furthering of greatness is *the* honouring wherein what is most worthy belongs entirely to itself. Therefore, questioning in the sense of inquiring into the most question-worthy is no idle intrusiveness but the unblending of all knowing-awareness unto what is sole and unique. Honouring as a thinking honouring is neither currying a favour nor transgressing, but a dissociating exposition that must venture its own foundational distress. Dissociating exposition exposes questioning to be-ing in such a way that the latter is honoured as what is interrogated and its response is taken over into the grounding of Da-sein.

Through mindfulness – inquiring-musing – man enters the truth of be-ing and thus takes man "himself" unto the fundamental transformation that arises out of this truth: the expectancy of Da-sein. Mindfulness means at the same time becoming free from the "freedom" of the "subject", from the self-entangled 'dis-humanization' of man.

Mindfulness means overcoming "reason", be it as mere receiving of what is pre-given (νοῦς), be it as calculating and explaining (*ratio*), or be it as planning and securing.

"Reason" remains closed off to the sway of truth; [G49] it only pursues a thinking that is turned towards beings and is always a superficial thinking.

Mindfulness is attuning of the grounding-attunement of man insofar as this attunement attunes him unto be-ing, and unto the groundership of the truth of be-ing.

Mindfulness transfers man unto Dasein, provided that mindfulness itself is already en-owned by be-ing. But be-ing longs for that *word* which always sways as en-owning.

Philosophy: this sole struggle for the imageless word "of" be-ing in an epoch of asthenia and lack of enthusiasm for the swaying word.

Mindfulness: in the epoch of the planetary lack of mindfulness.

I. Philosophy in mindfulness of itself.

II. Philosophy in the dissociating exposition of its history (as metaphysics).[a]

---

[a] For II, i.e., on the being-historical unfolding of the sway of metaphysics as the sway of the history of the truth of "beings as such in the whole" (Plato to Nietzsche), cf., "Die Überwindung der Metaphysik", in *Metaphysik und Nihilismus*, (GA 67).

Both are one, history of be-ing, and grounding belongingness to that history.

I.
14. Philosophy in Mindfulness of Itself

Philosophy's mindfulness of itself belongs to philosophy because mindfulness is demanded by that which philosophy, as foundational thinking, has to think: by being. Such mindfulness does not serve the purpose of provisionally securing the concept of philosophy so that philosophy could then begin to be carried out and pursued. Such mindfulness does not exhaust itself also in a supplementary "reflection" of philosophy upon itself in the form of [G50] a "philosophy of philosophy" which marks the end of all possibilities of philosophy, and only 'historically' counts up philosophy's past figures in an indifferent "typology".

Philosophy's mindfulness of itself belongs to the thinking of being. Be-ing sways solely in the clearing which is be-ing itself. But this clearing remains sustainable only in a projecting-opening that throws itself unto the opening of this clearing and 'owns itself over' to the openness of this opening and ventures to ground it. This grounding projecting-opening en-thinks the truth of be-ing and – however different and contrary this may seem – is thereby nonetheless en-owned only by be-ing itself.

The "development" of philosophy is always the unfolding of the ownmost of philosophy via ever simpler gathering unto the unique thought of be-ing.

Its goal is neither to communicate a knowledge, nor to set up a doctrine. To *be* the foundational knowing-awareness (preserving the grounded truth) but never to be "effective" remains philosophy's ownmost. Only in this way does philosophy find itself in its ownmost which belongs to be-ing. If philosophy succeeds in this, then it also takes for granted the danger of misinterpretations, because philosophy's ownmost is necessarily estranging and misleads to constantly recurring attempts to fix philosophy's ownmost by fitting it into an inappropriate, but seemingly more intelligible, context.

Because philosophy – non-deducible from beings and belonging to the uniqueness of be-ing – can only know what is its unblended ownmost, philosophy is also most frequently, directly and thoroughly threatened by a loss of what is ownmost to philosophy, a loss that always and even in different ways looks like enrichment, consolidation and corroboration of what is ownmost to philosophy. That is why philosophy now counts as science, now as art (poetry), now as world-view.

Because philosophy *is* foundational knowing-awareness and thus sustains the hidden glow of the sway of truth, philosophy is lured [G51] into drifting into "sciences", and like these and apparently supported by their results, into making scientificality the distinction of knowing-awareness. And yet this is always a lapse into what is subordinate. All scientificality of philosophy becomes a denial of its incomparable rank in spite of an apparent gain on splendour and richness of knowable beings and their manifold presentability in the forms of explaining and proving.

Because philosophy *says* be-ing and is, therefore, only as word in word, and because its word never merely means or designates what is to be said but precisely in saying is be-ing itself, philosophy might hurriedly try to cross directly over into *poetry* as help in need and especially as receptacle. And yet this always remains an entanglement at the roots of what is of equal rank to philosophy and which on account of its most ownmost sways by itself, and from time immemorial incessantly avoids the thinking of be-ing. For, the ownmost of poetry also grounds history but differently; poetry's "times" do not coincide with those of thinking. Approximation of philosophy to poetry and consequently to art endangers thinking knowing-awareness not because on account of this approximation thinking relinquishes the rigor of "scientificality", which indeed is inceptually inappropriate to thinking. Seeking refuge in poetry means fleeing from the keen boldness of the question of being, which always shatters machination of beings and its denial of be-ing and must persevere in the unease and cleft of a breakage so that thinking of be-ing never dares to come to rest in a "work". To philosophy belongs the serenity of the mastery of imageless knowing-awareness.

Because as thinking of being, philosophy has always already thought 'beings in the whole', philosophy easily succumbs to the presumptuous demand to raise itself henceforth to *"world-view"* in order to satisfy expectations of "life" and thus above all to corroborate the truth of philosophy. And yet this flattery of the "actuality of life" always continues to disguise that illusion [G52] behind which the lack of courage is hidden – the courage to persevere within the ownmost of the thinking of be-ing. For, such thinking can neither provide a ground for the "active life" that would directly nourish it, nor offer a goal to which "life" could attach its purposes. Thinking of be-ing does not fit into the role of a world-view, equally less is it able to replace the faith of the Church. Thinking of be-ing has to bear such incapability and, with it, the semblance of a fundamental lack, and all this out of the knowing-awareness that the grounding projecting-opening of the sway of truth by this thinking *is* only the swaying of be-ing itself which thus maintains the clearing that is thrown among beings, and from which all acting and all yielding obtains its times and its spaces, its eternities and its disseminations. Untouchable by such things and repelling their onward pull, only be-ing bestows to all beings and even to the non-beings above all and always the domains in which human realms are erected and destroyed.

No being is capable of lending be-ing a ground, because be-ing is the ab-ground wherein the distress of everything groundless has its depth and the necessity of every grounding has its peak. Philosophy belongs only to the clearing of the ab-ground, insofar as philosophy undertakes to say the simplest and the stillest, that is, the word of the truth of be-ing, the 'saying' [*Spruch*] of a knowing-awareness that is without science, has never the power of a decree and does not know powerlessness.

But because *thinking* of be-ing as thinking of *be-ing* is thrown into the ab-ground, it lies "between" beings, and is exposed vehemently to beings and to their pursuit – a vehemence from which every being as a rule is protected. The fundamental danger to the thinking of be-ing shows itself in the fact that, although sciences, poetry (art), and world-views, according to their nature, rank, origin and effect are among themselves basically different, they nevertheless equally crave for deforming or even replacing the unblended ownmost of philosophy. However, in truth these three that come from the predominance of beings are at times [G53] delegated with the task of distorting philosophy with the pretext of improving and rescuing it so as to subject be-ing to the domination of beings and to provide forgottenness of being – needed by all representing and producing of beings – with exclusive right.

But thinking of be-ing is mindful of itself since this thinking en-thinks that in its truth to which this thinking belongs because this thinking is en-owned by that which is *en-owning*.

This mindfulness is not a means of knowledge, it is not a reverting to a thinking that has come to a halt in the direction of knowledge, and is left behind, and organized like the extant. Rather, this mindfulness is the deciding leap ahead into the prolonged advancing for leaping into the origin, into the "leap" (rift) that is of the ab-ground and lights up, which as be-ing sways 'in-between' beings, so that beings *as such* may be preserved and forgotten; so that at times beings may join the sheltering-concealing of be-ing and its decisions, at times evade that sheltering-concealing, and at times sink into a lack of decision.

Thinking of be-ing does not come to an end with such mindfulness in order to cut itself off from be-ing, and so to speak, only to think about "itself". As mindfulness of itself, this thinking begins *as* thinking *of* be-ing. And in this manner philosophy begins with itself and thus it begins itself: philosophy *is* beginning. But philosophy is now a beginning that is other than the first beginning which for the first time en-thought being and called it φύσις.

Everything depends on there being again a beginning of philosophy wherein philosophy is itself this beginning so that be-ing itself sways as origin. Only in this way the power of beings and their pursuit, and along with it every purpose-oriented calculation, will be shattered. Only in this way an inkling arises again of that which does not need any effect, but towers through everything in that it *is*. But what is peculiar only to be-ing is to sway as be-ing. *Therefrom* thinking of be-ing has its own swaying origin. (cf. 67. Thinking of Be-ing).

Philosophy is *of* be-ing; it *belongs* to be-ing, not merely according to the manner in which philosophy grasps be-ing, but as the swaying of the [G54] truth that *belongs* to be-ing. Philosophy has its history in this truth, but because the truth of be-ing is the ab-ground this truth entangles itself beforehand and for a long time in the illusion that being as beingness exhausts the sway of be-ing (cf. XIV. Be-ing and Being); and that representing being is merely an obtrusion into being which be-ing may do without. Beingness becomes the object of the most general representing and this becomes the framework for "sciences" as the basic forms of knowledge. The sciences, however, appear as achievements and products of "spirit" and as "cultural" goods. Thus it is not surprising to come upon the history of thinking as the history of spirit and as the history of culture or as the history of its "problems", whereby the history of thinking itself is held to be what is most unquestionable. What continues to be banished is any inkling that philosophy could belong to the history of be-ing, indeed solely to this history, to the history of the struggle of ab-grounds and groundings of the truth of be-ing and nothing else. Instead of that inkling, there is the dominant claim on philosophy (as "wordly wisdom", as a "morality" that sets values, and as a "science" that solves the "mystery of the world") to account for beings and for the security of the extant man. At the end, this twisted and presumptuous claim plays itself out as the court of arbitration that decides the failure and usefulness of philosophy. One could view these sort of things with indifference, if therein an unrecognizable and stubborn representation of philosophy would not always consolidate itself, and degenerate into a hardly noticeable but unassailable repelling of any inquiry into what is ownmost to philosophy.

The consequence of this misinterpretation of philosophy expresses itself in the state of an epoch that allows this epoch to know everything 'historical' about philosophy and its history but to have no knowing-awareness of the one thing that is entrusted to philosophy's ownmost, namely to ask the question of the truth of be-ing and in the midst of the disarray of beings to set up this question in its inevitability.

[G55] As philosophy's mindfulness of itself, such knowing-awareness unfolds itself as thinking of be-ing. But this mindfulness reaches into the sphere of grounding what is ownmost to man, who, since long ago, is intensely engaged in an unfathomable flight from his ownmost – a flight that he always makes easier and more fleeting for himself with the illusion that he makes progress towards the completion of his domination.

By contrast, mindfulness – giving least importance to the "I" and the "we" – is primarily mindful of the fact that man is an interminable mystery unto himself. However, this being-a-mystery does not let itself be restrained and organized: man can only submit to this mystery to the extent that he does not ward it off by veering into the subterfuge of a presumed "science" of "man". But that mystery, in whose preservation man grounds the returning unto himself, is the sheltering-concealing of the allotment of man unto the truth of be-ing which holds itself ready for the free-play of decision, wherein the countering of man's ownmost and the godhood of gods is en-owned. This sheltering that conceals is something simple; it does not need anything unusual in order to be encountered, but throws a restlessness unto the ab-ground of Da-sein that remains the hearth of all history.

The inauguration of the question of the truth of be-ing in the midst of beings' abandonment by being must know that its grounding of history is inconspicuous. And the more originarily [Ursprünglich] its saying grows out of the en-thinking of be-ing, the more it must experience that in every attempt the poet is always capable of achieving the highest in grounding. The charm of what is near and inflaming shines through the poet's word. This word finds the most listening ear directly in the heart and does not need the keen boldness of questioning that throws itself unto what is most question-worthy. The word of the poet speaks unto what is intimate and kindles its fire in it. Thinking-saying rends unto what is strange by leaving that which is to be known within that which makes no impression and lacks effect. Thinking of be-ing grounds the unconditioned, still undecided aloneness of the 'in-between', which though undecided, fosters [G56] decision; grounds the origin that rends a clearing that remains an imponderable lonesomeness. The imponderable is be-ing. Only in en-thinking of *that* clearing does the thinker acquire that venture, which without prop and protection inquires into the sway of truth. Only in venturing can the imponderable, be-ing, be experienced: the en-owning that in the distress of decision lets the counter-turning swaying allotting of man's domain and the godhood resonate and thus keeps in reserve for beings the intimate discord of the world and the earth, so that beings as such could have a claim on being, and emerge in the openness of that discord and consolidate themselves into non-beings. Be-ing is not only incalculable (never to be represented and produced): as the incalculable it also remains imponderable insofar as it does not let itself be put on a scale that measures only beings against beings. What is an 'other' to be-ing is not even a being, be-ing has no 'other' to it, for, even 'nothing' is thoroughly of the same sway as be-ing.

Be-ing renders itself lonesome, *is* as this lonesomeness. And, therefore, only a thinking is capable of reaching be-ing which as a mindful thinking that inquires into the truth of itself is en-owned by be-ing unto Da-sein, unto the groundership of the sway of truth, and is assigned to aloneness and to the fundamental lack of any need for having any effect.

Philosophy's mindfulness of itself is not a movement that counters its threatening and undetainable eradication because even this eradication arises out of the sway of be-ing to which philosophy belongs as it grounds and forgets the truth of this sway.

Philosophy allows its eradication in a twofold manner, each of which is ambiguous: on the one hand philosophy at least relinquishes its name in favour of a serviceability that was once practiced in the Medieval Scholastic. On the other hand, philosophy succumbs to the illusion that with the erudite practice of traditional disciplines (logic, ethics, etc.) it is already sufficiently saved and secured for the future. Both manners of eradication of philosophy could combine [G57] and their insidiousness might be warded off so that within the culture-industry philosophy will be taken up as a desideratum and item of decor.

This eradication of philosophy is more radical than any blatant debasing and explicit abolishing of philosophy. This eradication is the promising indication that someday be-ing requires an inceptual inquiry and calls upon man to set free his still ungrounded ownmost. But this indication points far ahead. Meanwhile a long time has to pass before the grounding word "of" be-ing can be said. What alone matters up to such a moment of the history of be-ing is to prepare, from afar and unrecognized, the unique possibility that be-ing sways from out of itself and casts its truth around itself without thereby ever needing effect, success, extolment and defence.

Man can continue to be in the sphere of this possibility (in Da-*sein*) only if he has transformed his hitherto un-ownmost; only if his grounding-attunements encompass his closed-off and pressing earthbound way of being, and only if he can raise this into a world that is built from the hint of be-ing (from en-owning). This possibility confronts man with the struggle for deciding between belongingness to be-ing or an ultimate loss of his ownmost.

Without anyone ever being able to notice and record how and when it has come to this possibility, this possibility brings about that Da-sein is grounding and the swaying is happening: the countering of godhood and man's domain. The utmost unobtrusiveness of preparation of the truth of be-ing corresponds to the sway of be-ing, to refusal. Seemingly "only" preparatory, that is, merely paving the way without grounding anything, philosophy's mindfulness of itself is the closest shape that this preparation takes. This mindfulness puts into question *the ownmost* of philosophy and remains unaffected by the affirmations and negations of what is 'historically' current, that is, the un-ownmost of the philosophy-industry.

Philosophy's mindfulness of itself *is* philosophy itself, is the thinking that is en-owned by be-ing. Mindfulness is always [G58] historical and enacts a decision of the history of be-ing. In the epoch of metaphysics which shapes its end in the unquestionableness of being, an unquestion-ableness that has conceded everything to the omnipotence of beings ("the actual", "the effective", "the living"), the first word of mindfulness – the first word which calls out unto the sway of be-ing – must be said with a 'saying' that metaphysics indeed has already uttered in its end: *be-ing is 'nothing'*. (cf. 78. Be-ing and "Negativity".) Hegel's metaphysical thought, which determines being as beingness of the immediate, undetermined representation, that is, only as the not-yet of the utmost absolute actuality (of idea), differs infinitely from the being-historical content of the 'saying', which utters that be-ing is never a being. In contrast to all beings, this non-being is refusal, wherein be-ing withdraws unto its ownmost sway and gives a hint of itself as the origin, in which 'nothing' has its provenance.

The 'saying', 'be-ing is nothing' utters the utmost ambiguity insofar as it passes off be-ing as what is specifically most worthy of 'nothing' and puts forward be-ing's sway as what is most worthy of questioning. The 'saying' is the admission of the superfluousness of all philosophy insofar as philosophy counts as thinking of being. This 'saying' transfers mindfulness into that which lacks prop and support; it tells of the freedom unto becoming free in the ab-ground as the distress of the sway of the truth of be-ing which is to be grounded. Without this sway man will be denied the capability for god and along with it the possibility of once again taking a stance in a being-historical decision, and thus to counter the grounded belongingness to be-ing by creating a history of gods' distress. Without this sway man will be denied the possibility of submitting his ownmost to the preparation for the godhood of gods, so that man's ownmost may be extinguished in the glow of be-ing and this glow may find itself lighting up the stillness wherein – from the simpleness of its uniqueness – whatever is worthy of being bestows itself to whatever is worthy to be, and out of refusal arises a bestowal that creates the richness of what is rare and noble and [G59] takes this richness back into the hidden, wherein – withdrawn from the publicness of machination – the moments of be-ing turn unto each other and first create for "eternity" *its* time.

Mindfulness would be meaningless; it would be deprived of the sphere of truth that is allotted to it, if since long ago an uncanny and reticent sheltering-concealing of be-ing were not to enact itself in the history of be-ing – a sheltering-concealing that only now must be experienced and acknowledged by throwing free the question of the truth of be-ing.

However, no one knows what this other beginning of the history of be-ing "means". Only one thing is certain, namely that since long ago every 'historical' reverting (Christianity) and every 'technological' progress proceeded outside the path of possible decisions. No explanation of beings (with reference to a creator and redeemer god) and no glorification of beings (by a mere affirmation of the extant "life in itself" which is 'historically' burdened a thousandfold) can ever catch up with be-ing and remove man into that 'between', in whose perseverance he remains infinitely far from his ownmost and, equally, from the godhood of gods so that out of this farness he experiences the nearness of the venture of be-ing and its necessity.

The falling of be-ing into beings that were already unconcealed long ago (throughout the history of the first beginning) is the en-owning of en-ownment to which only those can be equal as guardians who come from the great disenownment of 'beings in the whole' (their abandonment by being) and who, through this disenownment, become those who – in startled dismay – are set free; for whom this dismay remains the grounding-attunement from out of which the truth of the 'saying' dawns on them – a 'saying' that says that be-ing is 'nothing', and that no power can reach the swaying rank of be-ing.

Thus speaks the law of the other beginning.

Philosophy's mindfulness of itself places philosophy unto its ownmost, and does not provide philosophy with any subterfuge into what is fortuitous and supplementary. Mindfulness means necessitating unto what is necessary, namely the grounding of be-ing.

[G60] Philosophy is grounding.

Those who ground – the founders – are those who, by transforming the *sway* of be-ing, transmit its *swaying* to the ground of an originary sway of truth. By contrast, the creators always renew and augment only beings. In a succession that is indifferent to him, every founder is a creator. No creator is already a founder. The founders are the rare ones among the lone ones. They "possess" their uniqueness in that they never find ready for them what gives them rank and support, but rather project it open as the most question-worthy, which they have to bear without protection and prop.

The founders determine the barely graspable 'times' of the beginning and the 'going under' of foundational epochs.

In the clearing of what is grounded by them blows the storm of those decisions which do not judge the pre-given, but only raise to its sway what is decidable and is to be decided.

Considered 'historically', those epochs from which philosophy has to withhold the distress of decision in order to let them move towards their own completion are *without* "philosophy". The unmistakable indication of this is the situation in which with some reservation "philosophy" continues to be desirable as decorative pieces in cultural competitions (cf. above, G54).

In such epochs (cf. the Middle Ages) "mindfulness" of philosophy is through and through a mere sham that consolidates itself on a conceptual definition of philosophy and is content with calculating philosophy's usefulness. This gives rise to a polymorphic "interest" in philosophy and its 'history' and thus to that ambience and attunement that make one insensitive to any actually questioning mindfulness.

But to the one who knows, such sham points to shelteredness-concealedness of be-ing. It – *er*[+] – is be-ing's most unwilling and most unsuspecting witness.

[G61] Mindfulness as well as philosophy always belongs solely to 'the ones to come'. However, there may be times in which lack of mindfulness is promoted and pursued simultaneously by the powers that dominate the epoch and by those that are dominated.

On the other hand, 'the ones to come' are indeed of a rugged stock that rescues the Germans by urging them unto the distress of their ownmost. 'The ones to come' are the reticent ones: they say what they say only as the distressing occasion of reticence. They thus force an intimation that, after all, something decisive rests somewhere in knowing-awareness but has not yet become knowable. At the same time they demand from the intimating ones – provided the latter are strong enough – to bear the nearness of the hidden, and to obtain the unboundedness [*das Freie*] of the question-worthiness of that knowable. 'The ones to come' do not escape into substitute-worlds and illusory appeasements; they get shattered at what "is", so that be-ing may rise unto the openness of its question-worthiness.

Foundational reticence is the firmness of a gentleness that reticently compels merely a few unto what is unique so that the latter know that without a knowing-awareness of the sway of truth, the realm of foremost decisions remains closed off to man.

The mere wordless ones are not the reticent ones, but neither are the 'talkers' nor the 'scribes'.

Those sayers must come, who habitually ponder beforehand every word so that all stress remains suspended in the word and the word resists consumption. But how do those come around who can listen? Only those who are capable of saying are capable of hearing [*hören*], without at once becoming the enslaved [*Hörigen*].

But perhaps the word "of" be-ing must en-own itself and remain in the stillness of the few; perhaps a decision is already made about a gulf between be-ing and what "they" hold as a being. Perhaps this gulf itself is the beginning, if once again the inceptual places itself between gods and man as the bridge for their countering.

[+] {Should be *es*.}

However, be-ing still continues to be overshadowed by beings [G62] and consequently any mindfulness of be-ing must venture, in manifold disguises, among beings and their pursuit.

The *thinking inquiry* into being as enowning can only begin by way of *historically* thinking-through the history of being, and this thinking inquiry must frequently retreat into the indistinct gestalt of a *'historical'* study of Occidental metaphysics. And this 'history' is content with the "treatment" of individual – seemingly fortuitously selected – "treatises" and works because a comprehensive presentation would appear too obtrusive and would be hooked into the industry called 'history' of philosophy. On the other hand, the momentum for mindfulness must lie ready in the impression made by what is fortuitous and fragmentary. Shaped in this way, the enactment of mindfulness can never arise out of calculation, but must be determined only by the unmastered question-worthiness of be-ing.

The 'historical' representation intends and always gives rise to the opinion that it dwells on what is historically effective. But thinking mind-fulness ponders solely what is: be-ing, that which does not need effect. The 'historical' impression made by thinking robs thinking above all of its ownmost and unique necessity and casts it among the traditional forms in which the past of "spiritual phenomena" are studied. Thinking mind-fulness remains inconspicuous among such forms, almost like a neutral curiosity for what has been. This, however, is necessary because any explicit emerging of a "philosophy" drifts right away into the public horizon of a "world-view", which, in addition is contrived. This horizon renders the actual questioning of thinking indiscernible. And yet, thinking cannot avoid "appearing" within a 'historical' representation.

It is not important to the thinking *into* whose enactment mindfulness must inquire, whether this thinking succeeds in making a statement on what is hitherto unrecognized; it is not important whether this thinking discovers something that [G63] serves "life", not important whether this thinking achieves a flawless explainability of all beings, not important whether this thinking obtains a cohesive guideline for self-orientation valuing. Rather, what is solely fundamental is whether be-ing itself en-owns itself in its truth and thus as en-owning throws the ab-ground unto beings and unsettles all machination, that is, the counterpart of the first beginning.

All the criteria for judging philosophy are destroyed, but beginning again, philosophy itself must first open up the struggle for the 'spaces' of the mastery of the most question-worthy. Vis-à-vis withholding of be-ing in the midst of effectiveness of beings, only little can occasionally endure.

No sooner does philosophy cease to think being in advance in the direction of beings and as their beingness, and instead inquires ahead into the truth of be-ing, than its self-mindfulness – seemingly only an *addendum* to philosophy – intertwines entirely with philosophy's ownmost. Philosophy means "love of wisdom". Let us think this word out of a foundational mindfulness by relinquishing the representational domains of everyday life, erudition, cultural concerns and doctrines of happiness. Then the word says: "*love*" is the will that wills the beloved *be*; the will that wills that the beloved finds its way unto its ownmost and sways therein. Such a will does not wish and demand anything. Through honoring, and not by trying to create the loved one, this will lets above all the loved one – what is worthy of loving – "become". The word 'love' calls what is worthy to be loved "wisdom".

"*Wisdom*" is foundational knowing-awareness; is inabiding the truth of be-ing. Hence that "love" loves be-ing in a unique 'fore-loving', [*Vor-liebe*]. This: that be-ing "be" is this love's beloved. What matters to this beloved, to its truth and its grounding, is the will to foundational knowing-awareness. Be-ing, however, is the ab-ground.

Out of a self-reliant exertion, the "will" "unto" be-ing does not turn be-ing into an "object" of striving so as to grasp be-ing representationally-explanatorily and to set be-ing aside as a possession. This "will" is the will of be-ing, [G64] en-owned by be-ing itself unto what is ownmost to this will. This "will" is not an autocratic self-seeking and exertion; the "will" here means the ardor, the grounding-attunement of persevering in the destiny of acquiescing to the distress of ab-ground. Such an acquiescing lies outside inactivity and activity – mere tolerating and wallowing in "anguish" is unknown to it. The ardor for that foundational knowing-awareness is en-owned as this acquiescing. And this acquiescing is the decidedness called forth by be-ing and held in the trajectory of the hint that sustains the 'owning-over' of man – from the ground of Da-sein – to the truth of be-ing. That ardor is the conveyorship of the settlement of countering and strife – the settlement wherein the last god announces its abodes.

And yet, philosophy is not a human contrivance, but a passageway of the *history* of the truth of be-ing – the history in which be-ing's 'turning to', and 'turning away from' man's ownmost happens. To put this "philosophically" it means that primarily and actually it is being itself that en-grounds the ground of the truth of be-ing; it means en-grounding the truth of be-ing as finding of its ground, a finding that refuses all support of beings; it means the ardor of en-ownment, the lightening of the truth's sway in the midst of beings when a being, after the thunderstorm, has found its way to beings and soon thereafter has forgotten the lightning.

Because be-ing is "philosophical", man must venture into philosophy and through philosophy into the whole, so that the allotment unto be-ing as ground of man's possible history is 'owned over' to him. Only through the like is the like raised unto the clearing which is ownmost to the like.

Philosophy does not deal "with" something, neither "with" 'beings in the whole' nor "with" be-ing. Philosophy *is* the imageless saying "of" be-ing itself. This saying is not statements made "about" be-ing, rather be-ing sways as this saying. Philosophy *is* such a saying or it is nothing at all. The rest is complicated erudition which has mistaken its object and is therefore neither "useful" and productive for science, [G65] nor does it ever even touch upon a decision in philosophy.

Amidst the confusion that is spreading now, the highest measure comes only from what is most profoundly – being-historically – ownmost to philosophy and promises mindfulness a direction.

Thus the most exacting test faces the thinker, namely that as long as he makes statements "about something" the thinker does not even operate within the field of questioning.

This field of questioning, which is not in need of an object, is avoided like a plague by all usual opinions and beliefs. And yet, this avoiding does not resolve the enigma that continually besets philosophy also, namely that sometimes a self-destruction surges within philosophy, so that its pathways of thinking and their means will be misused in order to compromise philosophy itself before the bleary eyes of Christians and non-Christians as impossible, and as tragicomical (more "comical" than "tragic".) This destructive compromising would be explained, but not fundamentally established, if one were to trace it back to the jealous asthenia for the questioning leaps, and to the failure to venture the questioning leaps. It is rather so that everything that is allotted to the beginning is accompanied by that which desires destruction, since beginning is the grounding of the ab-ground, and this grounding disseminates the semblance of annihilation. Where beginning does not begin, but is merely entangled in and seized by opining and reservation, annihilation appears in the misshapen form of incapability for grounding, which – employing the forms of judgement of the educated cultural fanatics – one can characterize as "tragic" and "comical" simultaneously. The measure for such a discordant attitude towards philosophy – an attitude seemingly seriously engaged in thinking but in fact only negating it – does not originate from within philosophy itself, but rather from a flight enacted beforehand into its denial.

But this spirit of self-destruction that encompasses every inceptual thinking would remain merely a superfluous "sophistry", if one wanted [G66] to take it into account as the unwilling and unknowing confirmation that the inceptual is preparing itself. Beginning never needs such a confirmation. Only the god of cultural Christianity needs the devil as confirmation of its godhood.

En-thinking of be-ing does not have anything with which it "occupies" itself because it is en-ownment of be-ing itself and nothing else besides.

Philosophy, which prepares the other beginning, does not obtain its basic stance and thereby its ownmost by crossing out of metaphysics and adjusting it, but only through a leap into an entirely different questioning that lays an abyss between being-historical thinking and metaphysics. Because adjusting is alien to this thinking, it also does not know an over-throwing ("revolution") by means of which only an uprootedness is set in motion that sooner or later brings its destructive character to light. Neither adjusting nor overthrowing but the grounding of a hidden, awaiting "ground" that is not propped up by any being – the grounding of an ab-ground which sways as be-ing – is the only ardor of being-historical thinking. To the extent that for the sake of a history-grounding encounter, and *not* for the sake of a 'historical' discussion, being-historical inquiry must think within the "destruction" (*Sein und Zeit**), this destructing dis-mantling has everything as its "object", which, in the course of the history of metaphysics, had to be a displacement of the first beginning, and a falling off from this beginning, and an empowering of the consequences of a necessary want of grounding the truth in this beginning. "Destruction" is not "destructive" in the sense of annihilating for the sake of annihilation; it is the "laying-free" of the beginning in order to restore its unexhausted fullness and strangeness that is still hardly experienced in the beginning's earliest inceptuality. From the outset, the *question* [G67] of a renewed inceptual mindfulness that is concerned with the "meaning" of be-ing lies beyond the metaphysical "nihilism" and consequently also beyond the

---

* See *Sein und Zeit*, ed. F.-W. v. Herrmann, GA 2. (Frankfurt am Main: 1977), section 6.

attempt at, and the striving for, the presumed overcoming of this "nihilism" within metaphysics, especially within modern thinking. The "radicalism" that lies within every beginning and inclines to its innermost threat and uprootedness claims a genuine sway only, if this "radicalism" understands itself as *preservation of the origin*.

Inceptual thinking in the other beginning en-thinks the truth of be-ing. En-thinking does not mean simply a thinking that autocratically contrives and invents, but means a thinking that is en-owned and enacts itself as enowned. The prime leap [*Ur-sprung*] of be-ing is en-ownment of its truth and along with this en-ownment the opening of the still undecided decision unto the grounding of this truth – undecided 'for' this grounding, 'against' this grounding or 'without' this grounding. The failure to enact the grounding is the necessary destiny of the first beginning. As long as being sways and a being as such "is", truth does not and cannot disappear. But truth goes astray in the errancy of the "un-ownmost", which is truth in the sense of correctness; and being loses its prime leap, rescues itself in machination and, at the end, forces philosophy into the semblance of "radicalism" that, as the self-certainty of the "I think" raises forgottenness of being to an implicit principle, and disseminates the groundless prototype of an illusory beginning of philosophy, which even that metaphysics cannot avoid that presumes to have overcome Descartes and the prehistory of modernity up to the nineteenth century by returning to "life".

[G68]   II.
15. *Self-mindfulness of Philosophy*
*as Historically Dissociating Exposition**
(Dissociating Exposition of *Metaphysics* and *Be-ing-historical* Thinking)

History of thinking is the history of be-ing; it is the history of the ways in which be-ing gifts its truth unto beings in order to let beings as such be. Right from its first beginning onwards and throughout, this history of gifting becomes a history of failing the sway of truth with the result that a

---

* See Part XXIV, Be-ing and "Negativity", for the dissociating exposition of Hegel. See also the conclusion of, and the supplements to, the lecture-course on Nietzsche delivered in the summer semester 1939, that is, *Nietzsches Lehre vom Willen zur Macht als Erkenntnis*, GA 47 ed. Eberhard Hanser (Frankfurt am Main: 1989) p. 277 ff. Cf. also "Destruktion" as the preliminary step in the dissociating exposition in *Überlegungen* XI, 24 f., to appear in *Überlegungen* B. GA 95.

grounding of the truth of be-ing is left out and is replaced with evasions, which finally lead to an indifference towards the sway of truth and to securing the claim that declares that the true is whatever is effective as "actual". Such arbitrariness and helplessness proliferate as soon as the failure of the sway of truth delivers 'beings in the whole' unto the unrecognizable abandonedness by being. But the abandonedness by being can become the earliest dawn of *refusal* – a hint unto the swaying of be-ing as en-owning.

Self-mindfulness of philosophy arouses the suspicion that it is a knowing of knowing which we abhor as a groundless circling around one's own emptiness.

This misgiving is legitimate if mindfulness is taken mindlessly in the sense that it describes and explains knowing as an extant process, and detects conditions behind knowing [G69] that proceed to further familiar and familiarly occurring extant things.

But knowing of knowing can also be a returning to the brightness of the swaying of knowing (in its belongingness to the truth of be-ing).

There – in the domain of the extant – knowing turns into what is seemingly known, *here*, knowing becomes more knowing because it leaps into the history of be-ing itself.

The historically dissociating exposition (in the "Echo" and in the "Playing-Forth") displaces unto those basic positions, in which and out of which thinkers are no longer "in agreement with each other", where "agreement" on foundational matters is prevented from happening since no agreement on opining about the same is still capable of carrying a truth.

The dis-sociating ex-position displaces into a foundational, and in each case, unique attunedness by the grounding-attunement. Grounding-attunement is not a diffused feeling which additionally envelopes thinking, but is the silent attuning unto the uniqueness of the one particular basic thought. However, as long as thinking remains metaphysical, the basic thought does not receive its fullness from the range of its possible application but from the fundamentality of the projecting-opening of beings unto being. Dissociating exposition, therefore, is never the same as calculating the correctness and incorrectness of doctrines and opinions. The notion entertained by schoolmasters that thinkers, also, occasionally "make mistakes" that must be removed has its place in the "schools", but not in the history of be-ing and never in the dialogue between the thinkers.

Because since long ago erudition and pedantry determine public opinion on "philosophy" and on "philosophical directions" and on the "debate" between them, and because as a consequence of the final triumph of historicism the present epoch, increasingly and decidedly – meaning here, increasingly without decision – holds on to such views, what is needed is an explicit dissociation from the present. And that means [G70] that we need to know how the present comports itself to philosophy and its history.

In spite of its importance, this knowing operates still within a marginal sphere, which, viewed from out of foundational thinking, could be left entirely to its own un-fundamentality.

However, since en-thinking of be-ing is never an analysis of what is extant, nor an aloof observation of "spiritual currents" and "situations" but rather an *acting*, we must undertake the unpleasant task of becoming mindful of what transpires presently and, in so doing, risk appearing as if after all we are merely analyzing and stripping the extant into "kinds" and "types", possibly even suggesting that *through* such a procedure we might subsequently arrive at another attitude. But in truth what seems to be an analysis is only the enactment of a dis-sociating ex-position that runs through the present and its exterior, and in which, acted thoughtfully, a decision on be-ing must be grounded and sustained. As long as the actual reality of our history (distress of the lack of distress) is not experienced, one *can* seize every mindfulness solely in terms of the knowledge that it yields and thus by-pass what is charged with deciding. *That* one *can* do this without upsetting and endangering the presumed security concerning the human being that one takes over and is one's own, is one of the many unrecognized testimonies to the fact of how groundlessly philosophy fluctuates within the un-fundamental: now as a "cultural" phenomenon, now as a pedagogical means, now as an all too early failed substitute for faith. Craving for the "actual", philosophy becomes everything that surrounds it, except philosophy itself. Where does this destiny come from?

Since long ago the relationship of our epoch to philosophy has become muddled because of the increasing educational possibilities of modernity whose consequences above all also include the increasing lack of education and a pretentious and rigid pseudo-education. [G71] Possibilities of "education" in advance consign philosophy to the "objects" of "education", whether this education is taken in the fundamental sense of shaping life that is sure of its measure, or in the un-fundamental sense of a fragmented educatedness. In this way, philosophy remains constantly an "object", a "force", a means that is heeded, seized and used within the established circles of organizing the power-positions of man.

One can try to disentangle this confusing relationship to philosophy through a renewed effort at understanding the "works" of great thinkers. Such a labor is unavoidable, but it is exposed to the danger of blinding again by the light that it kindles. For, all too easily, this labor favors seeking refuge in one of the earlier thinkers and calls for renewals that occasionally obscure the flight from the question-worthy.

A stronger attention paid to the "works" can claim a greater seriousness for itself than could be mustered by a superficial 'historical' comparison which goes back and forth between all standpoints.

Seeking refuge in the works does not yet guarantee a clear and firm attitude that is capable of sustaining a historically dis-sociating ex-position.

Therefore, a mindful and thorough scrutinizing of the prevailing forms of relationships to philosophy is required. We find:

1. The 'historical' adoption of an earlier philosophy (Kant, Hegel, Thomas Aquinas, Nietzsche) and its approximation with variously perceived situations of the time. The "point of view" and the "principle" of the adopted philosophies are "represented" with various degrees of insight, often transformed and even enriched by presentation and application that are appropriate to the times. However, this happens,

   (a) in order to continue driving "philosophy" further as a traditional "cultural good" through scholarly occupation with philosophy. This happens,

[G72] (b) in order to employ philosophy as a means for defending, developing, and intellectually justifying a posture of faith. This happens,

   (c) in order to have in philosophy the means available for a moral-personal clarification and at the same time an accumulation of points of view and perspectives for interpreting and organizing the appearances of the "world" and "life".

We find thereafter:

2. the 'historical' reckoning with the philosophy that is 'historically' handed down without explicit, decisive and justified preference for a single thinker. What is intended here is:

   (a) calculatively to work out a new and 'historically' more encompassing philosophy, in the course of which a strange "objectivity" considers [as] "valuable" what is different in the "intellectual good" of individual thinkers;

(b) to foster "philosophy in itself" and its "scientific progress". To this end one is led by the notion that a philosophy "in itself" hovers over and operates in the "temporal" fortuity of individual thinkers and their unavoidable standpoints – a philosophy "in itself" in which all "that is right" will be collected in time through a proper and timely elimination of "mistakes".

That 'historical' adoption of certain individual philosophies and *this* 'historical' reckoning with all philosophies hitherto can be brought together in the philosophy-industry of philosophical erudition that is in vogue in most high-schools and universities in all countries of "culture". This industry nourishes the plant of "liberal philosophizing" which is at the service of daily writing of newspapers and takes "timeliness" as the measure for the selection and method of treatment of "problems". Here "problem" counts as the name for questions that are no questions at all. We find further:

3.   a rejection of philosophy, firstly because it is held to be useless since it is capable neither of immediately delivering scientific knowledge [G73] nor of replacing it in the least; secondly because as mere "reflection", philosophy blocks and disturbs the direct and novel course that the craving for knowledge takes; and finally because as the breeding-ground of an obsession with doubt philosophy is held to be "dangerous". This discarding of philosophy even in the form of simply ignoring it is often more sincere than the business-enthusiasm of philosophical erudition. This rejection arises mostly from the points of view of religious, political and artistic assumptions. Here the historical appearance of philosophy is acknowledged as 'historically' remarkable, occasionally even explicitly recorded in order to warn against philosophy, whereby the referral to philosophy's constant change of standpoints and to its conflicting results is developed into a particularly impressive means of fright.

Additionally, we find:

4.   an indifference vis-à-vis philosophy. Although this indifference flourishes predominantly within the philosophical erudition, it does flourish also there, where "vitally important" spheres of tasks (technicity, economy, sciences and finally the general "culture-industry") claim exclusively man's calculation and effectiveness. Here, neither an effort is made in favor of a philosophical decision nor does it come to a rejection of, and taking a stance towards, philosophy. At most the birthdays and anniversaries of the death of

the great thinkers present an entirely non-committal occasion for commemorations, in the course of which only the fact is commemorated that one has not yet forgotten those dates. To mention such a recent "commemoration", it is not clear even to the most intense scrutiny what the Hegel-celebration of 1931 and the Descartes-convention of 1937 have significantly brought to light for philosophy, besides mutual corroboration of all parties involved in the philosophy-industry.

Finally, we find that [G74]:

5. all these – the 'historical' adoption of individual philosophies, the 'historical' calculation of all philosophies, the rejection of philosophy, the overt and covert indifference vis-à-vis philosophy, get muddled up so that now the one, then the other "posture" predominates arbitrarily, and remains ungraspable in its ground. The predominance of this hotchpotch, in which each 'scribe' and 'talker' can present himself and in which each can hide and so can contribute to the augmentation of "literature" – this is the actual sign of the lack of mindfulness. This state of affairs is no less true for Europe than it is for America and Japan. Today we cannot see through the sway of such planetary lack of mindfulness, over against which the point of views of political and religious assumptions are only evasions and no mastering. It would be disastrous, if we were to put aside this state of affairs of the world simply as something worthless, a decline and incapability. And more erroneous still would be the view that in the epoch of asthenia for and lack of joy in the foundational word one could ever eliminate this state of affairs overnight by publishing a "book".

Why do we say "lack of mindfulness"? In all these "relationships" to philosophy there prevails nowhere a *mindfulness* of the ownmost of philosophy *in such a manner* that *that* which philosophy has to think would be put into *question* and taken over in its *entire* question-worthiness without prop and protection, without evasion, but with the *single most* willingness to encounter philosophy's *own necessity*, which arises out of the uniqueness of philosophy's ownmost. If such mindfulness were at work, then for decades no "philosophical literature" would be proliferating.

Such mindfulness is possible only as a *dissociating exposition of history*, in which philosophy alone "*is*". Therefore, we must learn to know more and more clearly what such a "*dissociating exposition*" means (specifically in contrast to 'historical' refutation). Indeed, this knowing is [G75] a

fundamental prerequisite for the enactment of dissociating exposition –
for realizing that this exposition does not "refute" and cannot aim at
refuting.

Every foundational thinker is irrefutable (a foundational thinker is the
one who has already gained an originary and therefore unique *basic
position* in the history of being). *Irrefutability* here does not mean merely
that one cannot do anything with "a system", and cannot by-pass it with
counter-reasons to prove falsity and incorrectness, but means that such
intention in itself is already inappropriate and consequently a falling out of
philosophy.

Why? Because along with every basic position *the sway* of truth and
with it the *philosophical truth* is already co-posited. *No* foundational
determination of truth stands "*opposed*" to another philosophical truth *in
the sense* of a mere *rejection*, and no foundational determination of
truth stands therefore to another philosophical truth in relation of a mere
adoption, be it partial or complete.

But depending on their originariness, the basic positions do stand "over
against" each other in that each by itself, that is, in its *respective uniqueness*,
grounds and raises to distress the fundamentally *historical* uniqueness
of being and its truth. From this follows the demand to come back again
and again to such basic positions so that through a dissociating exposition
of these positions they can be cast into the uniqueness of an originary
question.

Dissociating exposition is an encounter through questioning:
1. so that both basic positions "*exclude*" each other and thus for the first
   time obtain the "over against" and in this way compel themselves
   into uniqueness;
2. so that this *excluding* is simultaneously *the allotting* unto the
   necessary belongingness to what is *uniquely worthy of questioning* to
   thinking.

(For this kind of historically dissociating exposition there is consequently no dialectical progression in the sense of 'elevating, cancelling,
preserving' [*Aufhebung*], but *unadjustability from out of the respective ground
of uniqueness*.)

[G76] We obviously need a *historical* knowing-awareness (not mere
'historical' knowledge) that comes out of an originary questioning so
that we experience, in what is fundamentally unadjustable as such, the
belongingness to *the unique* (and to its incalculability) and avoid the danger
of adjusting to an empty commonality in all that is to be thought –

a "commonality" that is suggested simply by the sameness and conformity of basic words and of the prevailing word-concepts. (But the *word*!)

However, it belongs to the sway of all that is historical – especially to the sway of what is created in thinking and poetizing – that "one" *can* take the historical arbitrarily this way or that way without having to be responsible for the consequences. And for the modern epoch of *historicism*, such possibilities are endless.

For example, Kant's philosophy (what does it consist of?) *can* be held to be *wrong* (and what does this mean?). Out of proving the wrongness of Kant's philosophy, one can make a career and a life's work. Except that this is not philosophizing, not an inquiry into the sway of being.

Where philosophizing is fundamentally and properly enacted, Kant's thinking does not appear as an "object" at all, but as inquiring along with, and ahead into, the same question. Therefore, what is under discussion is not whether *Kant* is right or wrong, but whether *we* are *capable* of meditating on the *truth* of his thought, that means, whether we are capable *of thinking along* with him *more originarily* (not *more correctly*).

Thoughtful dis-sociating ex-position is: *questioning disclosing unto the allotedness into the question-worthiness of be-ing.*

To question and to say *more originarily* does not mean to think "more correctly" but always to regain the necessity of questioning what is most question-worthy and out of it to venture a uniqueness.

Thoughtful dissociating exposition is not and can never be a refuting (which is an actual "blasphemy" against philosophers, and the worst violation of their ownmost), but is always solely the en-grounding of ground, venturing the ab-ground of be-ing, venturing be-ing as ab-ground.

In each case, the dis-sociating ex-position is, on the one hand, fundamentally an *overcoming* [G77] but on the other, overcoming should not be thought – possibly in favor of a progress – in the sense of refuting and leaving behind. It is not the thinker with whom dissociating exposition is engaged who is overcome, but always those who venture such exposition: what is overcome is the danger of, and the mania for, merely relying upon 'the decided', and taking 'the decided' over, no longer questioning it but only appealing to it. By contrast, in questioning, the thinker with whom dissociating exposition is engaged eases into his basic position and becomes worthy of questioning in such a way that his ownmost questioning detaches itself from its boundedness to the apparent "results", "doctrines", and "propositions" and, as so unbounded, sets thinking above all free unto the free play of the question-worthiness of the most question-worthy: it becomes a questioning disclosing allotedness into "being" ("*De-struktion*" in *Sein und Zeit*).[*]

The historically dissociating exposition does not 'historically' thrust history into what is past and does not at all tolerate history as the past, not even as the "happening" that is timely and always makes up the present. The historically dissociating exposition does not set up only "prototypes" within what has been, because even these "prototypes" all too easily remain only counter-images of a present that needs to mirror itself. The *historically* dissociating exposition frees history of thinking unto its future and thus puts on the path of the 'ones to come' the fundamental, unsurmountable resistances that can be matched only by the dissociatively exposed uniqueness of an inceptual questioning-thinking.

Only when we are adequate to *this* measure are we thinkers who *precede* futural thinkers. And perhaps one possible way for *us* to be adequate to this measure is the clear and strong renunciation of all that is inappropriate to this measure, which is the measure of what is ownmost to a thoughtful thinking. The prolonged education for *such* renunciation kindles a knowing-awareness that fundamentally surpasses everything that is newly calculated out of the hotchpotch of [G78] what hitherto is not thought through and leads further unto the remoteness to be-ing as the primal nearness to the decision between godhood and the human domain.

The dwelling in questioning what is question-worthy must appear strange to us, simply because, due to a prolonged habit, we only "think" in such a way that we are either on the lookout for the 'results' in order to get settled comfortably in them by appealing to them, or we resort to preconceived convictions in order to explain everything with their help and thus to obtain a general satisfaction. Last of all, this dwelling can open up – or it can never open up – as what it is: the *knowing-awareness* in the sense of inabiding the sway of the *truth* of be-ing (cf. 97. Be-ing-historical Thinking and the Question of Being).

The dissociating exposition of Occidental philosophy that is ahead of us, decides according to its fundamental trait on the very possibility of philosophy in the entirety of its history. Thereby the entirety of this history will not be determined by the completeness of the 'historical' presentation of doctrines and their interdependence, but by grasping the

[*] See GA 2, § 6.

beginning of this history, its inevitable falling away from the beginning, the self-rescuing of the falling away of this history in Descartes and completion of this history in Nietzsche. When grasped in the entirety of its basic positions, the history of Occidental philosophy is philosophy as *"Metaphysics"*. Here this word does not designate *one* "discipline" of philosophy among others: it does not at all mean a discipline to be taught and learned. Rather, it means the fundamental 'style' [*Grundart*] of thoughtful thinking in the history of thought hitherto, which, as the thinking of being, thoroughly prevails and sustains everything that could be divided into "logic", "ethics", "aesthetics", and so on – a division which itself is indeed a consequence of the metaphysical 'style' of thinking although not a necessary consequence. And yet the peculiarity of metaphysical thinking is the fact that often the most fundamental thinkers (e.g. Leibniz, Kant) enact this thinking within the framework of disciplines ("logic", "ontology") [G79] and they do so even at those junctures where the metaphysical thinking had to burst open such a framework. In the same vein, *Science of Logic*, the title of Hegel's work, which paves the way for the completion of metaphysics, cannot at all be taken as indicative of a superficial and accidental reliance on school philosophy. Rather, this title characterizes most precisely and completely this modern metaphysical basic position, namely that philosophy is "science" in the sense of the unconditionally certain propositions (of mathesis) in their grounding interconnection. And this science enacts and grounds itself as "logic", which means that *the known* in this science is projected-open and unfolded following the guideline of λόγος in the sense of the unconditioned thinking of absolute reason, and is thus the unconditioned *self-knowing*, which admits no condition for itself *within* itself and according to its own kind. Metaphysics prepares its completion in the gestalt of absolute logic. This completion becomes entire with the depreciation and dismissal of "logic" in Nietzsche's thought. However, this dismissal does not amount to an elimination of logic, but, quite on the contrary, in order to "think" being as "becoming" and to posit the actual "being" as "life" in "becoming", "logic" becomes that which as opposition is necessarily required.

The dissociating exposition that is ahead of us, and by virtue of which philosophy can first of all begin again as philosophy, is the dissociating exposition of metaphysics in its history as such. That means, the metaphysical basic positions must above all and immediately be eased into the freeness of the uniqueness of their questioning and they must bring their futurality into play. (Their futurality always sways in accordance with the "echo" of *the truth of be-ing*.)

In each case the historically dis-sociating ex-position places those that are variously situated within this ex-position into their own, unique and unrepeatable basic position within the inquiry into the question of being. The historically dissociating exposition is never an occasionally acquirable *addendum* to the "actual" thinking, rather it is [G80] a fundamental thrust of being-historical thinking itself. By contrast, the 'historical' refutation of philosophical "doctrines" and "views", which easily and ceaselessly looks like the historically dissociating exposition, remains an inexhaustible "issue" that concerns the historians of philosophy – inexhaustible because with every succeeding present it is filled up with new "points of view". The *historically* dissociating exposition becomes a *unique* necessity, simply *because* the overcoming of historicism is *the* distress for philosophy, but not *the* distress for the 'historical' erudition in philosophy.

Dis-sociating ex-position: the one between metaphysics in its history and be-ing-historical thinking in its future.

IV

ON PROJECTING-OPEN BE-ING

(Words that Hold Sway)

(The Be-ing-historical 'Saying')

16. Be-ing

Who thinks it exhaustively: be-ing – the enowning?

The en-owning – that which 'owns over' to each other and unto settlement, the countering and what counters in it, the strife and what is at strife in it; and as the en-ownment of this 'owning-to' lights up the ab-ground and grounds for itself in the clearing the sway of the countering and what counters, the sway of the strife and what is at strife, and that means the sway of the most inceptual truth.

Be-ing – nothing godly, nothing human, nothing worldly, nothing earthly, and yet the 'in-between' to all these in one – inexplicable, without effect: be-ing sways outside power and powerlessness.

Be-ing is unavoidable for man, so that he – himself a being – resides in the opening of beings, comports towards them, and holds onto them.

Because the swaying of be-ing points to what holds unto the ab-ground that refuses any appeal to beings – the ab-ground that solely distresses unto be-ing – be-ing is never explainable out of beings. Therefore, the grounding of the truth of be-ing does not belong to the extant and "living" man, but to Da-sein for inabiding, wherein at times being human must transform itself.

Being is never thinkable, initially and exclusively, *in orientation towards* beings, even though beings initially and constantly claim such orientation.

That could be the reason for the inceptual advancement and pre-eminence of *presencing* and the "present" and constancy – the advancement wherein be-ing as (enowning) refuses itself for a very long while.

Thereupon, appearing itself as a mode of presencing becomes a guise and semblance of what is simply constant (cf. 17. Being as φύσις).

The being-historically and originarily grasped constancy as well as the originary presencing do not arise out of a widening and enrichment of the "now", but rather, together with the "now", they are the *counter-hold* to falling and revolt within [G84] the countering and strife. As counter-hold they are fundamental, but in their fundamentality they nonetheless drive from enowning, which, however, is the *struggle* – without war and without peace – between the countering and strife (i.e., the alternatively gifting and helping unto swaying).

Countering is the fundamental decision between gods' allotting godhood and man's domain of humanness.

Strife is the 'owning-to' of the sway of the world and the earth.

As they sway, *their struggle* lights up – clears – and in the end what is lighted up – cleared – is the struggle itself as that which refuses itself: the ground that holds unto the ab-ground.

This clearing is the *truth* of be-ing, be-ing that itself *is* the truth.

Be-ing as enowning can and must be thoughtfully inquired in the direction of the "world" and of the "earth", of man and of god, but simultaneously also in the direction of their strife and their countering and, above all, in the direction of their struggle.

Be-ing sways as *the settlement* of countering and strife in the manner of enownment of the 't/here' [*Da*] as enownment of the ground of the clearing that prevails in en-owning.

Lighting up, the settlement sustains above all the countering as well as what thus light up, that is, what en-counters [*Er-gegnetes*] in the countering (godhood and man's domain), and in the same vein, in the intersection of this countering, settlement sustains within the "sway" of this countering the self-opening strife and what is thus open (the earth and the world) which means that settlement sustains the countering as it towers unto the ab-ground that enowns itself as be-ing. Settlement is en-owning.

The inquiry into be-ing never comes upon be-ing as an inquiry that is cut off beforehand from be-ing, and, so to speak, suddenly takes be-ing by surprise, but comes, above all, as pondering the beingness of beings, a pondering that primarily forgets itself, is serviceable to beings and is basically en-owned by be-ing.

Settlement does not mean finishing and eliminating, but en-opening, *lighting up of the clearing: en-owning* as settlement. *Settlement[:] fundamental to ab-ground.*

[G85] This inquiry is itself already enowned by be-ing, which means this inquiry is enactable only out of inabiding Da-*sein*.

With such inabiding, the decision is already made that man *no longer* thinks being with a view towards *himself* and according to *his condition* as a competent subject that thinks being in the sense of a supplementary general accessory to beings (as beingness), whereby "thinking" means representing in general. Prior to all and beyond every subordination of be-ing to the already interpreted "beings", man "thinks" be-ing inabidingly, that is, enacts a thinking charged with Da-*sein* by a projecting-opening-leaping unto the clearing itself. In and through such a thinking, man leaps over what hitherto is his *ownmost* (*animal rationale*). Thinking away from himself out of the leap unto en-owning, man does not think be-ing with a view *towards himself*, but in advance thinks *himself* fundamentally unto be-ing and its clearing. He has not left behind the transformation of his ownmost but laid this transformation ahead into his still ungrounded sites, which will become Da-*sein* only as the history of the guardianship of the truth of be-ing (cf. VII. Be-ing and Man).

Be-ing now demands the struggle for what is its most ownmost sway. The beginning of another history of man lies sheltered and hidden in this most quiet distressing. The decision remains, whether man is capable of experiencing the distress that is prepared in advance by such a distressing, whether he has that strength and patience which fundamentally surpass all power, coercive force and hardening.

17. Being as φύσις

The advancement of the present (of presencing and constancy) and with this the mania for "preserving" and the will to "eternity" in the sense of duration, and the preference of actuality and effectivity that is at the service of actuality, arise out of being as φύσις (out of a rising that places itself in constancy).

Within the purview of this swaying of being, man appears initially in his bodily conditionedness as [G86] the enduring, that means, as a being and *thus* animality – when thought metaphysically – becomes the first determination of man, and simply by experiencing the frailty of animality, animality becomes the object of preservation. The immediately experienced relation to beings (i.e., what is present and constant) is grasped as νοῦς – or receiving – and the receivable itself is seized as a possible footing and support within change.

Following various modifications, that initial truth of being as φύσις is in play in all manner of ways. Hereby what is "elementally natural" [*das "Natur"hafte*] in the reified sense remains only a form of the nearest *presentification*; it is not what is metaphysically deciding, but receives its importance from the sway of the being of φύσις.

18. "Be-ing" as "Word"

Be-ing – finally degraded in metaphysics to a used-up empty word that hardly still says the unactual detachment of thought from all that is actual and the detachment unto what lacks effect and is unactual – informs the total desolation of the representation that has no object.

In be-ing-historical thinking be-ing obtains the unique rank of a basic word of reticence that holds unto the ab-ground. The 'saying' that is sheltered-hidden in this word (which says that the sway of truth is to be grounded in Da-sein and as Dasein and that the 'in-between' of the settlement of the most unembellished and the most decided counterings is to be inaugurated) is the rupture through which unyieldingly and precipitatingly any being falls off against the ab-ground which alone restores be-ing to beings again and in the allotment to be-ing returns destiny to man.

Be-ing – metaphysically an indifferent hollow sound – be-ing-historically it is the stillness that holds back every storm and belongs to incalculable decisions.

In its sway, word as such belongs to settlement and can be known only as what belongs to en-owning.

[G87]   ## 19. Be-ing

Be-ing: in the first beginning the *rising* (φύσις), the self-unfolding (opening) presencing.

Be-ing: at the end of this beginning, in "*life*", the last vapor of an evaporating reality, *the self-overpowering machination as empowering of power*.

Be-ing: in the other beginning the *en-owning*, the struggle of countering and strife as the clearing of the ab-ground of the 'in-between'.

The rising and the enowning meet in the be-ing-historically dis-sociating ex-position.

Ungrounded in its unconcealment and sheltering-concealing, rising becomes a constantly *present* cause and condition and the unconditioned, and at the end it becomes the "life" that recoils unto itself.

The en-owning is the ground as the ab-ground of clearing, the struggle that struggles in the countering of god and man with the strife between earth and world.

20. The "Finitude" of Be-ing

In contrast to the inquiry heretofore, the expression "finitude" is chosen within the framework of an unavoidable *'historical'* understanding and demarcation. This "word" is subject to many misinterpretations: one can think of the distinction between the "relative" (Kantian) and the "absolute" idealism. Along with this, one can draw upon the Christian representation of createdness of all "beings" as one falls at the same time into the trap of the dialectic by "considering" that whenever the "finite" is posited, an infinite is also already thought. One takes the "finite" here generally in the sense of what is limited, indeed in the sense of a limitation of beings – one thinks "finitude" metaphysically.

[G88] However, the "finitude" of be-ing means something entirely different: the ab-ground-dimension of the 'in-between' to which the 'not-character' by no means belongs as a lack or a limit, but as a distinction. If the "finitude" of be-ing is thought at all as a demarcation from others, then it does not refer to the *infinity of being,* but to *the infinity of beings,* that is, to their unconditionality, which in turn means that the "finitude" of be-ing refers to the preeminence of beings vis-à-vis being that consequently reduces being to an *addendum.* The "finitude" of be-ing is a loaded expression that in an easily misunderstandable manner should guide mindfulness not to presuppose be-ing's "dependence" on beings, and not even to assume a limitation of representing being, but to assert the *uniqueness of be-ing as enowning* that is held unto the abground.

However, "finitude" of Da-sein—the inabiding the clearing of settlement of countering and strife—is a fundamental consequence of Dasein's foundational enownment by be-ing. By focusing on the referral of humanness into the relation to beings as such, one can *indicate* – without ever enough reservations – this finitude of Dasein 'historically'. But *such* indication is not the same as en-thinking the swaying of be-ing itself, that is, enacting a thinking for which right from the outset the characterization of be-ing in terms of finitude remains superfluous and disturbing.

The attempt undertaken in the treatise *Kant und das Problem der Metaphysik** at elucidating and rendering understandable, by way of a 'historical' approach, an entirely different beginning of the history of be-ing necessarily had to fail. This attempt led to adjusting 'historically' and thus fundamentally destroying the effort at inceptual thinking. The consequence is a remarkable situation: on the one hand *Sein und Zeit*** [G89] is interpreted as a continuation and complementation of the *Critique of Pure Reason* and its "anthropology" and is thus 'historically' reckoned with and rendered innocuous. On the other hand, my interpretation of Kant is condemned as one-sided and violent. Considering the "historical" "effect" – which, seen be-ing-historically, is of course unimportant – this is neither an appropriate elucidation of *Sein und Zeit*, nor an interpretation of the *Critique of Pure Reason*. Of course, whoever is able to think out of a knowing-awareness of the question of being will understand differently and will not get stuck in "historical effect". What the guide-word "finitude" would like to say and name is not a finished, assertable "property" of be-ing and of Dasein, but the title that is inappropriate for the utmost question-worthiness of that which shelters and conceals within itself the question-worthiness as a distinction.

According to Kant, being is always beingness in the sense of the objectness of the object. However, "objectness" itself is not an object and, as the non-objective, it is also only a fundamental consequence of be-ing, so that be-ing in its *ground*-character can never be en-thought out of such a consequence. "Metaphysics" is never capable of overcoming itself. As the first history of the first beginning, metaphysics demands another beginning, which immediately places metaphysics into its historical truth.

21. The 'Saying' of Be-ing-historical Thinking

The 'saying' of be-ing-historical thinking reads: *"be-ing is, a being is not"*. Only gradually, and with difficulty, can we overcome the prejudice of all

---

* See *Kant und das Problem der Metaphysik* (1929), GA 3, ed. F.-W. v. Herrmann, (Frankfurt am Main: 1991).
** See GA 2.

metaphysics according to which a being "is" and only beings "are" and can "be". Hereby, the "is" and the "be" always originate in a statement which states that something generally "is" (occurs and is extant); that such a being always "is" in this or that way (presences and stands vis-à-vis). The "is" which so to speak is innate to beings, indicates being [G90] in the sense of constant presencing. Remaining unquestioned, and encountering no resistance, this "is" seizes up the determination of being and steers all modes of being and their modifications (for example "modalities"). However, being as the "noun" of the familiar "is" reveals itself as beingness which was projected-open in the direction of "beings". This projecting-opening does not know the inquiry into the truth of be-ing itself and maintains itself outside any experience of a possible necessity of inquiring into what is called here the truth of be-ing.

By virtue of this lack of experience that is even inceptually necessary, the projecting-opening of be-ing as constant presencing takes beings themselves as the pre-given support and site of be-ing. That all the while a being is itself a being to the extent that it towers already within the unexperienced clearing of projecting-opening – this is recognized in certain ways (that of πρότερον τῇ φύσει, of "a priori" and of 'having been thought'). However, the peculiarity of this recognition is used only to finalize, for the entire length of the history of metaphysics, the failure to recognize the question-worthiness of the truth of be-ing's projecting-open. But to the extent that being itself is nevertheless "thought" and its determination is grasped as a task, three directions of metaphysics consequently open up:

1. Being is heightened to the most being (ὄντως ὄν) because being bestows beingness upon any being (ἰδέα). Being is the "outward appearance", which bestows upon beings their particular 'look' as such. In this sense and in this domain, ἰδέα is δύναμις: the empowering of the extant in presence and constancy, and as this empowering itself the power of presencing. (The Platonic Greek "idea" is not merely representedness of a subject-oriented opining in the modern sense, and nevertheless the ground and the force behind 'idea' as *perceptio* and "concept").

2. Being is explained with a view to that which being by its power (of distributing capability) renders efficacious (explained in view of ἀγαθὸν ἀκρότατον), what has already been equally strived for with ἐπέκεινα τῆς οὐσίας. [G91] The *Summum bonum* is thought in a

Christian way as *ens entium creans* (*Deus creator*). Being is "explained" in terms of the highest being.

3. Being is relegated to representedness and interpreted as objectness of objects for the subject that is charged with representation, whereby at times the "subject" plays its role of "origin" as conditioned and at times as unconditioned.

Thus metaphysics derives being either from a highest being or it makes being into a contrivance of a being and its mere representing, or it conjoins both explanations of being derived from beings.

(For Hegel, absolute *idea* is the thought of *the creator God* prior to, and for the sake of, this creation – a God who is thought of as the unconditioned *subject*. After Hegel and within a process of final completion of metaphysics that is supposedly free of metaphysics and reverses everything, all forms of explanations of being – out of 'idea', out of 'God', and out of the 'subject' – return in some kind of confusion and blending. The ur-swamp that holds these thought-less bubbles together is indicated by tracing everything back to the "all-life", [*All-Leben*] – ("life"). Thereupon, in the muddy self-evidence that sits well with the masses, even the last clarity which still distinguishes all fundamental metaphysical thinking is once and for all effaced.)

'*Be-ing is, a being is not*'. This 'saying' would like to say straightaway that, regardless of how a being may be given, only seemingly a path leads to being, whose truth can be experienced only through a leap as the clearing and the ab-ground that lights up.

By the very manner of questioning inquiring into the truth of be-ing, be-ing is already freed from any and all metaphysically fundamental binding to beings.

'Be-ing is' means: be-ing and only be-ing en-sways its own sway, enowns itself as enowning unto the ab-ground of the clearing that as the 'free play of time-space' acquires for be-ing the sites, [G92] which allow the settlement between countering and strife to become the moment and the ground of history.

Be-ing does not give away its swaying to beings, but fulfills this swaying as itself and thus lights itself up as the ab-ground, wherein, on the same plane, *that* which man calls beings may tower, may fall away and may linger.

Da-sein does not form and does not bind be-ing to man, not only because Da-sein itself above all becomes the ground of the be-ing-historical man, who begins beyond the history of metaphysics, but also because in its ownmost Da-sein itself is enowned by be-ing.

However, nowhere and never can beings count as mere image and reflected splendor of be-ing. Beings cannot be compared to being, and are turned away from being. Only the historical 'arrival-in-between' of man unto the truth of be-ing necessitates und makes possible a relation by virtue of which man comports himself to beings, which as such are pre-served in the constancy and presencing, because beings seem to bring about the nearest and the unique counter-holding ground against the ab-ground. The highest form of constancy and presencing is sought in "becoming" which inceptually appears as the opposite and the exclusion of being; in truth, however, "becoming" seeks the constancy of the per-manently other and still wants to rescue unto being the changing and the drifting.

In the epoch of the completion of metaphysics which simultaneously comes along with a complete distortion of metaphysics, the be-ing-historical 'saying' can hardly be said without avoiding the misinterpreta-tion, whose most adamant form always consists in explaining, out of the heretofore, something that has been thought and making it intelligible out of the heretofore.

Therefore, be-ing-historical thinking can try to make do with an 'in-between saying': 'a being is, be-ing sways'. But this 'in-between-saying' bespeaks instantly the intention of metaphysics to the extent that this 'saying' attributes being to beings [G93] and thinks the sway as the con-stancy of 'swayness' (ἀεί of the ἰδέα), regardless of whether this happens in a Platonic, a Christian-theological or a transcendental-subjective way.

Therefore, the 'in-between saying' is incapable of raising into a deciding knowing-awareness what it actually thinks and what it has to en-think. Therefore, it must be abandoned.

The strangeness of the actual be-ing-historical 'saying' offers at most a hint at the necessity of a thinking-leap, for which beings of metaphysics and man as experienced metaphysically are only historical occasions for the leap-off: these no longer set the measure for en-leaping the clearing of be-ing and its swaying but in turn come back above all to their historical uniqueness and inevitability via the metaphysical thinkers' fundamental groundings.

En-thought as enowning of settlement of the countering and strife unto the 'in-between' of 'the free play of time-space' that holds unto the ab-ground, be-ing cannot be elucidated and made understandable through approximation with, and vague resonances to, the wording of the metaphysical thinking hitherto. The keenest threat to be-ing is understandability.

Be-ing as the en-owning of the settlement of the intersecting of countering and strife that is held unto the ab-ground is en-thought neither in view of beings as their left-over and *addendum* nor in view of beings as their cause and condition.

The path of thought of be-ing-historical thinking runs outside any "metaphysics", whether ancient, Christian, or modern.

Whence comes the decision that is to be made between the pre-eminence of beings and the grounding of the truth of be-ing? It comes only from be-ing, out of the manner in which be-ing refuses and gifts itself. Be-ing itself *is* the en-owning of this decision and its 'free-play of time-space'.

Be-ing *is* more originary than the mystery of the earth, more worlding than the inaugurated world, more swaying than god, and more grounding [G94] than man, and yet "only" the moment of the 'in-between' for 'beings in the whole'.

22. Ground
(Be-ing and ἀλήθεια)

The 'in-between' as the ab-ground; the ab-ground which as ab-ground is the clearing for beings, and above all enfolds beings in grounding.

(In the attempt I made with *Vom Wesen des Grundes**, ground is grasped out of "transcendence" and transcendence is grasped as ground; transcendence, of course, is still within the perspective of the transcendental and thus under the purview of "consciousness", which in turn is replaced by *Da-sein* – all expediencies for simply familiarizing the knowledge hitherto of being with what is interrogated in general. Thus everything that is charged with ground – even if in the manner of a *surpassing* – is *piled up* on beings and thus posited nevertheless as a stage.)

The *temporality-spatiality of the 't/here'* does not arrive, as the 'in-between', at a placeless place that is first grounded by the 't/here' itself.

---

* See, *Vom Wesen des Grundes* (1929), *Wegmarken*, GA 9. ed. F.-W. v. Herrmann (Frankfurt am Main: 1976), pp. 123–75.

Although entirely differently inquired into, the swaying of be-ing, in spite of everything, still stands under the semblance of the *a priori* and consequently under the semblance of an *"addendum"*.

Be-ing does not sway as ground, it is not what grounds [*das Gründige*], that is, it is not what in the ab-ground of clearing prepares *that* for all beings unto *which* a being can*not* collapse because it is too "light". The being of a being is the prior prop unto which a being collapses out of the lightness of the lack of collapse; is the ground that out of the ab-ground grounds the *constancy* of a being, by virtue of which a being can find its way unto what is simple and rare and thus has to remain *the groundless*, and in itself without the 'in-between'.

However, be-ing can become the un-grounded and [G95] it will be recognized and becomes recognizable as such primarily through the be-ing-historical remembering of (*genitivus objectivus*) metaphysics.

For being's abandonment of beings is the ungroundability of being, as a consequence of which being lets itself be raised to the level of a mere *addendum*. Ungroundability arises out of the collapse of ἀλήθεια which itself is *not yet* held unto the ab-ground.

The ἀλήθεια is capable only of the swaying of sheltering-*un*-concealing, of appearing into openness: in ἀλήθεια openness itself does not hold sway as *clearing* and clearing does not hold sway as be-ing.

At the end, the ἀλήθεια is still the "yoke" and the bridge, but a *bridging* that is without abground; that means, ἀλήθεια is also not the bridge and the yoke and therefore it must forfeit what it possesses *inceptually-*foundationally and become correctness.

Only when inquired into as the 'in-between' of the en-ownment is be-ing of such swaying that it is charged with ground and grounding.

To know: the ungroundability of being of the groundless beings. Hence, the lack of mindfulness in explaining and planning everything. The "space" of the total 'de-spacing'.

Only where be-ing's chargedness with ground is en-grounded, that is, in be-ing-historical en-thinking, is the buildable possible once again. ("The constructive" of the mere arranging and planning is only what is cease-lessly *designable*; the design, however, is the (emptily extended) plan of the ungrounded plane of what is 'always the same'.)

At the plane of what cannot be grounded, a swaying of godhood out of the response of man's domain is impossible.

All *explaining* is the denial of what is charged with ground. Sciences confirm and pursue what is groundless in beings.

23. Be-ing

At the beginning of Occidental history and as its beginning there is the rising (φύσις), the rising prevailing (the self-lighting presencing). However, because of the [G96] preeminence of presencing, this rising is already the concealing of the ab-ground of be-ing and the relegation to beings themselves. The rising begins with the ab-ground and, that means, with *'going under'*. When do we "see" the 'going under' in this beginning, when do we intimate the uniqueness of this first beginning, when do we free ourselves from misinterpretations which have been forced upon us by the subsequent, prolonged and always widening history of the first beginning, and by the prolonged hesitating completion of this history? Inceptually, φύσις appears like a being itself and is then seized in the 'having-been-seen' of the ἰδέα. The rising does not become the breakthrough of the ab-ground which as the *'between'* casts itself amid beings, so that in the direction of the ungrounded open all beings, simultaneously *overgrounded* by the open, rend themselves unto the strife of the earth and the world and tower and close themselves in the silent glow of what is unblemished.

Inceptual being is the rising and thus already the 'going under' because the clearing that is ungrounded and is no longer promising overwhelms it. What the rising was and what remains ahead of all the history of be-ing as its 'going under' must be experienced *as the enowning of the ab-ground*. But to experience this is difficult, because beings – familiar and forgotten at the same time – have overgrown being and now brace themselves against being without letting being "count" as "more" than an empty, undeterminable concept.

Beings are *too much* of 'a being', and have become a confused fluctuation between power and powerlessness, and take refuge in the protection of an actuality, which in the calculating frenzy of man secures for itself above all a prestige as effectiveness.

Because be-ing as refusal is beyond power and powerlessness and is especially the distress of distressing unto godhood of gods and guardianship of man, man must come towards be-ing differently than he ever did in its first beginning, but not as though he could ever lay hold of be-ing and its truth. The *'arrival in coming towards'* [*Entgegenkunft*] is only preparing the [G97] readiness for the scarcely enquivering tremor, with which the ab-ground places itself between all beings and fosters decision between gods and man. As its unobtrusive sign, the 'arrival in coming towards' has the power which holds itself back, and wants to be known only by the 'knowing few'. Is man's domain still capable of this 'arrival in coming towards'? Must not here the refusal have become already a withholding gifting unto the storm of poetizing, thinking projecting-openings?

The unleashed *effectiveness* of beings that are abandoned by being still overpowers be-ing in all manner of ways: the *holding back* of refusal, which *beyond* power and powerlessness holds ready for the freest of decision the inevitable leap into the far-reaching depth of the ab-ground.

In order that holding back of refusal "grounds" as holding unto the ab-ground – because only thus does refusal compel into the distress of poetizing, thinking grounding of the word – this holding back of refusal lights up the open which is never the open of what is empty, but indeed the open of the fullness, which unperceivable by the measures and pincers of beings, allows its jointure only to become differentiable for the decidedness unto be-ing and unto *its* remembrance. The latter does not let what is to be remembered fade away, but raises it up into uniqueness as its keenest joining. The jointure of fullness is likewise the simpleness of the few, appropriate to what holds back. This fullness knows no rushing that comes from the manifold; rather it has its fullness from the open that is uniquely unshiftable, and that is the en-ownment that only broadens the open unto its openness to the distress of the exuberance of the decision wherein history has always already begun, that is, the decision between godhood and man's domain. History is the allotment unto the truth of be-ing and therefore achieves its apex with the 'going under' of those who ground the open and are privileged to be the precursors to grounding.

However, because thinking-saying is a 'not-saying' [*Entsagen*], only seldom does it succeed a trifle in its fundamental word.

[G98]   24. The Stillest Crossing unto the other Beginning

In the stillest crossing unto the other beginning, being, hitherto still an *addendum* to beings and overshadowed by them, is experienced as the ab-ground of en-ownment of Da-sein unto the swaying as 'the free-play of time-space' of the decision between man's domain and godhood – a decision for and against what is ownmost and 'un-ownmost' to man and what sways and un-sways in godhood.

The experience of be-ing urges into the initial distress wherein be-ing lights itself up as the refusal (of its sway) and fosters for itself a uniqueness to which – in the attempt to ground the truth of such a sway and to prepare for beings a site for appearing out of the simpleness and graveness of themselves – only a passage through a moment of history can be appropriate.

That which in the swaying of *be-ing* – from afar and held into the abground – solely en-owns man unto the guardianship of the truth of be-ing, *that* can never have the effect of the gigantic machination of *beings*, because gigantic machination of beings submerges man in the flood of his unleashed 'un-ownmost' and lets diminish all capability for god.

25. Be-ing

Be-ing is the en-owning of truth.

Truth is the clearing of refusal, which in refusal and as refusal is a prime-leap – an out-lay of lighting up.

En-owning is the originary allotting of human beings both unto the truth (of be-ing) and thus, simultaneously, unto the distressing-need of the godhood of gods.

The strife of the world and the earth arises from within the en-ownment to enowning, and things that are in strife arise above all from that *strife*.

[G99]   ## 26. Be-ing: the Ab-ground

Be-ing is the ab-ground, the cleft of the lighted 'in-between', whose "rocks" and "bluffs" and "pinnacles" keep themselves sheltered-concealed. Only from time to time in *a leap* of fundamental inquiry (in inquiring into the allotment unto be-ing and in inquiring unto be-ing itself and its clearing) does man leap the ab-ground and, as Da-sein, becomes the bridge and the crossing for a passage through en-ownment of man's domain unto the contentiousness of the godhood of gods.

Be-ing is nowhere and never fixed, affixed, propped up, and layed down. Be-ing is the "ground" that as such is always already turned *away*, because as *en-ownment* be-ing is the self-refusing allotment unto what is not propped up and protected – because be-ing means only this.

27. Be-ing is the Ab-ground

As ab-ground, being "is" specifically the nothing and the ground.

Nothing is *what is different* from be-ing, a difference that holds onto the ab-ground: nothing is the nihilating of all ground (of all prop, all protections, all measures, all goals) and it *is thus* en-ownment unto the open of the refusal and, therefore, is *of the sway* of be-ing, but it is never "the same" as be-ing because it is never the foundational fullness. Nothing is, above all, not the fullness because it is thus no *ground*.

Annihilatingly, *ground is the en-ownment* unto the distress of grounding as the inquiry and en-saying of the truth of refusal so as to obtain the truth of refusal as the 'between' wherein godhood and man's domain decide for and against each other.

[G100]   28. Be-ing – Distress – Care

Be-ing-historical thinking does not understand distress as a need and a mere lack vis-à-vis a metaphysical "ideal" but, in accordance with the nothing, understands it as ab-ground: the freedom of exuberance and mourning, both, however, not as feelings, but as grounding-attunements.

The announcing and direction of the tune unto the ground and its grounding – *clearing and joining*.

In accord with Da-sein, attunement is neither psychological nor biological nor "existential".

Hence, "care": the guardianship of the distress of be-ing.

Whence the constant intrusion of the mere *psychological* and *evaluating* thinking?

Why at the same time the constant staring at what is annoying? Because even here one always reckons with explanations that come from beings.

29. Being is En-owning

In en-owning,
be-ing holds sway as *freedom*

be-ing holds sway as *ab-ground*
be-ing holds sway as *refusal*
be-ing holds sway as *truth* (time-space).

Every word here says en-owning and what it says holds sway in en-owning. No alien and no familiar concept from metaphysics can be thought unto these words.

In refusal be-ing surpasses itself, it always sways more than itself and hides itself thus above all in the simpleness that no one fathoms.

The clearing of be-ing is of be-ing's own sway and removes be-ing instantly unto darkness.

The open of clearing is never something public, but is held back unto the unique aloneness of be-ing.

[G101] Be-ing remains ungraspable to all mere beings.

However, man has the distinction of being able to be that being that is not only a being, but grounds his "is" in en-ownment by be-ing.

Only that which like be-ing – while holding sway – takes itself back into the sheltered-concealedness, towers infinitely over every power and powerlessness. This towering over does not need eternity.

[G101]   30. Be-ing and Freedom

Be-ing is en-owning and is *thus* the ab-ground and *as* ab-ground the "ground" of ground and therefore *Freedom*.

Freedom is not somehow the "essence" of be-ing as though be-ing could be classified and subordinated to "freedom", but rather "freedom" sways in and as be-ing. Here freedom is understood more originarily than the metaphysical freedom, but more specifically than moral freedom.

(Schelling's concept of freedom is a metaphysical one. The transition into the "system" of negative and positive philosophy proves this.)

But the ab-ground is the "ground" of the ground because only the ab-ground can be the *distress* of grounding – of erecting the ground – and determine the necessities of grounding.

31. 'The Free-play of Time-Space'

How do we account for the fact that since long ago we know "space" (place) and "time" only as the extant and fleeting empty forms of the extant, and perhaps even admit them as means of objectification (of producing-representing) of the extant? What has happened that we know nothing of their originary onefold – of 'the free-play of time-space' whose holding unto the abground belongs to the ab-ground of be-ing itself?

[G102] Why are space and time only what is 'discarded' from "beings" and not the unassailable, intimately swaying fullness of the *'in-between'* that, while holding unto the ab-ground, grounds every nearness and remoteness, every refusal and gifting, every concealing and clearing, and is neither in man's discretion as power of representing, nor in the discretion of beings as the form of appearances? Why it is so difficult for us to detach ourselves from the traditional desolation of space and time wherein only calculation and planning rave – why are we blind and insensitive to this desolation? Because either we seek ourselves always merely as thinking animals, or we seek 'beings in the whole', or we seek the inter-penetration of both the thinking animal and 'beings in the whole' and strive for "explanations" (which are again productive derivations from the extant). Because unknowing as we are, and fleeing from be-ing, we have no inkling of the sway of truth.

32. Being and Space

Consider the ownmost of space as indicated in the spatiality of Da-sein in *Sein und Zeit.*[*]

Only out of the clearing is there space. And this requires in advance the overcoming of the metaphysical interpretation of space.

In metaphysics space counts as "emptiness", and "spacing" means making empty, giving up, and abandoning.

Looked at more deeply, space is just what is to be occupied, what is to be taken, because it is what receives, what holds in and what grants closure.

Space makes room in the manner of yielding a place, of granting the specificity to 'removals-unto' and thus to what in granting *'charms'*.

In the same vein, χάος, the gaping-opening, is not the emptiness that presses forth, but the ab-ground.

---

[*] See GA 2, sections 22–24.

[G103]   33. Be-ing and 'Letting-be'*

One is of the opinion that 'letting a being be' as how and what it is, is to be simply achieved by being indifferent to beings, by undertaking nothing about them and by taking nothing away from them.

But, on the contrary, 'letting be' presupposes the utmost inabiding the truth of the sway of be-ing.

The more fundamentally man's ownmost is wrested free of animality and spirituality, the more he is allotted unto the inabiding, understood as the intimate persevering in the grounding of the truth of be-ing.

'Letting-beings-be' must be kept furthest removed from any cajoling of what is presently actual, effective and successful.

34. The Be-ing-historical Word

The be-ing-historical word is ambiguous and at the same time does not "mean" different "objects", but says be-ing non-objectively, because be-ing, the sustaining en-owning that sways specifically and ceaselessly in manifold ways, nevertheless demands simpleness from its word. Here explanatory "definitions" achieve as little as indefinite and symbolic speaking through signs.

This manifold ways of saying of be-ing-historical words is creative within the stillness of the contexts that are inaccessible to a calculative systemization, because, as historical, these contexts, moreover, continuously and necessarily reserve what in them is sheltered-hidden and still undecided. However, this unsayable is not the irrational of metaphysics, but that which in the grounding of the truth of be-ing 'is-first-to-be-decided'.

---

* See the 1930 lecture on truth, "*Vom Wesen der Wahrheit*", to appear in *Vorträge*, GA 80.

V

TRUTH

(Clearing) "Moment"

AND
KNOWING-AWARENESS

(Inabiding the Yes)
Nearness and Remoteness

35. Question of Truth: A Directive

1. *Vom Wesen der Wahrheit* (lecture of 1930);[1] in addition, interpretation of the simile of the cave in the lecture-course of 1931/32.[2]
2. *Vom Ursprung des Kunstwerkes* (Freiburg lecture of 1935).[3]
3. *Vom Ursprung des Kunstwerkes* (Frankfurt lectures of 1936).[4]
4. *Vom Wesen der Wahrheit* (lecture of 1937/38).[5]
5. *Die Grundlegung des neuzeitlichen Weltbildes durch die Metaphysik* (lecture of 1938).[6]
6. *Anmerkungen zu Nietzsches II. Unzeitgemäße Betrachtung, Abschnitt VI Wahrheit und Gerechtigkeit,* lecture-seminar of 1938/39.[7]

---

[1] To appear in *Vorträge*, GA 80.

[2] See *Vom Wesen der Wahrheit: Zu Platons Hölengleichnis und Theätet,* lecture in the summer semester of 1931/32, GA 34, ed. Hermann Mörchen (Frankfurt am Main: 1988).

[3] To appear in *Vorträge*, GA 80.

[4] See *Holzwege*, GA 5, pp. 1–74.

[5] See *Grundfragen der Philosophie. Ausgewählte "Probleme" der "Logik",* lecture in the winter semester of 1937/38, GA 45, ed. F.-W. v. Herrmann (Frankfurt am Main: 1984).

[6] Published under the title "Die Zeit des Weltbildes", in *Holzwege*, GA 5, pp. 75–113.

[7] See *Zu Auslegung von Nietzsches II. Unzeitgemäße Betrachtung,* lecture-seminar in Freiburg in the winter semester 1938/39, GA 46, ed. Hans-Joachim Friedrich (Frankfurt am Main: 2003).

7. Lecture-course of summer semester of 1939 (Nietzsche, *Wille zur Macht*, III. *Buch, Der Wille zur Macht als Erkenntnis*).[8]

8. *Beiträge zur Philosophie*, 1936, section: *Gründung*.[9]

9. *Zu Aristoteles, Physik B* 1 (φύσις), third term of 1940, pp. 22 ff.[10]

[G108]   36. Clearing[*]

In the other beginning of en-thinking and saying, it is the clearing that we must ground.

But the clearing in its double swaying: clearing as *the dim glow* of the attuning attunement out of the ab-ground of be-ing and as *the simple brightness* of the knowing-ingrasping [*Inbegriff*] for inabiding the 'in-between'.

Both are not yet achieved in their originary onefold.

Both require the fundamental transformation of man into Da-sein.

The dignity of the truth of be-ing over against the preeminence of beings and over against the *addendum* of "beingness", ("idea" and "value") that is tolerated and needed by being.

The swaying of the 't/hereness of the t/here' [*Daheit des Da*] that holds unto the ab-ground, and the inabiding of Da-*sein* that as such grounds into beings.

To be Da-*sein* means to ground the clearing unto enowning – the clearing in its double sway towards history – in the 'in-between' of beings.

Thrownness and projecting-open are thrusts of the clearing that are already grasped out of the truth of be-ing but still viewed out of the provenance of the crossing of metaphysics into be-ing-historical thinking.

Clearing is never the empty, but the most originary thorough swaying of en-owning as the settlement of the countering and strife – the 'in-between' held unto the ab-ground.

And every 't/here' of a historical Da-sein obtains only an abyss of the ab-ground.

---

[8] See *Nietzsches Lehre vom Willen zur Macht als Erkenntnis*, lecture of the summer semester of 1939, GA 47, ed. Eberhard Hanser (Frankfurt am Main: 1989).

[9] See *Beiträge zur Philosophie* (*Vom Ereignis*), GA 65, ed. F.-W. v. Herrmann (Frankfurt am Main, 1989), pp. 293–392.

[10] On the 'fore-concept' of "metaphysics", elucidated out of Aristotle's concept of φύσις, see *Metaphysik und Wissenschaft*, to appear in GA 76.

[*] See above G 83 ff.

[G109]   37. Truth as Clearing

Clearing says an en-opening that 'removes unto', and shelters-conceals in itself both the 'charming-moving-unto' and the open of the opaque.

Clearing enowns what is light and calls to mind light and its shining and the radiating brightness.

Light and what is charged with light are both the quiet glow.

Therefore, grasped be-ing-historically, clearing always says the englowing of the open, the thorough attunement. The saying of the clearing is attuned.

As englowing en-opening, clearing is *of* be-ing which, while holding unto the ab-ground, is reticent on the distress of the ground and enowns the groundership of saying as the necessity that gives rise to freedom as history – history in the sense of the struggle between fundamental decisions.

The first beginning of the fundamental projecting-opening of truth unto *clearing*, as well as the fundamental delimitation of truth as *correctness*, begin with what is un-unfolded, that is, with what the early Greeks named ἀλήθεια after the name and the gestalt of the goddess – a word that we readily and aptly translate with *sheltering-unconcealment*, and its inceptuality we nevertheless intimate the least without proper historical distance.

"Uncoveredness" [*Entdecktheit*] and "resolute disclosedness" [*Entschlossenheit*] (in "*Sein und Zeit*") are held within the foundational domain of ἀλήθεια, and yet they do not succeed in obtaining the full be-ing-historical knowing-awareness of the inceptual which lets ἀλήθεια and φύσις remain within a onefold swaying.

And correspondingly, in Plato's simile of the cave there is already a falling away from the beginning (cf., the attempt to interpret it in 1931/32).* Although the simile (cave and the climbing up into the sphere of light) fundamentally refers to the relation between ὄν – οὐσία – ἰδέα – ἀλήθεια, ἀλήθεια is nevertheless carried over into a "representation" of the soul.

[G110] In Aristotle's ἀληθεύειν τῆς ψυχῆς, sheltering-unconcealment has become an unconcealing of the soul (in spite of *Metaphysics Θ10*): ζωή and νοῦς dispose over, and carry out the sheltering-unconcealment. Thus,

---

* See *Vom Wesen der Wahrheit. Zu Platons Höhlengleichnis und Theätet,* lecture-course in the winter semester 1931/32, GA 34.

as the decisive possibility for preserving the beginning, the significant but never accomplished – not even by the inceptual thinkers – grounding of the soul and man unto sheltering-unconcealment is finally lost. Since then, *correctness* takes its course, presses forth and dominates the fundamental determination of "thinking" and "reason" and, along with it, the interpretation of beingness of beings in the sense of representedness.

Correctness is the adequateness of representing to "beings", respectively accessibility of "beings" to and for representing.

Insofar as it comes down to man as the subject, adequateness *secures* beings, and makes man certain of beings. Truth has become certainty and, through certainty, the securing of the constancy of the subject. This securing has to turn itself into a stabilization and consolidation of beings, whereby it is no longer that important *what* each being is, *how* it shows itself. What is important, rather, is that beings surround us and are secured as something stable.

The question of adequateness in the sense of agreement and reproducing loses its importance and meaning; what counts is what is stable and secure even if, measured by the preceding measure of *adaequatio*, the stable and the secure reproduce nothing at all from beings as they become.

Seen in this respect, the stable is simply a deception – an imagination – an illusion – a falsity – an error. But this characterization has fallen out of the sway of truth. When at the end Nietzsche characterizes truth as "error", then what is decisive is not that he reverses the truth into its opposite, but that as the consequence of the preeminence of machination, *the sway of* truth transforms itself once again from certainty to stability. The characterization of truth as "error" is, so to speak, only the historical differentiation of the knowing-awareness of truth itself and [G111] by no means the knowing-awareness of truth that is awake in the "will to truth". Revering truth is not revering an "illusion" as such, but revering, within the purview of the concept of truth hitherto, the "truth" that "appears" as illusion. And this concept reveals itself in the same way also for the will to power as heightening, poetizing and transfiguration. That is why in this empowering, the adequateness to "being", namely to "becoming" as the will to power, still continues to be powerful. In spite of everything and without evasion, Nietzsche stays on the path of truth as *adaequatio* of which consolidation is only a variant.

Nietzsche conceives truth metaphysically unto the completion of correctness and certainty, but he does not think at all, and least of all inceptually. However, just like the inceptual thinking, the *one* thinking that *counts at the end* of metaphysics has its own foundationality and greatness.

Hence, truth can no longer be the "most supreme power" (*Wille zur Macht*, 853[1]), although for the will to power it continues to be unavoidable. By contrast, sheltered-concealed within the first beginning, φύσις and ἀλήθεια "are" the same and the unique.

Truth as correctness and stabilization is fostered, valued, revered and wanted because in the midst of beings man as a subject comports himself towards beings and, through all these, he comports himself above all towards himself.

The Will to constancy and presence is even the most sheltered-concealed and the actual ground for the projecting-opening of beings as "becoming" (cf. above G 25 f., and section 92, below, G 395) insofar as becoming is to grant both at once: the continuity of overcoming, and a *presencing* (of what is to be overcome) – indeed the overcoming of the rigid that stands still so that within this continuity a constancy sways (that of the overcoming).

[G112] But the will to truth (as correctness) is in this way, of course, not yet grounded, because correctness itself lacks the ground. Ground is the ab-ground of the clearing understood as the glowing en-opening of the 'in-between' of the moment (en-opening of the 'in-the midst' and 'amongst').

What in the first beginning (φύσις – ἀλήθεια) only arose and appeared as beings in general becomes here in the other beginning the *en-owning of the ab-ground of decision*.

Now in the other beginning, being no longer holds sway as *a being* "in itself", but – fundamentally remote from and free of all subjectivity and objectivity – being is the mastery of the stillness of all originary history: *the truth of be-ing is the be-ing of truth, and only be-ing is.*

38. Truth

Truth – the clearing of be-ing as the refusal that enowns within the intersection of countering and strife – is the be-ing of errancy.

Error in the sense of *un-abiding* in the clearing arises from out of

---

[1] See Nietzsche's *Werke* (Großoktavausgabe). *Zweite Abteilung. Band* XVI, *Der Wille zur Macht. Drittes und Viertes Buch.* (2nd ed, Leipzig: Kröner) 1922, S. 272.

errancy; errancy, however, arises from out of the truth. Errancy is not the result of mistakes and failures and entanglements: errancy belongs to the ownmost of the clearing and is grounded in its dignity, which is also irradiated by the refusal of be-ing – a dignity which no Da-sein is ever capable of outlasting.

Hence, errancy is nothing "human", rather it holds sway in the 'in-between' of god and man as 'the free-play of time-space' of the strife of the earth and the world.

The true as what is correct has already degraded errancy into incorrect-ness, that is, into a contrivance of man. Correctness, that powerful meta-physical being of truth in its manifold shapings, is the distortion of the inceptual sway of truth that is yet to be seized and is thus the collapse of all the paths of inquiry into be-ing.

[G113]   39. The Clearing of Be-ing and Man
                     (The "Moment")

Why is this sudden moment, "world-history", fundamentally and 'abgroundingly' different from all the "millions of years" of 'world-less' turn of events? Because this suddenness lights up the uniqueness of be-ing and what neither was nor was not outside of being and non-being receives the ab-ground of a grounding unto beings. Less than nothing compared with what is most fleeting in that moment is the presumed duration of being-less "beings" that subsequently one would like to ascertain as already extant out of the clearing of that moment and to call "nature" in order to figure out the fleetingness and illusoriness of that moment. But illusoriness is still the clearing, is still be-ing, illusion is still the clearing, is still be-ing, that is, that which alone gifts man unto his ownmost – into that which exempts him from any comparison with the animal and with the merely living.

But decision implies: whether we 'hear' and we 'say' be-ing or whether in a remarkable forgottenness of being we proceed primarily to calculate man out of beings – be it even by assuming catastrophes. For "catastrophe" remains a figure of speech, when by misconceiving the enownings of

---

ª That is, the *inceptual* be-ing-historical concept of decision and what in fact is be-ing-historical, but already enowned and inabidingly charged with Dasein (cf. above G 83, 45 f.).

fundamental origins that are held unto the abground we attempt with this figure of speech to derive everything from out of the same *ur*-mix called "life".

But decision implies: whether we preserve the inabidingness in be-ing as the ab-ground of all groundings of beings and refuse to submit our ownmost to a rational calculation.

'Decision is' means: decision is already the enownment by be-ing. Decision is not a mere choice, but attunedness by grounding-attunements, by virtue of which the ownmost of man is removed from animality, so that it can first become abiding in the midst of the strife of the earth and the world. This removal is en-ownment from out of [G114] be-ing. The moment of world history, in other words the moment of the enowning of the truth of be-ing, can never be assessed with the 'historical'-technical calculation of time. What is important is not duration and fleetingness, nor the mere fullness and emptiness, but the ground that is held unto abground and is the ground of the counterings of the mutual allotting of gods and man in their ever-groundable fundamental decidedness.

The "moment" is the suddenness of the down-fall [*Ab-sturz*] of everything that is not yet grounded at all but is groundable unto the clearing of be-ing.

The "moment" is the suddenness of man's up-rising [*Aufstand*] into inabiding the 'in-between' of this clearing.

The "moment" has nothing to do with the "eternity" of beings in the sense of the *nunc stans* of metaphysics which carries within itself all the right and wrong signs of calculated time.

The "moment" is the origin of "time" itself – this as the onefoldness of the 'removal-unto' that itself enjoins the clearing and *therefore*, although unrecognized, can be taken over as the realm of projecting-opening the very first interpretation of being.

The moment does not need "eternity" – the mere subterfuge of the transitory of the always-finite – which under the guise of the pre-eminence of the extant as "actual" beings remains extant, because the extant is after all the "permanent".

On the other hand, the moment should not be degraded to the most transitory of the transitory which obviously remains merely the seemingly heroically affirmed reverse-side of "eternity", the mere reversal of metaphysics through which the unavoidable is falsified into the fundamental. All mere doctrines of destiny, including the *amor fati*, are outlets conceived by metaphysics – they are attempts to 'say' something about beings, without inquiring into be-ing. Just as the originarily ("ecstatically") grasped time is only the closest to the clearing of be-ing – "the closest" that overwhelms us while we are mindful of the metaphysical interpretation of being – just so the "moment" remains only a temporal naming – temporal in the sense of originarily grasped time – of the *suddenness* of the clearing of be-ing.

[G115]   40. Clearing[a]
                        Nearness and Remoteness

We are accustomed to taking nearness and remoteness always only calculatively, and from the viewpoint of distance, and retro-related to the "body" when it is taken as corporeal. Straightaway we carry the spatial that is grasped in this manner over to the "temporal". Is this a carrying over? Or do not both arise out of the same root, except that space receives a priority, and this not by virtue of its space-character but on the basis of what is temporally ownmost to space – on the basis of its *"simultaneous"* presencing in all its *stretches*? And *presencing* has temporal priority because *it* seems to unfold be-ing above all and maximally. But what is the reason for this? From where comes this inceptual intimate connection between be-ing and presencing in the twofold sense of staying and "present"? (Cf. VII. Be-ing and Man.) Having obtained a preeminence through time, "space" dominates time itself with respect to grasping *the sway* of time and that means subsequently, with respect to the interpretation that takes "time" as a "line", and the "now" as a "point", and correspondingly takes the arrival and going away of this "point" as changes of location – except that this interpretation suppresses the question concerning the "space" that belongs to these time-locations.

Hence nearness is what can be reached in a *short* segment of time (span of time), that is, what can be reached as immediately present, produced and represented; correspondingly, remoteness. Both nearness and remoteness are calculated in view of the means available in each case for overcoming the distance. But to the extent that in the course of time everything becomes near in this way, it loses right away the character of "nearness". In this connection, *nearness* means *that* remoteness that is

---

[a] Clearing is the clearing "of" the settlement of countering and strife.

grounded in the swaying of be-ing and cannot be eliminated through the overcoming of distance – it means that the holding back that arises out of the refusal and is yet retained by the refusal is something entirely other than the empty extantness, and is the 'other' as a hinting of the ab-ground of be-ing.

[G116] Considering the primership of their sway, [*Wesenserstlingschaft*] nearness and remoteness are not measures, and above all, not measures for the spatio-temporal determinations of distances, but swayings of be-ing itself and its clearing. This clearing lends an openness to the familiar "space" and to the usual "time", that is, an openness which in truth (when grasped in view of be-ing) is no openness, but is filled up and thoroughly distorted by the calculating that comes from the unleashed and self-assessing representing and producing. The disappearance of the "nearness" and "remoteness" into the distantial – their levelling off into the numerical and quantitative differences – is simply the hidden *consequence* of the unconditioned mastery of being understood as machination of producibility and representability of beings.

In their sway, nearness and remoteness are to be grasped only as held unto the *ab-ground*, that is, from out of the sway of be-ing and for be-ing as en-owning.

Nearness is the ab-ground of remoteness, and remoteness is the ab-ground of nearness. Both are the same: the ab-ground of the clearing of be-ing.

However, any attempt at a "dialectical" conceptual reckoning would shatter what here is to be thought into a merely superficial back and forth of differentiating and relating, and would destroy any inkling of the leap unto the swaying of be-ing.

Nearness and remoteness belong to the clearing of be-ing as en-ownment. But they are not seizable properties that come in handy for describing the sway of the clearing and are useful for making this sway understandable. Rather, over against machination of beings that are abandoned by being, nearness and remoteness *initiate trajectories of decision* towards the truth of be-ing: in be-ing they are *the sites without location of the countering* of godhood of gods and the domain of man – a countering that throws that godhood and this domain back unto their sway which is held unto the abground.

The entirely concealed origin of the time-space of the 't/here' is that from which metaphysics in advance and initially has rent the spatiality-temporality in order then to make this spatiality-temporality self-reliant for interpreting everything out of them and to pass off what is uninterpretable as supra-spatial and supra-temporal.

[G117] Nearness and remoteness are not subordinated to any measure, and as far as be-ing itself is concerned, a being is never capable of offering a measure.

In their onefold that holds unto the ab-ground, nearness and remoteness are the 'resonating in-between' of all countering and the limits – held unto the ab-ground – of all blending that is needed by calculation and machination.

Nearness and remoteness are the preserve of the refusal as the highest gifting. They light up be-ing, which sways only in the 'in-between' but is never to be demonstrated from out of beings.

41. The 'In-between' of the 'T/here'*

The 'in-between' of the 't/here' is to be taken as *pre*-spatial and *pre*-temporal, if "space" and "time" indicate the objective realm of the extant and its re-presenting's locational-temporal juncture. Specifically indeed, the "in-between" bespeaks of the twofold intimacy of the '*in-the-midst* of' and the '*meanwhile*' (the moment of the ab-ground).

This 'in-between' is the clearing understood as the thorough-glowing (attunement) that opens.

The inabiding the 't/here' is standing-free towards beings and thus also first of all towards man as the one who can become his own and be a self.

Selfhood is grounded in inabiding. Self is the ground of the "you" and the "I", of the "we" and the "I".

But subject is of metaphysical origin and subjectivity means extantness of what is absolutely secured for representing.

[G118]   ## 42. Truth

The sway of truth does not lie in correctness and reproduction of beings; it does not lie in certainty and security of beings, does not lie in "beings" as 'what is reliable-valid-stable', and does not lie in the unconditionality of thinking. The sway of truth lies in the *clearing of being* as the distress of

* See below, G 321 ff.

the en-owned groundership and godhood, a distress that holds unto the ab-ground. *Only as the clearing of be-ing* is there manifestness of beings. The clearing of be-ing – the en-owning of the ab-ground.

Consequently, an entirely different relationship to *truth* is *demanded* from us. And what is the fundamental consequence of this demand? Inabiding the 'in-between'.

43. Truth and the True

Is the true to be merely skimmed off things and beings just like cream off milk?

Is, via human opinion, the true and what something is to be only attributed to a being as an object, and talked about?

Is the true what is left over of the objects or an *addendum* of the subject, or is it in part objective, in part subjective or neither of the two? Does the sway of the true move within the subject-object-relation at all?

From where do we obtain the sway of truth? What guarantees the finding of the sway of the truth? From where does the necessity for mindfulness of such a sway come?

In determining the truth of the true – analogous to the comportment in delimiting the being of beings – why do we appeal directly to what is simply accessible and intended by everyone? And why do we appeal to *the actual?*

[G119]   44. Be-ing and Truth and Dasein

Inabiding Da-sein is the steadiness of a grounded affirmation of the sway of truth as the clearing of the shelteredness-concealedness of a refusal of the domain of a decision concerning the countering of the domain of man and godhood.

However, affirming and approving are not the same. Approving surrenders itself and is a rescue.

Affirming frees unto freedom vis-à-vis what is unavoidable and is known in its necessity via sustaining a distress – the unavoidable that must be denied approval because approval trails endlessly behind it.

What succeeds approval is fanaticism, that is, the extreme form of an escape into a possibility that is offered for rescue.

Affirming refers to decisions that are not-yet-fulfilled, and have to be created for the first time.

Approvals are easy to bear and there is a multitude of what is to be approved.

Given their actual futurity, the affirming ones remain necessarily unrecognized and strange even among the likes of themselves.

What is genuine, what suffices the sway, is only among the affirming ones: they safeguard the *ur*-leaps, although they themselves do not always initiate the leaping of these leaps.

The approving ones lie because first they must lie to themselves, insofar as their approving is passed off as affirming, passed off as the freeness unto being-free, which is simply what they must evade.

Affirming means 'saying yes' to the nihilating of the ab-ground; it means taking over a de-cision which is be-ing itself and which necessitates the distress of the groundership of man and the distress of the godhood of gods.

Amor fati is still approving '*beings* in the whole': it is not yet the fundamental will to the truth of be-ing that is en-owned by be-ing itself. [G120] *Amor fati* still means loving the obscure in advance; it is not venturing the uniqueness of the clearing's lighting up, it is not venturing be-ing as refusal.

45. Knowing-awareness and Truth

Knowing-awareness is questioning-inabiding the sway of the truth of be-ing, it is the actual Da-*sein*.

Knowing-awareness is more originary than any kind of "cognition" and any kind of "will".

Knowing-awareness is inhering the clearing that resonates through and through with the sheltering-concealing of be-ing.

Knowing-awareness is what exclusively, and actually, is thoroughly attuneable by the grounding-attunements.

Knowing-awareness has nothing to do with "consciousness", which entirely and exclusively maintains itself in the forefront corner of the subject-object-relationship and presupposes man as the thinking animal that has become the subject.

This consciousness as "self-consciousness" can unfold itself into the absolute consciousness and encompass and determine *everything* that is taken into consciousness [*alles Bewußte*] in its 'having become conscious' [*Bewußtheit*] and consign any being to the absolute reason 'having become conscious'. Beingness is thus laid apart with the help of 'having become conscious', and brought into accord with what consciously stands together as what belongs together.

We will never arrive at a more originary interpretation of be-ing and truth in this manner. On the contrary, the semblance of the unconditioned covers and blocks every other questioning. By setting out from beingness as 'having become conscious', truth of be-ing is decided, and in fact decided so ultimately, that this determination cannot even be inquired into and thought as a determination of *the truth of be-ing*. As the highest determination, 'having become conscious' is so absolute that it *deems* itself equal to "be-ing" and hence for Hegel (in his "*Logic*") it can take over the inceptual designation, the "idea", [G121] that is, the 'having-been-seen' of an absolute 'seeing' which is thoroughly transparent to itself, and is the perceiving of reason or the "absolute idea". Insofar as here the talk is of "knowing", it means representing beingness of *beings*; it does *not* mean inhering the clearing of be-ing, and attunedness in this clearing.

Knowing-awareness is 'affirming' [*Ja*] the question-worthiness of the most question-worthy wherein the approval of "beings" always originates. To 'stand out' within this question-worthiness while inabiding means exposing *the ownmost* of man and *the ownmost* of decision about him to the preparedness for an allotment to the grounding of *the truth* of be-ing. This 'standing out' means awaiting the enownment so that man's ownmost may find in be-ing the time-space of the settlement.

46. Truth and Acting

Where "acting" counts as the true and where "acting" counts as "action", that is, as the intervention of a human contrivance into the extant, a long time must be given in advance for acting to unfold into something useful. To a present that is confined to the quotidian and the unexpected, "successes" and "advantages" might very well become discernible all of a sudden, indeed so that the consequences of these "successes" and "advantages" do not yet let the harm hidden in them become public. Thus acting does not follow usefulness at all and it remains to be seen whether a usefulness that can be ascertained at one time confirms what is true in an acting. But perhaps one should not refrain from asking whether the ownmost of acting can ever be fulfilled by all "activities" and "doings", however extensive and impressive they may be. Acting is acting only if, instead of begetting the true which has to hang onto the useful, it lets the sway of truth as the question-worthy be lighted up in the midst of the undecided. The genuine acting sets free unto freedom, that is, unto the inabidingness of belonging to be-ing.

[G122]   47. Truth and Usefulness

"There is no attitude, which could not be ultimately justified by the ensuing usefulness for the totality" (Adolf Hitler 30. January 1939)[1].

Who makes up this totality? (Eighty million-strong extant human mass? Does its extantness assign to this human mass the right to the claim on a continued existence?)

How is this totality determined? What is its goal? Is it itself the goal of all goals? Why? Wherein lies the justification for this goal-setting?

When is the usefulness of an attitude ascertained? Wherein lies the criterion for usefulness? Who determines the usefulness? By what means does this determination justify itself in each case? Can and should the one who adopts an "attitude" also judge its usefulness and its harm at the same time?

Why is *usefulness* the criterion for the legitimacy of a human attitude? On what is this principle grounded? Who determines the ownmost of the domain of man?

From where does the appeal to usefulness as the measure of truth acquire its comprehensibility? Does comprehensibility justify legitimacy?

What is "totality", if not the quantitative expansion of a particular conception of man as an individual?

What does *attitude* mean? Does one arrive at what is fundamental to human being through an attitude? If not, then what does justification of an attitude by the totality and by the ensuing usefulness for the totality mean?

Is there not in this concept "attitude" already a renunciation of every fundamental questionability of a human being with respect to its hidden relation to be-ing?

[1] See "Rede des Führers vor dem 1. Großdeutschen Reichstag am 30. Januar 1939", Druckerei der Reichsbank, Berlin 1939, p. 19.

[G123] Is not man beforehand and ultimately tied here to the pursuit and control of beings in the abandonment by being? And what are "ideas"? Do they not count as names for the final 'dis-humanization' of everything that man still and always creates beyond himself, so that through "ideas" he inevitably falls below his ownmost? Are not "ideas" phantoms that serve solely the "eternal" forth-rolling and up-surging of "life" and fully close off man in his animality as a "living being"?

Is not all "attitude" together with totality of a "people" shoved down the yawning abyss of "beings" insofar as attitude and totality always merely spin around themselves?

And does not such a 'casting-oneself-away' to beings entail the ultimate renunciation of every inceptual, fundamental calling of man for struggling – with a knowing leap unto *be-ing* – for *the sway* of gods and for 'the time-space' of their swaying?

VI

BE-ING
(Ab-ground)

48. Be-ing

Even if the circumscription of the word and the concept of be-ing is to be provisional; even if this provisional circumscription is misconstruable anew insofar as it creates the impression of a mere conceptual analysis, given the general apathy of thinking, we should nevertheless decide upon a preliminary view of the meaning of the word "be-ing". Remarks made in this context still operate entirely within the conventional view of language according to which language is the expression of a "meaning" that is spoken or written, whereas basically language is determined initially only from out of the sway of be-ing (cf. 71. Gods and Be-ing, G254).

Right from the beginning of Occidental thinking, being is grasped in opposition to "becoming". A final consequence of this determination of the sway of "being" as "the permanent", "the constant" – a determination which is still at work in Nietzsche – is Plato's "metaphysics", nay metaphysics itself.

But this view excludes from be-ing something that is indeed not nothing but "*is*", namely that which becomes, that which comes into being and ceases to be, the un-constant. By no means can be-ing be determined in opposition to "something", not even as the opposite of 'nothing' because be-ing itself is still the origin of the 'nothing', and that too, given being's sway, not incidentally, but fundamentally.

Only when we thus begin to think be-ing originarily, do we stand enquiringly outside all metaphysics and thus outside any preeminence of beings.

But this shows right away that the approach through elucidation of the concept is insufficient, and in truth we have already fundamentally abandoned such an elucidation without simply being able to say what has happened. And yet there is no need for another domain of inquiry. Rather, it is enough to be mindful of the word and of be-ing. And this indeed is most difficult.

[G128]   49. Be-ing

The metaphysical determination of being as beingness grasps beingness as presence and constancy. In the light of this interpretation, beings count as ἀεὶ ὄν and, applying this retrospectively to being, being itself becomes 'the most being', thereby being becomes the most constant and the most present. This is the case especially in Hegel when he 'conceives' being as the immediate and the undetermined whose "concept" is not eliminated from the absolute concept but is only sublated therein in such a way that the absolute determines itself *out* of, and along with, the immediate, and is at the same time purely extant and empty.

According to this metaphysical interpretation of being, it must be a violation of the conventional ways of thinking and representing when being is thought in its singularity and uniqueness. However, being in its singularity and uniqueness is not the simple opposite of the metaphysical concept of "being", which by contrast is posited through "becoming", and in terms of counter-positing belongs *to* the metaphysical thinking's sphere of positing.

Be-ing's singularity and uniqueness are not qualities attributed to be-ing or even subsequent determinations that could result from being's relationship to "time". Rather, be-ing itself is uniqueness, is singularity that always lets its time emerge, that is, lets its truth's 'free-play of the time-space' emerge. This uniqueness does not exclude a repetition, but the contrary.

But what is meant here is also not the "sudden" and the "moment", that is, things that still belong to the domain of metaphysical determination of being.

However, the truth of being in metaphysical interpretation refers already to something unique whose uniqueness is not touched by the duration and resiliency of metaphysical thinking. And yet speaking like this is to speak defensively.

And yet, with this way of speaking we do not want to ward off "opinions" and doctrines and standpoints, but to indicate the repulsion from a history of [G129] be-ing itself wherein be-ing was overpowered by *beings* that were *of* be-ing's ever-first-inceptual but un-retained sway.

This repulsion is still merely the reverse side of a questioning that has ventured into what is uninquired. We call the uninquired the 't/here', the clearing wherein no longer any *support* from beings (for determining being) can be invented nor a *refuge* unto beingness (the self-evidence of being) can be sought – beingness as what is lastingly fixed since long ago.

However, the clearing of the 't/here', wherein what needs no support and is not a refuge prevails, is not the empty. If we take the 't/here' in this way, then we would still be casting *a furtive glance* at beings and beingness. In that case, we do not *inquire* into, and do not venture the undecided and that which comes towards us by itself. But if we inquire, if we are wholly the listeners who listen to, and are bounded by this clearing – then we *are* also already enowned by that which sways within this clearing, that is, by the *refusal*.

What if be-ing itself were to be this: the en-owning that allots man to *itself* (to be-ing) by directing him back unto the inquiringly inabiding the 't/here', so that therein he inquires into, and inquiringly encounters, the sway of his historical human domain, that is, his allottedness unto be-ing as the guardianship of the truth of be-ing.

What if be-ing itself were to be this: enowning as the refusal that forthwith 'owns' man 'over unto' the undecidedness of that which needs this lighted refusal – man who is directed back to the grounding of his ownmost – in order to let the hiddenness of the godhood of gods and their siteless nearness and remoteness wink at him?

That which in the clearing of the 't/here' is "unsupported" and "is not a refuge" is neither a deficiency nor a possession but that enthralling, which vis-à-vis every 'having' and 'not having' (representational production) becomes a hint unto the refusal that sways through the enthralling – a refusal which gifts man unto the question-worthiness of his ownmost, while gifting gods unto the needfulness of be-ing.

In the course of his utilitarian way of representing-producing beings, man *comes upon* being as beingness [G130] of beings in order to forget it (being) soon, and with this forgetting to have a sufficient relation (as non-relation) to being. The subsequent determination that is made of being from time to time out of such forgottenness then posits being necessarily as what precedes (the *a priori*) – a positing which renders being increasingly a matter of indifference and as *indifferent* increasingly constant and finally as the sheer extant, as the immediate: the empty. But man does not deem the empty worthy of even a disregard – man who on account of metaphysics has in the meantime become the midpoint of beings. With this shunting, forgottenness of being just completes itself and in human domain becomes a "condition" which simply does *not* seem *to exist.*

However, man never *comes upon* being as be-ing – as the abground of all beings – because be-ing comes unto the open only insofar as be-ing en-owns itself to man in the manner of 'owning' him 'over' to the question-worthy allotedness unto that which as refusal (as be-ing itself) is the needfulness of gods.

As enowning of the refusal, be-ing shelters its singularity in the uniqueness of its clearing wherein what is fundamentally *powerless* becomes something estranging vis-à-vis whatever merely and usually is (the effective) and disperses whatever merely and usually is unto the hidden lack of groundedness and grants gods the time-space of a nearness and remoteness.

The unusualness of be-ing is never manifest in that which among beings is solely unfamiliar and exceptional: the unusualness of be-ing has the whole of beings against itself. Strictly speaking, the talk about the *un*-usualness is inadequate insofar as be-ing sways outside the usual and the unusual and claims a seldomness out of its uniqueness that eludes all 'historical' calculation. If we consider that in the history of being, being itself *for once* became the beginning, and is the beginning, and that the history is still a consequence and an imitation of the beginning, then we appraise approximately what claim be-ing itself puts on the man who ventures to inquire into be-ing so that its truth may become the ground of human being.

[G131]   50. Be-ing: the Ab-ground

Thus we think be-ing with a view towards the ground, and with a view through the rupture that we think unto the ground. But how can such a thinking take place, without thinking being before everything else? But do "*we*" think being? Or is it so that be-ing "*is*" and en-owns thinking

(thinking not as an arbitrary representing, but as en-thinking of being[a]) and thereby en-owns man's ownmost?

En-thinking of be-ing is never a matter of "generating" being, so that being would even become a matter of 'having been thought'.

En-thinking is the en-owned reaching unto the clearing of the refusal, unto a clearing which, without having a support and a refuge, broadens itself *as* the clearing of the *refusal* into the ab-ground which *is* the swaying of be-ing itself as its truth.

It is not we who "bring about" a rupture to be-ing; it is not we who interpret it "as" the ground. Rather, within the sway of be-ing as the refusal, there opens up first, *along with the ab-ground,*[b] what is charged with ground as well as the 'nothing' that prevails through all nihilation and arises together with the prime-leap.

For be-ing, we will never find a "place" – something that is "over-against" and "above" man. Be-ing never lets itself be allocated into an "order".

En-thought as the ab-ground, be-ing is not interpreted from out of something other than itself. Rather, *be-ing* first of all gifts the sway of the ab-ground, to which, depending on the direction and the span of its venturing, thinking of be-ing belongs differently. (The 'free-play of the time-space' of the 't/here' is the foreground of the ab-ground. From the 't/here' initially only "time" – in the onefold of its 'swaying removal-unto' – is the foreground and is thus fundamentally projected-opened as the truth of being and is historically experienceable in the truth of οὐσία – φύσις).

---

[a] En-thinking: the enowned inabiding the clearing of settlement.
[b] To what extent?

VII

BE-ING[a] AND MAN[b]

---

[a] φύσις—φάος
  (Clearing)
[b] Cf. 54. Man's Flight from the Ownmost; "anthropomorphism" – "subjectivism": grasped be-ing-historically; word and language.

51. Be-ing and Man

If be-ing inceptually came to word as φύσις and if φύσις and φάος say the
same in the manifoldness of the same, that is, the rising clearing within
the interlocution [Zwiesage] of opening and en-glowing, then the inceptual metaphysical experience of the living being who has λόγος, entails at
the same time the experience of man as a being that "has" the glow, the fire
– the experience of the one and only being that can make "fire". In that
case "fire" is not only, as conflagration and brightness, a "means" of τέχνη
(cf. 63. Technicity), but is also as the clearing – ἀλήθεια – the swaying
ground of τέχνη. In that case, Prometheus did not bring "fire" to "man" as
an extra, but rather man became man only through this action of the
Titan – the action of the older god against the younger one. In that case,
right from the beginning, the history of man and the possibility of
machination as the possibility of the groundlessness of the clearing[a] are
decided in τέχνη. In that case, the first beginning of the *history* of man
would have to retrieve its un-unfolded inceptuality entirely from out of
the en-saying of the other beginning. In that case, the relation of man's
ownmost to be-ing and the sway of being itself would have to be thought
more inceptually than metaphysics had been hitherto capable of doing
with respect to its own beginning.

However, this would not be a mere improvement of the 'historical'
knowledge, but a thrust towards man's fundamental remembrance by
virtue of which he would come to dwell in the near remoteness to be-ing

[a] Truth of be-ing as metaphysics.

and to its refusal and out of this stance could have taken over an inabiding the truth of be-ing from be-ing itself.

Be-ing-historically, this inabiding is then the powerless mastering of machination—machination whose power flounders only when it obtains that empowering of its superior unlimited power which can no longer by-pass what is sole and unique and as such [G136] is withdrawn from the coercive force of machination and can no longer by-pass the ground-lessness of the truth *of* being, that this groundlessness itself is machinationally.

52. Be-ing and Man

Being (beingness) – contrivance of man and posited by man. And man? The possible en-ownment of be-ing (as Da-sein).

Be-ing? The en-owning of the refusal that is free of power; the en-owning that lights up the ground, the ab-ground as the 'in-between', as that from out of which in the "meantime" the open as a being is carried over unto the strife.

But why everything is poised towards *that* 'either-or'? Is this 'either-or' the actual one?

Or perhaps only this: 'either' *be-ing or a being. Man as the guardian of the 'in-between'* – not a guardian that is 'prior to', or 'looks over' the 'in-between', but one who is within the 'in-between' while *standing out of it.*

The word.

No longer in terms of subject–object in modernity, but rather in terms of *Da-sein – be-ing.*

Man is at play each time and each time in different "ways" which in truth are incomparable because here subject is not replaced with Da-sein and object with be-ing; because here this very juxtapositioning of the word formulas misleads and particularly fills up or covers over the abyss that exists between both "ways".

Subject–Object: here man is put on the stage and secured in the pursuit of his security.

Da-sein–be-ing: here man is risked as the guardian of the most question-worthy.

The "pure" "objectivism" of being wholly absorbed into the 'all-life' is the most hidden completion of "subjectivism" in the sense of the unconditional domination of man's power as the "subject". The objective and the subjective are now equally self-evident. [G137] The total lack of questioning as the disguise of powerlessness.

We ask anew, why is there the 'either-or' between being as contrivance and man as the enowned?

Can there not be a part–part relation, being, in part a contrivance, in part "something" of *its own accord*? Wherefrom this possibility of a division?

Why be-ing and man at all?

Let us leave everything to "beings"! And this leaving – is it not somehow a decision?

Could then something like a necessity of decision be in play? And can this necessity count as absolute or only count under *the* condition that man is he himself and thereby he is the one who ventures and thus is the *one who breaks through* – be it as the one who flees, be it as the one who attacks – or be it even as the *one who lets* things be in accord with being's 'letting-be'?

*

'Dis-humanization' of 'beings in the whole' from out of 'dis-humanizing' man which is grounded in positing man as animal; man's forgottenness of being and consequently the self-unfolding of being's abandonment of beings.

To be lost in questioning through which man is transferred to transforming his ownmost is not retreating of the self into the circumstantial. And yet *how* is he to be lost in questioning? Does comporting "humanly" (mean?) the 'what for' of comporting itself and is this comporting also "human"? *The grip into 'the over' – whereunto as 'the over'?* [Unto the] abground: something that is *'in-between'*! *Be-ing*!

53. A Being–Be-ing–Man

Having become rigid unto what is without the clearing (a being), everything "is" merely "a being".

[G138] There is no one thing that belongs to be-ing; be-ing is not even approachable through a being as such.

And where a being *seems* to open itself up to a being, as in the animal, there everything is overlaid by the mere environing, which is called such, because it can never 'give' anything to a being that is incapable of 'taking' and 'renouncing'. Then, such "having" holds sway only in the clearing of being that grants openness to a being.

Belongingness to be-ing is peculiar only to man because he is en-owned by be-ing and because (be-ing) itself is en-owning and "only" en-owning.

And hence the prolonged dis-enowning; hence the ceaseless incursion of the semblance of be-ing as the emptiness of beingness, which is degraded to an addendum to the mere representing of objects.

54. Man's Flight from the Ownmost (Body–Spirit–Soul)

Selfhood is *not* retro-relatedness to oneself – or to 'I-hood' or 'we-hood'.

Selfhood – the inabiding of the truth of be-ing. The "relation" to being. Every talk of a relation to be-ing is erroneous as soon as and insofar as something like an *object*, something that is set aside, is implied.

Flight from the ownmost. Whence do we know man's ownmost, and from where can we know this ownmost? And wherein do we 'see' and posit the ownmostness of *the ownmost*? Neither *preserving* nor heightening nor overcoming "of" the man (hitherto), but in the first place knowing his ownmost and knowing the history of the fundamental consequences; history of man as animal, hence body–soul–spirit, and spirit only as the consequence and the blockage of animality.

Indeed, much of what is handed down as actually experienced and appreciated moves in a 'space' that is criss-crossed by the flight from the ownmost.

Be-ing only from Da-sein. But how has this nonetheless been up to now? To what extent [G139] is *beingness* still a trace of an uninterpretable, traceless trace? The consolidated dispersal unto beings. Keeping oneself ceaselessly within this dispersal. The semblance of freeness of this attitude. This freedom: that which compels into what is blocked in the clearing.

That man can do without be-ing, that he can disregard be-ing, that be-ing does not heed this: the wholly un-necessary which thus is the ground for the lack of distress.

The aloneness of the countering. The reticence of the attuning. The powerlessness of enownment.

Only man flees from the ownmost and this flight determines his history.

To the flight from the ownmost belongs not only evading oneself in the sense of mere self-forgottenness. Rather, the self can be sought and protected thoroughly, nurtured and heightened, and nonetheless man flees from what is ownmost to him.

55. Be-ing and Man

Be-ing depends on man. That means: the sway of be-ing reaches unto itself and falls into the loss of the ownmost depending on whether man's *ownmost* – man's relation to being – is fundamental to man and is the ground of "humanity". Thereupon, be-ing is delivered over to man, in each case to his ownmostness. But how is this?

Is be-ing thereby at man's beck and call, or does man merely fall victim to his un-ownmostness, the un-ownmostness which is a counterpart of be-ing, a counterpart of the refusal?

But how then does be-ing depend on man? Be-ing tolerates this dependence in that be-ing as enowning grants the enowned (the allotted unto the belongingness to be-ing) a freedom that is to be grounded first through a relation to being. Here freedom becomes self-determination whereby [G140] the self as the already extant (i.e., the rational that represents and produces beings) is nevertheless opted upon by willing and planning. Thereupon, freedom amounts to giving up the freedom instantly and finally, because everything here is decided by *renouncing* the inquiry into the ownmost of the self – ownmost in the sense of belongingness to being: man 'closes' himself 'off' to the truth of being and its question-worthiness.

However, unnoticeably, this 'closing oneself off' to the truth of being becomes falsified into 'letting oneself into', and 'freeing oneself for' the pursuit of beings ("world") whose midpoint (that is, laid as the ground) becomes and remains the subject.

The more beings are taken as actual, the more effective must also the "subject" become, and by the same token the less the "spirit", and the "knowing-awareness" and knowledge. And the more effective the "subject" becomes, the more fulfilled by life ("body" and "soul") the "subject" would be comporting itself, so that one day "life" puts itself on the same plane as 'beings in the whole' and determines man's ownmost as life and from out of "life".

Now the animality of man (ζῷον, animal) triumphs. But this does not mean that henceforth everything will be conceived in terms of "animality". Should this happen it would also be harmless because it is clearly crude. *Animality* triumphs means that "body" and "soul", that is, the inceptual and the lasting determinations of *animality* (whichever other way they are grasped), take upon themselves the role of ownmostness in what is ownmost to man. As old as animality of man is also *thinking*: reason, νοῦς, *ratio*, "spirit" as fundamental determinations of man. Since long ago and indeed for different reasons the sequence, *body–soul–spirit*, as a ranking of body, soul and spirit counted, and it counted up to the end, because the spirit as the "soul" of the understanding and the reason is indeed the most actual and the most effective (*actus purus*) in producing and representing until, with Nietzsche's reversal of Platonism, spirit could be disempowered and become the powerless adversary of the soul (of "life"). To be sure, the triumph of animality shrinks from simply setting the "spirit" aside and passing it off as "life's" secondary manifestation. [G141] Therefore, one instigates a mock battle between those who want to defend the "spirit" and those who basically want to deny it. However, since long ago both parties are in agreement with each other without knowing why. Those who deny the "spirit" still want to protect it and those who defend it deny it nevertheless by rescuing themselves into a trick and rearranging the sequence of rank so that the "spirit" comes right in the middle between the animality of the body and the soul: now the sequence of rank reads: body–spirit–soul. And yet everything remains the same as before. This means that the forgottenness of being that since long ago has been raving forth, heads towards its completion. One can know less and less what the "spirit" actually means because since long ago spirit has become a 'soul-like' version of the *ratio*, and is grounded in the subject.

One believes oneself to be active in a "struggle" for the ownmost of man and of "life" but one has no inkling that this "struggle" is only the flight from the question-worthiness of be-ing.

The struggle against the "spirit" and the ultimate embarrassment of simultaneously affirming and negating the spirit means pursuing the forgottenness of being.

But even the defence of the "spirit" plunges into the forgottenness of being insofar as the "spiritual" is only a sphere of "culture", of taste, of morality and of faith. Here as well as there, "spirit" receives its determination from the animality of man.

The familiar fundamental formula for determination of man along the line of animality is: the unity of body–soul–spirit. The spirit has the highest rank and, therefore, it also determines this "unity", even if only vaguely (or does this unity lie *before* this threefold and as what?).

In this fundamental formula the animality of man is seemingly subordinated and tied to the "spirit", although given its ownmost, the "spirit" is still experienceable only *with a view towards animality*.

The formula currently in use, that is, body–spirit–soul, is more clear with regard to [G142] the claim of animality and thus more decisive in lapsing into the hitherto. *Body and soul*: the animalness as such encloses and dominates and limits the "spirit".

However, this formula which, while expressing a lapse, also wants at the same time to be simply "novel", is necessarily more ambiguous, and that means, more indecisive and more cowardly vis-à-vis a thoughtful decision. Although this formula is apparently directed against Christianity and what is Catholic, it is Catholic in the most genuine sense insofar as with this formula one can do anything and at the same time be protected against everything. One forestalls the predominance of spirit (at the same time as one misinterprets it still as "intellect") and preaches "character", "animal" and "instinct". But one does not eliminate the spirit at all, one instead puts it in the middle such that it looks as if only now spirit is protected and defended. One does this because one has to protect oneself against the blame of barbarism.

Now everything is in order: under the protecting roof of animality (body–soul) one can cheerfully (so it seems) attend to all spiritual achievements of all history, that is, one can now surrender oneself to such an extent to historicism that, in comparison, the historicism of the nineteenth century seems stunted.

A tremendous satisfaction now prevails in "sciences", especially in humanistic disciplines over the newly offered possibilities of discoveries and refutations of the science hitherto. One feels oneself confirmed and needed in one's "spirituality", one feels that it is a pleasure to "live", and yet all this is, within the growing abandonment of beings by being, merely the outpouring of reckless and lasting urges of man's lack of decision. The highest triumph of this lack of decision is man's lack of an inkling of himself: man's flight from his ownmost increasingly becomes a hidden "panic".

[G143]   ## 56. *Da-sein* and *Sein und Zeit**
           ### *"The Da-sein of Man"*

The Da-sein of man could mean the extantness of the rational animal here and now; it could also mean *that* there "is" such a being. It could also mean the same indeed but conceptually differentiated: the manner in which man is the quality of his *existentia* as different from his *essentia*.

Here man is always the subject to whom a particular manner is attributed.

However, what in *Sein und Zeit* and later on is called Da-sein is separated from all this by an unbridgeable abyss.

Da-sein is that which grounds a fundamental transformation of man – is that which is possibly "of" man in an entirely different and still to be grounded sense of this "genitive".

Da-sein: the site of man's ownmost, preserved for him from out of the inceptual grounding of the truth of be-ing.

*

The Da-sein**

What is so named and inceptually grounded in this naming is:

1. *not* at all a "finding" in the sense of an extant that one lights upon. Rather, Dasein is that which evolves into swaying only through the projecting-open that 'leaps into' – enacts a 'leaping into' – and projects-open (designates itself *hermeneutic-phenomenologically*; does not understand itself as the "Platonic" beholding of the essences, but [G144] as a projecting-opening that inquires and interprets, is guided by a *perspective* and by a fore-grasping, and is *"philosophical"*, that is, "loves" the truth of being and is fundamentally *historical*).

2. This projecting-open as such *is not* merely a projecting-opening of human-*being*. (If this were the case, then for some reason, perhaps following the contemporary-anthropological intentions, man would be singled out and observed "philosophically".) But the broadest and the most inceptual projecting-opening unto Da-sein is man's pro-jecting-opening *unto*, and *from out* of, the allotment into the truth of

---

* Cf. 79. Being and Time.
** Cf. *Sein und Zeit*.

be-ing. However, *be-ing* is the *most question-worthy*. (Overlooking everything that is decisive, one "*can*" "read" and use *Sein und Zeit* as "anthropology" and as a kind of "existential ethics" and so on. But all this has nothing to do with the *exclusive thinking-willing* of this attempt, that is, with the enquiring unfolding of the question of being as the question concerning the truth of being.)

3. Da-*sein* means grounding the truth of being through a transformation of man out of a decision for *be-ing*, that is, what is exclusively worthy of all honouring, although be-ing is neither the "last" nor the "first", but rather the ab-ground, what is sole and unique in the 'in-between'. Therefore, "*Da-sein*" is incomparable *in every respect*; it is *not an object of a "doctrine"* (in *Sein und Zeit* "investigation" means fundamental *questioning*, not "explaining" the extant). Da-sein – itself en-owned in en-owning – is nothing that we contrive, but rather what in honouring the most question-worthy we *reverently* take over and in taking over we just "find".

Because the question of being and along with it also Da-sein is not yet grasped, because one still takes Dasein as the "subject", one arrives at the ridiculous demand that now the individual subject (in *Sein und Zeit*) would have to be replaced by people as subject. Poor simpletons!

What is fundamental about the resolute disclosedness does not lie in a presumed "subjective" "activity" of the individual but [G145] in the groundership that is charged with Da-sein and belongs to the transformed man; lies in the fundamentally other openness that is primary and is the openness to the truth of being as such; lies in the destruction of the subject-object-relation that sets the measure and founds the ground; lies in the overcoming of all metaphysics.

Groundership means inabiding the exposedness to the 't/here': the Da-*sein*; it means taking-over '*the t/here-ness*' as the clearing of being's ab-ground; and this as the '*in-between*' to all "beings".

To understand the inabiding "of" man in the sense of *genitivus essentialis* is to approach inabiding by taking it as a quality that hangs on to man – it means presupposing man as a subject that is already determined. In truth, that is, in accord with *this* thinking, *inabiding* means the anticipatory determination of the fundamental ground "of" man in the direction of which he can first be experienced *inabidingly* in his ownmost. Inabiding constitutes the "*essentia*" out of which the title "man" first draws its fundamental naming power.

In spite of all superficial *moral* impressions and *considering* the exclusive question of *Sein und Zeit*, that is, the question concerning the truth of being, *ownedness* [*Eigentlichkeit*] is to be grasped exclusively and always beforehand in relation to this truth as a "manner" [*Weise*] to be "the t/here" wherein the en-ownment of man unto the belongingness to being and to its clearing ("time") enowns itself.

"Ownedness" is a determination that overcomes metaphysics as such. Correspondingly *un-ownedness*, [*Un-eigentlichkeit*] which, thought "existentially" unto and out of the question of being, means lostness to *beings*, that is, means the predominance of beings themselves and their overshadowing of being to such an extent that the distress of the question concerning the truth of being has to stay away.

Any approach to this determination that comes from anywhere and serves arbitrary purposes (comes from some anthropology and "philosophy of *Existenz*") is at the mercy of any whim – only that such an approach never thinks-*along with*, which is always a thinking ahead into, that which is to be solely [G146] enquired into. In the best case of a scholarly pursuit of calculation, such an approach corroborates historicism as an occupation.

*

"*Sein und Zeit*"

Extrinsically approached, the beginning made with *Sein und Zeit* can be taken as an interpretation of man *as Da-sein*. However, this interpretation already reverberates only in projecting-opening man as Da-sein.

Da-sein unfolds fundamentally in "understanding of being", that is, again as projecting-open being unto its truth ("time") whereby this truth as such need not come to a halt in the knowing-awareness.

As always in *Sein und Zeit*, it is *from out of the truth of being* and *only* thus that man is inquired into. This inquiry belongs entirely to the *enquestioning of what is most question-worthy*. But how is this most question-worthy, be-ing?

Transformed *fundamentally* into "What" *and* "How", the grounding-experience is this: being is not the leftover of the emptiest universal that fills itself up with categories; being is not an "addendum" that is then as "idea" admitted on command; but rather, *being is the ab-ground as en-owning*.

Therefore, *Sein und Zeit* is:

1. *neither* a particular kind of "anthropology" (man as such in the midst of beings, be it *as a* being among others or be it as the relational-midpoint),

2. *nor* a particular kind of "metaphysics" (being as beingness *unto* a being).

Therefore, *Sein und Zeit*, which can only be *one* exigent pathway among other possible pathways, *must* unavoidably look like "metaphysics" and "anthropology", nay it has to make itself initially "understandable" with the help of "metaphysics" and "anthropology" by going through them, which means that *Sein und Zeit* has to reckon with all possible and proximate misunderstandings. And yet, all this leads nowhere and is not sustaining (cf. 61. Anthropomorphism).

[G147] The decisive insight is this: in its truth being can never be obtained from *beings*. What *follows* from this insight? The necessity of venturing a leap unto *be-ing's* sway from out of an initial clearing of be-ing itself.

57. The Metaphysical Grounding-Experience

Grounding-position, *grounding-experience*, grounding-distress.

Grounding-experience:

1. is not enacted by *anyone*, but by "individuals" [*Einzelenen*], that is, by those who are marked in advance. But as the marked ones, these "individuals" belong to be-ing: each for itself is less "ego-istic" than any "community" is ever "for itself".

2. Hence the grounding-experience is also not *"enacted"* in the sense that the "individuals" would invent it, concoct it or assemble it from isolated pieces.

3. Rather, grounding-experience en-owns, (is) and draws an individual unto the ground of the grounding-experience which the grounding-experience opens.

4. Accordingly, depending on the originary, inceptual and the non-inceptual swaying of being, the grounding-experience is also different. In the epoch of metaphysics, grounding-experience can assert itself only as a preview of the 'beings in the whole' and as projecting-opening their beingness as the φύσις that has become rigid.

In modernity this grounding-experience is guided specifically in view of the subject for experiencing the 'beings in the whole' as "life": the idealists, Schopenhauer, Nietzsche (*Leibniz*).

Grounding-experience is an *enowning of man*. In the grounding-experience man enowns and dis-enowns his ownmost.

And, therefore, within the domination of *animal rationale* there is the unavoidable impression that the grounding-experience is a "manner of lived-experience" and is an "affair" *of man* – "anthropologism".

The swaying of be-ing along with its *truth* enowns itself in the grounding-experience. The grounding and fundamental circumscription of this truth [G148] is the distress. [To unfold] the necessity which is adequate to this distress. [To unfold] what is humanly demanded, is put forth and claimed as "ideal".

58. The Question put to Man*

1. "What is he?"; 2. "*Who* is he?" These questions themselves are already answers, that is, decisions.

'What is man?' This question wants to determine that which is of 'the nature of a what' [*das Washafte*] and determines it as animality.

'Who is man?' This question is to posit that which is of 'the nature of a who' [*das Werhafte*] and . . .? Actually, the '*who*' is to be thought only in the *singular*. What is meant by this? The directive to the *self*hood of man, which selfhood is grounded in the 'owning-over-to' a "self" because 'owning-over-to' is grounded in the en-ownment by being. Man's belongingness to being determines him in terms of the *guardianship* of the truth of be-ing, which means that man as a being is *not* an occurrence among the rest of beings!

The question concerning the 'what' falls in the sphere of the explainable and assertable.

The question concerning the 'who' transforms and transfers man unto the belongingness to the hidden-sheltered – this question transfers unto the relation to being.

---

* See, *Überlegungen* X, p. 70 ff., to appear in GA 95 as *Überlegungen* B.

59. Be-ing and Man

Be-ing (enowning), the *elusive*, gathering midpoint and the ground of each and every 'in-the-midst'. Be-ing as en-owning is the *conveyance of this midpoint* (i.e., of Da-sein).

The en-owning as en-ownment, and the prime-leap as enstrifing the strife between the world and the earth, that is, enstrifing *these in their sway*.

Here is the provenance of venturing, of having to venture [G149] (the truth of be-ing) as man's ownmost. *From* here, that is, out of this provenance, comes primarily all *the swaying* and allotment.

Man as an occurrence within nature – within 'beings in the whole'. Is *this* 'beings in the whole' a representation of man?! And *whence* this representation? And is the *truth* of this representation of man by man within *nature*, out of nature – or is it a *decision*, and this decision from where? Thus, man as well as nature lose the preeminence.

It is in *truth* wherein both man *and nature* "move".

The decision [is] between the truth of be-ing (be-ing) and the pre-eminence of beings, ("life") but in such a manner that neither a retreat into anthropomorphism nor an appeal to "nature" is any longer possible. Rather it is man who decides. What *kind of a decision?* On *man's ownmost* that does not lie in the human domain, if this domain is that of *animal rationale. Da-sein.*

*

Overshadowing of being by beings. The *question-worthiness* of the most-question-worthy (of be-ing) as the inceptual truth. The distress of *honoring*, venturing ahead unto something whose nature is such as to require venturing.

Pindar: "ἄνθρωπος σκιᾶς ὄναρ"[1] – the dream that a shadow dreams, or (that which casts shadow – that which dreams), or: a shadow that is dreamt by a dream; the shadow – the dreamed.

---

[1] *Pindari Carmina cum Fragmentis Selectis.* Iterum edidit O. Shroeder. In aedibus B.G. Teubneri Lipsiae, 1914. Pythia VIII, v.95 sq.

VIII

BE-ING AND MAN

60. Be-ing and Man

Every determination of man's ownmost is tied up with the question, "How do we grasp 'beings in the whole' unto which the being called man is allocated?" The task of the fundamental delimitation of this being is thus rescued by delivering it over to an interpretation of 'beings in the whole' – an interpretation that is either already carried out or the conditions of whose enactment are hardly thought through. If this interpretation were to arise out of mindfulness, then immediately there arises the counter-question: "*Who* are 'we', who straightaway determine 'beings in the whole' and even assume the 'beings in the whole' to be sufficiently determined by an explanation in terms of a supreme cause?" Thus, the question concerning man comes back, except that this question is now either changed or is at the threshold of an unavoidable transformation – unavoidable, of course, only for the will to mindfulness. If we renounce this will, then everything remains within a barren back and forth between an interpretation of 'beings in the whole' and an interpretation of the "particular" being that we believe to know as man.

However, the experience to be mindful of is this: only on the basis of allottedness unto the truth of be-ing can man determine 'beings in the whole' and himself as the being that he is. Considering man's ownmost ground, be-ing itself has to have 'owned' man 'over' unto the truth of be-ing. This en-owning alone yields that clearing wherein 'beings in the whole' and man can encounter each other in order to assess their remoteness.

If man evades that mindfulness – and who wants to prevent this? – then at the end he rescues himself into an explanation of all beings as a product of human "imagination". In that case, 'dis-humanization' of beings in general is the first and last wisdom. And the more unconstrainedly the 'dis-humanizing' of man bears itself; the more exclusively he explains himself in terms of that which is neutrally extant and objectively found in him; the more he explains himself in terms of [G154] the animal which occurs as *animal rationale*, the more unconditionally and stubbornly 'dis-humanization' of 'beings in the whole' asserts itself.

However, devoid of any goal, the unbridled 'dis-humanization' of man is the cloud of dust that trails behind the hidden and reckless flight of man from his ownmost – a flight which flaunts the mask of a victory that proclaims a liberation of man for a total self-determination that accords with the species "man animal", and claims self-evidence as designation for its truth.

'Dis-humanization' of man is not only the ground of '*dis-humanization*' of 'beings in the whole', but also at the same time the ground of de-godding of the world. In this insidious gestalt, "anthropologism" obtains its illimitable metaphysical ownmost.

But how can the 'dis-humanization' of man be overcome? Only from out of the decision to ground the truth of be-ing. With this grounding not only will man be distinguished as a being from other beings, but he will be transferred into the clearing *of be-ing* and beforehand placed together with be-ing on the ground of an enownment of human *being* by be-ing that has already taken place, but not yet en-grounded.

But does not this underscored and exclusive way of putting be-ing and man together and putting them against each other already decide on the distinction of man, namely that *he* abides [*west*] within the belongingness to the truth of be-ing and accordingly interprets himself this way or that way as the being that he is, and thus positions himself towards 'beings in the whole'?

What justifies this decision? Or perhaps here no decision is made at all? Does a mere 'finding' announce itself here? And who finds this 'finding'? Does man come upon be-ing, or does be-ing attune man so that he comes upon be-ing?

Whereunto must man be shifted and to what must he be related, so that there is a guarantee that he would come upon his ownmost? Who [G155] draws here the boundary of the unavoidable relations? To what extend is man the one who is dragged into relations?

Does man then ever know "immediately" anything at all of himself, or is every immediate "self"-observation simply the first and most frequent 'excursus' in the course of which he certainly finds many things and yet thereby distances himself more and more from his ownmost?

Does not man revolve around that illusion of himself that he creates of himself? But how to account for this illusion?

Why don't we simply relinquish man to the predominance of that opinion of himself that prevails from time to time?

But when and how is man *he* himself?

He is indeed himself when he is 'owned-over to' his ownmost. However, this 'owning-over to' 'enowns itself' in the enowning of be-ing, which is grounded and preserved in the ownedness of Da-sein.

But each of these determinations seems again to be arbitrary – perhaps "flashes of ideas" that cannot do anything vis-à-vis the power of the "*actual*" human domain that now begins to "dominate" the planet and announces to it – daily and penetratingly – the actual ownmost of this domain. Certainly, but whence comes the proof and justification that the "actual" is also of the nature of the ownmost and even guarantees the sway of being? This remains no less questionable than the preceding "flashes of ideas" can be. But when the questionable stands against the questionable, then how to make a decision and by whom? Or what is to be experienced before all decision is this: 'beings in the whole' and their claim on "truth", and the determination of the ownmost of selfhood of man are equally question-worthy within *the questionable*? And why are they *equally* question-worthy? Is it because both have to belong mutually and fundamentally to each other in what is hidden-sheltered and because this belongingness is the hint to what is fundamentally question-worthy, that is, to be-ing itself? So that being can never and nowhere be evaded unless we sink into the forgottenness of being, which seemingly takes for granted an acting and an attitude [G156] that apparently tolerate the appeal to the effective, that is, to the actuality of the actual, but as forgottenness nevertheless thinks be-ing insofar as in truth "actuality" is thought.

That such forgottenness of being unceasingly makes a mockery of itself and "contradicts" itself, and that "the contradictory" in the usual sense cannot be tolerated according to the rule of "logic", is not what is disturbing here. For, who justifies such a yardstick of "logic" and "the logical"? (Most likely that appeal to the actual as the rational, that is, to that which corresponds to useful purposes.)

It is not the "contradiction" that disturbs here: one does not let oneself be disturbed by it. It could also be that this "contradiction" in the meantime brings about a *destruction* that amounts to a devastation in such a way that devastation becomes at that point least discernible where forgottenness of being threatens to become complete. Sinking into forgottenness of being is to pursue a devastation through which that ground peters out upon which alone man's mastery over beings is able to stand: the inabiding the truth of being.

Man is the one from whom thinking must 'think-*away*' in order to think him in his ownmost. But whereunto?

And yet, this question 'whereunto?' *belongs* to the 'thinking-away' but does not make this 'thinking-away' helpless and groundless. Rather, this question 'whereunto?' confirms man himself as *the questioner* that can be strong enough for affirming and negating the decision which rules before all agreeing and approving.

Only as the questioner of that question can man be the true guardian of the truth of being itself, that gifts itself as the most question-worthy to him, and only to him as the questioner. And this most question-worthy is the ground that is held unto the ab-ground as the ground of every "creative prowess" whose ownmost we must think more originarily, not as producing of products, but as the grounding of the sites and pathways of *Da-sein* through whose 'in-between' the struggle of countering and strife secures for itself the "moment" (cf. truth–clearing–"moment").

IX
ANTHROPOMORPHISM*

---

* Cf. 60. Be-ing and Man.

61. Anthropomorphism*

Anthropomorphism is an explicit or implicit, acknowledged or unknowingly adopted conviction that 'beings in the whole' are what they are and how they are by virtue of, and in accordance with, the representation that, among other processes of life, proceeds in man, the animal endowed with reason. [Thus] what is named and known as a being is a human contrivance. Anthropomorphism pretends to be less than a well-rounded doctrine that requires a grounded presentation. Anthropomorphism promptly assures itself approval as a "belief" which prior to everything teachable is evidently intelligible – a belief which is ceaselessly sustained and strengthened by the opinion that what man is in his ownmost can by no means become the object of a question. At any time and in a manner evident to everyone, anthropomorphism can retreat to its first and last proposition, according to which everything represented, stated and inquired is indeed merely "human". And yet, what is essential to anthropomorphism is not the 'dis-humanization' of beings, but rather a variously announced and shaped resistance to any possibility of a fundamental transformation of man. That is why anthropomorphism eagerly assumes the role of a subterfuge vis-à-vis *any* demand for a deciding questioning.

* Cf. the "Conclusion" of *Schelling: Vom Wesen der menschlichen Freiheit* (1809), the lecture-course given in Freiburg in the summer semester 1936, GA 42, ed. Ingrid Schüßler, (Frankfurt am Main: 1988) § 28, pp. 282 ff.

As long as mindfulness does not arrive at a fundamentally more originary grounding position, the illusion of the unassailability of anthropomorphism deceives to such an extent that even attempts to ward off anthropomorphism are forced into a plane and trajectory that are suitable to anthropomorphism. But the condition for all this lies in the insight that the 'dis-humanization' of beings – whether it is affirmed or negated – arises out of 'dis-humanizing' being. Specifically, this means: the question concerning the truth [G160] of being remains unknown and uninquired. Man's comporting relation [*Verhältnis*] to "being" counts in advance as decided via explaining man's human ('dis-humanizing') relation to beings. Hence, the actual prop of anthropomorphism is metaphysics as such. Metaphysics provides above all the 'space' for the claim of anthropomorphism and for warding it off. This may be demonstrated by the opposition between "subjectivism" and "objectivism" in modern metaphysics, an opposition that degenerates forthwith into total unproductivity. In this connection "subjectivism" must, of course, be understood in its full sway, that is, metaphysically. Subjectivism is the positioning, in the sense of the sub-ject, of man (be it as the "I", the "we", the "individual", the "community", the "spirit", the "body", the mere living being, or the "people"), that is, *of that* being from, and in view of which, all beings are "explained" in their beingness. Likewise, taken metaphysically, "objectivism" necessarily turns out to be the reverse side of "subjectivism" as soon as subjectivism's sway becomes totally un-transparent and self-evident. Man, the *forgotten* subject, belongs to the 'whole' of the "objective" beings and is within this 'whole' merely a fleeting speck of dust. The heightening of man to an unbounded being of power and surrendering him to the unknowable destiny of the course taken by 'beings in the whole' belong together, they *are* the same. The differences between the ancient and modern "anthropomorphism" proceed *within* the metaphysical grounding position of the Occidental man hitherto. Although those differences are important for the individual stages and courses of metaphysical thinking, they can be left out of consideration in the present reflection on anthropomorphism.

Since a "systematically" unfoldable account cannot fit anthropomorphism insofar as anthropomorphism is nothing but a retreat into the one guiding proposition, mindfulness must make sure that, from different "sides", its questioning [G161] always comes upon the same grounding position and renders it question-worthy in all respects:

1. Can human comportment in general and human "thinking" in particular ever be other than what they are, namely constantly rooted in "man"?

2. Is with the assumption that, in this way, man is the enactment-ground of his comportments, also a decision made on the 'dis-humanization' of everything to which his comportment and thinking always relate, namely beings? Are 'beings in the whole' in advance and irredeemably subjected to the encroachment of 'dis-humanization'? Is the semblance of the opposite merely a plain illusion within this dislodgable state?

3. And what counts here for actually dislodgable? Is it not since long ago the ever-powerful and increasingly emptier self-evidence of positing man as the thinking animal? Is not then the 'dis-humanization' of 'beings in the whole' already the consequence of a preceding and unrecognized *dis-humanizing* of man? 'Dis-humanization' of man means above all the erecting of that which distinguishes man as man by basing it upon animality (that is, by taking what distinguishes man as a differentiation *within* the sphere of the living beings). But this animality simultaneously redefines the living beings and thus man as a being that one comes upon, and that is equipped, ever differently, with lower and "higher" faculties ("organs"). 'Dis-humanization', therefore, means man being pressed into an extant animal-being that also occurs among other living beings. The variety of assessment of human faculties and achievements does not change anything concerning this metaphysical consolidation of human being.

4. However, if anthropomorphism consists in such 'dis-humanizing', and not primarily and solely in the 'dis-humanization' of all beings, then should not mindfulness of anthropomorphism first of all raise the question concerning [G162] what is ownmost to man? This demand seems to be self-evident and yet it conceals within itself the most question-worthy decisions, because it is not decided how in general, and with what intentions and in which respects, we are to inquire into man and in what way here a decision is enactable.

5. In terms of direction and scope the question concerning man's ownmost must indeed be so laid out that this question in advance measures up to everything that mindfulness on anthropomorphism can bring to light as question-worthy.

6.	Anthropomorphism asserts the 'dis-humanization' of 'beings in the whole', and that means 'dis-humanization' of beings *as such*. By the grace of representing, being as representedness is a contrivance of the rational animal. There lies in anthropomorphism a prior decision on being as a contrivance of the 'dis-humanized' man. How, where and when is *this* decision *as such* ever enacted as a decision on being? But if up to now this decision is nowhere and never enacted, must not then, above all, such a decision concerning the sway of being itself be decided upon beforehand? Must not then the question concerning man also take up the question as to how man can be allotted to the truth of being at all so that such decisions can for once become a distress for him and in this sphere of decision questions can become a necessity? What if this question-worthy allotment of man unto the truth of being were to announce man's ownmost before everything else? But why has this hint so far simply remained unperceived?

7.	What is this allotment of man unto the truth (clearing) of be-ing? Where does this allotment come from? Is it an invention and will-fulness of "man" and in that case what does "man" still mean? Or is man en-owned unto [G163] his ownmost above all and solely by be-ing? And does be-ing hold sway as this en-owning itself and only as this?

8.	In order to rescue his ownmost, that is, to shape this ownmost as it behoves vis-à-vis be-ing, must he then not become the grounder of the truth of be-ing? The rescuing of man's own-most is then a transformation into that groundership whose swaying we call Da-sein. The 'dis-humanizing' of man collapses in itself and the 'dis-humanization' of beings proves to be without ground.

9.	The knowing-awareness "of" Da-sein as Da-*sein* itself is, by itself, necessarily the knowing-awareness of the manifold being-historical conditions that secure anthropomorphism its apparent "natural-ness", "indestructibility" and "popularity". These conditions are:
    a) the undiminished preeminence of beings vis-à-vis being in metaphysics; indeed simply the undiminished preeminence of beings on the basis of the metaphysical inquiry into being (as beingness);
    b) in the horizon of this preeminence, and at home therein, the experience of man as *animal rationale*;

c) the consolidation of the extant "essence" of man in the Christian way of thinking (the *ens creatum – homo* – as the "pilgrim on earth";

d) the intensification of the extantness of man through the interpretation of man as "subject";

e) the final harnessing of man into the unleashed machination of beings (technicity – 'history').

10. However, if the swaying of be-ing is grounded in en-owning – in the en-ownment of man unto Da-sein – is it not then be-ing more than ever, and no longer only beings, that is exclusively and properly determined in the direction of man, and that means, from out of him? Not at all, since the en-ownment unto Da-sein is in itself already an 'owning-over-to' be-ing as that 'in-between' that holds on to the ab-ground, and in whose 'free-play of time-space' the countering of god and man crosses itself with the strife between the earth and the world.

X

HISTORY*

* Cf. 64. 'History' and Technicity; concerning Nietzsche's *II Unzeitgemäßer Betrachtung* (man – 'history' and history – temporality) see the Freiburg seminar text of the winter semester of 1938/39, *Nietzsches II. Unzeitgemäße Betrachtung*, GA 46, ed. Hans-Joachim Friedrich (Frankfurt am Main: Klostermann: 2003).

62. History

Steadfast in the truth of be-ing, we must obtain that originary historicality through which all 'history' is overcome.

Not restraining 'history' but overcoming it. When is 'history' groundless and un-necessary? When history has become fundamental, which happens when the grounding of the truth of be-ing is enowned by be-ing and unfolds for the sake of be-ing.

An epoch that still needs 'history' for its "history" – that is, an epoch which has already mixed up in advance both 'history' and history – proves that a fundamental history is refused to that epoch and, therefore, proceeds towards the lack of history (devastation).

In the face of the 'going under' that is set at the beginning, inceptual decisions – whether enacted, taken over or by-passed – cast suffering and rage unto beings: in *the grounding of the truth of be-ing* (Da-sein), *history is* the en-owned swaying of be-ing (settlement). History alone endows a people with national cohesion and distinctness of its ownmost. "Space" and "land", climate and blood, never have the power to shape nor the will to cohere. Transmission of decisions and decidedness brings forth the basic thrust of futural questioning and commanding; brings forth the style of inabidingness in beings, the ability to have destiny and the determination for 'going under'. Only where such things prevail is there history – everything else is a 'historical' cacophony that reports the results of lived- experience and passes off what it reports as "history".

*

[G168]   History and 'History'

Is 'history' the 'only' fundamental possibility of relating to *history*?

And what is "history"? It is achieving the truth of be-ing for preserving it in beings[a] and thus for rendering beings manifest by residing within the *clearing*.

Or does man become fundamentally historical only when he has overcome 'history', indeed any kind of 'history'?

What does this overcoming presuppose? It presupposes overcoming the 'dis-humanization' of man.

It presupposes transforming man into the founder of Da-sein.

History is the trace left in the clearing of be-ing by the decisions on differentiating be-ing from "beings" – decisions that are enowned by be-ing.

"Culture" in the sense of fostering and realizing[b] "values" – and values in turn as "goal" or as "means" that belong to a people and are national or human "means" that belong to the domain of man or are "expression" of the "life" of a people – always presupposes a view of being as machination (represented producedness) and consists only of the domination of man as the subject. Finally, the thinking in terms of values is the most superficial superficialization of being as objectness. (The critique of culture *as such* that is carried out in *Sein und Zeit* is grounded in the fundamental determination of historicality; in the differentiation between history and 'history', and in the interpretation of truth as *resolute disclosedness* of 'being-in-the-world', that is, Da-sein.) Domination of culture-consciousness and consequently domination of cultural politics pursues a growing consolidation of modernity in the direction of that which modernity pursues, namely the forgottenness of being. The uprootedness of man does not consist in a specific shaping and degeneration of culture and cultural-consciousness. Rather, [G169] culture as such is this uprootedness and indicates the severance of man's as yet ungrounded ownmost from history. This rejection of "culture" is not an advocacy of the state of "nature". Rather, this rejection renders the distinction between "nature" and "culture" invalid, because culture presupposes nature.[c] However, the exclusion from history cannot be immediately

---

[a] Grounding of be-ing in Da-sein.
[b] ("culture") ("historicism").
[c] The Aristotelian model: φύσει ὂν and ποιούμενον, πρακτόν.

overcome through "politics" because politics on its part, and specially in its "total" claim to domination, means merely turning culture over to modern man's completed technical-'historical'-machinational ownmost.

The consequence of the political-'historical' conception of modern man is that only with the help of this conception will *historicism* be brought to completion. Historicism is the total domination of 'history' in the sense of reckoning with what is past in view of what is present with the claim to specify thereby once and for all man's ownmost as *'historical'* – not as *historical*. One day historicism must bring about its own end insofar as historicism, through 'historical', psychological analysis and "biological" explanation deduces everything from "life", and allots "life" to itself as the provenance of historicism, and thus appears as an "expression" "of life". The political historicism becomes a victim of cultural-'historical' historicism only by way of a reversal. By thus falling into the arms of its own adversary, historicism confirms its belongingness to modern man's ownmost, and brings about its own *termination* which, insofar as it exhibits the highest form of historicism, has removed itself *furthest* from the *overcoming* of historicism. The domination of 'history' will be overcome *only through history*, through a novel decision and through an ever-first inquiry into the truth of be-ing. Indeed, this "overcoming" is already something fundamentally different and specific [G170] so that what this overcoming accomplishes can be and continues to be indifferent to this overcoming.

Metaphysically, the sway of "culture" is the same as the sway of "technicity". Culture is the technicity of 'history' – culture is the manner in which 'historical' reckoning with values and 'historical' production of goods arrange themselves and so spread the forgottenness of being.

XI
TECHNICITY

63. Technicity*

We succeed best in discovering the fundamental sphere of technicity when we realize that τέχνη is a word of "knowledge", and when we grasp "knowledge" as inabiding the truth, and when we understand truth as openness of beings from out of the clearing of be-ing. Thereupon we avoid the danger of inquiring into the "purpose" of technicity and of explaining its "sway" out of this purpose. Τέχνη neither consists of producing tools and machines, nor of the mere use and application of them within a procedure, nor of this procedure itself, nor of being well versed in such a procedure (cf. below, G 177 f.) On the one hand, the way τέχνη is named inceptually hits upon τέχνη itself, and, on the other hand, this naming does not penetrate more originarily into the sway of τέχνη. The reason that such an originary penetration of τέχνη did not happen is that in the epoch dominated by this word τέχνη, the sway of truth – to which belongs what τέχνη names – remained ungrounded and has remained ungrounded ever since. Since, metaphysics shares with "technicity" the same sphere of swaying, this makes clear, why all metaphysics can never measure up to the sway of τέχνη and technicity. Metaphysics does not dispose over any domain that metaphysics could leave to the grounding and overcoming of technicity. Technicity itself becomes the destiny of metaphysics and its completion.

---

* Cf. above, G135.

All modern control of technicity, all claim to wanting to be its master, is thus only an illusion that covers up – pretty badly at that – the metaphysical enslavement to technicity.

Technicity is producing beings themselves (producing nature *and* history) unto the calculable makability; unto the machination that thoroughly empowers the producibility. However, machination as the swaying of being calls technicity forth. And insofar as [G174] man's ownmost is decided upon as the "subject", the pursuit of technicity is withdrawn from man's willing and not willing. The subjectivity in the domain of man shapes itself most purely in nations; the community of a nation pushes to the extremes the individualization of man into subjectivity. *Technicity* attains mastery precisely there where being of beings is grasped from out of representedness and producedness of what is objective and situational. And again this mastery is not what marks one cultural area among others or one form of civilization, but is that "inabiding" the truth of beings that has forgotten the truth in favor of beings and in the interest of the unconditional mastery of their machination – the inabiding that as a component of this machination has surrendered itself unto, and submitted itself to, machination. This surrendered and never grounded "inabiding" the "truth" as the certainty of representing and producing 'beings in the whole', gives rise to all invention, all discovery, and all interpreted creative prowess, arrangement and conveyance by taking – in every respect and discretion – the "simplest", (i.e. shortest, fastest and cheapest) way.

The sway of the "machine" becomes graspable primarily out of the sway of technicity, which as a basic form of the unfolding of truth in the sense of securing the objectness of beings is grounded by Occidental metaphysics and determined by its history. In the machine (as what sways, not as what is an individual thing) nature becomes primarily the secured, and that means the "actual" nature. Similarly, history becomes primarily the secured 'history' whose highest modern form consists in propaganda. In the same vein, even man himself becomes primarily the secured, who through breeding and schooling becomes trained for arranging all beings into calculable makability.

Unsure of itself, technicity is "inabiding" the forgottenness of being – being that continues not to be experienced since it is overshadowed by machinational beings. That endows the technically grounded openness of beings with the transparency of the arrangable and trainable, and with the character [G175] of simplicity understood as the unique controllability of the groundless, the empty.

In the epoch of technicity numerous and ever more blusterous "symbols" arise, that is, they are now "made" and produced more than ever, because symbols are not needed at all by 'beings in the whole' and man. Symbols are the specifically arranged agreement to the effect that searching for meaning (for the truth of beings in their being) is meaningless. As that form of securing (i.e., technicity) wherein technicity secures itself against itself, that is, against the incursion of truth, this agreement requires that technicity should not be merely the destruction of beings, but the *devastation* of be-ing itself whereby every beginning and grounding has to peter out in what is groundless in being's abandonment of beings. The landscape of technicity that henceforth one finds rightly "beautiful" per standard of the dominating "truth" of beings is not at all a destruction of "nature" because along with and through technicity, "the sway" of nature does transform itself into the machinational machine-appropriateness and *therefore* only now emerges in *its entire* "beauty" within the technical arrangements. By contrast, what is *not yet* surmounted purely technically appears as discordant and tasteless and therefore deserves to fall prey to destruction and elimination. Technicity also brings the "aesthetic" view of the beautiful to total mastery. And it is only a misunderstanding, nurtured by retrograde feelings, when one believes that with the technically "beautiful" one has overcome what the entire pleasure-enjoying middle class considers "aesthetically" beautiful: the "aesthetically" beautiful is not overcome but, per plan, is arranged according to the lived-experience that is common to the "people".

Technicity entails and arranges the unconditional mastery of the decision that is taken long ago on the sway of truth as security and on the sway of being as machination. The contrivance of [G176] the mastery of truth as the security of what is objective and situational is securing machination. Technicity is the highest and most encompassing triumph of Occidental metaphysics. In its dissemination throughout 'beings in the whole', technicity is Occidental metaphysics itself. The faith in Christianity's Church-regulated grace-mediating institution is merely a prelude and a subplot to modern technicity for which, in return, engineering constitutes the one-sided 'pre-form' insofar as engineering only *seemingly* differentiates itself from 'history', propaganda, and other forms of "mobilization". However, "mobilization" does not only "set in motion" what is hitherto unused and is not yet serviceable to machination. Rather, "mobilization" primarily and beforehand transforms the entirety of beings into the machinational. And man neither masters "mobilization" nor will he simply be mastered by mobilization. Instead, the domain of man, already posited as the subject, is simultaneously marked and defined by the machination of 'beings in the whole'. Differentiating man–the experiencer of the "lived-experience" of life – from 'beings in the whole' as the 'all-life', is only the lagging confirmation of the onefold that is *of* being [*seinshaft*], the onefold of the makable (in the broad sense of the mechanical) and of "the maker", that is, the "living" forces. The fact that in the epoch which beforehand is the epoch of unconditional "organization", that is, in the epoch of a readily accessible arrangement of all beings, "the organic" simply has to become what is exclusively called upon, and appealed to as desirable, only shows that the long-held guise of a difference between the "mechanical", in the broad sense of the plannable-makable, *and* the "living" is now shed. Both are originarily already one and the same in the sense of what is machinationally ownmost to all beings. That is why efforts finally to explain all "living" "mechanically" surface in the same way as the assurances one gives that one is still inclined to recognize the "psychic" besides the "physical". Here the 'life-less' and the living and their possible "unity" and their co-currentness are thought in advance metaphysically-technically. [G177] "Materialism", "vitalism" and "spiritualism" are metaphysically the same: each is always the selective and distinctive positioning of a being as a thing and as an object for "explaining" being that is neither inquired into nor considered question-worthy and is nonetheless, since at least Plato's ἰδέα interpreted in orientation of what holds sway machinationally.

(What is still clearer – even though its consequences are hardly thought through – than the inner connection between εἶδος – μορφή – ὕλη and τέχνη in the Aristotelian "metaphysics" that sets the norms not just for the Middle Ages, but for the entire Occident? Where else can the almost unignorable distinction between "form" and "content" be rooted than in the "technical" interpretation of ὄν and οὐσία that is in line with τέχνη? In this regard, see the Frankfurt lectures on the work of art given in 1936*.)

However, the sway of τέχνη does not consist in manufacturing, but in representing producing, such that what is handed over and what is deliverable secures calculating availability of not only what is produced right now, but also beforehand the calculating availability of the whole of everything with which what is produced right now is interconnected

---

* See "Der Ursprung des Kunstwerkes", in *Holzwege*, GA 5, p. 1–74.

above all according to its producedness. Producedness entails a distinct nearness (presencing) of what is constantly present in beings.

The domain of producedness that is projectable within the horizon of τέχνη (which is always μετὰ λόγου) becomes normative for the later interpretation of all beingness of beings. This later interpretation reaches one of its summits in Hegel's determination of "being" as the "absolute idea", that is, in a presence that brings itself to presencing in what is present. This allusion to Hegel is not intended somehow as a rough "technical" interpretation of his metaphysics. Rather, what counts here is to grasp the metaphysical consequences of τέχνη and firmly to [G178] extricate τέχνη from the superficial distinction between "mechanical" and "biological". (The metaphysical consequences of what ensues from the sway of the Occidental metaphysical art – and all Occidental art is metaphysical, let alone the related "explanation of art" and the discipline of "aesthetics" – cannot be pursued here.)

One points out with enthusiasm that the machine is powerless without the power of man and then concludes, equally enthusiastically, that the overcoming of technicity by man is thus already and fundamentally accomplished. However, on the one hand, the machine is not the same as technicity, and mastering the machine still does not mean controlling technicity. And, on the other hand, there arises the question: what is this power of man that utilizes the machine? This power is nothing other than the empowering of engineering to the fundamental form of organizing beings. And this empowering is grounded in the includedness of man into being insofar as being is determined as machination (cf. 9. Machination).

XII
'HISTORY' AND TECHNICITY[a]

(ἱστορεῖν – τέχνη)

---

[a] From this point of view "history" is considered in a narrow sense and "technicity" in the modern sense. [Cf.,] "historicism".

64. 'History' and Technicity*

The concept of historicism: its "overcoming" only via rendering 'history' inoperative.

Historicism: the view that the past is always to be seen out of a present situation so that the past is exchanged with this situation – "relativism". Historicism as a way of grasping historical knowledge and what is fundamental to this grasping is the relation to history as such, so that this relation is (pre-scientifically – scientifically) determined by *'history'*. But instead of grasping history out of 'history', should not history be grasped from, and *as the truth of be-ing*? How is a liberation possible from *'historical'* history? Historicism: nearness and remoteness [to history].

Historicism: that domination of 'history' through which 'history' masters the fundamental completion of modern man as the subject and unfolds the *animal rationale as animal historicum*. The 'historical' animal does not somehow mean the animal that has become 'historical' and belongs to the past, but the animal that produces everything, and for whom being of beings amounts to (. . .)+ producedness and hides itself at the same time in its machinational character.

Historicism reaches its completion in *"organic construction."* "Completion": not the same as adding a missing piece! Rather, completion is the unbounded and therefore the simple empowering of the sway.

---

* Cf. 62. History.
+ {Two words are unreadable.}

Historicism: the title means many things that derive from the mastery of 'history' in the domain of modern humanity. Primarily and actually it means an attitude that comes along with, and maintains itself in such a mastery.

*

[G182]   History and 'History'

'*History*' in the broad sense: the representing producing of "history"; a representing producing of the past and what is always of today for today and for the future, an objectification of the past into what is situational in the present.

History: the happening of the domain of man insofar as this domain – a being in the midst of 'beings in the whole' – on the ground of its hidden allotment to be-ing "comports" itself towards 'beings in the whole' and towards itself.

The ground of the historicality of the domain of man is its *allotment unto the truth of be-ing*, which as the domination of *ratio* and thus as the domination of "irrational" "lived-experience" can prevail on the foreground for a long time.

History and lack of history is only there, where there is a comportment to beings as such.

Can man also be without history? Only if he becomes "animal" without ever being able to be one.

'History' is grounded in history. Only that which is fundamentally historical *can* – but need not – *be* 'historical' and enact 'history'.

Only that which is 'historical' can also be 'un-historical'. The 'un-historical' remains fundamentally different from that which is without 'history' since that which is without 'history' lacks history, for example, the animal and all forms of "life".

However, the historicality of the domain of man is grounded in the enowning-character of *be-ing*. Therefore, depending on the belongingness to being (forgottenness of being or groundership of the truth of being), the *historicality* of man (not just his history) is different. Therefore, the unbounded domination of the 'historical' animal can go hand in hand with the un-historicality of the domain of man – a way of being that modern man pursues ever more willfully.

*

[G183]   'History' and Technicity*

'History' and technicity are *both* the same. The foreground *illusion* that they are utmost *opposites* to each other is produced by they themselves. Why? Because, from all main domains, beingness of 'beings in the whole' accomplishes in this way its machinational sway. For 'the same' is pursued most securely when it can appeal to *itself* as something different from itself and so defend itself.

What basic meaning reveals itself from out of these considerations in respect of the sway of all "culture"?

'History' in a broad and fundamental sense can in this way be grasped as encompassing technicity and in a narrow sense *'history'* can be placed in opposition to technicity.

The same is true for *"technicity"*.

'History': an enquiring producing in general. 'History': "technicalization" of the past as such for the sake of the "present", and of "life".

Technicity as the 'history' of "nature", and as the 'history' of what lacks nature. *Technicity* as producing beings as such *with expertise*.

'History': the producing of the past and the futural. Both the arrangement of the present as object and condition.

                              *

                          'History'

1.   As a reckoning of the past onto the *present*.
2.   As producing a mirroring (of the present).
3.   As consolidating in the subject all relations to beings.
4.   As an evasion before history (in the sense of a decision from out of be-ing).
     [G184]
5.   As the destruction of the grounding-attunements (cf. *Überlegungen* VII ff.; IX, 40 ff., 44 ff**).
6.   As pursuing, without knowing, the ungroundingness of being out of the groundlessness of beings (all explanation is the denial of what is of the nature of ground [*Grundhafte*]).

                              *

* See, among others things, *Überlegungen IX*, 86 ff., to appear in *Überlegungen B*, GA 95.
** To appear in *Überlegungen B. GA 95.

Overcoming of 'History'

Overcoming of 'history' can be achieved only when mindfulness takes the place of 'history'. Its place? No! For no mere exchanging of the one with the other can make us free; for, because of a prolonged habit, mindfulness could be taken forthwith as a kind of 'history'. Overcoming 'history' must be a liberation of history from the orbit of objectification by 'history'. But mindfulness can be enacted only by the founders as grounders insofar as mindfulness means inquiring into the sway of the truth and the decision of be-ing.

Mindfulness brings forth a transformed liberation of history or an actual liberation of history unto the truth of be-ing and immediately needs solid trajectories for preserving. In its representing producing, 'history' will be replaced by the *inquiring initiation* of the *decision* between be-ing and beings.

XIII
BE-ING AND POWER*

---

* For being as "actuality" and "idea" see 9. Machination.

65. Be-ing and Power*

According to the conventional estimation, what in the highest sense "is", is a being as *actual*. What supremely counts is "actuality" in the sense of extantness of the effective; effectiveness and nothing else. Actuality translates – not merely in language – *actus* and *actio*, which translation on the other hand has claimed ἐνέργεια by *misconstruing* it. (The misinterpretation of ἐνέργεια conceives it in view of "energy" understood as the power of enactment and *actio*, whereas ἐνέργεια means presencing in "work" and as work, that is, presencing in what is produced and is constant and permanent in such produced things. The Latinate *agere* and *actus* are not at all capable of naming this presencing, which shows that the Romanization of ἐνέργεια is a completely uprooting re-interpretation.)**

Actus purus: ἐνέργεια seen in view of action, in view of actualization, of providing, (a) activity: creative prowess (in *movement*), (b) *effectiveness*: (*success*) producing.

That which is of the nature of object for the producing comportment [is a being]. [Hence] the *veering* into ποιεῖν taken in the rough sense of the mere enactment of making. *Objectness* as *objectivity* instead of retreating unto itself as retreating unto *constancy* and *presence*. From here on only one step to *what is capable of effect and is capable of being effective* (*power – will to power*) *will as power.*

---

* Being as power – power as *success* and *effectiveness*: the true; thereupon, being and beings and non-beings.
** Cf. 76. A Being as "the Actual" (Being and Actuality).

Actuality as the measuring-midpoint of modality, the powerful – the effective – a being. Possibility as the preliminary stage, and necessity as the highest stage of actuality. But in each case both are modes of actuality.

The order of stages: matter – "spirit", powerful – the powerless: *actus purus* in the Christian perspective. Nietzsche's *reversal!*

Be-ing: the *powerless – beyond power and lack of power* – better, [G188] what is outside power and lack of power, and fundamentally unrelated to such.[a]

*

The Powerless

The power-less is not the same as what is without-power which while it is deprived of power and lacks power nevertheless and simply remains related to power.

The origin of power-character of beings.

(Power of φύσις – the power of be-ing. From today's perspective of thinking, what could be attributed to be-ing as *fundamental* is its *powerlessness*.)

Hence disempowering of φύσις bespeaks of divesting the sway; of 'not-finding-the-way' unto enowning as the powerless. This has a double meaning: 1. disempowering of φύσις means divesting the sway, 'not-find-ing-the-way' unto enowning; but 2. it means that φύσις should not be capable of grounding ἀλήθεια.

The grounding-attunement vis-à-vis the *powerless*. The power-less: what is power, what is the lack of power? How to understand the *-less*? From out of *refusal*. The *swaying consequences*.

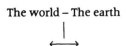

The world – The earth

Machination as the ground of the overpowering of beings and of *power* itself – powerlessness of being; yet, this powerlessness is the *guise* of the refusal.

In our earlier deliberation (in *Contributions to Philosophy*) we speak of

[a] Such things [power and lack of power] amount to measuring the immeasurable – *falling away*.

disempowering of φύσις.* Thus, inceptually and actually [φύσις] is "power". But to what extent?

[G189] Why then dis-empowering, if not simply empowering, but empowering not as empowering of φύσις as such but rather as the empowering of οὐσία to *actus*?

Power: the *capability to be effective*, to make secure, to calculate and arrange *successes*. *The effect* as being effective without directly *effecting*! Power out of *"effect"* – simply not out of possibility!

*

Be-ing and Power

Since "actuality" counts as *the* determination of beings and since *actuality* is no longer grasped as the presencing of the constant, but rather as *actus*, "action", and power of effectiveness, and since the actual in this sense is finally determined as power and as the powerful, one has come up with the strange opinion that the *higher* a being stands within the metaphysical order of stages from the material-physical to the spiritual, the more powerless a being becomes. Accordingly, the powerful is what lies lower – the powerful in the sense of that which is capable of *actualization*. What comes next? The *actual* whose *ur*-image is seen in *matter*. (The subsequent scholarly exploitation of this Nietzschean thought that originates in Nietzsche's reversal of Platonism, for the purpose of playing certain "categorial" games with the "layers of being" and the like, is meaningless and can never render the deciding question discernible.)

(In the same vein, even when in the order of "modes" within the metaphysical doctrine of "modalities" of actuality, possibility and necessity, a seeming equality is taught, such a teaching is still "oriented" to *actuality* and its preeminence. Because both "logic" and "ontology" already presuppose the fundamental decision on the beingness of beings, and express this beingness always in their own way; and because in addition "logic" and "ontology" are retro-related to *each other*, it is a matter of indifference whether this equality in the order of modes is treated in "logic" or in "ontology". What is not a matter of indifference is that [G190] the entire Occidental metaphysics determines beingness along the guiding-thread of "thinking", that is, as *representedness*. Perceivedness cum receivedness [*Vernommenheit*] is the unexpressed and ungrasped sphere and domain

---

* See *Contributions to Philosophy (From Enowning)*, p. 88.

of projecting-open – unexpressed and ungrasped because they are necessarily un-inquirable.)

The opposing view that the spirit is what is the most actual (*actus purus*), together with the previous view, belongs to the same sphere of metaphysics insofar as metaphysics has determined beings *generally* and thoroughly by means of objectness, withstandability and effectability. The most extensive structure of "categories" – if it would be worthy of a thoughtful attention at all – cannot hide the fundamental failure upon which metaphysics rests and whose unfolding metaphysics is, namely the failure of not inquiring into the truth of be-ing.

Those "theories" that advocate the increasing loss of power with the increase in the height of the 'layers of being' are incapable of saying anything about being itself because they are not even capable of addressing what alone is addressable by them, namely the metaphysical presupposition and interpretation of beingness of beings.

However, what makes the basic gestalt of this doctrine significant for be-ing-historical thinking – the doctrine of Nietzsche's metaphysics as the reversal of Schopenhauer's doctrine of "life" – is something else.

A final consolidation of the interpretation of beings in terms of the effecting-effectable and, correlatively, the consolidation of the interpretation of the true in terms of the effected and effecting success, gets enacted in this completion of metaphysics. However, even in this way the decisive process is not yet reached: that the consolidation in terms of the actual as a being and as the true – prepared since long ago, but not yet brought to a successful conclusion–must nullify *being*, and make it into what is not even worth being specifically forgotten. In the history of man only now does the forgottenness of being achieve full position of power. But what if this abandonment of beings by being would be the beginning of an originary history wherein being is be-ing so that [G191] what is increasingly actual would be ever more hopelessly cast off by being – by being as refusal which refusal cannot be matched by any power and super-power because power and super-power must always necessarily and *from the ground up* mis-cognize the sway of that which is power-less? The power-less can never be disempowered. But the irrelevance of disempowering to the power-less is not hanging onto the power-less as a deficiency; rather this irrelevance is only one consequence of the *nobility* of the power-less – a consequence that is not even necessary for, and appropriate to the power-less. Whether as the lifeless matter or as the absolute spirit, everything powerful as what is actual is the lower – so low that in relation to being it should not even be brought into comparison.

However, in the first beginning of the history of be-ing, being (φύσις) had to appear as "power"[a] because beforehand and in general the hidden refusal could only be manifest in an overflow. But *disempowering* of φύσις did not somehow eliminate this ever first necessary fore-grounding power-character (which is charged with encountering), but only weakened it, so that it could then be transferred into the character of ἰδέα and objectness. This had the initial consequence that with the mis-interpretation of the Aristotelian ἐντελέχεια and ἐνέργεια as "actuality" of the effecting-effectable, an interpretation that was to set in soon, beings came to be viewed thoroughly in the gestalt of "the actual" and by them-selves indicated ahead to what in the future would have to be held for being in all the metaphysics that was still to come. Within this history, Leibniz's monadology of *substantia* as the doctrine of *vis primitiva activa* obtains its significance that is retrospectively and prospectively equally essential.

Insofar as metaphysical thinking, which is grounded in the 'not-hold-ing-unto' the first thinking-beginning, passed off for being the power-, the force-, and the effect-character of beings, it so happened that "life" pushed itself to the forefront as what really 'is' and as what is really "actual" and demands the "sacrifice" of the "lived-experience" as the sup-posed height of humanness that henceforth does not experience itself as the victim of, and the adherent to [G192] being's abandonment of beings, but as the "triumphant" yea-sayer to "life". The first thinking-beginning did not at all grasp beings simply as *"actuality"*, but grasped them rather as the *rising presencing*; as that wherein a being as such gathers itself unto its 'counter-turning' and presences and remains as what 'counter-turns' [to man]. Power was not yet force, or effectability, or *coercive force*, nor was power also already specifically the unavoidable "semblance" of the power-less that does not need power. What power was, was in fact still undecided, such that power was soon decided upon as *the effective*. And this decision, without ever being able to bring into the open what is the originary sway of the χάος, immediately let loose the malicious and the confounding. The metaphysical determination of beings as the will to power and the metaphysical determination of beingness as the eternal return mark the end of a beginning that at the very beginning has fallen

[a] In what sense? The recognizable enownment.

off from the beginning. *Every beginning* is without effect, and while returning to itself must remain a beginning if it wants to preserve itself.

Being and only being "is". And being is thus beyond both power and
powerlessness. And yet being is not *something that belongs to the 'beyond'*
[*Jenseitiges*] since being does not need first to posit for its truth the secular
[*Diesseitige*] powerful (actual) beings in order that being or the be-ing-
historical projecting-opening of its clearing can have a leap-off.

However, because since long ago man, and modern man in particular,
calculates everything (and even being) according to power and powerlessness, usefulness and disadvantage, success and uselessness, he is not
capable of hearing any word of be-ing and of thinking its truth without
initiating his *calculation*.

65 a. Be-ing and Power

Considering its swaying ground, be-ing is never power and, therefore, it is
also never powerlessness. If nevertheless we name be-ing the power-less,
this cannot mean that be-ing is deprived of power. Rather, the name
power-less should [G193] indicate that given its sway, be-ing continues
to be detached from power. However, *this* power-less *is* mastery. And
mastery in the inceptual sense does not need power. Mastery prevails out
of the dignity; out of that simple superiority of the fundamental poverty
that in order to be does not need something under itself or over against
itself and has left behind every assessment in view of the "colossal" and
the "tiny". On occasions we use the word "power" in the transfigurative
sense of *maiestas*, which means the same as "mastery", although even this
word frequently gets lost in vagueness and approximates what is of the
nature of power in the sense of coercive force. Hence we can never see
immediately the swaying direction of the saying by considering the
isolated usage of the word. And therefore the unequivocality of the choice
of a word within which simultaneously an equivocality resonates can be
obtained only through historical mindfulness.

However, if power-character is basically foreign to the sway of be-ing,
how could it then happen that in the course of the history of metaphysics
being is grasped as actuality? And does not this interpretation of being
also correspond to the conventional opinion and experience according
to whose estimation the actual counts in the highest sense "for what is"?
And does not the last basic position of metaphysics say the same, when

metaphysics completes itself in the doctrine of the "will to power" – a will which must be grasped as the empowering of power to its constant over-powering? And what does power mean here other than the capability of effectiveness in the sense of what is fundamentally effective? Does not then the familiar equation of "being" and actuality in metaphysics and the interpretation of being that unquestioningly arises out of this equation in the doctrine of the will to power speak in favor of the power-character of be-ing? And did not *Contributions to Philosophy* grasp the inceptual history of be-ing in the sense of "disempowering of φύσις" and thus assign to φύσις an inceptual, and that means [G194] a fundamental power-character? Indeed, but the talk of disempowering here is ambiguous. Disempowering means that in the first beginning of its swaying be-ing neither gifts itself in its own truth nor does it specifically ground the sway of truth (cf. the lecture-course of the winter semester 1937/38"). By con-trast, inceptual be-ing leaves mastery to the beings which for the first time enter into manifestness as rising in being. The preeminence of beings that has ever since set the goal and the measure for determination of being results in disposing of rising in the direction of the sway of self-showing and manifesting. This sway of being is the ground of the later interpretation of being as beingness in the sense of κοινόν or ἰδέα. Being-ness is "countenance or sight", 'outward appearance' and 'sightableness'. Here nothing is left of a rising that gapes-open and immediately seizes and en-opens the open and grants what is present and countering with pres-encing and constancy. In that be-ing inceptually holds back the mastery of its sway and henceforth refuses to grant clearing to the full sway of rising and thus denies already the possibility of a knowing-awareness of the refusal, the holding back of the swaying dignity of be-ing in the first beginning brings about a historical consequence that is to be grasped as the empowering of power-character that is hidden in such a deter-mination of being. Φύσις is not dis-empowered, as if in its swaying ground φύσις were power. And yet be-ing discards the preeminence vis-à-vis beings and leaves it to them to bring to the fore the power-character in being that is grasped only superficially. Of course, this power-character comes to light in unrecognizable signs, so to speak only cautiously and initially, until it breaks loose and prepares that which (in be-ing-historical

---

* *Contributions to Philosophy (From Enowning)*, p. 126.
** See *Grundfragen der Philosophie: Ausgewählte "Probleme" der "Logik"*, ed. F.-W. von Hermann (Frankfurt am Main: 1984), GA 45.

thinking) must be grasped as conveying being unto the sway of machination.

[G195] Aristotle still preserves the last remnant of the inceptual sway of be-ing's clearing as rising. In the sway of rising lies held back the constancy of presencing. However, in that Aristotle grasps beingness as ἐνέργεια, he succeeds in naming this constancy of presencing. What this metaphysical basic word, ἐνέργεια wants to say is the presencing which holds sway in work as work; the presencing that preserves what is produced and in this way makes up its constancy. However, even this metaphysical basic word that seeks to rescue the last glimmer of the sway of φύσις becomes the impetus for the final loss – that was to spread soon – of the inceptual sway of be-ing. For, ἐνέργεια is no longer grasped with a view towards being and out of the remembrance of the hardly lighted swaying in the sense of the constancy of presence. Rather ἔργον is explained by looking back at that which is itself extant, namely that which is to be made and its maker (ποιεῖν). And again, still a fundamental step further away from being as the constancy of presencing, the interpretation of ποιεῖν deteriorates into an emphasis of enactment: Ἐνέργεια is relegated to the word *actus*. This translation that in advance decides the future of Occidental metaphysics up to Nietzsche is not an insignificant matter of an insignificant and supposedly incidental process in the usage of language. On the contrary, this translation is the unavoidable consequence of the fact that being conceals its own sway and entrusts the determination of its concept to a thinking that henceforth has forgotten all question-worthiness of be-ing. From this thoughtlessness of thinking lives above all that "philosophy" that calls itself "Christian metaphysics" and brands everything that is not of its kind as a history of errors and presumptions.

The Latin word *actus*, from *agere*, is not in the least capable of naming what addresses us in the Greek saying of the word ἐνέργεια. The Romanization of this basic Greek metaphysical word enacts a completely uprooting reinterpretation of the concept of being in such a way [G196] that the Roman interpretation determines modern metaphysics right away and forces the grasping of Greek thinking into the horizon of Romanization. All future interpretation of Greek metaphysics, including Nietzsche's, is Christian.

XIV
BE-ING AND BEING

66. Being –
Framed in Predicate ("the Categorial")

Be-ing is and will nonetheless never be a being. Being of a being – as what is *spoken to* and from this being, that is, the predicate – claims be-ing insofar as the asserting pronouncement always already has to hold itself in the open and address what is un-covered beforehand as a being in its "that" (it "is") and "so" and "so" ("is"). That which is framed in the predicate and only in it (being as beingness) is the "categorial". The "categorial" can and must be framed in the predicate because predicating will be subsequently determined as an assertion that the "subject" makes about objects, and this assertion proceeds along the track and the bridge of the subject-object-relation, and is *especially* grasped as "subjective" (belonging to the subject) *and* as "objective" (as determinedness of the object) and precisely *because of this*, it is sometimes grasped only as the subjective *or* sometimes only as the objective. And finally, as a finite relation, the subject-object-relation can begin out of an infinity that overcomes both the immediateness and the one-sidedness of the mere object- and subject-relation, and through such a fundamental overcoming it achieves the sway of the absolute subjectivity.

Subject–object-relation itself is grounded in truth as *correctness* and correctness is grounded in representing beings in their beingness (man as animal).

But what does it say about *be-ing itself* that be-ing leaves it to beings to be named through beingness and to be interpreted exclusively *as being* out of beingness?

Beingness (constancy and presence) claims to make up the sway of being and thus to determine "beings", and in opposition to itself to determine that which becomes. But whence the "opposition", if an 'other' is not posited through beingness? And how can this be, if beingness itself is not a decision in favor of a measure that beingness itself wants to give (that only the "eternal" and "that which is present" actually "is")? And how can this decision be [G200], if this decision does not separate possibilities and does not withdraw itself from the separation as well as from the separated by not heeding the sphere of decision (of time-space) and fundamentally forgetting that it has nevertheless claimed the temporal?

But where does the decision come from regarding beingness as the sway of being? Does be-ing foster a decision by relinquishing being as beingness to beings? And if so from whom? From man as ζῷον νοῦν (λόγον) ἔχον – from the one who only *through* this decision and upon this decision as a ground comes to his ownmost without grasping and taking over the swaying ab-ground, perhaps only to begin thereafter a *flight from the ownmost* (cf. there).

But of what sway is this decision, that is, the decision that concerns the choice of the sway and the taking over the sway? Which "being" can then take over what is ownmost to itself and at the same time also flee from it?

What must "enown" itself here? Must not man himself be 'owned over' unto the allotment to his ownmost and must not this ownmost be grounded in the allotment unto the truth of be-ing – as yet undecided but steadily to be decided – so that in this way the thrownness unto the swaying of be-ing be grounded; so that be-ing is simply that enownment of the domain of man unto that which is necessitated by the distress of the godhood?

Why does enowning (the sway of be-ing) always foster a decision about its truth and this above all in such a way that even the truth as such remains in forgottenness? And why is this decision ever-first-inceptually a decision about φύσις and thereupon about οὐσία as ἰδέα?

In that be-ing entrusts beings to beingness, that is, in that *be-ing* admits beingness *as being*, be-ing refuses itself and thus hides-shelters itself as refusal and preserves itself – traceless and power-less – for the unique gifting.

The refusal enforces the 'gathering', the 'taking together-unto-one' [G201] and the 'receiving' of the rising presencing (φύσις). It is this 'gathering', 'taking together-unto-one' and 'receiving' that *be-ing*, out of hiddenness-shelteredness, still leaves to the receiver *as being* so that the receiver comes upon being itself in what lies closest to and furthest from the receiver and therefore confirms being itself as the determination of beingness for beings.

Since then all "is" and being arises out of beings; since then beings enjoy the preeminence of the starting point; since then beings enjoy this pre-eminence even there, where the "origin" of beingness (always categorial) is displaced into the "I think" and into its 'having been thought'.

Φύσις is that be-ing that is barely rescued straightaway as beingness and beings, that is to say, it is the inceptual hiddenness of the refusal which sways as enownment.

Consequently, man's ownmost increasingly and securely advances towards animality, and the godhood of gods becomes divinity, understood as the prime cause and as that which conditions, that is, as that which explains and includes all calculating.

In a final fading, being itself becomes a "word" and an empty framework for representedness as such, a framework that perhaps encompasses men and "gods" and all things as a refuge that is no refuge but is only used insofar as representing asserts itself as the first and the last manner of relating to "being" (and to beings). Representedness in turn is wrapped up in the expressed and expressible predicate (the category), and speaking and language are tools and means of the animal "man".

Here, being and the sway of being are referred to supplementarity and depend on *beings* as that which actually "is".

It is not only disconcerting, but remains completely unthought and uninquired that only be-ing *is*, and that being as beingness is its inceptual and necessary semblance wherein what is called a being can presume to be the guise of what is genuinely "a being"—can presume to be the guise, of the actual, of that which "is".

[G202] Here the drama of metaphysics is played out, that is, the drama of the metaphysically grounded history of Occidental man. What transpire here are the alternating reversals that put forth as actual beings at times the non-sensible idea and at times the sensible which lacks idea – the alternating reversals that *within* this history thus give rise to different and yet always similar standpoints, and at the same time let the inceptual forgottenness of be-ing via self-evidence of being remain once and for all forgotten.

This forgottenness preserves the distress that necessitates a decision about the truth of be-ing – this forgottenness denies be-ing the ever-first distinction: question-worthiness.

66 a. Be-ing and Beings

We think that, because beings are named after be-ing or because even being is only that which is extracted out of beings, be-ing is to be found "in" beings and is to be calculated from out of beings.

But be-ing never leaves a trace in beings. Be-ing is the trace-less; is never to be found among beings as a being. At the most it could be found in be-ing's inceptual semblance, that is, in being as beingness. But how then do beings come to this name, being (i.e., beingness)?

Beings come to this name, being, because a being (what "is" it then?) comes within the sphere of be-ing's clearing while clearing holds sway only as the openness of enownment.

This "coming" into the clearing happens with *en-owning*. Clearing is not extant as emptiness into which, so to speak, subsequently beings always stream. Rather, clearing 'breaks in upon' 'that' which because of this 'breaking in upon' becomes first "that" which can be present and absent as a "being".

Seen from its own purview, a being remains always in beingness. [G203] By starting from beings, beingness is the highest and the only one that can be said and thought about being. For to start from beings means to be simply satisfied with the produced and the representable, with what presences *and* absences and thus, at the same time, with "what is a being" and what becomes.

But why does *be-ing* solidify itself to *being* in the shape of *beingness*? Does be-ing solidify itself then? Or does not be-ing leave beings to themselves and to the openness that is incomprehensible by beings?

Enowning lets beings as such arise in that it refuses itself without a trace, and so simply *is*, while at the same time enowning leaves to beings as claim the naming by being (that "it" is and be).

What raises no claim, is trace-less and power-less, is hardly credible to the representation that knows only beings. And when such representation concedes that 'the claim-', 'the trace-' and 'the power-less' *is*, representation must assess it right away as what is feeble and nothing and thus lacks what distinguishes beings as the actual (the effective).

Enowning (that is, its mere semblance in the shape of the represented guise) appears easily as a fleeting *addendum* to beings, an *addendum* that does not even accept beings but makes an appeal to them as a mere shadow (what is meant is being as objectness). Even when being is distinguished as *"a priori"* (subjective and objective), it is degraded to, and lies in, an *addendum* (what is supplemented).

Why does man think being so seldom in its sway as *the prime-leap* and the cleft of the ab-ground which above all *settles* beings as such with beings?

Because man above all has consolidated his ownmost in such a way that "in the midst" of beings and as a being among other beings, he stands over against beings as the one who represents and produces. It is out of such *positioning* that he determines his *stance* and his "self" as what is conditional.

Thus, being counts either as a veneer (objectness and [G204] representedness and live-experienceability of the representing live-experience) or it is simply explained as what is most effective, is the cause of itself, and thus all the more the *"existing"* "cause" of beings.

Both interpretations of being (the veneer and the 'doer') are correlated and betray in their own different ways the hidden confinement to beings, the present-constant. Even in that case in which representing beingness (thinking of being) is raised to absolute thought, being continues to be determined as "idea", and thinking continues to be determined as that to which self-manifestation of being (objectness) *appears* in such a way that the completion of representedness gets enacted in and for this thinking and the conditions for the constancy of the object and for the over-againstness, in their alternating relation, are taken back unto the unconditioned which in turn determines itself from out of the completed inventory of the whole of conditionedness – determines itself out of the conditioning thought.

XV
THE THINKING OF BE-ING

67. The Thinking of Be-ing

What does it mean that in manifold and even enormous variations all sorts of beings force themselves upon man, captivate him and lead him to unusual achievements without be-ing ever announcing itself in beings or even vanquishing the superior power of beings?

Does this speak for the specific right and the exclusive "truth" of beings or is this only the still unrecognized sign of the ultimate impotency of beings which is protected by the guise of the unimpeded dissemination of their machination? Was here a decision made long ago in favor of beings (in favor of that which without an explicit assessment [*Festsetzung*] always counts in an epoch as beings)? Must not then being put up with getting determined in conformity with beings and must not this determination be satisfied with being barely tolerated as a mere appendage? Or is there behind that preeminence of beings (of "actuality", of "deed", of "life") already a decision made about being? But perhaps this "decision" is also only a lack of decision that from time to time be-ing allows to occur in order to entrust beings to groundlessness and thus to the consolidation of an even not noticeable errancy, namely that *beings* should say what being is?

But if being can never draw its truth from beings, even if the mindfulness of how the currently dominating beings are meant and understood *as* beings only succeeds in asserting what as beingness already guides all relation to beings – even if this beingness is taken for be-ing and distorts be-ing's sway and holds as unnecessary the search for the sway because beingness passes off this sway as decided – even if the thinking of being remains therefore submissive to the preeminence of beings as long as this thinking only represents beingness, then this thinking in the end must remember its unique destiny [G208] and by taking over this destiny it must transform itself and be what it is out of its most ownmost necessity and *only* out of it.

If the thinking of be-ing does not originate from within the distress of the experience of undeterminedness and ungroundedness of the truth of be-ing; if this thinking does not choose as its sole and unique task the specific grasping of the domain of projecting-opening the understanding of being merely as the unavoidable foreground of the truth of be-ing thus also already thinking through that within which this foreground sways; if all thinking-mindfulness does not focus on the one thing, namely that beings are lighted up and inhere in the openness, or within a 't/here', and that man himself errantly wanders through this openness without either being familiar with, or belonging to, the sway of the clearing, then all pursuit of philosophy that is still underway continues to be lost in endless imitations of metaphysics whose 'un-sway' (inseparable from the sway) disseminates in such a manner that it lets the question concerning the truth of be-ing remain ungraspable.

The dominating commonsense opinion, held since long ago, that "being" (what is meant thereby is always beings) can surely never be grasped, let alone be produced, by "intellect" is indeed always already the *consequence* of the defusion of the sway of metaphysics. Both common sense and metaphysics agree that what is decided is the impotence of thinking vis-à-vis being (what is meant is beings). Metaphysics too is of such an opinion since it merely claims to conceptualize the beingness of beings – their *a priori* – a business which the familiar but also exclusively active, and actuality-producing "life" eagerly entrusts to metaphysics.

And wherever one still tries to think being metaphysically, such a thinking remains incapable of even reflecting that once, in its beginning, this very thinking was capable of en-thinking what this thinking now represents as the emptiness of the most general, because this thinking still obtained and possessed its determinedness (the direction and the manners of projecting-opening and the style of the initial preserving [G209] of the projected) out of the attunedness to the grounding-attunement of wonder.

Since long ago, and especially in modernity, wonder *about* being and "*of*" being (*genitivus "objectivus"*) – the Middle Ages remained without "philosophy" and worked out such questions only theologically – are replaced by slurping the lived-experiences of beings. "Thinking" had forfeited its necessity which can only arise and be preserved out of the freedom of the beginning. Thinking now has entered into the apprenticeship of shaping "culture" and, just as in Nietzsche at the end, philosophy is reckoned with in view of what it can mean to "culture". But to the extent that determination of being could still matter, this determination becomes totally dependent upon the pursual of beings at the service of securing and unfolding of the human domain, that is, securing and unfolding *of* a being of the 'midpoint'.

Inclusion of philosophy within "culture" marks the final state of metaphysics insofar as within this state the "un-sway" has become master of the sway and thus has nullified a possible transformation of the sway.

Only as en-thinking the truth of be-ing does thinking return into its most ownmost necessity. From the point of view of modernity this means that only if philosophy, necessitated from out *of its* distress, grasps that it has absolutely nothing to do with "culture", can philosophy initiate a mindfulness of itself which is strong enough to venture more inceptually into its ownmost beginning. This thinking of be-ing *neither reckons up* being out of beings, nor does it "demonstrate" beingness which counts already, but positions itself in en-thinking, that is, in en-quiring the *truth* of be-ing—positions itself unto that clearing in the midst of beings *from* out of, and *unto* which, this thinking alone can be determined by be-ing itself, that is, can be thoroughly attuned to, and thus be thrown-forth unto the sway of be-ing.

Be-ing itself en-owns thinking unto the history of be-ing, unto this: be-ing is *en-owning*. In this way, thinking becomes be-ing-historical thinking. Thinking "of" be-ing neither lets being emerge as the most general determination of the representable, that is, [G210] as un-determinedness out of thinking as the subject – where being becomes "object" for this subject (the genitive in the phrase "thinking of be-ing" is not an "objective" one) – nor is be-ing itself that which thinks, that is, the actuality that has determined itself as reason and spirit in order to enact thinking as the manner of its self-actualization within itself understood as the underlying addendum (*subjectum*) (the genitive in the phrase "thinking of be-ing" is also not a "subjective" genitive).

The be-ing-historical thinking of be-ing is en-owned by be-ing as what is wholly strange to this thinking and this thinking is allotted unto the truth of be-ing in order to ground this truth. Be-ing is never an object, but en-owning in whose clearing, which belongs to en-owning, thinking becomes inabiding.

What be-ing-historical thinking en-thinks above all is *Da-sein* insofar as such a thinking is destined to found a ground for the ab-ground of be-ing. However, Da-sein is not man but that through which the 'dehumanization' of man (the overcoming of the 'historical' animal) becomes possible, since Da-sein above all provides beforehand the site for the exposedness of man unto beings. What is mentioned here is only an initial leap of be-ing-historical thinking. Because Da-sein is enowned by be-ing as settlement, Da-sein is not just the ground of man.

Only in and as the projecting-opening-grounding of Dasein is be-ing-historical thinking always "also" immediately capable of "thinking" be-ing itself, that is, is capable of throwing itself – as a thinking that is thrown into this domain of projecting-open – against 'undergoing' enowning.

This makes clear that here the ownmost of thinking is no longer obtained through logic, that is, in view of assertions made about beings. Rather, the concept of thinking determines itself from out of the grounding-experience of belongingness of understanding of being to the truth of be-ing itself.

Thinking in the emphasized sense of thoughtful thinking is projecting-opening-grounding of the truth of be-ing: inabiding in [G211] sustaining the guardianship of this truth. Thinking is no longer representing beings in general. Moreover, thinking is not a tool that is used in order to obtain something else, for example, to bring to a "concept" an intuition and the intuited.

Metaphysical thinking can never become the thinking of be-ing by somehow exchanging its "object" or by a corresponding expansion of its inquiry hitherto. For this is the core of all metaphysics that in metaphysics the determination of being's sway continues to be decided upon as beingness no matter how beingness is grasped in accordance with the determination of the one who thinks (determinations of man as ψυχή, *ego cogito, animus, ratio* – reason – spirit – "life"). Metaphysics ties itself necessarily to the chain of "categories" whose essence is decided upon since Plato and Aristotle and whose deduction, order, number and interpretation ("subjective" – "objective") are alterable *within* the decision made about being as beingness and about beingness as the categorial.

With the decision to determine the sway of being as beingness, metaphysics as such remains installed in a basic stance which, regardless of possible modifications, offers a security and a protection against any impetus to another questioning. The metaphysical thinking can never realize to what extent another thinking of being could still be possible at all and even be necessary. And even the attempt to lead this metaphysical thinking in itself only to its own "presuppositions" and thus to initiate its self-overcoming out of itself must fail, because such an attempt (*Sein und Zeit*)* will be interpreted *again* inevitably metaphysically. And this not in order to obtain a higher standpoint for metaphysics, but to descend to a lower standpoint. Because the sway of being is established as beingness and [G212] because beingness can only unfold and shape itself as "the categorial", the remarks about the domain of projecting-opening of *this* metaphysical understanding of being must instantly be subjected to the crudest misinterpretation that it can possibly be subjected to. Thus addressing the *"understanding* of being" would mean returning to the "anthropological" and so to the one-sidedly grasped conditions for the enactment of thinking – roughly put, would amount to a "psychology" of metaphysics and so would prove to be anything but a contribution to the enlargement of the stock of categories. Since metaphysics can only expect a progress of "ontology" and since "ontology" investigates "being in itself", addressing the "understanding of being" must be depreciated in metaphysics as "subjectivization", and thus as endangerment of the "objectivity" of thinking and of "logic" in general.

The attempt at initiating the self-overcoming of all metaphysics arrives at the opposite of what it wants as long as it just falls prey to a metaphysical interpretation, that is, to an anthropological interpretation in the broadest sense.

The self-overcoming of the thinking of being understood as representing beingness means nothing less than giving up *this* thinking by leaping into something entirely different. Here "self-overcoming" does not have the metaphysical character (somehow the Hegelian one) of a steady progression towards an as yet un-unfolded but nevertheless still *metaphysical* standpoint. Here self-overcoming does not mean a more enlightened adhering to the self as conceived heretofore and thus an obtaining of a purer self. Rather, self-overcoming means here *the decided abandoning* of the metaphysical basic position as such – decided by a decision in favor of an entirely different inquiry.

---

* See GA 2.

However, this other inquiry (into the truth of be-ing) is determined by the belongingness to be-ing itself which means something entirely different than beingness in itself. *Sein und Zeit* arises out of an already enacted leap into this belongingness to be-ing – be-ing that is neither thought as beingness nor calculated as the "absolute" (in the Christian or un-Christian sense). [G213] Initially, the leap is shaped as an attempt at grounding and thus as the only possible determination of the *truth* of be-ing. And the next thing included in this grounding is the fundamental unfolding of the sway of truth which in metaphysics could be grasped always only as correctness and validity of representing – correctness and validity which at the end had to degenerate into the subject–object relation and had to be built into this relation.

But the fact that the enactment of be-ing-historical thinking "of" be-ing can be understood neither in the sense of *genitivus objectivus* nor in the sense of a *genitivus subjectivus* indicates the incomparability of this thinking with all metaphysical thinking.

XVI

[G215] THE FORGOTTENNESS OF BE-ING

The forgottenness of be-ing is the forgottenness that is held unto the ab-ground (that is, it is the forgottenness that is turned towards be-ing). What remains forgotten in this forgottenness (in a distinguished *not-retaining-retaining*) is first of all that which is *constantly* retained in the understanding of being and which, above all else, must remain preserved in a peculiar retainment, [*Behalt*] in such a way that the retained in its retainedness gives man as such the ground upon which he – inabiding the midst of a clearing of beings and comporting himself towards these beings – can stand firm in sustaining this clearing in order to be a *self*. The belongingness to the truth of be-ing and consequently the exposedness to beings is co-grounded in a forgottenness of being.

However, a forgetting in the quotidian forgetting of being sinks into forgottenness along with the forgotten (the vortex). If it is seen at all, this forgottenness looks like the mere nothingness.

The forgetting of being is not a lapse of memory and not a loss of the retained; the forgetting of being cannot be demarcated vis-à-vis the rememberable, and is not a turning away from the remembered. What is it then? Is it a mere overlooking of being which is constantly pre-understood? Is it merely "not-thinking-of being-specifically"?

This forgottenness seems to be almost a matter of utmost indifference, since explicit attention to what is besides forgotten and indeed is constantly retained leads nowhere further, be it that with this attention the unencumbered immediacy of the relation to beings – granted hitherto through forgottenness of be-ing – will be disturbed without offering any gain on fundamental insight. For, this forgotten being gives itself away always only as the empty and the most general, which is to be equated with 'nothingness', and about which nothing further can be said, and seeing it in this way amounts to the most appropriate grasping of being. Must not then the forgetting of being be called the most superficial forgetting? The talk of an ab-ground of forgottenness appears as a groundless exaggeration.

[G218] Certainly what initially can be said of the constant understanding and forgetting of being looks like this. But what guarantees that the initially and constantly understood and forgotten being is nonetheless only a semblance, indeed one that has a ground that is held unto the ab-ground? This: that in this forgottenness, being is taken as the most empty and the most general and is unceasingly held fast in this determination which especially can be proved at any time and has proved itself in this sense in the completion of Occidental metaphysics although in different ways: in Hegel as the undetermined immediate, and in Nietzsche as the last haze of a fading reality.

Metaphysics has brought about this interpretation of being and in this interpretation maintains the security of its own stock. Through metaphysics the forgetting of being is indeed shoved into forgottenness, *because* metaphysics as metaphysics has "raised" being to the indifference of the most general.

The fact that if we come across the forgottenness of being this forgottenness does not "touch" us any further and at most occupies us fleetingly as something remarkable that can be easily explained, this fact is a *consequence* of the domination of metaphysics and a hint that points backwards to metaphysics' own ground, and shows that metaphysics owes its permanence to the failure to raise the question of being (cf. lecture-course text of the winter semester of 1937/38.)* But this is the juncture of a unique and most simple decision along and out of which the future history of Occidental man is decided: whether this interpretation of being has to stay and along with it the indifference of the forgottenness of being, or whether this forgottenness shakes man up (in his hitherto ownmost, that is, *animal rationale*) and sets him free unto an unsettling dismay through which he gets displaced into the distress of an entirely other

---

[1] See *Grundfragen der Philosophie: Ausgewählte "Probleme" der "Logik"*, lecture-course given in Freiburg in the winter semester 1937/38, GA 45.

fundamental grounding – a displacing that nevertheless cannot be man's contrivance and organized by him [G219] but must be grasped as the enownment by be-ing itself.

In that case, the forgottenness of being would be suddenly something different – no longer the superficialness of a mere 'not-thinking of being' (as not-thinking the empty), but rather the 'not-inquiring' into the truth of being as the ground that itself sustains even the superficiality and the indifference of the forgottenness of being. In that case, this forgottenness would be a lapse into the lack of questioning vis-à-vis the most question-worthy – vis-à-vis the most uncanny, that disseminates itself unto the ab-ground beneath the thinnest surface of the self-certainty of man who forgets being. And, *therefore*, forgottenness of being would never be a mere oversight of man, rather it would be enowned by be-ing itself and a puzzling hint into be-ing's sway. It would be a hint into the refusal that as such gifts itself seldom to man so that his ownmost reaches out into the belongingness to be-ing and finds therein the supreme necessities: to create a site for be-ing's truth in beings so that be-ing as the ab-ground of the countering of humanity and godhood helps gods in their sway.

For this reason also, man can never eliminate the forgottenness of being: even when he honors the most question-worthy by inquiring into its truth and so confirms that he has to be the en-owned of an en-ownment – even then the refusal remains and fosters the turning towards *beings* and the inabiding in them and thus again a forgetting of being remains, which with the inquiry into be-ing is not alleviated, but only established in its uncanniness. In be-ing-historical thinking only the superficiality of the forgottenness of being is broken through but *the forgottenness* itself is never overcome but "only" enopened in its abground-dimension. This forgottenness belongs to inabiding the *clearing* of beings, that is, to *be* the '*t/here*' wherein beings dwell and at the same time to be able, within the clearing of the 't/here', 'to be away from' being itself and its truth. This 'being-away' belongs to [G220] Da-sein and makes possible and necessitates man as that being that is capable of taking over the guardianship for the truth of be-ing while preserving, shaping and disclosing beings. 'To be away from' the hidden refusal *keeps* man *away* from the ground of his most ownmost – the ground that for this reason is in itself the ab-ground which is held open by the forgottenness. However, this forgottenness of being is at the same time the ground for the possibility and necessity of all that forgetting that as not-retaining of beings dominates human comportment. That is why the forgottenness of being can never be explained as the outcome of manifold forgetting. This forgetting as not-comporting towards beings and as not-relating to them as such is grounded in that 'being-away' that is held in the ab-ground, and resonates in the ownmost of Da-sein.

In 'being-away' Da-*sein* attests to the deepest belongingness unto the openness of refusal, in fact so that on the ground of this openness and only in this openness this refusal is capable of sheltering-concealing itself. Inexhaustibly thinkable is be-ing, and the one who thinks being '*is*'.

And this is the case only when thinking has overcome metaphysics for which being has to dissolve itself right away into 'having-been-thought' so that nothing remains that could be unthought or even be inexhaustibly thinkable. For all "categories" and systems of categories are only the corroboration of that which already decides for metaphysics – the corroboration that ceaselessly arrives late – namely that being is the most general and the most empty and, therefore, has to be filled up and filled out with and through the "development" of categories.

But do we enthink the origin of 'the nullifying' at the same time as we are knowingly aware of the originary forgottenness of be-ing (that belongs to be-ing itself)? (Cf. 78. Be-ing and "Negativity".)

XVII
THE HISTORY OF BE-ING

69. The History of Be-ing

By realizing that the ownmost of "the tragic" consists in the beginning being the ground of the 'going under', and the 'going under' not being the "end" but rather the rounding of the beginning, we also realize that the tragic belongs to the sway of be-ing.

And this makes it possible that "tragedies" are there where in the history of beings, and indeed exclusively in the history of a being whose ownmost is rooted in the relation to be-ing, a being reaches unto the primal leap of be-ing. The great fundamental poetry – fundamental in the sense of laying claim on be-ing – is "tragic". And perhaps the "tragic poetries" hitherto are only arenas in the forefront, because in accordance with their belongingness to the metaphysics of the Occident, these poetries poetize beings and only mediatingly be-ing. However, the designation "tragic" plays no particular role in the context of the present deliberation, above all not in the sense that here a "philosophy of the tragic" is to be concocted. What is fundamentally important is only the knowing-awareness of the beginning as the ground of the 'going under' that rounds the beginning. If in the thinking of beginning we speak of an "end", then this "end" never means a mere cessation and lessening but means rather the completion that equals but falls away from the beginning – a completion of that which the beginning posits and decides as possibilities by leaping ahead of its history.

The first ever history of being – from φύσις to the "eternal return" – is a beginning that 'goes under'. But this history in its progression remains hidden and the scenery of representing and producing beings does not even know this history as a background. Because beginning can be only experienced inceptually, the first beginning and its history only come into the open – but never into the openness that is the public – from out of the other beginning of the history of be-ing.

If philosophy is the thinking of be-ing as an inquiry that thinks ahead into the grounding of the truth of be-ing, then the title "the philosophy of the tragic" says the same thing twice. Given the just-mentioned content of this word "tragic" [G224] philosophy by itself is "tragic". There is here no reason for proceeding from the familiar emotional ways and conceiving of philosophy as "tragic". Considering the fact that this word tragic is burdened by "literary-historical" and "erudite" opinions, it would be better not to use this word. What alludes to the fundamental designation of the beginning (the already decided inclusion of the 'going under', and the already decided "beginning" with this) can also be grasped without this word and held fast in the posture of thinking.

*

The History of Be-ing

As a rift that lights up wherein beings can come to a "halt", be-ing, the prime leap (*Überlegungen* X, 47 ff.[*]) is the enownment of man unto the allotedness to the truth of be-ing. Allotment is attuning, is the forth-throw that throws man into a grounding-attunement wherein his directive to allotment should be grounded and according to which he is allotted unto the groundership of the truth of be-ing.

The enowning is rare and with enowning, rare is also the possibility that man is thrown into *the care* for his *ownmost* and thus wrested from engrossment in himself as extant, that is, as individual and as community. Rare is en-owning and with en-owning, rare is also *the* history wherein man becomes "familiar" with his ownmost as that which he has to acquire out of the allotment unto be-ing and thus out of be-ing itself and its truth. In order for the human domain to be thrown into *that* question for which be-ing is the most question-worthy and for which in the hidden history of be-ing a still more inceptual inquiry is the adequate response – an inquiry

---

[*] See *Überlegungen* B, to appear in GA 95.

that comes to face the sway of being as refusal (en-owning – prime leap) – there happens what is sole and unique and worthy of happening, namely be-ing as the prime leap [G225] becomes more inceptually the beginning that it is. Between these rare en-ownings, which determine their own "time", *that* history takes its course *which*, out of the respective dominating beings, is the forth-flowing foreground of these en-ownings, and which by exploiting and using 'history' first becomes history and raises man himself more and more as "humanity", as "people", or as "life" to their purpose.

In his excludedness and expelledness from belongingness to being (that is, out of the struggle for the groundership of the truth of be-ing), man is left to himself and handed over to the machination of beings, so decidedly, that the expelledness as such can no longer be thought at all and drawn to mindfulness. Rather, the imperiousness of the human domain goes so far that in its "history" this imperiousness does not even leave the judgement on itself to the future but calculates already in the present and makes secure its own "greatness". The indication that *this* history of man has begun is the rise of "anthropology", that is, the ultimate stabilization of the determination of man as "animal", that is, as "life". This process of the rise of "anthropology" is decided in advance by the determination of man as ξῷον λόγον ἔχον and by interpreting this determination in the sense of representation of man as *animal rationale*.

The process of the rise of "anthropology" is not meant here as the emergence of a particular direction and trend in the 'history' of "philosophy" and "metaphysics" but is grasped as the be-ing-historical consequence of being's abandonment of beings. Whatever is specifically contributed to anthropology; what is said and "written" about it; whoever pursues this exposition in whatever explicit or implicit form; all this is immaterial here because it all has to be the utmost proliferation and [G226] usability of a process of which the "representatives", "advocates" and "pioneers" of anthropology have never an inkling, and "fortunately" can never have an inkling. The be-ing-historical thinking that has to ponder the processes of the consequences out of being's abandonment of beings as the necessities of the history of *be-ing*, must always know that such pondering easily and unavoidably is misunderstood as if here a "dissociating exposition" of these "directions" and "trends" begins – as if with such exposition *thinking* could and should experience fecundity. With such a "critique", the be-ing-historical thinking would attest already that it has fallen out of its ownmost insofar as it is incapable of grasping the history of the 'dis-humanization' of man as a necessity that comes from the refusal of be-ing, which is to say that this thinking would not be capable of thinking be-ing fundamentally.

XVIII

GODS

Projecting-opening What is to be Thought Beforehand
in Every Inquiring Naming of the Godhood of Gods

70. Gods
The fundamental Knowing-awareness

Thinking gods and speaking of them already requires inabiding a *funda-mental knowing-awareness*. This thinking and this speaking do not require certainty which, as such, lies outside the fundamental claims of funda-mental knowing-awareness. For, every certainty is always only the additionally reckonable warranty in accord with which the 'not-knower' at first consents to accept "knowing" and its advocacy. The fundamental knowing-awareness is unwaveringly steadfast in the revering inquiry, which, as a consequence of incertitude, is usually merely mistrusted. The strength for revering the most question-worthy arises out of an unsettling dismay, that is, out of the grounding-attunement that displaces man unto the freedom towards all mere beings and surrounds him with the abground-dimension of be-ing. Allotted to be-ing, a being can endure only as a being that belongs to this allotment when in the unsettling dismay this being is capable of honoring the abground which prevails only in a 'revering-turning' that turns to the grounding of the truth of the hidden-sheltered ground. And this unwavering 'turning unto' is the inquiry into the most question-worthy. Considered calculatively, this uncertain "certainty" lies beyond the reach of any science. The funda-mental knowing-awareness can never become confused and gloomy through the kind of mania resulting from a mere intellectual zeal that is associated with 'world-views'.

Specifically, this knowing-awareness inquires into three possibilities through which, and in different ways, the differentiation between beings and be-ing is kept open as *the* decision.

The order in which these possibilities are named here is not important, because these possibilities do not logically exclude each other as they are simultaneously in force since long ago, and because the one who knows has to inquire into each of these possibilities by being decided, especially when it is kept in mind that here only the attempt is made to allude to the realm wherein gods are named, forgotten or remembered.

[G230] [The first possibility is this:] whether in laying claim on being, beings once again are grounded inceptually and appear in the simpleness of their ownmost. Whether, therefore, out of an *ur*-inceptual unimpairedness, the earth is surrounded by the stillness of a world of noble ventures and in strife with that world the earth attunes man's attunedness unto the grounding-attunement of be-ing and brings this tune to language, which gives rise to an inceptual dialogue between those who as gods overcome their godlessness and those who as men have left behind their 'dis-humanization' ('dis-humanization' in the domain of the subject and the 'historical' animal). Whether in order that such things enown themselves, be-ing, truth, godhood, human domain, history, and art succeed to reach, primarily poetically and thinkingly, the origin of their sway and their ownmost through the grounding of *Da-sein*. Whether in poets and thinkers 'the thinking-ahead-remembering' of the truth of be-ing enowns itself, that is, in those who have a burden to lift, whose weight escapes any and all numerical calculation.

And the other possibility is this: whether beings hold on to the chains and conventionalities of the hitherto historically mixed up and inextricable beingness and compel to a total lack of decision; whether within the sphere of this lack beings then pile upon beings in ever-newer arrangements and ever-faster controllability; whether under the guise of an intensified "living" a being chases another being, takes its place, and settles the haze of an amusement over all beings – an amusement that is sure to succeed but is wanting in validity – until the end of this mastery of beings (of "actuality that is close to life") has become endless.

And still the other possibility is this: whether the first possibility stays away, and though the second one does assert itself, and given their admitted appearance, beings dominate all being but still something else happens: whether the history of be-ing (the grounding of its truth) begins in the unknowable hiddenness-shelteredness within the course of the struggle of the 'alone ones' and whether be-ing enters its ownmost and strangest history whose jubilation and sorrow, triumphs and defeats beat only in the sphere of the heart of the most rare ones.

[G231] When in the transition out of the second possibility, the first possibility stays away and displaces the second possibility into nothingness, then the indicators of the first possibility (Hölderlin and Nietzsche) are allusions to the third possibility, that is, to the process that insofar as we and the coming ones are swept away into the second possibility, we lose the first possibility and the echo of the third possibility will cease.

Fundamental knowing-awareness does not reckon "with" these possibilities in order to forecast the "future", but inquires into these possibilities in order to become strong in the still coming inquiry into remembering the decision between the exclusive predominance of beings and the originary grounding of the truth of be-ing, be it that this grounding honors beings once again in the whole of an inceptual be-ing, be it that being withdraws its own history into the sheltered-hiddenness of what is sole and unique, which again is still preserved reticently for the rare ones.

This fundamental knowing-awareness alone errantly traverses that realm wherein gods are still nameable, even if merely out of the remotest forgottenness. However, here "gods" are not thought of as the 'highest' in the sense of metaphysical poetizing and thinking hitherto but as belonging to the distressing need of be-ing which reverberates in everything since be-ing alone is capable of tolerating nothingness 'about itself' [um sich] as the purest purity of making room for a moment of the primal leap.

Now if a mindfulness of gods is to arise out of the fundamental knowing-awareness, then this mindfulness can think only in the direction of the first possibility, because only in this way does the question concerning be-ing instantly force the distinction between be-ing and beings into a decision and thus by enthinking be-ing this question thinks that which gives a primary and fundamental relation to the naming of gods. Nonetheless, the inquiry into the first possibility stays in the knowing-awareness of the other two possibilities, especially when as a preparatory questioning, the inquiry into the first possibility can never claim to begin decidedly the history of be-ing in the sense of an overcoming of the other possibilities. Thinking "about" gods and be-ing describes [G232] nothing pre-given. It only inquires into that which an originary questioning, which through dismay is set-free of beings, has to allow to allot to itself. But the setting-free of beings through dismay, that is, the setting free from the exclusivity of the preeminence of beings which have forgotten being, must be endured in the knowing-awareness of this preeminence without ever deviating into the mis-attunement of indignation over situations that are in the foreground. In its revering questioning, fundamental knowing-awareness is already too near to the remote nearness of be-ing to tolerate a distortion that comes from what is merely a being. But this knowing-awareness should not close itself off to what is "actual" in the second possibility, because the "actual" in the second possibility does transform itself into what is passed over when decision occupies the first or even the third possibility. The fundamental knowing-awareness of the second possibility is a knowing of be-ing, but in the gestalt of a knowing-awareness of an interpretation which is necessarily hidden to itself as an interpretation of 'beings in the whole'. The knowing-awareness of the second possibility means inabiding the "epoch" of the beginning of the completion of modernity and thus the termination of the first Occidental history. To be sure, the fundamental knowing-awareness of the second possibility destroys all "illusions" concerning the "cultural progress" and improvement and elevation of humanity, because this knowing-awareness grasps "culture" and "mass's being" as consequences of the human domain hitherto. But this destruction of "illusions" would be no knowing-awareness, would be no inabiding a more originary ground of truth, if this knowing at the same time would not leave to the epoch that begins the enjoyment of its own glory; if it would not see through the unavoidability of the machination of this epoch and its live-experience and if it would not advise against any disturbance of this unavoidability and live-experience. Indeed, knowing is fundamental knowing only when it prepares what is known for transformation into what is to be inceptually grounded. Therefore, alien to fundamental knowing-awareness as be-ing-historical is the 'historical' calculation according to progress and decline. What is grasped as the completion of an epoch and is removed to a distance by the thinking that thinks ahead and crosses to the other beginning, should never be reduced to the paltry formula of [G233] turning away from the present and dreaming up an undetermined future. Equally, the fundamental knowing-awareness is not to be confused with the compulsion to acknowledge as "good" anything that happens because it just happens. For this appraisal, too, lacks the standpoint of inabiding the truth of the distinction between being and beings and maintains itself only in the comparison between beings and beings. The enactment and the sustaining of the fundamental knowing-awareness of the second possibility is the most difficult to achieve, because the quotidian 'historical' viewpoint unexpectedly comes in between and reduces all mindfulness to a mere judgemental discernment. The fundamental knowing-awareness of the commencing epoch of modernity is a remembrance of 'that which already sways' – 'already has been' – in this epoch. However, this remembrance preserves from beings the truth of their be-ing and hands over this truth to the decisions of the history of be-ing. This remembrance above all brings into what is 'historically' present and promising the genuine and hence the oldest future, which instead of dawdling in the emptiness of the merely concocted, merely desired and merely planned maintains itself in stillness in 'that which already sways' – 'already has been' – and draws its gatheredness out of the nearness of the simple decisions, and in a revering questioning keeps awake in itself the restlessness of the originary.

Beings manifest themselves to the fundamental knowing-awareness of the second possibility in the following manner: as soon as man becomes the subject, and in the whole range of extantness (of "living actuality" as people) he takes the position of the extant midpoint of the 'beings in the whole' and interprets his "life" as an expansion of this position, 'history' in the fundamental sense of explanatory exploration must make up the basic form of all representing. In this way 'history' evolves as the technicity of producing a history that is necessary for such a human domain (the history of the past and the present as they give rise to further plannings). On the other hand, technicity is the 'history' of nature, that is, the 'history' of the course of the exploitation that returns unto itself as the exploitation of the earth not [G234] only for satisfying the needs but also for steadily steering them – the steering that corresponds to that technicity of representing history.

'History' as the technicity of representing the past and the present, and technicity as producing the 'history' of exploitation of nature, are therefore both unified procedures through which and increasingly without exception the individual man always eliminates every inquiry into the 'whereunto' and the 'why' as aberrant and superfluous. 'History' tolerates and puts up with itself still only as the exploration of what in advance is taken to be self-evident.

Seen from the Occidental point of view, the commonsensicality of democracies and the rational plannability of "absolute authority" will one day find and recognize each other as the same.

Through 'history' the animal "man" has become the subject for which the world – 'beings in the whole' – has become a single object of representing-producing which in turn includes the subject. What until recently counted and at times still counts as the "ideological super-structure" of material conditions of production ("culture" and "spirit") is today the 'expression' of the forth-flowing life. What is deciding in each case is the same: whether man finds his first and last justification in the extantness of an extant (matter, "life", "race") and the exclusive domain of positing goals and providing conditions for their realization, or whether the extant, the "permanent" is interpreted in terms of matter, in view of the body and soul or with respect to the spirit. The truth of being that as such underlies all beings and as such is their unknowable ground is decided in the sense of extantness and objectness. Here, with respect of this epoch, there remains only the possibility of crossing into the other and older beginning, or the third possibility of which no one is capable of having an inkling who has forgotten being and who even puts forth 'history' as calculating the planning of the future.

[G235] However, mastering the second possibility requires the security of the gigantic in every conceivable undertaking and calls for an increasingly shallow but equally unerring "optimism". Errability has become impossible because otherwise man would have to encounter errancy, that is, the sway of truth as the most question-worthy.

Modern man remains insulated from this thrust the closer he drives himself towards his own fundamental completion. His lack of need also prevents him, the midpoint of beings, from ever having an inkling of what is held back from him: the swaying of be-ing.

71. Gods and Be-ing

Gods: those who incalculably necessitate man unto inabiding Da-sein so that the swaying of be-ing announces the uniqueness of the most unusual as enowning; so that enowning brings about the sphere of that countering wherein *that* comes into itself *which* first lets the distressing necessity of Da-sein arise from out of the distressing need of be-ing.

Neither do gods create man nor does man invent gods. The truth of be-ing decides "on" both but not by prevailing over them but by enowning itself between them and thus by first enowning them themselves unto the countering.

Knowing and naming gods get enacted depending on the manner in which be-ing finds truth, depending on the manner in which this truth is grounded as clearing for the withdrawing enownment of that countering, depending on man's gestalt which fosters such a grounding, depending on man's belongingness to be-ing, and thus depending also on man's representing and calculating lostness among beings and on the interpretation of their beingness.

God is never a being about which man knows something at times this way and at times another way; god is never a being whom man gets closer to in varying distances. Rather, gods and their godhood arise [G236] from out of the truth of be-ing, which is to say that, for instance, the thingly representation of god and the explanatory reckoning with god as the creator are grounded in the interpretation of beingness as produced and producible presence.

But man can neither steer nor force the manner in which, at any given time, be-ing enowns its truth or holds it back in order to leave beings entirely to themselves and to their raving in machination, because according to the belongingness to be-ing that is fundamental to man and without fathoming this history and having an inkling of it, he is attuned by be-ing to determine his ownmost.

And yet it depends entirely on the freedom of man, on how and to what extent he transforms and grounds that attunement into his destiny – an attunement which comes upon him from be-ing – and so at any given time shapes his ownmost into a definite gestalt. In fact freedom is nothing other than this ab-ground that is addressed to be-ing and destines itself to ground the truth of be-ing in the sense of preserving this truth in beings.

(Whether *wonder* as grounding-attunement places [thinking] before beings and grasps φύσις as ἀλήθεια and unto which it enjoins all the domain of man – or whether the *dismay* that *sets-free* lets be-ing's abandonment of all beings break forth into an openness and undertakes as necessary the grounding of the truth of be-ing.)

Wonder and dismay that sets-free are the utmost, that is, most inceptual attunements that attune to groundlessness and groundability of the truth of be-ing. Their uniqueness and rarity correspond to the sway of be-ing. Hence all the more varied are misinterpretation and modification and weakening of these attunements. But as the result of the long-held anthropological interpretations of man ("biological", "psychological", "spiritualistic" and "moral" interpretations) all of this has reached an unrecognizability such that any saying about gods now seems arbitrary, appears as intellectual zeal or mere imitation and worn-out habit, or as empty pretension. For the basic representation of the so-called gods posits them as "objects" [G237] to which man has either a mere representational relation or no relation at all.

But as long as man is not sundered beforehand from all beings of being-ness by the swaying of be-ing and its dismay that sets free, and as long as he is not transposed unto the groundlessness of the truth of be-ing and out of this transposing once again does not fathom the clearing wherein a refusal opens to him which is the hint of be-ing itself that has thus enowned him already, so long gods cannot come to language, because every 'time-space' for their godhood is covered over and buried. What is left then is only the reckoning with the hitherto, and that exhausts itself either in the impotent and baseless modification of the Christian creator god or exhausts itself in the mere counter-Christian, that is, the pagan imitation of the "mythical". In the historical domain of the mastery of metaphysics which encompasses both reckonings and which in graspable and manifold ways of 'historical' reconstruction is still all too familiar to us, gods have become impossible. Put historically, the flight of gods is decided within these epochs and these epochs are molded by this flight as well as by its cover-up.

Hence all naming and reticence of gods resonates in the mindfulness of the history of be-ing. And only when the venturesome ones of man let themselves be attuned to the tempest of this history; only when the dismay that sets-free is no longer misinterpreted psychologically and morally, but instead re-grounded on a path of inabiding Da-*sein* (as awaiting the clearing of refusal), only then is a footpath stepped onto, which leads to the regions for preparing man for grounding a different ownmost to his own self and which allows a quiet intimation to arise that the flight and nearness of gods once again may lead to a decision. Every other way – that of calculating beings, explaining and obfuscating them – is only seemingly a pathway. Godlessness does not consist in the denial and loss of a god, but in the groundlessness of the [G238] godhood of gods. Therefore, the pursuit of customary worship and its consolations and uplifting can all the time be godlessness; equally godless is the replacement of such worship by enticing "lived-experiences" or paroxysms of emotion.

Since long ago man is without attunement, that is, without that which at times enjoins his ownmost to the relentlessness of preserving an openness wherein be-ing enowns itself. Thus far lack of attunement is replaced by enticement of emotions and lived-experiences which merely 'dehumanize' man into the fortuitousness of what he happens to pursue and obtain through calculation. But attunement throws from out of itself the 'time-space' of fundamental decisions and throws the attuned one into this 'time-space' and surrenders the attuned one unto the "t/here", which *to be* amounts to nothing less than bearing up the care for the truth of be-ing in fundamental saying, in fundamental thinking and in fundamental acting (fundamental in the sense of belonging to the "t/here" and its swaying) and protecting the attunement of be-ing in the attunedness of Dasein as the site for the countering of gods and man.

Since long ago man is without attunement. Without their night and without their day, gods flee from the swaylessness of their godhood. But man still relies on his opinions and achievements and on their desolateness he pastes the images of his confused flickering "lived-experiences". And nevertheless already a hinting comes to pass; nevertheless the dismay that sets-free strikes into the machination of beings, and nevertheless another history has already begun, which perhaps the man hitherto will in the long run never experience because he puts his trust into his hithertoness, which, given the growing upheavals and alterations of his undertakings, he has only seemingly left behind.

Still there are a few as well as those of the deep awe who, for the sake of a moment of the necessary 'going under', bear up the dismay that sets-free – bear it up indeed so that because of them dismay does not lose its dismayedness but will be received instead as a hint of the foremost shifting-apart of be-ing's 'time-space' [G239] and will become transformed into the imperceptible attempts at displacing man into Da-sein. It is not as though Dasein stands ready like a reservoir and a sanctuary. For Da-sein *is* only in the en-ownment of man to the guardianship of the truth of be-ing which as the distress of the godhood of gods necessitates them unto their new sway.

Since long ago man is without attunement and the godless gods have fallen prey to the 'dis-humanization' of man and have become a 'filling' in the hidden emptiness and boredom of "live-experience". Only when man learns to have an inkling that it is not for him to decide on godlessness but that godlessness is the highest loss for gods themselves, only then does he enter the path of mindfulness which shows him how godding as retro-attainment [*Rückfindung*] of godhood enowns itself solely out of be-ing. Only where explaining and obfuscating dominate; only where beings press forth unto the beingness of the represented, can the opinion arise that gods are the result of *divinization*, be it divinization of "nature", or of human drives and powers (*animal rationale*). Where at the mercy of such divinization gods are merely the object of opining and procuring, one day it must come to de-godding, that is, to that state of affairs where gods and the (Christian) God – shaped into a means of explanation – will appear as that "authority" to whom one appeals when one simply needs the "ultimate" and the 'inexplicable' in order to rescue all explanation and the whole explanatory operation. (For example, one explains everything as emanation, and expression of ever-varied types of man, the rational animal, and "finally" one "explains" these types themselves *as* the *unexplainable* and as "willed by god". Hereby the pretension to know the "will" of god is the least complacency whose consequence is the 'dis-humanization' of man.) The de-godding is the inexorable counterpart of *explaining* the godhood of gods, that is, derivation of gods from a diviniza-tion. Even the Christian God has arisen from a divinization, however much the theology that befits this God [240] opposes gods that arise out of divinization. The Judeo-Christian God is not the divinization of just any particular cause in a causation, but is the divinization of 'being-a-cause' as such, that is, the divinization of the ground of explanatory representation in general. In this most subtle divinization of "causality", as such, lies the ground for the apparent *spiritual* superiority of the Christian God. In truth, however, this divinization is the glorification of the crudest explanation. That is why the de-godding that corresponds to this divinization still serves best the transformation of explanation into the planning-arranging pursuit as well as the representation and live-experience of all beings – a transformation that first begins in modernity. Christianity increasingly becomes capable of fitting into culture and in spite of its seeming aversion, at the end agrees with everything that is invented in the interest of the pursual of the "live-experience". By virtue of that most subtle divinization of the most crude, namely the divinization of 'being-a-cause' for 'effects', which the "idea" of the creator God and interpretation of beings as *ens creatum* reveal, Christianity still retains, over and beyond "life", the securing of arrangements.

In the preparation for the godhood of gods through divinization and through de-godding there rules a unique belongingness of man to be-ing, which is best characterized with the words forgottenness of be-ing. This forgottenness gives preeminence to beings themselves as "the most actual", and marks them as representable and producible. To the extent that representation and production reach *their* limits, which they grasp right away as the limits of beings, and insofar as the explainable comes upon the un-explainable, the explainable must either be glorified or explained with the help of the un-explainable itself. In each case representation arrives at a higher being or at a being that is beyond beings [*Über-seiende*]. Here the godhood of gods never arises out of the swaying of be-ing. Indeed, gods who arise out of divinization lack godhood altogether. In their case godhood is replaced [G241] by subsequently hurling at the god who arises out of divinization the attributes of being the cause and object of a drive or of being the cause and object that stir the feelings. In all cases here the godly is merely that which lies 'over- and-beyond man' [*Über-menschliche*], whereby the direction and the locus of this 'over' and 'beyond' are represented and produced via representing beings out of the forgottenness of be-ing. But insofar as this forgottenness is not to be completely erased it is continually retained in molding *being-ness* as the most general of all beings. It is no accident that this beingness right away coincides with *the highest being* (cf., the coupling in Aristotle of πρώτη φιλοσοφία and θεολογικὴ ἐπιστήμη – a process whose meaning is not grasped if it is only worked out in the direction of the concept of philosophy and metaphysics and its Occidental unfolding. Rather, underlying this process is what is being-historically deciding, namely that finally here within the Occidental metaphysical history, be-ing is deprived of the possibility of a grounding of its truth.)

Only via a fundamental overcoming of all metaphysics and its ground will the possibility for a 'time-space' be created wherein the godhood of gods arises out of the swaying of be-ing, and divinization and de-godding become null and void. Rigorously thought, divinization and de-godding are not capable at all of preparing for a godhood of gods; they only lead – in conformity with the forgottenness of be-ing, and with the ensnarement by beingness – to a general representation of the "godly" as 'the beyond human' and 'the sublime'. For godhood is the swaying of that en-owning which necessitates gods' coming back, from having no night and no day to the countering with man in such a way, that vis-à-vis 'the nothing' that arises simultaneously, the uniqueness of be-ing becomes the source for the moments of actual history. Not that *beings* are, but *that* "is" sways as the still refused en-ownment – this is what surges as the quiet abground of the waves of the ocean with the most abounding overflowing of pure intimacies that most reticently 'turn-towards' us. [G242] When the grounders of the abground – those who 'go under' – come, the abground bears that which – different in the sway – as 'work', 'deed', 'poetizing', 'thinking', 'gifting', 'building', shelters-conceals the truth of be-ing in things – in the growing things, in the pliable things, in the things that light up – and in the open space of the ones that are at strife lets the sheltered-concealed, and only this, to emerge *as a being.*

That be-ing is–this most hidden hearth-glow inflames history as be-ing's struggle for the countering of gods and man–a struggle which only struggles for the ownmost swaying of be-ing out of be-ing itself, and thus rekindles the glowing of its glow unto the most sheltered-concealed stillness. Gods are those who necessitate Da-*sein*, that is, the guardianship of man, but in such a way that gods' distressing need, the need of their own godhood, arises out of be-ing as enowning.

But will the grounders of the truth of be-ing come? No one knows. But we have an inkling that such groundership as preparedness for the thrust of be-ing should be prepared in advance and protected a long time. To this end, thinking of be-ing needs a power of thought that sustains the inter-play of all those in the present epoch who prepare and cross, and that inclines their hearts to one another even if each wanders on a path that leads far away, and never runs into the path of the other.

Only in this way may an hour strike in the history of be-ing which is granted a grounding.

Seen from within the history of the first beginning (i.e., seen in Platonic – Christian – Occidental and modern terms) god, as the unconditioned and the infinite, is the ground of being (beingness) and cause of beings.

Thought within the prehistory of the other beginning, be-ing is enowning of the abground of the countering of the distressing need of gods and the guardianship of man. Therefore, everything depends on the grounding of the truth of be-ing and on preparing the grounders.

These grounders are the reticent sites of the foremost stillness of the hint of the gods' decision. For, insofar as for a long time [G243] god ultimately served already merely as the most transitory expedient and as the limit of calculation as well as of its termination, godhood of gods must primarily, exclusively and incessantly be protected in, and borne out by, the aloneness of the alone ones until *Da-sein* as preservation of the truth of be-ing is strong enough to put this truth into work and deed.

All those who wish for a direct involvement with gods and for some-thing graspable and handy; those who ponder upon organizing "religions"; those who foster the visibility and intelligibility of gods' worship and thereby refer to what is past, have no inkling of the deep stillness wherein for a long time the ear of the lonesome hearers will have to catch up with the song of the flight of gods. For first there should be those hearers who, away from all spurious founding of "religion", are consolidated in a knowing-awareness which thwarts every short-lived desideratum whose paths are still directed at "religion" and "religiosity". Tying back man and his producing-representation on a superhuman object and a superhuman sphere entails indeed the mis-cognition of the futural truth according to which the countering of gods and man must always enown itself out of be-ing as the swaying of the truth of be-ing. Otherwise neither gods nor man find their way to the freedom of a fundamental transformation which alone disseminates out of itself what is solely necessary for their countering. However, such countering cannot be "religion" any more just as the guardianship of man in the sense of the groundership of Dasein cannot be any more the same as human beings living their life to the full as *animal rationale*. Here again, overcoming any wish for "religion" (as sinking deep into some form of divinization of beings) gifts gods the most marvelous of gifts, namely the possibility of grounding gods' godhood by virtue of which they can *inceptually* return to their sway. This re-turning no longer comes upon what is past. What this re-turning finds again is the sway of the truth of be-ing which has never been grounded and never taken in possession, and in whose swaying the last god futurally finds itself.

[G244] There is no longer any possibility for gods *apart from be-ing* since beings, broken loose in their machination, are only capable of serving the de-godding.

But the uniqueness of be-ing encompasses further such abundance of 'the unsaid' and 'unquestioned' that the last god completes above all a rich prehistory of the grounding of its godhood.

In its sway this prehistory is different and profounder than any history of "religion" hitherto. Indeed, that prehistory and the history of religion cannot be 'historically' compared at all, because the prehistory of the grounding of the godhood of the last god already needs the man of Da-sein who no longer computes 'historically' in order to produce something "new" but is attuned by longanimity and equanimity to intimate and experience already the fundamental decisions as foremost hints.

At first all this happens unrecognized and still entirely overlaid by the domination of the last epoch of the Occident hitherto (i.e., by the domination of modernity).

Although nowhere seized in the domain of lived-experience and machination, the thrusts of be-ing that at such times of preparation occasionally touch man and drive him (that is, his ownmost hitherto) to the verge of Da-sein – and that are in various ways thrusts whose "meaning" still remains hidden – are nonetheless thrusts that are preserved in the memory of that mindfulness which sets its inquiry's unhurried and dependable steps on a path to which the foremost guardians of the truth of be-ing find their way again and again out of the varied entrapments in the hitherto that are alien to each other.

And perhaps for the sake of any possibility of the other beginning of history it could happen right away that those who since long ago are destined to prepare for the other beginning would be unequal to this destiny insofar as they would rescue themselves in the diversions offered to them by what is still contemporary: evoking something new; organizing something promising, and reckoning with discipleship. Should this happen, then all of it had to speak of a disloyalty [G245] to the destiny of a prolonged awaiting and of a denial of that knowing-awareness that knows that man neither comes upon gods, nor invents them; that along with the transformation of man's ownmost, gods immediately remove themselves unto their own sway; and that this simultaneous happening enowns itself as *the en-owning* whose swaying demands that this en-owning itself names *be-ing*.

Therefore, what is unavoidably most difficult and in its difficulty not at all mitigable for the crossing is this: under the thrust of be-ing no ought [*Müssen*] can and should make itself understandable immediately. But this does not mean exclusion from any shared knowing-awareness. On the contrary, the shared knowing-awareness must be inaugurated in those who mold their style out of the attunement that thoroughly attunes a dismay that sets-free from beings and bears and steers the displacement unto the inquiry into the most question-worthy. The prehistory of the other beginning is thoroughly dominated by a relentless direction that aims ahead at what is to be inquired into. The futurality of this prehistory is the *inner* unyielding attunement of the destiny for grounding the truth of be-ing. This futurality is entirely different from any kind of "eschatological" attitude, that is, from an attitude that is *not* attuned to grounding and aims at awaiting an "end of time" which awaiting pre-supposes already a complete forgottenness of being. All "eschatology" lives out of a faith in the certainty of a new state of affairs. But in be-ing-historical thinking as thinking ahead, the grounding ground of Da-*sein* is Da-sein itself: the inquiry into be-ing. Here the knowing-awareness of what is most question-worthy prevails—the knowing namely that the same ground that gives rise to the sway of the godhood of gods also gives rise to the beginning of the respective fundamental worthiness of man by virtue of which he overcomes the 'dis-humanization' as the most acute danger to his ownmost.

The hour of be-ing is not the object of a religious expectation. The hour of be-ing is refused to us, and for the same reason it demands from us the perseverance in the prolonged preparation for the crossing. It is difficult to bear trials and tribulations of the present; [G246] it is still more difficult to persevere in the crossing out of the knowing-awareness of the be-ing-historical possibilities of the epoch. Courage is required for struggling against what is near and visible, and yet venturing into the most hidden pathways and stages requires that boldness that remains reticent.

To ground a history for *gods and man* in their mutual beholding; to merely strive for such a grounding through many errant pathways and grounds even if from far away, or initially only to lead mindfulness to this hidden trajectory of be-ing-history and to pass over the metaphysical epoch – should this still be a goal for the unclaimed powers and unrecognized ventures of the Occident? Those who are *knowingly-aware* of be-ing respond as questioners, but those who pursue beings exert themselves, with their success, to prove themselves 'historically' before the future 'history'.

They say that mere thinking accomplishes and effects nothing. Certainly, mere thinking never immediately causes and effects a being. Nevertheless, the enthinking of be-ing is a deed deeper than any immediate veneration of god, because out of the most remote awe this enthinking lays claim [*stiften*] upon that which neither gods nor the calculative man are capable of claiming insofar as this enthinking brings the clearing to shine from out of the nearest glow—the clearing in whose simple stillness the countering enowns itself wherein be-ing is named to its ownmost sway.

But who are the grounders? We are hardly capable of conveying their trace, because everyone still thinks within the murky sphere of metaphysical explanation and no one has an ear for the never-ending resonance of the sound of the oldest words.

That is why we rarely know that the lack of decision concerning the flight and arrival of gods is not nothing but the unfamiliar field that because of the absence of decision has become different—the field on whose overcast borders the rumbling of unresolved battles is let loose. We take emptiness for "nothingness" in the sense of mere absence of beings and do not experience the reverberation of the still invisible bridge that refers new shores to new shores. Within the pursuit of beings, and not attuned to the truth [G247] of projecting-open, we hold this projecting for something provisional which lacks realization and at the end we hold this projecting for an unfulfilled dream. Not attuned to be-ing, we miscalculate ourselves with beings. However, what has swaying power and compels gods and man into mutual beholding is not what is actual as a being, but what is necessary through be-ing.

And what is necessary arises out of distressing need. And yet this distressing need arises from 'making room' for a 'time' of abground, which as abground forces the godhood of gods onto the bridge that leads to the domain of man and demands from him the grounding of that 'time-space' which as grounding lets *that* history takes its inception to which belongs what the guardianship of the truth of be-ing has ventured.

Here perhaps the most lonesome ones find the buried paths of the flights of gods without finding their way back to the winding roads of "beings" which cannot offer anything but the endless exploitation of beings in their desolation—an exploitation under the guise of the progressing happiness of the massive man and his confirmed needs.

Only an other "world" in strife with the earth could still rescue the earth from exploitation. Or is the process of destroying the earth under the growing appearance of constructing the modern "world" unique and therefore unstoppable? If we do not merely calculate in terms of centuries and millennia, and if we do not abandon ourselves so 'historically' to the simple replacing of one state of beings with another; if we think out of the slowness and rareness of the thrusts of be-ing-history, then the giganticness of the present and the giganticness of the still futural state of the world fall together with what is tiny in the ultimate abandonment of beings by being. An other "world" would have to measure up above all to the strife which flares up out of the admittance of the question-worthiness of be-ing and abandons the excuse of appealing to what is merely a being. [G248] For what is the point of making a solemn declaration concerning earth-boundedness, if the earth itself is set up for destruction? (*Destruction* here does not refer to what is in the forefront, namely violating "nature", respectively violating its "protection", but to the ultimate disruption of each and every relation of beings to the truth of be-ing.)

The world and the earth are not to be promptly rescued or created anew, since, all such attempts could only unfold within the interlinking of explanation, organization and adjustment, which in order to be sure of itself has to avoid all question-worthiness of be-ing. The epoch of the covert lack of decision would have to unlearn above all the belief in the "healthy reason" if this epoch wants to prepare a human being whose senses and mind are open enough to experience that enowning which in all lack of distress and decision, refuses itself to us and out of such a refusal hints at the swaying of be-ing and entrusts the hearts to the grand stillness of mindfulness. And yet, this epoch closes itself off to any denial of that which as 'drive' and 'reason' guarantees the power of man as the 'historical' animal. How else should the beginning of another history be prepared for, other than by decidedly *passing*-beyond what sways in the epoch, if this history is distinguished by be-ing's breaking through the preeminence of beings, and by be-ing's rendering impossible the utmost covert reckoning with gods out of and for explaining beings?

However, it cannot 'historically' be said whether, when, and for which hearts be-ing positions itself between the alienated gods and the disturbed human beings and allows the sway of gods and the ownmost of man to resonate in a creative mutual beholding. Indeed, to cling to such questions means mis-cognizing already the fundamental knowing-awareness.

The name "gods" should be 'said' only in order to raise the silent reticence of the question-worthiness of gods to a foundational attitude. Whoever turns a deaf ear to this 'saying' nonetheless often attests [G249] to a more genuine questioning attitude than those who are concerned with "satisfying" "religious needs".

In be-ing-historical thinking the name "gods" merely names the empty site of the undeterminedness of godhood that arises out of man's lack of attunement—the man who just intimates the distress of the crossing into a more originarily grounded history and will be thrown unto the beginning of another grounding-attunement. The name "gods" does not rest on the certainty that there are "beings" and spirits that are extant somewhere and that work in many ways – beings and spirits whom thus far we have somehow always justified to ourselves in compliance with human-*being's* total definiteness.

But to name an empty site means here making room in thinking for a domain of question-worthiness—a thinking that at the same time must be already attuned by an attunement that sets man free from every calculative bonding to beings.

This grounding-attunement, however, is not just the consequence of a "fortunate" or "unfortunate" frame of mind of a simply extant human being. It rather means the grounding of the removal of man unto a relation to be-ing out of which arises first every conditionality of comportment and attitude.

As little as such naming could inadvertently introduce new gods or even inaugurate a religion, as little is this questioning-enthinking out of the sway of be-ing – questioning-enthinking of godhood and of man's domain- – to be equated with a churchless and cultless yet by no means an "atheistic" piety in the sense of an enlightened pantheism and the like. For all these belong to the sphere of metaphysics. But what counts here is mindfulness of that which is most temporary in all preparation, that is, mindfulness of man's leaping into the grounding of a truth of be-ing – a leaping that does not need the help of beings, and does not degrade beings to the distortion of be-ing.

[G250] For this is the foremost non-propositional "truth" of be-ing-historical thinking: only in the grounding of the truth of *be-ing* does the countering of gods and man enown itself and never again does a god come to man and a world arise for him out of the objectification of beings.

Depending on the beginning, 'going under' and the course of the history of be-ing in the epoch of metaphysics; depending on the dis-empowerment of be-ing and the destruction of the being of truth that happens in this epoch; be-ing can enown its openness only when, via a grounding-attunement that is attuned by be-ing, the post-metaphysical man who undertakes the groundership for this openness is sundered from all ensnarement by mere beings. This grounding-attunement is the attunement of the dismay that sets-free (cf. above). In uncountable times, and prior to everything else, the grounders – and in different ways those "builders" – are affected by this attunement who set out to build a world on another ground. So that these grounders and builders can be seized by, and thoroughly attuned to, the dismay that sets-free, modern man (the 'historical' animal) has to have made all beings calculable to the utmost, along with he himself as their midpoint, as well as all forms of the available counter-possibilities of "rationalism", namely "irrationalism" ("mysticism", "myth" and "biological world-view"). The "lived-experience" is then merely an accessory of *calculation* through which beings, whose machinational sway is de-grounded, obtain ultimate dominance with the sheer exclusivity of coercive force and violence that are relevant to them. When the history hitherto as a whole proceeds towards the nearest margin of 'nothingness' – when in this history 'beings in the whole' are absorbed in calculation and subjugated by the will – only then does all representing and producing calculation whose ownmost is completed suddenly lose every support in that which as a task could still lie ahead of representing and producing. If this support and secret refuge falls away, then calculation, that is [G251] the 'historical' animal, is left to itself in the midst of beings, which no longer offer this animal anything for explanation. At such a moment everything suddenly caves into a unique emptiness. But this emptiness is nonetheless only the other side of 'nothingness', its 'un-ownmost', which conceals even the ab-ground dimension of 'nothingness' as the swaying of be-ing. However, that nothingness of emptiness is the foremost and *as such* not yet perceivable thrust of be-ing.

Therefore, with a view towards this course of the history of be-ing within the completion of modernity, all attempts must be judged as impeded impediments which want to renew the previously held basic metaphysical positions, and want to give the man of today a seemingly deep conception of life by offering him the mixed products of religious directions and world-views. By contrast, "deeper", that is, more fundamental, are all exertions that urge beyond the domination of dispassionate calculation of all beings and see the only criteria of actuality, that is, of beings as such, in calculability and in the volitionally organized average accomplishability. It is here alone that the sway of modernity – incipiently predetermined – comes to a head. Everything else is bad romanticism that may be chosen as a way out by the many and by individuals in order to get used slowly to what is already decided as swaying in the epoch or may be chosen perhaps in order finally to prefer the enjoyable imperturbability of the undisturbed hitherto to any departure into the 'time-space' of be-ing.

The foremost truth of be-ing-historical thinking (see above, G250) entails a decision whose originariness and yields cannot be calculated, because this decision has to fall in the history of be-ing for the first time and thus has nothing to be compared with.

This truth *is* only as the other beginning of history, it is not a declaration that is merely made out of a doctrine. However, the begin as such is in the beginning and it is most sheltered-concealed in the swaying of beginning's sway, indeed sheltered-concealed in a most unusual manner [G252] so that the more a 'beginning' and a 'becoming' and even a 'development' arise out of the beginning, the more this beginning conceals itself. But *what* does this beginning conceal and shelter by concealing *itself?* Only that thinking finds the response to this question which no longer considers beginning as an occurrence among beings but as belonging to be-ing. And since "gods" find unto their sway only through the distressing need for be-ing, this sway is akin to everything inceptual. This relation appears misinterpreted wherever gods emerge and are "treated" as the "first cause" and the like.

Thus, if after the metaphysically grounded history 'goes under' and out of its 'going under' gods ever again announce themselves, this primarily happens not as bombastic "theophanies" of some "vigorous" "prophets" and "myth-makers" but by unobtrusively and decidedly making room for the sites of the decision in favor of a struggle that strives for obtaining gods' glance in the beholding of those who inquire poetically and thinkingly. The quiet dissemination of these sites of decision goes beneath, elevates and encircles the human-being hitherto. When does this happen? When the ab-ground of be-ing opens itself under the swinging arc of an over-crossing bridge. Who spans the bridge? Those marked by invisibility, those who, having been thrown into Da-sein, transform the *animality* of man into the resonating 'play-space' of 'the charming-removing' grounding-attunement of an awe-inspiring dismay that sets-free – those who through questioning knowing-awareness leave behind all '*history*' (in the fundamental sense).

The still unseized signs of thrownness into Da-sein hint above all at the strangeness that settles on what is most familiar, most near and most current, and unveils their proffered certainty as the pursuit of a forgetting of be-ing.

Would man once again venture a prolonged reflection on the fact that perhaps his way of being has long become unbearable to gods not only because he can no longer include gods in the calculation of the gigantic [G253] tininess of his "lived-experience" but also because prior to that he cannot even bear be-ing in a grounded truth?

And yet the "beginning" of such a reflection begins only when man, out of his doings that covet success and are fixed since long ago, has found the way back to the pride in his still hidden-sheltered ownmost, and decides for be-ing against the machination of mere beings. Thereupon, he is the one already rent into the beginning. The sway of the beginning does not lie in the 'begin' – in the 'inception' – but shelters and conceals itself as the un-unfolded decidedness of a 'going under' that reaches ahead. Everything 'inceptual' begins by 'going under'. If there could be a talk of greatness at all in the context of the widely held opinion about it – the gigantic which quantitatively can never be surpassed in enormity – then the sway of greatness in the sense of the inceptual would have to be obtained from this sway of beginning.

Solely gods are great, great insofar as their godhood is out of the inceptuality of be-ing.

What does the beginning shelter-conceal in that it shelters-conceals *itself*? Its 'going under' that is kept ready and decided in the beginning. "Eternal" gods *are* no gods if "eternal" is thought of in the sense of ἀεί, of *aeternitas*, and even especially in the sense of *sempiternitas* of modernity's more desolate progressive 'so forth and so on'.

The loftiest beginning encloses in itself and thus begins with the most profound 'going under'. The last god arises out of this 'going under'. Because the last god is the one most rare, there belong to this god the longest time of preparation and the suddenness of its unpredictable nearness. To know this is already to intimate, out of the grounding-attunement that lies outside happiness and unhappiness, the remoteness of this god.

But what still counts is the distressing need of the crossing and that knowing-awareness "of" be-ing that is needed by the crossing. For only this knowing transposes one unto *the* 'time-space', wherein alone is granted an inquiring and renouncing naming of the name of godhood. This knowing-awareness "of" be-ing begins with a beginning that brings itself to words strangely enough as *being is be-ing*.

[G254] *'Being is be-ing'* – a proposition – and nevertheless the enowning wherein being above all resonates in its own swaying. *'Being is be-ing'* – an empty statement – and yet the fullness of the inexhaustible if only the inquiry puts up with its own surging restiveness. *'Being is be-ing'* – perhaps a fragment that only equals the same emptiness and yet is the grounding-in-itself of the ab-ground unto which nothing has an entry that returns as the same. *'Being is be-ing'* – a beginning that is not at the origin, but first initiates the crossing. For this 'proposition' wards off the search for a refuge amongst beings and thwarts the explanatory assurance through a cause of all beings – a cause that comes from a being that lies beyond beings. Both that search and this explanation have already cast be-ing off into the incidentiality of an *addendum*, which is also the ground of their superficial truth. How defying of all explanation and discordant is indeed the beginning of a crossing which departs from the preeminence of beings – from their self-exaggeration that they themselves generate – into the stillness of the mastery of be-ing.

'Being is be-ing' – here the knowing remoteness of man and of gods simultaneously enowns itself, but in such a way that in the mutual beholding sheltering-concealing both refuse gods' sway and man's

ownmost that belong to be-ing.[+] Be-ing – the longest bridge of the 'between' whose bridgeheads are hidden in the darkness of the 'not-yet-honored' and the 'not-yet-decidable'. Be-ing – whose swinging arc sustains itself in itself if the word no longer persists as a statement, an expression, and a sign, but instead remains the sustaining, elevating, exposing and comporting power of resonance of be-ing itself. Be-ing – the bridge in the 'time-space' of the stillness between the first beginning that stands before us and the other beginning that is ahead of us. Be-ing – that as *prime-leap* shatters what before the shattering could neither "be" nothing, nor a being, nor something manifest, nor something hidden.

In all manner of ways and since long ago the illusion rules according to which gods are the cause, the support, [G255] the ground, the apex and the disfiguration of beings, and dominate beings as if after all a god lets itself be reckoned out of beings. If this reckoning fails, then one seeks refuge in what is already proven since long ago and thus proves the opinion that god belongs to beings. But this illusion is so often and in so many ways proved by metaphysics as the truth that this illusion dissolves itself in metaphysics and becomes identical with what is self-evident but unnoticeable. What if gods could neither be reckoned out of beings nor be destined for beings; what if gods were not even the cause of being (of beingness); what if be-ing as prime-leap were to be their ground? In that case then, the en-thinking of be-ing could indeed yield this: that man learns to have an inkling why a protracted misunderstanding of the godly misleads him, and why since millennia no god appears any longer. In these two millennia no god appears any longer, perhaps because of the "divine" Plato's culpability, being and its truth have been buried under 'propositional' thinking (λόγος) and surrendered to ιδέα through objectification – because beings hindered being from becoming an ab-ground that above all is silently reticent about the call to ground and necessitates the stillness of a grounding into the word. Or could it be that beings are capable of *seemingly* overwhelming being only because being has relinquished beings to themselves and has surrendered its own semblance – beingness – to objectification by the representing man?

Gods do not need man, but are distressingly in need of be-ing whose truth – insofar as man is enowned in Da-sein – has to be grounded in Da-sein. Be-ing is the distressing need of gods so that, availing themselves of be-ing's swaying and in the complete detachedness unto the unconcernedness with each and every being, gods let come true, like the storm of a great flight into their godhood, the announcing of themselves as those who refuse themselves within the refusal of be-ing.

All metaphysics and every art that is grounded in metaphysics (all Occidental art of the history hitherto) poetized [G256] and thought gods as beings, at most as being itself. However, those who prepare must first come – those who, after all, are capable of thinking be-ing and this alone as the distressing need of the godhood of gods.

How undisturbed and owned will be then the path of the futural man to the last god; how completely devoid of all detours into the escape routes of the transformation of the hitherto will this path be, and how unconfined will it be by the prospects of the calculated?

However, at first gods will be more difficult and more rare, but therein more in sway, and yet thereby nearer in their swaying remoteness, and thus nearer to the en-opening of the most remote.

What is most remote in the hardly revealed 'time-space' of the truth of be-ing is the *last* god. The last god is inflamed to the highest distress by be-ing as the 'in-between' of beings that holds unto the abground. And be-ing throws between the world and the earth that necessity of simplifying to 'unblendedness' and the 'stillness' out of which all things proceed together in their most intimate self-belonging.

XIX
ERRANCY

72. Errancy

Errancy and erring in errancy is the simplest experience of thinking unto which thinking sees itself relegated when it has given up the support of beings and the escape into beingness. This errancy itself is the clearing (openness – truth) of be-ing. Errancy does not set itself up against the truth, and is also not removed by truth and made to disappear. Rather, errancy is the appearing of the truth itself in its own sway. Errancy is that within which a particular interpretation of be-ing must err, which erring alone truly traverses the clearing of refusal – traverses in accord with the clearing of what is lighted up.

The fundamental consequence of errancy as the sway of the truth of be-ing is that any being that enters into and stays within the openness and can possibly preserve this openness, simultaneously resides in 'un-truth' in the double sense of sheltering-concealing and dissembling (cf. *Sein und Zeit** and the lecture of 1930, *"Vom Wesen der Wahrheit"***).

* GA 2.
** To appear in GA 80, *Vorträge*.

XX

ON THE HISTORY OF METAPHYSICS

73. Schelling

Within the history of German metaphysics Schelling projected-open the most profound gestalt of spirit without, of course, making it last. For his negative-positive philosophy is a lapse into the rational metaphysics and simultaneously an escape into Christian dogmatics. And both have their necessity in the sway of Occidental metaphysics itself; in the categorial determination of beingness, in the causal and generally conditional interpretation of the "absolute".

Schelling was granted the profoundest grasp of the spirit because he begins with the philosophy of *nature* and straightaway recognizes its importance for the system. For as soon as "nature" is grasped more fundamentally it becomes 'the other' in the absolute whereby the negative of the spirit is at the same time determined positively, and is posited as the 'other' of spirit in a manner that had to be denied to Hegel.

Schelling does not want to "spiritualize" nature; his philosophy is not at all romantic, in any case not romantic in the treatise on freedom where this philosophy achieves its ownmost.

Schelling certainly retains the spirit and the absolute "subject", but if freedom is the ownmost of spirit, then with the capacity for good and evil he places a determination in this freedom which bespeaks something more fundamental than Hegel's "absolute concept".

73a. Relinquishing Philosophy

Relinquishing philosophy almost reaches the level of "triviality" where one declares, with seeming faithfulness to "phenomena", that being (that means here beingness and following beingness; actuality, possibility, necessity) is "indefinable".

The actual mindfulness of thoughtful thinking is here declared to be impossible so that following this declaration something is passed off as "philosophy", which has "in common" with the historical philosophy only the stocks of concepts, [G264] words and the so-called "problems in themselves".

Besides, to consider "definition" to be the highest that should be applied to being, but which cannot be done given the above-mentioned declaration, betrays the total desolation and groundlessness of this type of occupation with something, which following a remarkable drive sneaks off from philosophy an object to pass the time with and to achieve progress and ever-new discoveries. Here we come upon the last waste waters of the declining forms of metaphysics.

XXI
THE METAPHYSICAL 'WHY-QUESTION'[*]
(The Crossing Question)

[*] Cf. XXIII. Being as Actuality (The "Modalities").

74. Why?

'Why are there beings at all, and not rather nothingness?'* (Cf. below
G 376 f.) However deeply rooted this question may seem to be, it nevertheless lies in the forefront of the objectively represented beings. This
question does not know what it asks. For in order that nothingness sways,
which is what this question still knows – nothingness that this question
believes to know as the counter-possibility to the actuality of beings or of
beings as actual – be-ing, which *alone* is strong enough to need nothingness, must indeed sway.

   And if insofar as we do not yet grasp the question concerning the truth
of being we do not see a way for inquiring beyond beings by leaving them
behind, then even so there still remains a question: why then the 'why'?
Why and to what extent the mere necessity of the horizon of *such* a
questioning, even if we entirely disregard whether this question refers to
beings or not? The answer is: for the sake of be-ing[a] so that its truth, that
which belongs to be-ing, may find in Da-sein the ground and site.

   Inquiringly thinking ahead, we do not reach further than be-ing
because be-ing – more originarily than Hegel thought – '*is*' nothingness.
The consequence is that mindfulness of the sway of be-ing must unmask
that 'why-question' which lies in the foreground *as* a superficial question,

---

   * See 'Was ist Metaphysik?' in *Wegmarken*, GA 9/103–22); see also the beginning
of the lecture-course text of the summer semester of 1935, *Einführung in die Metaphysik*, GA 40, ed. Petra Jaeger (Frankfurt am Main: 1983) p. 1 ff.
   [a] Honoring *the dignity*.

and demonstrate how the origin of nothingness unveils itself from out of the sway of be-ing and that the ground of ground (of that which is to be inquired into in terms of the 'why') resonates within the ab-ground-dimension of be-ing.

But be-ing – never qualifiable as an object because never a being – can never be encountered, according to metaphysical thinking, as "the ultimate" and "the highest" in the sphere of νοούμενα – a sphere through which an ascending and a mere "transcending" extends itself beyond [G268] a being, as the conditioned, to being, as the unconditioned. On account of the co-occurrence of all thinking-saying with the familiar statements, although the impression always persists that even with the saying of be-ing through a pure demonstration an assertion is made about something that happens to be there [*Vorfindliches*], be-ing still sways differently than what the familiar thinking of explanatory and objectifying representation unawares wants us to believe. However, the actually thinking (not 'scientific') meaning of "phenomenological" inquiry that can be grasped only after prolonged mindfulness does not consist in transferring the representing demonstration of the explanatory grasping of beings on to the en-thinking of be-ing. This inevitably leads either to a misinterpretation of this thinking or to the corresponding escape routes where all thinking of being is taken as a play with signs whereby being is meant as the 'beings in the whole' and their transcendental ground. The meaning of phenomenological inquiry – the will to "things themselves" – obtains its ownmost necessity only when be-ing is interpreted to such an extent as to determine the fundamental character of the thinking that belongs to be-ing and to make this thinking recognizable not merely as an accidental and additional manner of grasping be-ing, but rather as its enownment that belongs to the swaying of be-ing itself and accords with be-ing.

Notwithstanding the contrary impression – ineradicable from the quotidian representation and communication – the saying "of" be-ing is not a statement made about something that happens to be there, but is an enowned en-saying of be-ing's swaying out of be-ing itself as enowning. Here the call "to things themselves" is solely a leap – here decisions are made only between ventures which do not need to make themselves understandable on a "neutral" level, because each decision, each time, knows what is unique about the other one and expresses it in itself in its own way. Within the metaphysical styles of thinking which, with increasing shallowness, fall victim to scientific calculation and analysis, the emergence of a leap is obviously something indiscernible or still disconcerting [G 269] and immediately disparaged by the tribunal of research as arbitrary.

"Why" are there beings and *"why"* are there all the things that want to be chased after and suffered for the sake of representing and producing beings? Why? *For the sake of be-ing.* But metaphysical thinking too could claim this response for itself. Certainly, but only so that when metaphysical thinking faces the "why?" be-ing continues to be unquestioned, whereas here the response to the originary inquiry can be given with the most question-worthy, that is, the response can be given so that for this inquiry be-ing only now becomes what is most question-worthy.

Beings as well as the "why?" itself are for the sake of be-ing, which tells us that be-ing sways in *the* truth – in the clearing – which is always sustained only in a knowing and in a mindfulness that are enowned by be-ing.

But what is this "for the sake of be-ing"? It is that lighted up and swaying 'between' that belongs to the creative mutual beholding wherein gods and man do not merely meet but beforehand first *be*-hold each other, initiating a glancing of the heart that awakens each to find the sway and the ownmost, and blocking the flight of gods from their sway and the flight of man from his ownmost.

So that be-ing obtains the preservation of the truth of its swaying, *beings* *"are"* in the contentiousness and unpredictability of their discordance and confusion; in the unexplainability of their upswing and luminance; in the usualness of their balanced flux and their occurrences which lack decision. For beings are beings only as be-ing's preservation. Just as nothingness encompasses be-ing and thus owns it [*umgeignet*] – the nothingness against which be-ing sets up its uniqueness – so 'not-being' interpenetrates beings and predominantly passes itself off as the "actual".

"Why?" This interrogative word names the clearing, advancing through which man fares through the dignity of the guardianship of the truth of be-ing.

"Why?" The actual response to the ownmost of this question and, that means, to what is fundamental to all questioning, can only be an inquiry into the most question-worthy. Only thus will there be clearing in beings; [G270] only thus will be-ing itself be guarded against the pull of the dullness and blindness of the mere animal. Except that man can, with a remaining, ravaged, remnant of that clearing and mindfulness, still "deliberately" submit to the blindness of a drive, and thus definitively cast into mis-cognition the fundamental dignity of his own self.

Wherever everything is claimed as possible and achievable; hence anywhere where explainability is already accorded to everything; there the sway of the "why?" is definitively abandoned, that is, the sway as that which has sealed within itself the blessing of the dignity of the most question-worthy.

The blind and gazeless "belief" in the "complete" prepossession of all responses; the belief in the sheer rationality and in the possibility within man's domain to be the absolute master of rationality; takes the place of the "why?" and of the fundamental inquiry. But with the help of the rational appeal to the rationally conceived and pursued beings the utmost *estrangement from be-ing* is achieved. This is the end of man in total 'dis-humanization'.

Does "why?" mean 'On what ground and towards which ground'? But the sway of ground is be-ing itself – the enowning of that 'between' which is lighted up and which holds onto the ab-ground; the 'between' unto which man (as Da-sein) is shifted; unto which as the openness, gods are necessitated for countering a counter-beholding of them, so that they should find to themselves.

On *what* ground? Herein is already en-opened that which has the nature of ground [*Grundhafte*]. And the en-opening is already the swaying of that which grounds, that is, that which offers the preservable for pre-servation, and that which lets beings as such "be" beings. Only be-ing itself has the nature of ground. The inquirable for the thinking of be-ing is kindled from out of be-ing – the inquirable that turns this thinking itself into an inquiring en-thinking and fosters this thinking as what belongs to the inquirable. What has the nature of ground as such repels every "why?"

Here mindfulness replaces a decision over ranking the stages of inquiry. This already shows [G 271] that ranking of stages is determined by the originariness and the style of the interpretation of being, that is, by that grounding-attunement that thoroughly attunes and determines the relation to "being".

The question "Why are there beings?" should have already left behind the question *"What* are beings?" How else could "beings" be questioned as to the "why?" of their "that"? With the question *"What* are beings?" their *'that'* is acknowledged and experienced in its superior power. With the "that" that a being *is*, a being becomes manifest as what it is – a being. But in wonder that attunes man and sets him before the 'that' and before the 'what' that shines along in the 'that', there gathers at the same time and initially the inceptual attunement into an enquiry in such a way that at first beings appear as the most question-worthy. "What is it – a being?" is a *questioning* response, which is to say that only now the 'what-question' – "What is a being *as* a being?" – bursts forth. This 'what-question' asks so little away from beings that it rather unfolds beings and bears them out in unanimity with the grounding-attunement of wonder. Thus for the first time ever, in this actual 'what-question', beings as φύσις are held into the ἀλήθεια that belongs to them in such a way that in wonder, for the first time ever, the relation to beings gathers itself in pure receiving, and out of such gathering (λόγος) brings the 'counter-striving' to presence, that is, "thinks" it as the one [*als Eines*] and as this specific one [*das Eine*]. From out of the grounding-attunement of wonder what is first-ever-inceptually ownmost to "thinking" is determined – a thinking for which the 'what-question' remains the foremost question that predominates everything. And yet here for the basic stance of the first beginning be-ing and *its* truth sway already hidden-sheltered, un-inquirable, and necessary. The un-inquirable, which nevertheless resonates throughout the first-ever-inceptual question and answer, constitutes the inexhaustible fullness of the first beginning. But at the same time, the un-inquirable determines the ambiguity which was soon to begin, never to be eliminated – because never explicitly addressed – and which stretched itself throughout the entire history of metaphysics: the ambiguity that being is *thought* in the beingness of beings (in what a being as [G272] a being is) and yet always only beings are *inquired into*.

We still have hardly an inkling of the promise which was sealed within the inexhaustibility of the 'what-question' that was attuned to wonder; hardly an inkling of the unique and increasingly rarer approaches through which pure wonder ventured itself before beings as such; hardly an inkling why then the 'what-question', in the shape of the inquisitorial question "What is this?" – which was eager about expertise and which while going forward turned back to check on itself – confounded the purely persevering wonder and finally destroyed it.

We know nothing of this history: mere lack of "sources" is not at all to be "blamed" for this not-knowing since here such sources fail altogether insofar as the knowing-awareness of this history is of another provenance.

This history of the first beginning is hidden-sheltered to us, because the enlightening power of mindfulness cannot match the simple relations of the inquiring grounding-attunement of wonder and the perseverance in this attunement. Because here, as a consequence of a convention that set in early on and increasingly proved to be stubborn, the *explanatory* 'why-question' of the researching ("historical") expertise (τέχνη) soon imposed itself until, at the end, the question concerning the first cause of all beings (*creator*) became *the* metaphysical question *par excellence*. In the domain of the first beginning the 'what-question' inceptually gained a preeminence over the 'why-question' indeed so that this 'why-question' could not at all determine the actual thoughtful thinking of beings as such. However, the 'what-question', "What is a being?" becomes in fact the *guiding*-question of the entire subsequent metaphysics, but the response to this question is attempted by way of explanation from out of causes[a] or out of conditions for the representability of beings that are pre-determined as objects.

[G273] But why does the explanatory 'why-question' gain the upper hand now? Because subsequent to the initial wonder, beings increasingly lose their strangeness, are pushed into the domain of expertise and draw from this domain the forms of their determinability (assertion–λόγος–categories–"four causes"). The incipient wonder is overpowered by the growing familiarity of beings, it makes way for this familiarity and thus abandons itself and coalesces with the mere amazement about what is astonishing (that is, that which cannot instantly be explained in τέχνη). The incipient wonder fails to retro-ground itself unto its own origin and thus become ever more bewildering. Although this incipient wonder again and again exclusively unfolds its attuning power among the rare individual and unique thinkers, and although this incipient wonder can never become the ordinary average state for everyone, nevertheless the transformation and the extinction of this grounding-attunement shows itself even in the historical sequence of the great inceptual thinkers from Anaximander to Aristotle.

In the inceptual question "What is a being?" being is interrogated and is already thought as "ground", that is, as the *swaying* ground of beings. This ground is never touched by the 'why-question', but only distorted. This means that historically the inceptual Greek relation to beings is increasingly covered over by the explanatory exploitation of that which this relation inceptually opened.

Modifications of the metaphysical basic stances cannot be pursued here.

---

[a] Cf., for example, the introduction of Thomas Aquinas to his commentary on Aristotle's *Metaphysics*.

And yet it is necessary to know that although in the course of that history the 'why-question' has taken on the appearance of the deepest and most extreme question, the 'why-question' is not an *originary* question at all, but rather remains trapped in the domain of explaining beings.

Should the guiding-question as such and in fact in its first-ever-inceptual shaping not be the originary thinking-questioning at all, but rather prepare another beginning for a [G274] thinking that must think be-ing itself (from out of the grounding-attunement of the dismay that sets-free), then the 'why-question' completely loses its presumed preeminence, and, given its horizon, does not touch that which has the nature of ground (be-ing itself).

The question of the other beginning (the actual grounding-question) is: 'How does be-ing sway?' or 'What is the truth of be-ing?'

Here the "how" does not refer to the explanatory mode: it refers to the ground that is to be grounded by man who experiences his innermost fundamental determination through be-ing as such. However, in this way be-ing is not traced back to man, rather man is sundered from 'dis-humanization' and transformed into Da-sein wherein the grounding of the clearing comes to pass in whose openness be-ing sways.

The thinking in the grounding-question 'How does be-ing sway?' undertakes specifically and for the first time what is most difficult, and had to be lost in the first beginning (the perseverance before the wonderment of beings as such), particularly in the shape of inabiding the grounding-attunement of the dismay that sets-free – an attunement that surpasses all wonder, and has nothing in common with the familiar feeling of mere dreadfulness.

Dismay that sets-free sets free unto the ab-ground over against mere beings, transposes unto the truth of be-ing as the ground of ground.

Here every attempted "why?" disintegrates into the pettiness of a calculation that is consumed with curiosity; into the pettiness of mere appeasing, and of contentment, as if such calculation, appeasement and contentment could be meted out to man if, by virtue of the guardianship "of" be-ing, he has to enter into a mutual beholding of gods; as if here, where what counts above all is the grounding co-swaying with be-ing itself, there should be room for businesses and for enlightenments.

If the 'why-question' is still raised in the domain of en-thinking be-ing, then it can only be enacted as the crossing question. Answering it no longer leads to a highest cause that, with the peculiarity of a primary technician, anticipates everything, holds everything together, and takes care of everything. Rather, the answer points to be-ing [G275] in such a way that now the responding one directly unveils itself as the most question-worthy, but question-worthy for an inquiry in which every 'why' either falls too short, or does not hold at all.

In metaphysics, a being was determined by a ground (cause – condition for an explanatory representation). In the history of the other beginning, be-ing itself determines first the sway of ground and excludes the 'why-question' as inadequate. The Da-sein, wherein the transformed man becomes inabiding, *maintains itself in the nearness to be-ing, a nearness that holds unto ab-ground.* But this maintaining can never become for man a customary permanent self-perpetuating state but rather holds sway in resoluteness, which is more originary and more difficult than any deed and any support provided by achievements. And this resoluteness is never a mere exertion of man's "will" but is his inquiring-venturing self-opening to the thrust of be-ing. [It is] the preparedness for belongingness to enowning in whose trajectory humans and gods contend for their own sake – for the sway of gods and the ownmost of man – and thus open the strife of a world with the earth and so within this clearing of contention let a being again be a being.

Insofar as a comparison between metaphysical and be-ing-historical thinking could be permitted at all – in truth it cannot – one could be tempted to contrast both in the following manner: metaphysical thinking maintains itself in representing beings as objects, be-ing-historical thinking abides in enthinking-inquiring resoluteness to enowning. The meta-physical thinking additionally reckons for itself its 'creator god' and this god's "almighty" "providence", and the be-ing-historical thinking ventures the remoteness of the 'self-refusing' as the ab-ground of unreckonable decisions regarding the flight and arrival of gods. The former rescues itself in the 'why?' and its irrational response, which is more than ever rational, the latter opens itself to the swaying of be-ing and does not expect any-thing fundamental from beings.

The former never understands the answer to the question concerning 'why [G276] the why', indeed it does not even understand that this question becomes possible only on the basis of evading beings as such, that is, only on the basis of not grounding the truth of be-ing. The answer to the first 'why?' – that is, to the question concerning its sway – lets this sway arise out of be-ing insofar as be-ing is grasped as the ground that holds unto ab-ground, and insofar as this ground itself is put forth as what is most clear and primary for the explanatory representation.

The 'why?' seems to express the utmost unrest of the profoundest inquiry. In fact, it only *seems* so. For, in truth, the 'why?' – and the inquiry that it intends – means ceaselessly turning away from pure inabiding in and before what is most question-worthy, that is, be-ing, which alone continues to be reserved and preserved in its dignity, as long as the heart keeps itself open to the pure swaying of that 'between' unto which removed, man anchors in his ownmost the relation to be-ing and takes over the belongingness to enowning and with it elevates to the unsettling knowing-awareness the uniqueness of his own self in the midst of beings, and thus grounds the guardianship of the truth of be-ing as the other beginning of a history into which all the hallways and gates of 'history' never reach. For 'history', and that means the metaphysically explained 'beings in the whole', will further control the 'un-ownmost' of the man hitherto and secure him the domination of a world that does not world [*die nicht weltet*] because it could never world. Ever louder and manifold will the 'why-question' flaunt its presumed answers. The historicizing of the rational man will become total and can be total only when it completes itself in the *explanation* that the instincts and the unintelligent [*Verstandlose*] are the driving and sustaining force in all that he does and does not do. If an actually major doctrine explicitly claims the unexplainable as the ground of explanation of everything, then the enlightenment of reason forces down 'beings in the whole' into the boundless representability and producibility. Only now all kinds of "irrationalism" flow freely, and mysticism and myths [G277] attend to their businesses, and the dispute between logico-scientific "spirit" and the mythic-mystic "spirit" produces the semblance of a living "intellectual life" and so supplies the self-sufficiency of the 'historical' animal with the highest confirmation of its supposed rank.

However, in the meantime something else comes to pass occasionally, and the resolute individuals see the glowing hidden hearth-fire of all beings and intimate what is futural to their guardians, which does not come like a romantic dream only *after* this present epoch, but *has* already come and has gifted be-ing to the historical recollection as refusal and has allowed man to know what is the 'other' to his own self.

XXII

BE-ING AND 'BECOMING'

(The Completion of Occidental Metaphysics)*
(Hegel—Nietzsche)

---

* Cf. XXIV. Be-ing and "Negativity"; cf. *Überlegungen* X, 55 ff., to appear in *Überlegungen B*, GA 95.

75. Be-ing and 'Becoming'*

Since the superficialization of the first beginning of Occidental thinking, the most traversed and traversable path towards determination of being is marked by the opposition of being to "becoming". In this way the interpretation of being as 'not-becoming' in the sense of permanence immediately comes to light. Being means constancy and presence. At the same time a twofold possibility of the relationship between being and 'becoming' is already given. "Becoming" counts as infringement upon, distortion, and diminution of being, as evident in all familiar Platonism. Or 'becoming' towers above being insofar as being, understood as *standing*-still, denies 'becoming', and that means "life". In place of each exclusion, be it exclusion of 'becoming' by being or being by 'becoming', there comes an interpretation which unifies both in the unity of the one and the other, but enacts this unification always according to the meaning of being and 'becoming' that is pre-determined from the beginning of metaphysics. Hegel's and Nietzsche's metaphysics, in opposite directions and belonging simply together as opposed, bring about the inclusion of being into 'becoming', without denying being its respective necessity within 'becoming'; without at the end addressing even 'becoming' itself by more or less disguising it and not thinking it through as the actual "being". Occidental metaphysics completes itself in Hegel and Nietzsche *because* without ever touching the already established first-ever-inceptual

* Cf. above, G 110 f.

interpretation of both being and 'becoming' and their relation to "think-ing" (representedness) both Hegel and Nietzsche think through the utmost possibilities of the alternating unity of being and 'becoming' (the absolute spirit – the eternal return in the will to power). This is to say that in the epoch when this completion begins, modern man, without specifically considering these basic metaphysical positions and their domi-nation, believes himself to possess all possibilities of [G282] interpreting "life" (Nietzsche) and "actuality" (Hegel). Modern man rescues himself in a selection and blending of such interpretations without experiencing this mixture as such and without even inquiring into its ground and un-ground. Or, on the other hand, modern man begins to grasp and interpret this possession as the fundamental fact that he himself (that is, life, people) is the goal, the domain, the measure and the fulfillment of himself. The unconditionality of Hegel's absolute becomes the basic determination of "life" in Nietzsche, individualized each time into peoples and races understood as units of life. Herein gets enacted the ultimate self-exclusion of man from any relation to being – exclusion from a relation that entails an inquiring, struggling grounding of the truth of being. The 'nothingness', that is, what arises first-ever as the highest from be-ing, is not grasped but distorted through total thoughtlessness, pushed aside as the most dreaded dread, not even feared in earnest, let alone experienced in the dismay that sets free.

Be-ing-historical thinking en-thinks not only the truth of be-ing, but also be-ing itself as the prime-leap according to its most hidden-sheltered sway which can never be measured by any determination of being-ness. Thought metaphysically, being moves out of the juxtaposition to 'becoming' and is itself the sway of 'becoming'. In the very 'ground' of be-ing the first thing that "becomes" is 'nothingness' to which, at the end, truth indeed accrues.

On the basis of Hegel's metaphysical thinking "be-ing" and 'nothingness' are the same, and consequently beingness as objectness (that is how he takes being) is the undetermined and the immediate in any intending [*Meinen*] (representation). For metaphysics, the sameness, that is, belongingness of being and 'nothingness', is grounded in the identity of being and 'nothingness' and is "thought" out of 'nothingness' as not-being pure and simple – "thought", that is, according to the already established and intended mediation within which being as well as 'nothingness' are what are to be 'cancelled-elevated-preserved' [*das Aufzuhebende*]. For Hegel, 'nothingness' draws close [G283] to that earliest nearness to being and into the sameness with being because within absolute actuality being itself has to be the last remnant of the foregoing dismantling, that is, something that still has to be acknowledged vis-à-vis not-being so that the beginning which is the willed end of the absolute itself does not somehow just begin but in its self-unfolding may *begin* from out of the immediate, may have a point of departure, and begin in the manner of that "becoming" that has to be already posited along with the absoluteness of the thinking of mediation of mediating. The 'nothingness', and even the 'negation' and the 'negative' that Hegel estimates so highly, are in truth not taken seriously by him, rather only admitted and presented piecemeal so that mediation may bring itself before itself in its most empty form and on the basis of the emptiness of this background unfold the triumph of its 'becoming'.

This, of course, does not come from Hegel's personal style of presentation and from the power of his dialectical destruction and construction (the former is almost more admirable than the latter), but, on the contrary, from the necessities of the history of *be-ing* that announce themselves here, in view of which Hegel's "being" can only become the utmost superficialization of objectification in representation that has taken place long ago. And this indicates that Hegel's entire *Logic*, as what is absolutely objective in the pure self-objectification of spirit, rests on this superficialization, and in spite of its richness ultimately does not find its way back to be-ing. This can also be elucidated in this way: all actuality and thus all being is displaced onto the absolute as the object of absolute thinking. The createdness of *ens creatum*, on the way that goes through Descartes, has transformed itself into the objectness of absolute thinking. "Being" has disappeared from beings and retreated into the unconditionally representing absolute spirit and is secured there as the absolute certainty of itself. However, the fact that "being" finds absolute "truth" in the "dialectical" unfolding onto the absolute concept, that is, [G284] in the freedom of the absolute spirit – this is not any grounding of the truth of being in the sense of an originary inquiry. Rather, it is merely the Christian-Cartesian consolidation of οὐσία as ἰδέα in the absolute *I think of myself as the one who in such thinking intends things*. The truth of be-ing is "decided" long ago so definitely that, as in the earlier stages of the history of metaphysics, it cannot be *questioned* at all. Here "decidedness" means the unconditioned transition of decision into a lack of decision, which is simultaneously *un*-aware of itself as a transition because of the unquestionablity of the truth of be-ing.

As the knowledge of the beingness of 'beings in the whole', the absolute knowledge that completes itself in Hegel's *Logic is* the total inability to be knowingly aware of be-ing, because *absolute certainty* of being as representedness excludes any possibility of another necessity of inquiry, and of another ability to be knowingly aware. But in the meantime that erroneous opinion has become commonplace according to which Hegel's philosophy – except in his "school" – has had no "effect" at all. But provided that one still thinks of something when one uses this word "effect", what does one imagine by this word? A thoughtful thinking's effectiveness in a "school" is the most indifferent thing that can happen to that thinking. The "effect" of Hegel's metaphysics, that is, the "effect" of the predominance of that absolute unquestionability of being – the predominance that increasingly becomes indiscernible and unrecognizable – consists in nothing less than being's abandonment of beings that in the guise of "positivism" passes itself off as the ultimately obtained nearness to "life" and to "actuality" and that lets modern man find his own "essence" in his greatest discovery, namely that the most important thing is to turn "life" into a "lived-experience" and to make all possibilities of lived-experience accessible generally to all in equal manner so that through this universality of "lived-experience" "life" may prove and actualize itself as the unconditioned whole. Insofar as here the unconditionality of "life" dominates, Hegel rules here; insofar as this life [G285] becomes certain of itself as the *ur*-extant, Descartes rules here; insofar as here beings and the actual are matters of lived-experiencedness [*Erlebtheit*] (i.e., representedness and producedness), Plato rules here. But what is intended here is not a 'historical' accounting. Rather, through such mindfulness we are overwhelmed by what is the most actual in this thoughtless actuality of lived-experience, namely the "effect" of the long since supposedly bygone and solidified thinking of Occidental metaphysics. Without initiating its own self-destruction, how could that which has made itself beforehand the goal of itself and has put all goal-setting at the service of this goal, ever *inquire* into a goal?

The unconditionality of the "life" of "lived-experience" means positing "becoming" as the actual "being" and thus simultaneously consolidating the unquestionability of being itself. In this way the 'nothingness' becomes the most indifferent 'nullity' which would have to be more questionable than being, if in the midst of all calculating and reckoning with "live-experience", the question concerning "nothingness" would still be given at least a most fleeting hearing.

In metaphysics being, 'nothingness' and 'becoming' are mere names for the questionless and the empty. With its completion metaphysics has rendered itself superfluous, which cannot mean that metaphysics has succumbed to impotence. Rather, the power of metaphysics is now the least noticed self-evidence within the sea of what is self-evident – the sea that floods the "live-experience" and ascribes to it the view that "live-experience" itself is the sea and the unconditioned. What is fundamental to the incipient completion of modernity is not that all goals are lost, but that the epoch becomes certain that it has found "the" goal and thus its own eternity in "life" itself – the eternity wherein being and 'becoming' become equal and exchangeable and "what becomes" testifies for being as its success and success brands everything that is not successful null and void, and prescribes the "principles" and "weighty measures" according to which alone success itself and the likes of success are to be calculated. Ever more violent and simultaneously harmless, [G286] ever louder and especially uncannier, "life", in its unconditionality rolls back into the predominance of "live-experience" so that within the frenzy of his "actions" and "contrivances" man finally forgets that since long ago he has forgotten being. The forgottenness of forgetting is the most hidden-sheltered process in the 'dis-humanization' of man. What corresponds to this 'dis-humanization' is that this *dis-humanization' itself* pursues that which disseminates the semblance of what is the counter-ownmost to this 'dis-humanization': 'history' in the broad sense which now unfolds in cultural politics, that is, in the feud between various claims to be the preserver and promoter of "culture". These claims too, be they nationally oriented or reckoned internationally, originate from within the indiscernible domination of the completed Occidental metaphysics wherein the representation of "culture" in the sense of a uniformly emerging and uniformly expanding fostering of all potentials of the creative *spirit* receives its first "justification" and determination for the unity and the unification of life and its actualities. Thus the 'historical' man of culture *fulfills* that doom, which within the forgottenness of forgetting of being drives the 'dis-humanization' of man to an ab-ground that can become a ground for a fundamental transformation of man, provided that man – having long since become blind to whatever lacks ground and to whatever especially holds unto the ab-ground – does not pass by the ab-ground, which, because there is indeed no longer anything besides the whole of "life", is not even 'nothingness'. Here again what counts is to see in all these the unrestrained power of the completed Occidental metaphysics and to keep its sway in view – the sway which has been made increasingly ordinary, even almost unrecognizable.

Indifferent to this process, however, is everything that belongs exclusively to the erudite renewal of Hegelianism or to the 'historical' "occupation" with Hegel; everything that belongs to the "literary" exploitation of Nietzsche. For all this is indeed a later and further *consequence* of the effect that is derived from metaphysics in its completion.

XXIII

BEING AS ACTUALITY

(The "Modalities")

76. Beings as "The Actual"*
(Being and Actuality)

It lies in the inceptual interpretation of being as presence and constancy that very early on beings are determined as that which later and today is called "the actual".

The interpretation of εἶναι as ἐντελέχεια indicates that in the presencing of what is present, presence is completed, that is, presence itself is present pure and simple.

Corresponding to ἐνέργεια is finishedness and *producedness*, sheer presence (presencing in the produced – in the erected, and the constant).

Here the inceptual interpretation of being gathers itself and solidifies itself unto that beingness, which, grasped as ἰδέα, is encompassed by the guiding perspective of the immediate representing, or pure intuiting.

But even in Greek thinking this Greek and genuinely inceptual interpretation of being is not retained in its summit and purity. Soon it is understood in the "popular philosophy" in terms of things [*dinghaft*] for instance in the Stoa. And thereafter it is instantly reconstructed in Christian terms – *ens* as *ens creatum*. The indication of this is the seemingly unimportant translation of ἐνέργεια and ἐντελέχεια with *actus, agere* – acting, creating, *actus purus*, the creator god – *ens creatum*.

[When a being is interpreted as *ens creatum* then] a being is what is

---

* Cf. above, G 187. For this interpretation cf. XXI. The Metaphysical 'Why-Question'.

effected, and its "cause", [is] the *effective* pure and simple [that is, the creator God. When such a being] is interpreted once again [in modernity] it is the "actual", but not "seemingly actual" as the object – objectness – thus [there is] only a *certain* returning to ἐντελέχεια, because now everything refers to the subject, to the consciousness. At the same time the actual [is grasped] as the effective – as *the effectual!* – and this also as the "true".

In their ownmost, possibility and necessity not only refer merely to being [G290] (actuality), but *along with* actuality in its threefoldness, they are also determined as such from out of the same root as the inceptual interpretation of being as presencing and constancy.

In other words, there is no problem of "modalities" at all; rather under the *guise* of an empty metaphysical astuteness this problem only conceals the origin of the inceptual interpretation of being, and hinders the originary question of being.

What applies to this "problematic" is the same that has to be said about the "doctrines of categories".

As seeming inquiries, the doctrines of categories originate from out of the flight into an as such unrecognized lack of questioning the most question-worthy.

Possibility – actuality – necessity could serve as the starting point for another overcoming inquiry into the truth of be-ing, in which case they are already no longer "modalities".

XXIV
BE-ING AND "NEGATIVITY"*

---

* Cf., 14. Philosophy in Mindfulness of Itself, G. 57 f. On *Hegel's* negativity cf., 78. Be-ing and "Negativity".

77. Be-ing – 'Nothingness' – 'Going-Under'

Where and when the sway of being is grounded in its utmost truth, the history of man reaches the stage that is marked by the ability for 'going under', that is, reaches the summit of the deepest *overthrowing* fall.

(That *in a certain way* Hegel recognized negativity but only in beingness, and that nonetheless and indeed for this very reason he wanted to be understood as fulfillment and permanence, that is, as an all-mastering adjustment of everything for ever, and not at all as 'going under' and decision – *this* most clearly indicates that negativity in Hegel did not arise from out of the *ground* of 'nothingness' and be-ing, but had to remain stuck in beingness as *representedness*.)

In Hegel *negativity* is already completely overcome in advance, rendered harmless, and only *thus*, and precisely for this reason, it is exclusively in play.

78. Be-ing and "Negativity"*

Hegel's "negativity" and Plato's μὴ ὄν are the same, except that Hegel's "negativity" is relegated to the "ground" of the absolute "*I think something*",

---

* Cf. XXII. Be-ing and "Becoming".

which thinking, as unmediated, is *not* yet the mediated of mediation and is therefore for itself always a *privation* of the *absolute*. Thus everything within absolute thinking which is not by itself absolute is determined by negativity. Hegel's "negativity" carries within itself simultaneously the absolute subject-object-relation.

However, this is not meant as a *justification* of *negativity* as the immediate in Plato but only as its displacement into the absolute thinking. The "origin" of the "negative" is so inadequately determined here that this origin cannot at all be put in question. Indeed, [G294] metaphysics as such blocks this question insofar as metaphysics cannot know anything about this question. But where and when metaphysics encounters the negative, it is evaluated as what is basically "null and void" – even in Hegel, in spite of his "positive" stance towards "negativity".

But why is "metaphysics" denied the knowing-awareness of 'nothing-ness', why is metaphysics driven to a depreciation of negation? Because in its inquiry into "being", metaphysics always starts off from beings and by holding beings in its regard takes being as beingness. Here 'nothingness' becomes immediately the 'nothing' of 'beings as such and in the whole'; becomes the pure and simple "negation" – indeed the "negation" of beings. However, where, as in Hegel, 'nothingness' becomes the negation *of being* (where negation is the "un-" of all determination and mediation – determination out of determining understood as *determinatio* in the sense of *praedicatio vera positiva* – determination of something *as object*, as *tale quale*, quality whatness), there, being as the undetermined immediate is for the absolute thinking that has not yet returned to itself the highest and thus the nearest and emptiest beingness. But 'nothingness' "*becomes*" – it *is* for Hegel already – the actual "affirmation" of that being that is already characterized – 'nothingness' in its "identical positionedness" ["*Gleich*"-*setzung*] with being determines being as that being which in the sense of "beingness" has to lower itself for the absolute thinking to what is merely immediate and *un*-determined. Thus 'nothingness' (i.e., being) becomes *privation* of the absolute actuality (i.e., "idea"). [But] 'nothingness' is not at all the *privation* of being; 'nothingness' does not at all break-up being, which if it were to happen would need being beforehand merely as the ground of the possible break-up. Rather, 'nothingness' is *the same* as being.

But what if 'nothingness' were nevertheless to be thought as the *privation* of being (and neither as the "negation" of beings nor as the "negation" of being), then would we not be thinking more fundamentally?

And yet, whence and how "privation"? How does be-ing itself come to this break-*up*? How else at all if *'nothingness'* would not already and right away offer the clearing for such a break-up of being?

'Nothingness' is neither the negation of beings nor the negation of [G295] beingness, nor is it the "privation" of being; it is not the deprivation that simultaneously would be an annihilation. Rather, *'nothingness' is the foremost and highest gift of be-ing,* which along with itself and as itself gifts be-ing as enowning unto the clearing of the prime-leap as ab-ground. Here ab-ground is not meant metaphysically as the mere *absence* of ground but is meant as the swaying of the distress of grounding, a distress that is neither a lack nor an excess, rather the *'that'* [*Daß*] of be-ing – the 'that' that is superior to both lack and excess – the 'that' of be-ing as the "that" of "is". [*Daß des Seyns als des "Daß" des "ist"*.]

The enownment of man's ownmost unto the allotment unto enowning that enowns itself simultaneously as the distressing need of gods is, in the manner of the highest *refusal,* the gifting of 'nothingness' as the gifting of ab-ground so that a *being* could never venture to come upon, and to fulfill, be-ing in its sway in order that be-ing then could nevertheless be meant as a being.

As long as man continues to be entangled in metaphysics, that is, as long as he holds on to the preeminence of beings as the actual in the sense of the effective and the "potent" (i.e., what has the capacity of being effective), so long does 'nothingness' remain what is worth nothing to him, and dread – the disclosing grounding-attunement of 'nothingness' – remains that which is harmful to every affirmation of "life", deserving only repulsion and rejection. And the other way around, as long as this rejection of 'nothingness' deems evident and is given the faintest approval, so long does man remain in forgottenness of being, that is to say, in that un-relation to be-ing that hinders him from honoring the gift of "negativity" and from fathoming the destiny of man's domain, and thus from entering into the 'free-play of time-space' of the simple decisions.

The be-ing-historical knowing-awareness of "negativity" is a pathway for en-thinking refusal; is honoring being as enowning; is inabiding the *'between'* wherein the countering of man and gods is enowned; is preparation of a readiness for *history.* The be-ing-historical knowing-awareness of "negativity" is never a "trick" in the exercise of "categorial" discernment: questioned as a question, this knowing-awareness *is* already more being than all "realities".

XXV

BEING AND THINKING

BEING AND TIME

79. Being and Time*

In the historical dialogue with the fundamental thinkers about what is most pure and simple in them, there emerges ever more decisively the intimation that they have never said what is fundamental to them, because their utmost successful word can still ward off the most concealed attunedness by what needs to be said.

Heraclitus's λόγος, Plato's ἰδέα, Aristotle's ἐνέργεια, Leibniz's *monas*, Kant's "I think" as "freedom", Schelling's "identity", Hegel's "concept" and Nietzsche's "eternal return" – all say the same: being. They do not make "propositional statements" about being as if being were an object that is set aside. Being itself is said; raised to the "word" as what is said; the word which here is not a random expression in language, but is be-ing itself that has become truth (clearing). The saying of the thinkers does not speak in "images" and "signs"; it does not try its hand at conveyable rewritings, all of which would have to be equally inapplicable. Being itself is said, but with the proviso that it is not said to the ear of intelligibility which, prone to approximation, wants to have everything explained.

That which is never said by the fundamental thinkers is still purer and simpler than what is said by them. That is why from time to time be-ing always summons thinking again unto the beginning. But this thinking begins only with the beginning when each time the enthinking of be-ing

---

* Cf. 56. "Da-sein and *Sein und Zeit*".

has become more inceptual and thus as something entirely different, has the strength to remain the same.

The other beginning of thinking inquires into the truth of be-ing.

*

[G300]   "Being and Time"

Be-ing-historical thinking enthinks the truth of be-ing (openness of clearing) at first as 'time-space', as that ground of the onefold of "time" and "space" that lets both time and space emerge in their mutual-belongingness as trajectories and expanses of 'removal-unto' of the clearing of ab-ground. However, insofar as it is "time" that at first manifests the onefold of *removal-unto* more strikingly than 'space' – "space" also 'removes-unto', not less but differently than "time" – the attempt to render the *truth* of be-ing (i.e., the "meaning" of be-ing) thinkable must start off from "time". Therefore, the nearmost unfoldment of the question of being that begins again stands under the title "being and time".

Here "time" names something that cannot be clarified by "merely" discussing the earlier and present concepts of time. Rather, here "time" names something that is predetermined in an incomparably different way by the *question* concerning the *clearing* of be-ing itself as the swaying that belongs to be-ing. Any detailed consideration of the "concept of time" can only have the limited task of elucidating that which arises out of the original time (which, incidentally, has not the least in common with [Bergson's] *durée*) and which by contrast, and without, of course, ever permitting a transition into the other "time", can serve to bring into relief that entirely other "time". The "time" that is launched in be-ing-historical thinking prevails already as the *horizon* – the *perspective* – which more specifically put is the uninquired and heretofore uninquirable horizon for the "presence" and "constancy" (οὐσία); for gatheredness (λόγος) and receivedness (νοῦς); for representedness (ἰδέα) and objectness, whereby throughout the entire history of metaphysics being was determined in advance as beingness. And this "pers"-pective is the one that primarily, and as if by itself and out of itself (why and to what extent?), suggests itself to *"thinking"* (νοεῖν – λέγειν) so that, reassured in this perspective – in this horizon – and sustained by it, this thinking never needs to ponder on itself, but holds unto itself as the *guiding-thread* for determining beingness and [G301] its constitution, and in keeping with the self-understanding of the one who thinks (*animal rationale*), unfolds itself as *"I* think" and as absolute thinking ("categories"). However, in spite of knowing the πρότερον, the *"a priori"*, the transcendentals, thinking of being never recognizes within the history of *metaphysics* the pers-pective – the horizon – that is allotted to this thinking as en-thinking. Rather, "philosophical" thinking considers itself sufficiently grounded with the differentiation according to which philosophy thinks *being* (beingness – categories) while "sciences" and ordinary opinion represent and explain *beings*. Yet even this differentiation is not decidedly clear everywhere and when *within* the history of metaphysics, in Kant, this differentiation attains maximum clarity this thinking of being is forthwith falsified as "theory of knowledge". The inner reason for this process is that Kant grasps beingness as *objectness* but limits objects to accessibility to experience – to mathematical knowledge of nature.

Philosophy, as inquiry into being, is at all time the same as *thinking*. Yet, precisely because of this, thinking as originary thinking must determine itself from out of that *which* this thinking en-thinks: from out of be-ing. Accordingly, if in formal respect "being and time" is preferred prospectively [*künftig*] as a title to "being and thinking", then this does not mean abandoning thinking in favor of "irrationalism" and "mood" but, *entirely to the contrary*, it means that only now is en-thinking compelled into the exactitude of the ab-ground-dimension of its hitherto unthought perspective, that is, into the originary truth of be-ing. Only now does en-thinking obtain its freedom so decisively that the naming of "time" can just be the immediate indication of what is question-worthy, towards which the more inceptual thinking knows itself to be *"on the way"*. Hence 'being and thinking', as the title for the *metaphysical* manner of inquiring into being, does not mean the commonplace opinion that "thinking" is just the form of enactment of philosophy, or even merely the form of philosophy's employment. Rather, this title is already thought be-ing-historically from out of "being [G302] and time", so that it indicates that the *metaphysical* 'thinking' of be-ing *does not yet ponder what is its most ownmost*, namely presentness (time) as the perspective – the horizon – of metaphysical thinking's own manner of interpreting beingness. Instead, without pondering on itself, 'thinking' simply considers itself as the sufficiently determined tribunal for all delimitation of the sway of being. This lack of pondering vis-à-vis the concealment of what is actually and fully ownmost to metaphysical thinking – an increasingly consolidated concealment – this peculiar domination of the 'thinking' that is evident to itself in metaphysics, is simply the reason for the frequent surfacing of all "irrationalisms" within the history of metaphysics, irrationalisms that distinguish themselves only by a *still* cruder "rationalism", insofar as this word indicates in the thinking of being the preeminence of 'thinking' that does not ponder upon that which this thinking itself is.

To ponder upon the thinking that inquires into clearing, wherein it moves as the en-thinking of being, it is obvious now that this pondering is not what we could call "reflection" according to the formula "thinking of thinking". For history of metaphysics in the epoch of German idealism has indeed enacted this "reflection" so decisively and in such a great style that even "reflection" was mirrored and taken back once again in to the absolute *concept* of unconditioned knowledge. But this happened in such a way that mindfulness of the perspective – of the horizon – of thinking became ever more impossible and ever more unnecessary because absolute knowledge knows itself as the truth of 'beings in the whole' and thus excludes every question-worthiness. Hence, through historical mindfulness we can see that here with the 'thinking of thinking', metaphysics removes itself from mindfulness of the truth of being that is to be en-thought, and as a result metaphysics removes itself from thinking itself. Therefore, the question concerning the "meaning" of be-ing as a question concerning the sphere of projecting-opening of en-thinking of be-ing is the en-opening and grounding of this sphere, never the matter of a "reflection" on thinking and "I think". Instead of 'reflection', the more inceptual [G303] question of being requires a leap-off from man as the "subject" and that means simultaneously a leap-off from the relation to "object" *and* from object itself. By turning towards "object", that "subjectivism" is not only *not* overcome, but is retained all the more in its imperturbability and firmness. (Let it be undiscussed here whether an overcoming of "subjectivism" and "objectivism" is a fundamental necessity of be-ing-historical thinking. For, one day this overcoming may have to unmask itself as a superfluous mock fight, staged only with an inexhaustible enthusiasm, so that metaphysical thinking may consider itself absolved from looking into its own question-worthiness.)

XXVI

A GATHERING INTO BEING MINDFUL

80. Enowning

The settlement means bearing apart of countering and strife unto the intersection of their sway. The bearing apart as en-ownment of the 'in-between' carries out the intimacy of the intersecting mirror-play up to a decision of a history of Da-sein.

The settling – bringing to maturity – is that 'swaying-stillness' whose tune lets all destiny depart from be-ing.

The destiny necessitates the distress of Da-sein, the distress turns the inabiding into what is its necessity and this necessity displaces Dasein into the unavoidableness of an 'owning-over' unto the truth of be-ing.

En-owning is settlement.

Settlement sustains the ab-ground.

The freedom of 'thinking-poetizing en-saying' rises up out of the ab-ground.

81. Settlement

The 'removing-lightening' counter-turning 'owning-to' of beings in the wholeness of their swaying within the countering [of godhood and man's domain] and within the strife [of world and earth] are always brought unto the 'ownhood'.

Be-ing is the 'onward-lead' into the clearing of the ab-ground that is en-opened by be-ing's 'settleability' – the ab-ground out of whose refusal the necessity for the counter-turning 'owning-to' the 'ownhood' of beings arises (as the swaying of what sways out of the godhood, out of the domain of man, out of the world and out of the earth).

*

The Settlement

'Settling' says both 'preserving' up to the maturity of swaying decision as well as 'deciding for' the sway [G308] – raising this 'deciding for' unto enowning and thus entrusting en-owning to its own sway.

Moreover, the fundamental character of 'settling' as 'preserving' and 'deciding for' is the grounding of the ab-ground that lights up, en-frees the free and shifts unto 'setting apart' [aus-ein-ander] and 'setting unto' [zu-einander].

"What" gets settled are "countering" and "strife": in themselves both are 'settleable' in their sway, and in their 'removals-unto' both are simply entwined in one another.

En-ownment is settlement.

Enowned unto their sway and unto their ownmost are above all the countering ones (god and man) and the ones at strife (the world and the earth).

However, in this en-ownment history "comes to pass", that is, becomes fundamental as the grounding of the clearing in the Da-sein "of" man.

82. The En-owning

The en-ownment unto the 't/here' and thus the 't/here' itself is refusal of being as beingness, is the failure of every producing-calculating representing as the comportment on whose path man could find his way to being as the site of decision of his swaying-attunement.

As en-ownment, be-ing itself destroys the pre-eminence of λόγος; tears away beings as such from power and thus from machination, and en-sways them unto 'ownhood'.

Only now does be-ing itself – and not just the calculability of beings – foster the genuine junction that enjoins the truth of be-ing; only now does be-ing itself foster the belongingness of the sheer earnestness of *thinking,* only now does thinking stand before the decision either to become en- thinking of be-ing or to be nothing at all.

*

[G309]   Enowning

For the initial knowing-awareness of what its naming says, the sway of en-owning must be indicated. That can happen only up to the "region" of thinking out of which the projecting-open that throws itself free becomes *possible* as *thrown* projecting-open. It is a gift of enowning *whether* this projecting-open enowns itself. The indication of the sway of enowning proffers the knowing-awareness of the sway of "time" that 'removes-unto and lights up' – "time" understood as the 'free-play of time-space' – for the determination of beingness as such, that is, beingness as presencing and constancy.

The clearing that 'removes-unto' points to something that can never be represented as the 'doings' of a being and nonetheless its swaying surpasses and is of more being than any being. The clearing that 'removes-unto' only indicates the ab-ground-character of being and the swaying of ab-ground – that being simply refuses any escape into the permanent, and as this refusal being simultaneously gifts the allotment unto the distress of a belongingness to being.

Being, while en-own-*ing* [*Er-eignend*], allots the countering of man and god and the strife of the world and the earth into the 'ownhood' of its sway.

But why these? To what extent is enowning simply the en-swaying of such things that holds unto ab-ground?

The question sounds as if be-ing (enowning) is meant above all as something that sways for itself from out of which then the rest should be deduced.

However, precisely the directive that ensues from out of "time" should indicate that be-ing as abground sways in the '*in-between*' of "beings", and certainly is not to be determined from out of *beingness* of beings, but from out of being's hidden-sheltered swaying that being itself constitutes.

What we *metaphysically* call "god", "man", "world" and "earth" belong be-ing-historically to be-ing insofar as what is so named sways as '*ownhood*' by holding on to ab-ground, and is ever variously allotted to belongingness to enowning.

Thus how can "we" decide on be-ing's sway? [G310] Do we have here a direction and a measure, and if not, is not everything arbitrary?

What distinguishes be-ing-historical projecting-open is neither compulsion nor arbitrariness but rather freedom as liberating the ground unto ab-ground, whereby in one moment the thrownness of projecting-open must enter the domain of this projecting's own knowing-awareness to the effect that this projecting *is* and can only *be* an en-owned projecting.

The projecting-opening of be-ing is a distinct enowning of the history of be-ing; it is not advancing an opinion about be-ing arbitrarily and forcefully.

As freedom, be-ing-historical projecting-open is *venture*, except that since long ago this word has had a false ring to it and is thus better to be avoided. For here the conditions of venturing are not what in the prevailing views concerning venturing are called circumstances that should be altered. Rather, the conditions of venturing are the distress of the history of be-ing itself – the distress that lets the venturesome ones right away become the ones who are weighed and found wanting.

The allusion to "time" that 'removes-unto', and 'lights-up' as the "truth" (openness of projecting-open) of being can initially and merely defensively give a hint that "being" cannot be encountered in representation as a subtracted and dissipated being and finally be emptied as a general or even the "most general" concept. This emptiness remains fundamentally what it is, indeed it is all the more confirmed when one ensures that this emptiness will be filled up by "concrete" "ontological" determinations.

Being (swaying in "time") announces itself as the "in-between" of beings that fosters a distinctly transformed relation to itself, that is, the inabiding Da-sein. But this fostering is only a representationally grasped and misinterpreted relation if we consider that be-ing as enowning [*Ereignis*] en-owns Da-sein as the swaying of being's grounding of its truth – which enowning [*Ereignen*] makes up just what is 'primary' in the enowning [*Ereignis*] that holds on to the ab-ground.

The clearing of time that 'removes-unto' is the indicator that points to the [G311] swaying of the 'unto-each-other' [*Aufeinanderzu*] that holds unto the ab-ground (necessitates de-cision) and is the 'unto-each-other' of 'what has been' [*des Gewesenden*] and 'what comes' [*des Kommenden*]. This 'unto-each-other' wherein the 'free play' of beings expands – the 'free play' whose be-ing determines itself first out of clearing – is the hint to en-ownment wherein the 'settling' of countering and strife enowns itself.

In order to have a knowing-awareness of this, what is immediately necessary is the insight into the time-character of the inceptually determined beingness (φύσις), and the experience of being's abandonment of beings – an experience wherein be-ing announces itself as refusal.

83. Beingness and Be-ing

Beingness and machination.

Machination in its unfolding: the unity of 'history' – technicity – 'discourse' [Rede].

This unfolding as letting loose unto abandonment by being.

Abandonment by being as a refusal of be-ing.

The refusal as the swaying of be-ing itself (the dis-enownment of beings – the holding-forth-withholding [Vorenthaltung] of 'ownhood').

The dis-enownment as the hint onto en-ownment.

The en-ownment onto settlement.

The settlement as en-owning.

En-owning as the swaying of the clearing of be-ing.

This swaying as history.

Be-ing and the ab-ground of the 'in-between' (the swaying of 'nothingness').

('Nothingness' originating from beingness, although not from "negation"!)

[G312]   83. Be-ing and 'Nothingness'

'Nothingness' as the ab-ground of the clearing of refusal. What in the ground is of the nature of "ab", [das Abhafte des Grundes] comes from refusal.

The refusal as en-ownment unto inabiding the persevering-awaiting [Er-harrung]; *this* as being-cnowned unto dis-enownment.

The dis-enownment as the swaying ground of *negation*. [But] "negation" *not yet as the mere* objectifying assertion about what is present and absent (the "no", the "not", and the "un-").

The originary negation as perseverance of *preserving* wherein refusal can and even must light up without thereby gifting away its full sway.

The negation as Da-sein's inabiding the refusal. No! It "is" "*not*" yet and yet it "is" so in the gifting of refusal. The "no" here is not meant as defense and resistance – these are not originary – but as inabiding, and yet not just as "affirmation" as "attuning"- approval [*Zu-'stimmung'*] of something extant, rather attunedness to the tune of stillness.

85. 'Nothingness'

1. *The metaphysical concept of 'nothingness'* (Hegel – the un-determined im-mediate);
2. *the be-ing-historically thought metaphysical concept of 'nothingness' – the nihilating;*
3. *the be-ing-historical concept of 'nothingness'* – the ab-ground as the sway of be- ing.
   Here 'nothingness' loses every semblance and superficiality of what is merely of the nature of 'not' [*Nicht-haftes*]. For ab-ground is the swaying of refusal as the swaying of en-ownment of gifting.

*

The more superficially – the more without the knowing-awareness of the truth of being [G313] – is thought metaphysically;[+] the more "nihilating" 'nothingness' becomes, the easier 'nothingness' is shoved away into the "logical" negation.

That and to what extent being and 'nothingness' are the same, namely on the basis of the swaying of the truth "of" being, can be grasped be-ing-historically.

Proposition counts for Hegel only to the extent that it empties "being" (what he calls "absolute actuality") beforehand up to what is merely thinkable for the absolute thought as it still limits itself to its utmost, respectively up to the residue of what is still represented in 'un-thought'. In its representedness, what is represented in *this* way is "something" in general; it is not simply nothing and yet at the same time it is nothing.

Metaphysics is capable of thinking the sameness of being and 'nothing-ness' only along the guiding-thread of a projecting-open that *represents*

[+] {sic}

(being and thinking) from out of the emptiest and foremost generality of what is most immediately general.

The be-ing-historical inquiry does *not* experience 'nothingness' merely as the 'nihilating', but, insofar as this thinking inquires into be-ing itself in the fullness of its swaying, this thinking experiences 'nothingness' as the en-ownment.

86. Truth-
Be-ing and Clearing

Be-ing and clearing are the same; so goes the inceptual 'saying' of Parmenides in the other beginning.

Formerly, beingness (ἐόν) had to be en-thought inceptually as rising presence so that beingness and disclosive receiving belong together.

Futurally, the ab-ground of belongingness itself is to be en-thought as what begins – be-ing, the en-ownment of the 'in-between' that lights up, gifts and refuses the clearing itself as its sway.

[G314] Decision onto be-ing positions all beings in another joining that retrocedes into another swaying.

Be-ing en-sways the clearing; the clearing enowns in the 'in-between' of settlement of the countering and the strife; clearing sways over [*überwest*] be-ing.

87. Truth

Truth is the clearing that belongs to be-ing as en-owning. Clearing: settling the countering and the strife unto the openness of their inter-section. Clearing is: clearing "of" settlement.

Truth is the clearing "of" settlement, that is, clearing of en-owning.

Clearing "of" settlement says: the 'removal-unto' and the 'making room' of what is released into separation as what is allotted to itself, is enowned in en-ownment, happens and is borne in settlement.

Clearing sways from out of settlement and renders settlement its own.

Clearing is never an empty openness bereft of determination; not even the openness that belongs to some sort of "a being" that is intended in advance [*vorgemeinten "Seienden"*].

This clearing safeguards and preserves the "sway" of the 'settling' and simultaneously the sway of the countering and of the strife.

As the "world" is at strife in innerworldly beings, the sway of clearing sways – only far away in the open [*draußen*] – as the *self-showing* of beings; the self-showing claims the inceptual sway of the clearing.

The sway of truth can never be enquired into by starting off from self-showing.

ἀλήθεια – *sheltering-unconcealment* – *openness* – *clearing*.

The context named by these names is a historical one and is thus determined by *be-ing*. What these names name cannot be established by a "definition" and arbitrarily addressed to everyone so that everyone with his "natural" understanding, which is lodged in the hitherto everydayness of opining [*Meinen*], understands it right away. What is required is preparedness [G315] for thinking being, even at the point where elucidating ἀλήθεια 'historically' is seemingly what counts above all.

That preparedness comes along simultaneously with the transformation of the relation to the word.

Within the Greek metaphysical thinking, this experience and knowledge of ἀλήθεια is concerned entirely with the unconcealed itself *as such*; what follows this concern and the unconcealment that is only thus experienced is the presencing of the constant. Satisfied and more than satisfied with the astonishing presencing itself, [Greek metaphysical thinking] does not ponder upon and does not question the presencing that already sways unto an "openness" and the constancy that is situated therein. However, εἶναι is nevertheless allocated to the relation to νοεῖν; and both are thought as belonging together. *Certainly* – but νοεῖν is the comportment of the self-present "man", and receiving as such is an unrecognized making-present of what is present which is equally unthought in its "time"-character. Furthermore, [in Greek metaphysical thinking] it is not thought and asked what that is, into which and through which receiving, so to speak, extends and spans itself in order to take and to have what is present as such.

But does not Greek thinking nevertheless succeed in taking a step "forward"? Does not ζυγόν, the yoke that subdues and bounds ὄν (οὐσία) and νοεῖν together, indicate that ἀλήθεια is not only represented as presence of beings (as being), but is simultaneously thought as that which in receiving, so to speak, resonates over what is present in order to grant this receiving the arc unto beings? At the risk of *over*-interpreting the matter, we must, of course, be prepared to experience how being is thought here. Simply put, being is not thought here as the most general property that is extant in beings, but as the presencing which above all lets receiving resonate unto the presencing and belong to the presencing (φύσις as rising prevailing). Obviously, the designation "yoke" seems to come from the outside and appears to strengthen the opinion that two extant things, namely "a being" and a "soul", are *under*-yoked and harnessed together. This does not merely appears to be so. For the Greek's, [G316] representing has to clarify this too from out of the presencing, whereby obviously the sheltering-unconcealment is not validated with a view to *openness*. And yet, what do δῆλον and δηλοῦν say? [They say] revealing, but indeed without inquiring into openness itself. Here openness is as little enquired (and is as little enquirable and *question-worthy*) as the *sheltering-unconcealment* that is represented along with *sheltering-concealment*.

And here just as little is inquired whether presencing as abandoning and relinquishing of sheltering-concealment is a specific "happening" in itself – something that cannot be put together and calculated from out of the properties of a being and "activities" of the "soul".

It remains outside Greek thinking *that* sheltering-unconcealment is presencing and this presencing is unconcealing and thus sheltering [*Bergung*] *and* concealing [*Verbergung*], and all this is *what* has thereby become experienceable. Hence, in spite of the directives that one gathers, for example, from the simile of the cave, still grasping the sheltering-unconcealment as *openness* of beings is already *un-Greek* in the noteworthy sense that, with this grasping, what is inceptually Greek in the thinking of being, for the first time becomes actually *ponderable* as what is 'owned-over' to us. For if we do not preserve the beginning, then we fall out of history: we belong no longer to be-ing and its necessity, but merely to beings that are 'historically' planned in good order and abandoned by being.

For the Greeks the unconcealedness of beings and manifestness of beings mean presencing, that is, being, and that means beingness, and that means a being as such, that is, a being.

Later on, however, neither *presencing* (*even* in its *inceptually* concealed time-character) nor *sheltering-concealing* and *openness* are interrogated and become worthy of thinking.

And insofar as we specifically name this [that is, presencing, sheltering-concealing and openness] as question-worthy, we are no longer thinking metaphysically.

However, what remains most remarkable is that in the Christian doctrine of faith and salvation, that is, where "revelation" is expected to handle the 'ultimate questions', the *"revealedness"* of [G317] *ens* is completely leveled off, and on the path of "Roman" and "juridical" thinking, everything is modified into what is right, and everything modified according to correctness. (Therefore, the manners of talking that Christian theologians have taken over today concerning the "revelation of being" are expressions and propagandistic constructs that are not at all adequate to that which these theologians have to think in keeping with their dogma as *ens creatum*.)

With the modification of ἀλήθεια into ὁμοίωσις and *adaequatio*, and with the modification of this *adaequatio* into *certitudo* and the certainty of 'having consciousness and being conscious of', and with the modification of this certainty as certainty of self-consciousness in the very essence of absolute knowledge and absolute "spirit", and with "spirit's" 'falling off' into the scientific-technical-'historical' experience, and with the incorporation of this experience in to "live-experience" – in short, through the *metaphysical* history of "truth" – every possibility within metaphysics is ultimately removed for thinking ἀλήθεια in the direction of *presencing*, sheltering-unconcealing, and the openness of the open. All of this already names something that is never accessible to the thinking of metaphysics (representing beings in their beingness) – something that by contrast is already said from out of the thinking of be-ing. In Greek unconcealment means presencing whereby [Greek thinking] neither enquires into nor grounds the time-character of presencing and the *sheltering-concealing*. And that is why *unconcealment*, too, had to give up its mastery soon – the mastery that unconcealment could have maintained only with the *unfolding* of its sway.

And now we might ask where the necessity of inquiring into the time-character of presencing and into the sway of sheltering-concealing and into unconcealing comes from. Whence the necessity of thinking the open and the openness of beings?

This necessity can only arise from out of a distress. And the distress itself? The distress belongs to the unliberated excess of the swaying of be-ing itself. That this is the case is what determines *this* moment of our history; that this is the case is what destines us into a history that as the history "of" be-ing not only does not admit any human measure but also [G318] blocks the divine insofar as the divine is misused as the ground of explanation and is depreciated as a mere refuge.

88. Be-ing and Measure

For metaphysics being as beingness is unhesitatingly ἀρχή and thus the measure, that is, the absolute, the unconditioned, which is what representing then calculates out of, and for beings themselves as the constancy of what is present. Along with the function which measure assumes, thinking in terms of "goal" takes the lead; τέλος – inceptually a determination of presencing and its rounding unto itself, an echo of φύσις – gets modified into *finis*, modified into the abstracted and presupposed "goal" of 'proceeding up to' [*Dahin*] and *progressing-ahead*. Ultimately this progressing-ahead becomes itself the goal. And this goal, wherever it is seemingly overcome, is then only hidden in the enactment of mere vitality of living for the sake of living (the "eternal people" and some such thoughtlessnesses.)

But be-ing is never a measure. For its truth above all else says that nowhere in beings is there a measure because as 'ownhood' beings are en-owned into the question-worthiness of decisions (en-owning) which alone grant the nearness and remoteness of gods and out of which comes the silent struggle for the strict transformation of man.

89. Be-ing-history

History of be-ing – en-ownment of truth as clearing; in the first beginning the gifting which had to be followed by a denial, because being itself as beingness is made serviceable to the preeminence of beings.

The denial unfolds itself as the reversal [*Verkehrung*] of the sway of truth into ὁμοίωσις – correctness–certainty–justice – *the leveling off* of truth into beingness as machination [G319] – the machinational openness of beings as "publicness" – the indifference vis-à-vis *the sway* of truth; the effective [*das Wirksame*] as the measure of effect-uality [*Wirk-lichen*], and this as actual beings.

The hidden abandonment of beings by being.

The en-ownment as dis-enownment.

The sheltering-concealment of refusal, and yet the hint at the refusal, and so out of inattentiveness [*Hintansetzung*] to all beings and their being-ness, the hint at the swaying of be-ing itself.

90. Enownment and Attunement

In the first beginning, neither en-ownment nor attunement enter into the unfolding of the sway of be-ing. And yet, unrecognized in their sway, both are nevertheless thought in other shapes. The enownment conceals itself in the belongingness of νοῦς and of λόγος to being, a belongingness – which as a result of the lack of knowing-awareness of the truth is not mastered and is not masterable – that ultimately leads to displacing being-ness (as objectness) unto man (as subject) so that the question of being and the swaying of be-ing hide themselves behind the "problematic" of the conditioned and unconditioned subject-object-relation. This relation at the end brings itself in the whole to predominance as machination, wherein the effective counts as the actual and this in turn as beings and as the "living" in a broad sense to which "live-experience" remains subordinated.

The φύσις of the first beginning becomes machination; the belonging-ness of νοεῖν and εἶναι turns into the relatedness of "life" and "live-experience" whereby "live-experience" appeals to the "organic" which it grasps as the sheer machinational calculation and planning.

Machination is the complete dissembling of en-ownment, and when it is experienced as such a dissembling it can indeed become a hint [G320] into the refusal – the refusal which lets beings rave in the abandonment by being.

Attunement belongs to en-ownment; as the 'tune' [Stimme] of be-ing attunement attunes the en-owned (what is attuned to grounding the truth of be-ing) into a grounding-attunement – an attunement that becomes the ground for grounding the truth of be-ing in Da-sein – the attunement that en-joins Da-sein as such while attuning it. This is to say that grounding-attunement not only is *not* a feeling – a capacity among other capacities of the soul and of the subject – but also that it is the "ground" of all comportments that thoroughly attunes them. This is to say also that grounding-attunement is not merely that within which one finds oneself [Befindlichkeit].

In the attempt that is made with Sein und Zeit this interpretation of attunedness does indeed think from Da-sein and for the sake of Da-sein out of the be-ing-historical question of being. And yet instead of taking seriously the enowning-character of attunement, this interpretation succumbs to what is insidious in the naming and the concept of attune-ment by shifting it, as an occurrence, to the "side" of human being. In this context the main hindrance is the ever-first-inceptual and metaphysical interpretation of attunement as πάθος and *affectio*. Even if we avoid misinterpreting αἰδώς, χάρις and every πάθος in a subjective modern sense, or just in a Christian psychological sense, even if we intimate that these "attunements", like νοῦς and λόγος, belong together with be-ing, even then the fundamental admission must be made that admits the undecidedness of the sway of attunements and recognizes in this undecidedness the ground for the subsequent displacement of attunement into ψυχή, *animus*, even "*cogitatio*" and into consciousness. If lived-experience takes full possession of the interpretation of the sway of "attunement", then every prospect disappears of ever being able, within the metaphysical interpretation of being, to render experienceable the en-owning-character of attunement.

Here too what is undecided from earlier on evades the one decision, namely the decision of the truth of being, that is, the decision which itself has to be enowned.

[G321] *Only the en-owned ones are capable of deciding.* That is, only out of the resoluteness towards the projecting-open that throws itself free unto the inabiding Da-*sein* are the en-owned ones capable of *bidding farewell* to representing and perceiving (intuition, *intuitus*). Resoluteness here reaches "only" so far as the preparedness for the en-ownment: resoluteness is never the same as mustering one's own contrivances.

91. The 'T/here' as the Ab-ground of the 'In-between'*

The "t/here" is never the "here, there" as a name for *presencing*, but rather that wherein such things as presencing sway. The "t/here" as the clearing for every possible 'where', "here" and "there", but also for '*then*' and '*when*', as in "at that moment, 'when' he came".ᵃ

The 't/here' lights itself up in Da-*sein*. However, Da-*sein* sways as the perseverance of the 'in-between', a perseverance that is grounded in the belongingness to enownment. The 'in-between' is en-owned by en-owning as that wherein enowning finds itself in its swaying. To this swaying belongs the originary onefold of the 'in-the-midst of' and

---

* Cf. 41. The 'In-between' of the 'T/here'; cf. "Grounding" in *Contributions to Philosophy (From Enowning)*, pp. 206–74.
ᵃ The temporal-spatial meaning of the "t/here"–*but?*

'amongst' (the temporal-spatial *clearing*.) The 'in-between' within which the trajectories of strife and countering cross among themselves, and radiate unimpairably in the clearing in all directions.

92. Da-sein

Da-sein is neither the condition for the possibility nor the ground for the condition of the possibility of "man" as what is now extant. Rather, Da-sein is *that belongingness that, holding unto the ab-ground, belongs to the clearing of be-ing.*

Although, all the works from *Sein und Zeit* up to [G322] *Vom Wesen des Grundes,*[*] as the threshold, still speak and present metaphysically, *the thinking* in these works is *not metaphysical.* And yet, this thinking does not succeed to reach the unfetteredness of its own ab-ground.

Therefore, what is communicated in these works is *ambiguous,* but not to the extent that because of this ambiguity a pondering would become *impossible.* Da-sein's ownmost is be-ing-historical.

93. Da-sein "of" Man

Here too the genitive "of" is to be thought be-ing-historically. Da-sein is "of" man, is 'owned-to' his ownmost in the sense of a transformation of the ownmost that is uniquely determined beforehand by be-ing. Given this manner of his ownmost, man is *en*owned unto be-ing, is *en*owned by be-ing.

Da-sein: the swaying site for shattering man's ownmost in the guardianship of the truth of be-ing.

Da-sein names the be-ing-historical distinction of man in such a way that it is nothing "human" as "contrivance", "attitude" and "comportment". But Da-sein is "human" only in the sense that Da-sein claims man for the transformation of his ownmost.[a]

Da-sein can persevere only as inabiding (in the history of be-ing as enowning) and only through grounding the ab-ground. Da-sein is never something we run into; it is never to be "demonstrated".

---

[*] See *Wegmarken*, GA 9, pp. 123–75.
[a] Da-sein in man – man in Da-sein.

The arising-en-owned inabiding in Da-sein is the indication of the extent in which man ventures forth in his ownmost history in order to be *in*, and to be *this* history.

[G323]   94. The Hint at Da-sein

Within metaphysics, the place of man as a being in the midst of beings as such is still indicated by the "understanding of being". However, considering all that is established within the guiding context of the question of the truth of be-ing concerning "understanding of being", "understanding" means: projecting-opening the truth of be-ing. And with this, we reach the axis of the turning in crossing (which is not a reversal).

'Understanding of being' does not count as a property,[a] nor does it count as the fundamental distinction of man in the propertied sense. In an onward-lead, 'understanding of being' does indeed look merely like a more fundamental version of "reason". However, 'understanding of being' is the swaying ground of man as he is already destined to an ownmost transformation.

The projecting-opening is thrown, is placed into inabiding the openness of projecting be-ing open. This placedness into inabiding arises from out of a displacement that originates as attunement from the tune of stillness (from be-ing itself): this placedness is what is enowned in enownment.

Within the crossing, the "understanding of being" is thus an ambiguous determination. Still, it points in the direction of reason and subject, but from within a clear knowing-awareness it is nevertheless the destruction of all subjectivity of man, and simultaneously the overcoming of the failure of the first beginning.

Being is no longer the unconcealment of the rising presence and thus itself a pure pre-sencing that is ungrounded in its "truth".

Being is in no wise "relative to" a representing subject and "life" (i.e., relative to what makes up the *a priori*).

The possibility of anthropomorphy is shattered.

*

[G324] But what does the ownedness [*Eigentlichkeit*] and the un-ownedness [*Un-eigentlichkeit*] of Da-sein mean?

---

[a] Property, a word, more appropriate than constitution and equipping.

The un-ownedness is grasped as 'falling unto', that is, being claimed by beings. Herein is indicated that the mindfulness of being is what is fundamental and exclusively guiding. The 'falling unto' beings is the affirmation of machination that is hidden to itself. However, what needs to be shown above all is that this "falling" is not an "error", but together with thrownness remains the *one* ground and shelters within itself an unmastery of being (beingness) that is nevertheless open.

Correspondingly, ownedness does not mean a particular existential interpretation in accord with a moral ideal. Here again ownedness bears merely a hint into the selfhood of Da-sein – a hint into the disclosing resoluteness as joining into the truth of being.

As "existentials", ownedness and un-ownedness are not labels for a "new" anthropology and the like, but rather the directives to the swaying of be-ing itself that attunes Da-sein for making the truth of be-ing its own [*An-eignung*] and attunes Da-sein to the loss.[b]

What is communicated here by itself assuredly gives the false impression that it is a particular anthropology.

However, equally assuredly, on the whole and from the outset and to the end and everywhere, is the fact that what is exclusively asked here is so unambiguously the question of being as the question concerning the "meaning" of being, that at least an attempt is made for once to think through what is said from out of *this* question and *only* from out of it and to set aside all the familiar opinions.

[G325]   95. Da-sein

Da-sein is incomparable, and admits of no perspective within which it could still be lodged as something familiar.

Da-sein forestalls all mania for explanation. Explanation (calculation) can no longer retain the claim to grasp being within the clearing that holds unto the ab-ground and in stillness arises from out of Da-sein; any yielding to the machinational has forfeited the ground and the sustaining domain. Explanation no longer 'says' anything, it merely gets entangled in the non-being and thus still retains a duration that is long since swept away in itself, while something else already and in a different way has let the truth become the 'time-space' of beings.

[b] Be-ing-historical decisions.

How then should Da-sein ever be "explained"? It should not even be declared unexplainable.

Strictly speaking Da-sein is to be thought be-ing-historically: it is the grounding that is en-owned by the sway of being as the grounding of that truth that is be-ing's own and is the grounding that inabides the knowing-awareness of be-ing as en-owning.

Therefore, although remotely, yet decisively, there is still the basic interconnection between *Da-sein and "understanding of being"*.

In no respect is Da-sein a determination of a being, neither of an object nor of a subject, nor of a being as such that is somehow thought.

Da-sein belongs solely to the swaying of be-ing that has relinquished beingness, and out of the truth *of* this swaying comes into knowing-awareness and word.

Hence, Da-sein cannot be found either in a being that is somehow extant, or in man: Da-sein is not demonstrable. It can never be shown and exhibited as an object, just as little in terms of "lived-experience". *Therefore*, right from the outset, "Da-sein" is to be thought "hermeneutically", that is, only as the projecting-opening of a *distinct* projecting-open, namely the projecting-opening of *being* unto its "meaning", that is, unto its truth as clearing.

[G326] Hence, Da-sein can also never be derived from a projecting-opening of 'beings in the whole' as a projecting-opening that in some ways has to be appropriate to the metaphysical representing.

However, that projecting-opening of be-ing takes the thrower itself along unto the en-opened clearing wherein the thrower recognizes itself as an en-owned thrower. This projecting-open that carries the thrower along and transposes it, enacts in itself a fundamental transformation of the thrower insofar as the thrower is called "man".

Thereupon the guardianship for the truth of being begins.

But why is Da-sein grasped as "temporality"? Because even from the perspective of metaphysics and indeed from its beginning the 't/here' as clearing becomes initially discernible within the swaying of 'time-space'. Hereby "time" and "space" do not mean "the place" and "the sequence" of the series of now, but rather the *beforehand* unifiedly swaying clearing of being. However, the fact that being resides in such a clearing is borne out by the interpretation of being as οὐσία – presencing and constancy. Of course, the inquiry into the "Temporality" [*Temporalität*] of οὐσία already resides outside metaphysics and can be inquired into only and already from out of the grounding-question concerning the truth of being.

Temporality [*Zeitlichkeit*] of the 't/here', means the clearing that 'removes unto'. That is why what mattered [in *Sein und Zeit*] was to offer a hint at *Da-sein* in and through "temporality".

Here "temporality" is thought neither in a "Christian" sense, nor in general as the opposite concept of "eternity", unless one would truly grasp "eternity" (the ἀεί) as determination of being and would inquire into what this determination and its preeminence mean within the interpretation of being and wherein this determination is grounded, and to what extent at all constancy and presencing overwhelmingly dominate the relation to beings as such.

However, if the "eternal" is taken in an exclusively metaphysical sense as an independent actuality, or if the "eternal" is thinned out as the "ideal" and the "validity" of values and if "temporality" is assessed in concordance with values, then any grasping of *Sein und Zeit* is in advance made impossible. Positions taken in this "direction" [G327] entirely belong to those positions that understand "Dasein" virtually as "extant-ness"–*existentia*–τò ἔστιν.

Indeed, within the crossing the word and the concept of Da-sein have an ambiguous meaning to the extent that we hold on to this word Dasein and insofar as "Da-sein" means something incomparably other than what it means in the phrase "Dasein, that is, existence of God" or what the word *da* means in Da-sein when we say "the uncle is *da*, that is, he is here".

There is nowhere a grip for grasping Da-sein other than in the inquiry into the swaying of be-ing itself, because Da-sein, without ever becoming "merely" "a being" (ownhood), is, according to the manner of the swaying of be-ing itself, always the enowned of be-ing.

Considering the early directives in *Sein und Zeit* that concern Da-sein, one gladly observes that what "gets established in this work" is already held in sight, and is already presupposed and is later on demonstrated as pure invention (as if in this domain there could be inventions.) With this objection one believes to have unmasked, as spurious, the core of the undertaking in *Sein und Zeit*. But one has no inkling that with this allusion to "what is to be demonstrated" as 'what is grasped-beforehand' one names precisely that upon which everything depends, that is, *the projecting-open*. Nowhere in *Sein und Zeit* does the opinion prevail that man is something extant that could be gaped at unconditionally; nowhere is it maintained that if this gaping is carried out enthusiastically and long enough, then one day "Da-sein" could be "discovered" in this extant being.

What ensues from this presumption then is that one contrasts this pre-supposed and one-sided "anthropology" with other anthropologies, and tracks down the author's personal presuppositions and valuations and tolerates the whole thing perhaps as the peculiarity which "in its time", that is, in the supposedly questionable 14 years, could only once become possible under the influence of the "metropolitan" conception of man.

Having in this way put together from all sides the 'one-sidedness' and 'limitations' of the standpoint of *Sein und Zeit*, one believes oneself to be finished with this work before one could succeed to enter even the remotest sphere of that *unique* question in whose purview the stages of this work are thought and said.

[G328] *Da-sein is the historical ground of the clearing of be-ing – a ground that is en-owned from out of en-owning.*

Da-sein is the reticent counter-resonance of the tune of en-owning as inabiding the stillness wherein what is of ownhood, [*das Eigentümliche*] is en-owned in its ownhood and beings are decided to pay tribute to be-ing.

Da-*sein* is to be grounded only as inabiding the en-ownment of enowning, that is, from out of be-ing. Therefore, any attempt at grasping Da-sein predominantly or even exclusively with a view towards man remains inadequate. The Da-sein is equally fundamental for god and is equally fundamentally determined by the relation to the world and the earth which preserve their swaying ownhood in Da-sein. Nevertheless, the relation of Da-sein to man in the sense of an 'owning-to, and hinting' mindfulness and naming has a preeminence that requires that the immediate projecting-open of Da-sein goes through man (see *Sein und Zeit*). But precisely hereby man is already in advance no longer thought anthropologically, that is, metaphysically, but rather is grasped from out of his 'understanding of being' which unfolds itself as the guardianship of the truth of be-ing. In this vein, right from the beginning, and in contrast to the entirety of metaphysics, every 'dis-humanization' of man through his mere self-assertion (the subjectivity) is overcome.

If man is no longer the "image" of the Judeo-Christian creator-God, does it follow from this that he is then the image of himself? Not at all! Especially not, when the relation to be-ing – the inabiding the truth of be-ing – makes up the swaying ground of man. The only conclusion to be initially drawn for be-ing-historical thinking is this: man is not at all the image of an other [*Andere*], but he has his most, indeed his distinctly ownmost, by virtue of his relation to be-ing. The 'own-ness' [*Eigenheit*] of man's ownmost is not the self-seekingness of a willful positing of the essence, but rather belongingness unto be-ing, that is, unto what is most unique, which as such does not know an 'other' like itself. [G329] All along Da-sein undertakes the history of the grounding of the be-ing-historical incomparability of human being. This alone also guarantees the expectation of god who, as the last one, has left behind all correspondences to what is of the nature of man.

Just as little as the "world" and the "earth" remain unaffected by the swaying radiation of god, just as little is Dasein – en-owned by *be-ing* as settlement – ever related only to *man* as his ground.

96. Da-sein is Always Mine*
(Cf. Sein und Zeit)

Especially now when every single scholar in philosophy endeavors to think from out of the "community" and for the "people", how offensive it sounds that Da-sein is always mine.

How convenient it is to deal out a decisive blow at "fundamental ontology" with which one cannot come to terms, since now "individualism" can be rendered obvious even to the most stupid eyes. And which objection is more unsettling to the thinking of everyone than the objection of "individualism"!

Look at the wretched simpletons who are always capable of discovering their own folly in the thinking of others and especially in the thinking of their "opponents".

'Da-sein is always *mine*.' What does this want to say? It wants to say that inabiding the 't/here' – the renunciation of all superficiality of the 'inner subject' and of the "I" – can be taken over and enacted purely and only in the *self*. It wants to say that only when the truth of be-ing is entirely and exclusively 'mine' is the warrant grounded that the truth of be-ing can instantly and only be *thine* and *yours*. For *how* can this truth ever be if *thou thyself* do not take this truth seriously with [G330] your *thou* – if with this truth *you yourself* do not bring into play *your* enactment of your 'most ownmost'?

Or, should the truth, like an unconditioned indifference, be immediately valid for everyone?

* See *Sein und Zeit*, GA 2, § 9, p. 57.

However, what should we expect from the "readers" who are not capable of thinking beyond the first *wording* that *sounds* from the first sentence of the first *printed* page, who, right from the beginning, refrain from resolving to *follow a pathway* of thinking that is presumably *not* their own and to bid farewell for a moment to their wrongly understood and permanent "mineness"? What should we expect? Nothing. Or, is it *also* not "something" that year in and year out one copies from the other the same thoughtlessness?

This is, of course, "something" that does not concern the "author" of *Sein und Zeit*, but rather bears witness to the end of philosophy, namely this: that the inceptual thought of being can no longer be thought in its simple distress, that the groundlessness of its truth can no longer be experienced, because everyone knows *much too much*, because everyone is capable of mixing up everything with everything else and of setting anything in a calculating and comparing relation to anything else and is allowed to lump together in a single operation anything with anything else.

'Da-*sein* is that which is always mine'; the grounding and preserving of the 't/here' is 'owned-over' to me *myself*. But *self* means resoluteness unto the clearing of be-ing. In other words, the self-perseverance of the self is 'owned over' to the *disenownment* from every vain and accidental egoism – is 'owning over' unto en-owning.

XXVII

THE BE-ING-HISTORICAL THINKING AND
THE QUESTION OF BEING

97. The Be-ing-historical Thinking and the Question of Being

The question of being is a question that inquires "into" being. Should this proposition count as an elucidation or is it only a rewording of the phrase "the question of being"? Whoever has attempted to elucidate the question of being as a question in order to put the inquiry solely on its track and enact it, will recognize how decisively this elucidation has already settled the question of being so that no reservations arise any more about the manner of this inquiry and its legitimacy.

The question of being that inquires "into" being, inquires into the being "of" beings – inquires into what beings are. The question of being questions beings with regard to their being and thus inquires equally decisively "into" beings. *Such* an inquiry "into" being moves from a questioning of beings back to being so that here being counts in advance as that whose naming as beingness of beings disputes the response to the question of being. "That" into "which" this question of being inquires and what is "questionable" for this question, that is, 'that' with respect to 'which' as the interrogated the response is still to come, turns out to be beings. It is from beings that the manner of asking the question of being and its response is decided. Specifically, beings are questioned with regard to their ἀρχή. And ἀρχή is that from which, as from the "first", beings as beings "are" and are *what they are*. The ἀρχή has the *twofold* meaning of γένος (κοινόν) in view of which beings are determined in what they are, and of αἴτιον, the prime-cause, through which beings are produced. Beings presence in γένος as "such and such" and in αἴτιον as 'that they are'. The twofold meaning of ἀρχή operates within the leading meaning that obviously does not exist "for itself" and according to which the gaze turns generally to what is present, that is, to that which lets beings themselves be present in their "being what", [Was-sein], and in their "being that" [Daβ-sein]. The primariness of ἀρχή is one of presencing and constancy. Why? (Cf. 104. Φύσις and Metaphysics, and 106. Being as Φύσις).

[G334] This brings to light the extent in which already the grounding-experience of beings as such becomes an occasion and impetus for letting the question of being become the question of ἀρχή. The fact that an inquiry is made into ἀρχή is not a form of questioning in general that is pre-determined from somewhere, and finds its fulfillment in equating ἀρχή with being. Rather, there lies in the question of ἀρχή itself the decision to represent being, without questioning it, as presencing and constancy and to experience beings as what are present and constant. To what extent? The inquiry into the "principles" – regardless of how they might be determined – does not have the 'indifference', 'non-bindingness' and 'self-evidence', that one would like to attribute to this inquiry. On the contrary, to inquire into the "principles" (ἀρχαί) means to raise the question of being in the elucidated sense, respectively to take this question over as the question that is raised and wherein one dwells, and to operate within the sphere of the possibilities of responding to this question.

In truth, *this* manner of inquiring "into" being inquires by passing over being, and as it passes over being takes it up in its not yet en-grounded determination (presencing–constancy), and thus supplies *the* response to the question – a response that, strictly speaking, counts only for beings.

This inquiry "into" being is made directly *by* and *for* a being (by man) in such a way that this being too is established in advance in 'what this being is' and 'in that this being is', and this again only on the basis of the experience of beings as what is present and constant. The questioner of the question of being is also the one who responds to this question. Responding in this context means: representing the ἀρχή of beings in the mentioned twofold interpretation, and *producing* the ἀρχή representationally, so that with the help of asserting the response beings may explicitly reside and be constant in the presence of the constancy of ἀρχή itself, that is, beings *may be*. Accordingly, the question of being moves in the direction of the explicit – articulated and sayable – securing of *being* for 'beings as such in the whole'.

This inquiry "into" being ceaselessly *passes being by* (passing by in [G335] the Greek sense of παρά whereby that which is passed by inquiringly indeed presences but not *as* such), so that being simply presences in this inquiry that passes being by and yet is not itself inquired into in the way and according to how it is itself already determined. This inquiry that passes being by represents presencing and constancy in a certain way, but never in the light of that which is experienced in such a representing, namely the present and the duration, that is, a specific temporalizing of time. For this inquiry "into" being that passes by being, being is what is unquestionable, and what absolutely needs no questioning. The question of being of the kind that inquires after beings as such by inquiringly passing by being, which also procures for itself the response, receives its history – the consequences and diversity of the basic stances that are possible from within this history – primarily and apparently exclusively from out of the ever-dominant direction of the experience of 'beings in the whole' as such, and thus out of the experiencing and questioning man. And yet, the allusion to the uniqueness of the so-shaped question of being gives an inkling of how inevitably this question is determined by the manner in which beings *as such* are shaped in advance – one does not know from where and why – in other words, how the unquestioned "sway" of being itself is interpreted, that is, laid out into presencing and constancy. In turn the question of being holds itself already in the specific way in which 'beings in the whole' as such are opened and have thus become knowable and questionable. *The jointure of this opening of beings into the openness of their sway* (that is, into the openness of beingness that is determined as constancy and presencing) is increasingly sustained by the question of being and shaped and consolidated in various directions and stages. The unfolding and shaping of that jointure by the question of being received, then, the name of "metaphysics". In its sway metaphysics "is" that jointure itself and is thus grounded upon that from out of which the jointure is enjoined.

The proposition, "the question of being inquires 'into' being" is a commonplace and yet at the same time contains a directive to [G336] what in Occidental history is most sheltered and concealed, provided that not only *this* history but also the sway and the mastery of history as such are grounded *upon that* which was indicated as the opening of the sway of beings as such.

Nothing supports the view that the question of being as a question that inquires "into" being in the manner just indicated exhausts its exclusive possibility or even satisfies its ownmost necessity.

Everything—the whole of metaphysics in its sway and throughout its history—necessitates that this very same question of being be asked in a fundamentally different way. However, this necessitating cannot originate from within metaphysical thinking itself since this thinking is totally consolidated in itself, and in its own way autocratically sticks to itself and, therefore, can only entangle itself more self-seekingly in its own way of questioning. The history of metaphysics, the manner in which in this history the question of being increasingly and decisively passes by being in its inquiry, the more the questioner (man as subject) with certainty depends on himself and arranges all beings exclusively as a 'producible vis-à-vis' (object) (the world as "image", as an imageable, representable producible view), all this is a single "proof" that the question of being is entangled in the jointure of metaphysics. The differentiation between being and beings is so worn out that it becomes tantamount to effacing what therein is differentiated – tantamount to superficializing "being" to mere wording of an empty "content" – and all this because beings that are not at all thought out in their beingness "are" everything that can count as beings in the sense of a makable actuality.

The necessitating for asking the question of being in a different way cannot be awakened and aroused out of, and through, metaphysics. Rather, the whole of metaphysics can become the impetus for becoming mindful of a distress that necessitates the question of being. However, even that requires that the whole of the enduring sway of metaphysics in its present shape as *the jointure of the openness of beings as such* is already experienced and overcome.

[G337] From where should this overcoming come, if not from that which enjoins and determines the jointure of the openness of beings as such? And what else is this but be-ing? The same be-ing that discharges beings as such into predominance till being is forgotten can wrest this preeminence away from beings. Meanwhile, the history of that discharging is of a different kind than the history of the wresting away that is perhaps already commencing. In this history, be-ing itself must obtain a unique mastery, which does not mean at all that be-ing publicly reveals this mastery and reveals itself in this mastery like the predominance of beings that are abandoned by being. Publicness is that gestalt of the openness of beings as such wherein any being is immediately accessible to anyone, even though this accessibility is mostly an unrecognized illusion.

What happens then, when beings and the beingness (the *a priori*) that is always appended to them lose their preeminence? *Then there is be-ing.*

[*Dann ist das Seyn.*] Then, the "is" and all language undergo a fundamental transformation.

But how does this happen? Which pathway leads to this happening and enables us to know this happening? Only by questioning be-ing itself and so by asking the question of being differently and by knowing which transformation we must prepare ourselves for, if we want to belong to the history of the transformed question of being.

Now, the question of being questions be-ing, so that be-ing may respond, may gift the word which says the truth "of" be-ing. Now we no longer question being by passing it by so that beings as such continue to be the questionable; we also do not question being by aiming at being [*auf das Sein zu*] whereby be-ing becomes an "object" in the manner of metaphysical thinking – we question be-ing itself. The questioning entrusts us to be-ing as what alone is responding. Such a response demands a different hearing out of a transformed hearkening that is pliant out of a belongingness to the truth of be-ing that is gifted by be-ing itself.

In metaphysics, beings become questionable with respect of being whose sway remains so un-questioned in metaphysics that being cannot even be called the questionless.

[G338] For the transformed question of being, be-ing becomes *the* question-worthy. And yet question-worthiness and questionableness mean different things. It is not the questioning that always exclusively questions be-ing itself that just renders be-ing question-worthy. Rather, questioning is honoring in the sense that questioning allots to be-ing the responding of its truth, indeed as enowned by be-ing questioning experiences itself as the question "of" be-ing.

This question of being that questions be-ing belongs to the swaying of the truth of be-ing which swaying is the originary history of be-ing. Hence, all en-thinking of be-ing from out of such questioning is be-ing-historical. The question of being of be-ing-historical thinking cannot be accessed or grasped at all from within and by metaphysics. The be-ing-historical "questioning" of be-ing is the overcoming of metaphysics, which as such an overcoming originates from be-ing itself.

Even as metaphysical, the question of being belongs to the history of be-ing, although for metaphysics and through metaphysics this history remains hidden and sheltered. Therefore, it is only an illusion when out of "one's" heedless opinion "one" ascribes "one's" own meaning to the phrase, the "question of being". Every attempt of this kind already depends on an interpretation of being that completely and continually eludes the undertaking to name and explain the wording of this phrase. One cannot come to an agreement on the sway of being and on what the "is" says by convincing others to the contrary. One can only forget and exclude oneself always from the knowing-awareness that a truth of be-ing as enowning determines the historicity of every history and that this truth has already decided on the possibility and necessity of the respective kind of the *question of being*. Whether we experience it or not, whether we want to "admit" what we experience or not, we stand now at the crossing from the metaphysical to the be-ing-historical question of being. This points to a singular moment of the history of be-ing. Measured by this moment the inquiries that metaphysically or otherwise dominate the question of being count equally. Only that has grounding power which exposes itself to the history of be-ing as well as [G339] to that singular moment in order to thus prepare a site for the *knowing-awareness* wherein, *according to its sway*, the truth is experienced as distress.

Whether the question of being inquires "into" the being (of beings) or "into" be-ing itself in its truth – this is an 'either or' whose deciding ground is kept in be-ing itself. As soon as this sheltering-concealing of be-ing itself enters the earliest clearing of a gentle hint, there arises the necessity of a *thinking* whose decidedness and bindingness leave behind all astuteness of "precise" "rationality" and leave to their usual gratifications the extant "sentimental needs" along with the "irrationality" of these "needs".

The be-ing-historical questioning of the question of be-ing is the passage through that history whose "enownings" are nothing other than decisions concerning man's capability to make decisions "vis-à-vis" the one who bears his ownmost as the guardian of the truth of be-ing, that is, the one who compels to the grounding of be-ing out of the gentleness of the gifting of what is most unique, namely the settling of the undecided within the countering of man and god in the strife of the world and the earth.

The utmost stillness of the hint of be-ing through which be-ing hints unto itself is the undecidedness of that settlement in the gestalt of the abandonment of beings by being – beings that assert themselves into predominance as machination (cf. *Überlegungen* XIII, 36 f.)*

To question be-ing means above all to take in that hint and not to seek refuge in makeshifts; it means further to have a knowing-awareness of

---

* To appear in *Überlegungen C.*, GA 96.

the mastery of be-ing without knowing the grounding of its truth, it means inhabiting the ambiguity.

The question of being as an inquiry "into" being projects-open beings unto beingness in accordance with a sheltering-concealing of be-ing.

The question of being as questioning "of" being, projects-open be-ing unto the truth through a projecting that is thrown into be-ing that lights itself up as refusal.

[G340] *That metaphysical* question "concerning" being that takes the path of passing being "by" by representationally taking it along is grounded in "being" that as *presencing* prevails over everything.

This be-ing-historical questioning "of" being in the sense of a responding-questioning is grounded in the sway of enownment that as be-ing already admits the *questioning* solely as the *history* of be-ing and thus more than ever predetermines the response in its ownmost as the swaying of be-ing.

In the metaphysical thinking of the question of being for which being becomes immediately the predicate of beings (is inferred from beings and again is ascribed to beings), it looks necessarily so that being is either found by man or even invented as a help in need. Being looks like "something" towards which man either proceeds or does not, "something" that via representation he procures for himself or even builds, as though being's sway 'is' like something extant in itself.

However, the indifference of being vis-à-vis the intrusion of man is only an illusion. This is to say that this indifference is grounded in a kind of self-refusal so that – experienced be-ing-historically – even the seemingly self-empowered awakening of man for ascertaining being is enowned *by being*; even the projecting-open of being that *represents* being as beingness of beings (a projecting that does not throw itself free unto the truth of be-ing) is a projecting-open that is thrown by be-ing itself so that in its sway thrownness has to remain *hidden-sheltered* to the inquiry "into" being. This hidden-shelteredness that remains unknown to metaphysics itself allows metaphysics, in the course of its unfolding, the unconditioned self-certainty of absolute knowledge which does not tolerate any conditioning and whose origin cannot be demonstrated from out of the law of a representing projecting-open. The self-empowering of the representing projecting-open (of λόγος, of thinking) of being goes so far that this projecting-open immediately and ultimately determines in which sphere alone (namely, that of "thinking") one may speak of beingness. The metaphysical thinking of the question of being is never capable of [G341] experiencing *that* this thinking itself is determined by be-ing; it is never capable of experiencing *to what extent* this thinking is determined by be-ing; it is never capable of experiencing that such determination is grounded in an "attunement" that arises out of a "tune" through which be-ing itself en-owns the clearing, "speaks" for stillness, and responds to a question that is still perhaps unquestioned.

The be-ing-historical thinking of be-ing en-thinks be-ing in its truth, whereby "*en*-thinking" is meant to say that man, beforehand and solely "attuned" (by "attunement") must allow himself to be led into the pre-paredness for inabiding the truth of be-ing, that is, into the preparedness for the *knowing-awareness* of be-ing. However, in metaphysics "man" does not count as some indiscriminate being and as a species of animal in general, but as a being that from within the jointure of metaphysics has delimited its ownmost as *animal rationale* in order to become, out of such a delimitation, equally decisively pure "spirit" and uninhibited "body". These molds, into which human being is cast by Hegel and Nietzsche correspond here to the concluding and final positions that metaphysics obtains. The confirmation of the finite subjectivity in favour of the absolute spirit, and the glorification of the body in favour of an un-conditioned "anthropomorphy" are *only seemingly* different ways for the self-empowerment of metaphysical thinking to get to the position wherein this thinking's lack of an inkling of being's abandonment of beings is ultimately to be secured – the abandonment that has occurred in the meantime.

The metaphysical question of being is no longer capable of taking itself seriously; that is why it seeks the favor of "sciences" and like them finds salvation in "what is concrete" and "proven", which the metaphysical question of being hands over to itself out of the "live-experience" of "beings". The strange striving for a "real" and a "realistic" "ontology" is not even the end of metaphysics any more, but merely the dying away of a phantom which scholarship has produced out of the scholastic form of metaphysics. However, insofar as the 'history' of philosophy masters this "kind" of the "question of being," the "history" – the mere past of the meta-physical [G342] doctrines – congeals in an "image" which presents neither a bit of metaphysical thinking of being nor of the possibility of mindful-ness of the question of being.

Thus, divorced from the metaphysical question of being and not seizable by the be-ing-historical mindfulness, an occupation with the "question of being" asserts itself, the 'doings' of which must surely be characterized as a rough semblance of philosophy but whose achievements should neither be made an object of critique nor the point of departure for mindfulness.

We should obtain all the more decidedly those basic stances out of which the "difference" between the metaphysical and the be-ing-historical question of being becomes experienceable in terms of decision, because here the simple course of the history of be-ing compels into the rigor of preparedness for questioning.

Out of the metaphysical thinking that occasionally ascribes being as a "predicate" to *beings*, the insight had to emerge that being itself can no longer be furnished with the predicates "is" and "be" because in that way, all of a sudden, being becomes a being. Instead, being is nevertheless elevated to ὄντως ὄν, which is why that which "is" is being. This is how Parmenides thinks pre-Platonically: ἔστιν γὰρ εἶναι. But here, of course, one has to consider how εἶναι is meant. Since μηδέν is immediately contrasted to εἶναι, it becomes clear that without further differentiation εἶναι means both *beings* that are, *and the being* of these beings. However, mindfulness of the inceptual saying, "being is", becomes vacuous as long as we do not let "being" and "is" have the inceptual meaning, namely 'presencing presences'. What is meant or intimated here is the presencing constancy of the constantness of presencing. However and how appropriately we still penetrate into the inceptual saying of being, we cannot fail to see that the metaphysical thinking of the beginning does not fail to attribute the "is" to being and knows being as the most-being. It is precisely by virtue of this knowing that being should be made distinct [*herausgehoben*] from all beings without [G343] falling prey to 'nothingness'. The inquiry "into" being as the most-being thus conceives being as "whence . . ." beings as such are *represented*. A question of being of this kind does not and cannot take up its abode by the most-being because in this way the most being would lose the distinction of being "*the first*" *for* whatever follows and would thus become merely something "in itself", which certainly would *presence*, but no longer as *the presencing* that surpasses the presencing of everything present as well as its own presencing. If adequately thought through, the metaphysical saying "being is" can become an indicator to what extent at all being itself brings its own sway to mastery within metaphysics.

The metaphysical saying "being is" wants to *rescue* being as the most-being and as what is 'first' in relation to beings.

The be-ing-historical saying "being is" thinks something else; it does not think the most-being as the 'first', and in spite of saying "is", it does not think be-ing as such as a being. The be-ing-historical saying says the pure swaying of be-ing; it says the granting of what is charged with decision as well as the taking back of be-ing unto the stillness of the ab-ground.

"Be-ing is" says: en-owning en-owns the clearing of the 'in-between' and grounds the uncommunal [das Unöffentliche] of the fundamental decisions and preserves its sway as incomparable and unapparent. [Here] "swayingness" no longer means distinguishedness that likes to foster prominence and predominance, but means that which shelters-conceals itself in the mastery of its hidden mildness.

The knowing-awareness of the saying "be-ing is" requires inabiding be-ing in such a way that be-ing enowns into their ownhood what is contended in contention *and* the 'counteredness' [Gegnis] of the countering.

The metaphysical question of being that drives metaphysical thinking even as a question that is no longer specifically asked has its "method". In representing beings with respect to beingness, the metaphysical question of being follows a kind of procedure which, as the case might be, indicates simultaneously the "categorial" being, the "actual" cause, and the "ground" of 'beings in the whole'. One can interrogate 'historically' the metaphysical basic stances with respect to [G344] the "method" that each explicitly names (Plato's ὑπόθεσις and διαλέγεσθαι; Aristotle's ἐπαγωγή; Descartes' *mathesis universalis*; Kant's transcendental and speculative-practical systematics; Hegel's "dialectic"). And yet in this way we do not come upon the actual procedure, which, as the case might be, consists in how metaphysics thinks *from* beings and *away from* them *towards* [zu] being but thinks past being (with respect to its truth) back to beings, and how in all manner of ways beings are distinguished beforehand as the "actual" and what specific field of the actual is preferred. This procedure of metaphysics cannot at all be grasped metaphysically-'historically' but only be-ing-historically as the manner in which beingness as the jointure of beings is traversed and held firm. Thus be-ing-historical thinking thinks ahead already in the manner in which being itself prevails over "thinking" (representing beings *as* such from out of beingness) and transposes thinking into its ownmost even though metaphysics holds the view that the being that "thinks", man, by himself persists vis-à-vis 'beings in the whole' and by himself investigates its causes and its makeup. However, even when metaphysics *includes* man also in its explanation of 'the whole' – *includes* this "thinking" being as a kind of living-being, as a kind of "spirit", as a "finite consciousness" and the like – even then because of metaphysics's own sway it can never arrive at the point of experiencing from out of the swaying of be-ing the belongingness of the one who raises the question of being to this sway of *being* itself and to make such an experience the grounding-experience. But to the extent that be-ing-historical thinking is capable of grasping the procedure of metaphysics and thus its innermost dynamics, this thinking re-thinks metaphysics in a more originary manner. From this we receive the directive that when thought be-ing-historically, metaphysics alone, in its *procedure and method,* has come into sway, that is, the content of metaphysics is thus taken back into the joining of the belongingness of "thinking" to being. [G345] We grasp this belongingness out of the insight into the ownmost character of "thinking" understood as the guiding thread for projecting-opening beings unto beingness. Insofar as being arises as φύσις, it prevails over man in such a way that he becomes the one who 'takes in' and 'gathers' (νοεῖν–λόγος) – becomes one in the "unity" with the swaying character of being. "Unity" here means the gatheredness *out* of and back unto the constancy of presencing; what belongs to this is the *one*, and that means what "*is*". The metaphysical thinking renders beings present with respect to their presencing and in their presencing. And the highest form of rendering present becomes necessary and is reached in the "dialectical" thought, which, "restive" and "dynamic", solely deliberates on the unconditioned rendering present of all that is conditioned as such in the unconditioned and on the unconditioned's own representing of itself. The predominance of "*thinking*" (as the trajectory of projecting-opening the determination of beingness as such) arises out of being itself that sways inceptually as φύσις and – provided that man takes over and claims the relation to beings as such as the basic thrust of what is ownmost to him – thus places man into the mold of the one who perceives, that is, 'takes in'. Once this inceptual decision is taken in favor of swaying (in favour of φύσις prevailing over man's ownmost) man rescues "himself" by claiming his ownmost as the "*thinking*" animal. Thereupon and in the future there remains the possibility of obtaining in thinking itself and in its unfolding the self-assertion of man as subject and – without the knowing-awareness of what happened in the beginning – of consolidating the basic relation to being in such a way that with "being and thinking" the sway of metaphysics may be ultimately named. The predominant positioning of *thinking* as the trajectory and domain of projecting-opening beings unto being is the distinctive mark of metaphysics. Wherever and as long as this predominant positioning of thinking asserts itself, every inkling and ultimately every preparedness for the be-ing-historical question of being fails to materialize.

The be-ing-historical question of being "has" no "method" for "investigating" the being of beings as well as beings themselves. [G346] Rather, the be-ing-historical questioning "of" be-ing *is* a pathway and only this. And pathway here indicates specifically a *"going"* and a *"way"*: it means submitting to a way. Here, way and stride simultaneously enown insofar as they are enowned by be-ing that throws forth its truth as en-owning: throws forth the clearing, wherein be-ing as such sways so that now a prevailing over man into a 'receiving' belongingness to be-ing no longer comes to pass, but the enownment of man into the *grounding* of the truth of being – man who in the meantime has forgotten be-ing. The en-ownment unto the distress of this grounding is the en-opening of *"Da-sein"* – the hitherto completely barred, and in its ownmost not only strange but also unrecognized, *"Da-sein"*. To hearken to the tune of en-ownment means taking that pathway of the question of being as a question that questions be-ing itself as the sole respondent. This pathway does not run "outside" and over against beings and their beingness. This pathway is *a vanguard* that admits be-ing itself unto Da-sein – is a thrust of be-ing itself. Da-sein is the submission to en-ownment – a submission that is enowned by be-ing. And, as this submission, Da-sein is the swaying ground of *history*, is the 'falling', 'grounding' and 'going under' of decisions on the sway of be-ing – decisions made out of be-ing in the realm of the truth of be-ing as such and its grounding.

Within the purview of the be-ing-historical question of being, the metaphysical question of being wants readily to appear as a mere *preliminary stage* of the be-ing-historical question of being. However, when in be-ing-*historical* thinking the sway of history is grasped for the first time out of the sway of be-ing and is grasped only thus, then this thinking obtains above all that knowing-awareness of the sway of "metaphysics", which returns metaphysics to its own eminence and in this way renders metaphysics incomparable—metaphysics as the foremost and indeed irrevocable enownment of man unto being.

Eminence is the grounded soaring into a decision concerning the swaying that endows its own law and measure, and above all and by itself, acknowledges and thus recognizes at all what is exclusively eminent in its uniqueness. The eminent never [G347] acknowledges the eminent through equalization but always out of elevatedness. Metaphysics never becomes for be-ing-historical thinking a preliminary stage that is caved unto itself. Metaphysics never becomes a stage at all, but soars in its own inceptuality and thus becomes inaccessible for the pathway of be-ing-historical thinking and as the inaccessible it thus becomes above all an en-owning, a hint of be-ing itself into the necessity of the 'other'.

Elucidation of the question of being through a differentiation of the metaphysical question of being from the be-ing-historical question of being always has the semblance of a mere "historical" "classification". The mere acceptance of such a classification leaves everything as it was. And as a consequence of the approximation of philosophy into "science", the question of being "was" already a task of erudition or at best of "intellectual creativity". But these two – erudition and intellectual creativity – are not domains that should house the question of being. We must venture to think the question of being as an enowning of the history of the truth of be-ing that cannot be housed anywhere. Thereupon, we should know that only the belongingness of man's *ownmost* – belongingness of his history – to the truth of be-ing decides whether once again the uniqueness of a beginning will be gifted to man.

And because the question of being is superficialized in the most vacuous erudition and the historical man nevertheless still continues to be allotted to be-ing – even if this allotment comes to pass in the abandonment of being – therefore if mindfulness of the question of being is to venture the innermost of be-ing itself, this mindfulness has to ponder every time what is most superficial.

What is most superficial is indeed that undecidedness of the question of being which lets this question appear just like any other question of investigation and "interest" in knowledge. Here undecidedness does not mean that a response to the question of being is still to come. Rather, it means that the question of being is nowhere posed as a question; it means that this question is never asked out of a necessity and is not referred to anything question-worthy and nevertheless still 'appears' as a "problem". [G348] And what must be more confusing than this appearance? By alluding to itself, that is, to its mere 'appearing' in the shaping of "world-views", "positions of faith", "further development of philosophy hitherto" – all of which are sufficient occasions for attributing, at times some kind of importance to this question as a form of "the theory of reality" and at times to deny this question any significance – this 'appearing' forestalls any approach to the experience of necessities. However, this groundless and ungraspable obtrusiveness of the undecided question of being that avoids every decision on distress itself originates from being's abandonment of beings and from the unbroken predominance of what is always simply "actual". The abandonment of being prevents beings from becoming an impetus to the question-worthiness of being, that is, the question-worthiness of that wherein beings are held, although still held in their 'un-ownmost'.

With the awakening of an "interest" in "ontology" and metaphysics, the question of being is not wrested from undecidedness but merely further solidified therein. On the other hand, the genuine mindfulness of the question of being must recognize in 'that which is' this overt 'appearing', because only in this way will the illusion be destroyed that a preparedness for the truth of be-ing can be awakened with the reproduction and transmission of the transformed doctrines of metaphysics.

Rather, the detachment of a mindful thinking must go far enough to sacrifice *philosophy* [hitherto] so that mindfulness gains a preliminary foothold from where alone a decisive leap lets philosophy be inceptual as the beginning of the grounding of the truth of being, and thus obtain a beginning "again".

Therefore, it is good to have a knowing-awareness of how little the "question of being" means the same as the "question of be-ing".

However, this knowing-awareness cannot stick to the differentiation of questioning as modes of comportment and representation. For the differentiation and its differentiated – similarly thinking itself as the knowing-awareness of this differentiation – think [G349] as a decidedness that man does not owe to a resolve since it is a decidedness unto which man is en-owned by being itself as enowning.

However, just as being in its beginnings occasionally relinquishes [*preis-gibt*] the sway of its history unto this history itself as well as the manner of its openness, so also the enownment always enowns itself. Being's relinquishing [*Preisgabe*] itself does not mean being throwing itself away to beings, but exposing of itself as the prize for the sake of which beings are beings. Therefore, this giving away of a prize [*Preis-gabe*] must be a refusal wherein the intimacy of the en-ownment is gifted and sheltered-concealed at the same time.

Only from afar are we capable of recognizing and interpreting the signs of the en-ownment and of preserving them in simple words.

One such sign is the inceptual word of Parmenides: receiving [*Vernehmung*] and being are the same. Here we have to think inceptually:

"that which is" [*das Seiend*] (ἐόν) and 'representing-receiving' belong together. "That which is" is experienced as φύσις, as the rising-prevailing, which also and specifically prevails thoroughly over that which must place itself unto what rises [*das Aufgehende*], (the unconcealment of beings). Inceptually thought, here the retainment is the retainment of 'representing' in a being – a 'representing' that itself as a being has to be of the same sway as that which enacts the retainment. That is why in the whole of what is thus unconcealed, *a* being that *'represents'* appears as ζωή (*animal rationale*).

In the first beginning, being is the unconcealing-prevailing that as sheltering-unconcealment only shows itself to that [thinking] which 'represents' the unconcealment in its presencing. In the first beginning, being sways and shelters-conceals its swaying – shelters-conceals the unconcealing and along with it beforehand the un-unconcealable swaying ground of unconcealing: the enownment. From out of the other beginning wherein being as en-owning enowns itself in its clearing, en-ownment lets itself be remembered as the swaying of φύσις and out of such remembering to know what here enowns itself, namely the *'that'* of the belongingness of receiving and being. *That* both belong together is what gives the history of [G350] the first beginning which we know as "metaphysics" that basic thrust in keeping with which the beingness of beings is held to be "true" in a projecting-opening that 'represents' (being and thinking). Out of the first-ever lighting up of enowning in the other beginning the following enowns itself: the transformed swaying of belongingness, which as the abground of enownment, is beforehand conceived with a view towards 'representing'. Formerly the 'that' of belongingness enowned itself, futurally, *this belongingness itself* will be *that which begins.* Be-ing no longer sways as the 'other' to receiving and no longer as the 'same' to receiving. That is why the alternating relationship between representing-producing and objectness that arises out of such beginning and which makes up the end, comes to an end. Be-ing sways as the ground of the sameness of the first-ever-inceptually differentiated. This ground offers nothing that is explainable and explains; it does not allow any refuge in, or a way out, to beings. Rather, this ground is the ground that casts off the predominance of beings and at times as en-owning itself fosters en-grounding in the sense of preparedness for the sites of the swaying of the decision on the undecided (on the settlement of the countering and strife).

The differentiated reside in the first beginning as the same, the undecided sway in the other beginning as the intimacy of the dismay that sets free.

Therefore, it is only from out of the other beginning that it can be known to what extent the terminating shapes of the alternating relationship between receiving and being have *machination* as their sway – machination which has subjected everything that "is", including representing and producing themselves, to the law of makability in order thus to delimit by all means that which could have still emerged in such a history as "beings". Thus, in the lingering shadow of metaphysics itself even that questioning that questions be-ing could look like monopolizing be-ing, while in the most sheltered-concealed ground of the enactment of that questioning, the joinability [*Fügsamkeit*] unto the other beginning must enown itself, otherwise everything becomes a contrivance. However, the more foundationally [G351] the question of being becomes the question "of" being, and the more it becomes actually historical, (i.e., en-owned), the less this question denies the 'inquiry into' being. Of course, this question that 'inquires into being' is no longer the only one and not the first in rank, but, on the contrary, it is the familiar question and the next step that is capable of upsetting – although never overcoming – the forgottenness of being.

However, 'questioning be-ing' is also not the next step that may be enacted after the first step; rather, the 'inquiry into' being is never capable of mediating the 'questioning of be-ing' but is undoubtedly capable of delivering an impetus for this questioning. This impetus is capable of doing what it does only insofar as it is itself already en-owned. And the 'inquiry into' being indeed remembers metaphysics and has seen through and avoided all "ontology", even in the insidious, but in truth already en-owned gestalt of "fundamental ontology" that seems to 'inquire into' being in a way that even metaphysics cannot. For metaphysics aims at beings and thus 'inquires into' beings. The inquiry "into" the truth of be-ing inquires into being, but only seemingly so, for "truth" as the clearing of the refusal is the foremost en-ownment of Da-sein and therefore, insofar as it is thought in en-thinking, it no longer tolerates a representing projecting-open, but attunes into throwing-oneself-free. The metaphysical and the be-ing-historical questions of being cannot be contrasted and placed in relation to one another like standpoints, and reckoned with as a manipulable relationship. Their interconnection is a historical one, and decides itself futurally from out of the abground-dimension of en-ownment that preserves what is still sheltered-concealed in meta-physics and in its history – the enownment that does not allow a calculable and 'historical' modification of the basic stances of metaphysics.

Throwing-oneself-free unto enownment means being vigilant over the undecidedness of the undecided and leaving the undecided to the discretion of its decidability that holds on to the ab-ground.

Throwing-oneself-free unto enownment is preparedness [G352] for *the sway* of truth to place itself in mastery, and prior to all "truths", that is, prior to all "goals", "purposes" and "usefulnesses" to decide beings unto the *ownhood* of be-ing.

The "renewed" raising* of the question of being ("*Sein und Zeit*") does not mean "repetition" in the sense that the same should be attempted once again, as if the history of the question of being would let itself be twisted back unto its first beginning, as if the originariness [*Ursprünglichkeit*] of questioning consisted in a 'historical' renewal of the past. To renew the question of being does not mean that it should be treated as a rigidified "problem". On the contrary, to renew the question of being means to awaken a necessity for questioning this inceptual question. This can only mean that the question of being will be futurally thrusted into an other beginning. But by what means may this occur? By means of that which had to remain uninquired in the first beginning, that is, by means of the truth of be-ing. But to the extent that this truth belongs to be-ing itself as the means with which be-ing – without effect and without needing to have effect – en-owns the grounding of the ground of its truth (the Da-sein), the displacement unto the question "of" be-ing comes from be-ing itself. However much, on the basis of the predominance of beings, the "inquiry into" the being of beings may still continue to be an occasion for the 'question of being' as such, the other question "of" be-ing remains separated from the metaphysical question by an abyss because of which only a "leap" that is tantamount to bidding farewell to all metaphysics leads up to questioning. Every attempt at a 'historical' mediation covers over the abyss and provides excuses for immediately weakening the uniqueness of the metaphysical questioning and for calculating the futural inceptuality of be-ing-historical questioning into mere modifications and into the hitherto. Besides, the questioning of be-ing-historical thinking cannot be communicated (in the sense of transmitting representations). Every questioning and saying here is always only a loosening up

* See *Sein und Zeit*, GA 2, p. 1.

of what is tied unto enownment but has not yet found its necessity in the sense of a [G353] pathway for the grounding of the truth of be-ing, a grounding that is only prepared but never fulfilled by thinking.

Hence 'questioning be-ing' means also this: to have to experience what *all* beings "are", while keeping in mind that a being needs no knowing-awareness of this experience; it means also to bear up that which humans normally believe to "experience" as their "life" while they remain, on account of a forgottenness of being, insulated against taking any step towards the brink of the ab-ground of en-owning.

Accordingly, the forms of "communicating" be-ing-historical thinking cannot be invented and planned: sayability and hearability are reserved for the swaying of be-ing. Here every coercive force and every intervention is nothing but cowardice. The courage for waiting prepares for expecting, which, however, is not the same as idly "waiting for" but is preparing for en-ownment through *mindfulness*.

Ask be-ing! And in its stillness as in the beginning of the word god responds.

You may roam through all beings: nowhere does the trace of god manifest itself.

XXVIII

THE BE-ING-HISTORICAL CONCEPT
OF METAPHYSICS*

---

* The φύσις, ("world-view" as offshoot of metaphysics) *"mysticism"*.

98. The Be-ing-historical Thinking

The Question of Being of Be-ing-historical Thinking

The *metaphysical question* of being as an 'inquiry into' the being of beings, immediately unfolds as the history of metaphysics in the manner of the questionless representing of beings in general.

The Be-ing-historical question as a questioning "of" be-ing questions be-ing as the respondent, *and* this questioning is *'of'* be-ing, arises now out of the swaying of its truth, and is questioned out of this truth.

In the domains of mindfulness, be-ing-historical thinking is occasionally called an *Er-denken, en-thinking* (cf. above, G46 ff. Philosophy as Enthinking of Be-ing). This gives the impression that be-ing is autocratically and merely wantonly "contrived", and "invented", whereas exactly the opposite is meant. The word *Er-denken* [*en*-thinking] wants to say: thinking that is *en-owned* beforehand by be-ing – by what is to be thought – and becomes enactable only in a history and as the history of be-ing. Thus, if the word *Er-denken* is understood according to the ordinary linguistic usage, it is thoroughly misleading and should, therefore, be avoided. In the meaning that is claimed here, *Er-denken* or en-thinking is that thinking that is en-owned by be-ing – a thinking that is to be differentiated from the metaphysical representing that places beings as such before itself.

"Metaphysics" as such will be grasped only when the history of be-ing has abandoned the "metaphysical" "period". Thereupon, metaphysics is the name for the history of the ground-lessness of be-ing amidst the pre-eminence of beings that is permitted by be-ing – the beings that being allows as beingness (κοινόν)

The be-ing-historical thinking is not a 'historical' style of thinking or such a style that exclusively and especially investigates the "history" of thinking.

The title 'be-ing-historical thinking' is meant to indicate that this thinking is en-owned by be-ing itself, an en-ownment that makes up the sway of history [G358] (cf. *Überlegungen* XIII).* This thinking perseveres in a *knowing-awareness* that cannot be brought about or even intimated out of a knowledge of beings. Not even metaphysics, as the manner of the hitherto "knowing" of being that aims at beingness, is capable of bringing forth something knowable from out of its un-knowingness.

The knowing-awareness arises out of the grounding experience of the distress of the lack of distress wherein being's abandonment of beings becomes manifest as it 'hints over' to becoming en-owned by the refusal as the sway of be-ing and the be-ing of the sway. By enthinking the swaying of the truth of be-ing, this 'hinting over' enjoins what must be called the history of be-ing. This history does not consist of events and of the comings and the goings of opinions about beings, but rather it *is* what the tune of stillness responds, which tune this history takes over unto the reticence of its own saying.

The history that *be-ing-historically* is be-ing itself, [is the history that] en-owns and enjoins Da-sein inabidingly.

This naming is not a designation according to a standpoint or an opinion, rather it begins out of an other beginning in accord with what is ownmost to thinking itself.

Thoughtful thinking is questioning. This thinking itself is never the respondent, not because the response has to be postponed further by an endless questioning that – one does not know why – only moves within itself and entangles itself in itself out of a suspicious pleasure that it takes in itself. The questioning of this thinking is something strictly different and therein lies the reason why strictly this thinking is never the respondent.

The response comes always only from out of that which the thoughtful questioning 'en-hears'. That is the tune of the stillness unto which

---

* To appear in *Überlegungen C*, GA 96.

thinking thinks ahead, but always only hearkeningly: all saying is hearkenable and attunable through this tune.

By contrast, the *representing* projecting-opening of that which stems from before [*das Vor-herige*] already anticipates [G359] the "rejoinder", and already says the other "word". Everywhere science takes over the responding and spreads and consolidates the claim on responding and on providing explanatory statements. Thus, wanting to "know" means to insist on such responses. This then leads to the erroneous opinion that interprets all questioning only as the preliminary phase of such responses, and degrades mere questioning right away as embarrassment and aberration (since mere questioning never arrives at a response).

In this way one avoids every attempt at thoughtful questioning because one merely lays in wait for a response, and for whether and how a response may succeed or fail.

Thus the excuse is readily at hand that one cannot wait until shrewd thinking comes up with the response, and, therefore, one must give up the questioning.

As if waiting for the response and expecting it does not mean *enjoining the swaying word* that comes from the interrogated itself and cannot be reckoned up by the questioner – as if waiting here is only a prelude and not the unique history (of be-ing itself).

Since this en-thinking of the truth of be-ing (en-hearing the tune of stillness) is still foreign to us all who come from metaphysics, we reckon with results and dismiss what lends no results. We do not receive the word in that saying in which, when considered calculatively, "nothing" is "actually" said. We have no inkling that here 'nothing' is already the veiled tidings of be-ing; we have no inkling that 'nothing' limits our hearing ability for awaiting for, and for exhaustively listening to, what is basically already familiar.

We never appraise 'the other' which can only be a "dialogue" here that is not a 'discussion about something' at all and does not rely on refutation and being right, but through alternating surpassing of questioning solely gives rise to and shelters an un-traversed pathway of mindfulness.

The en-thinking of be-ing never responds itself because it only awaits en-questioningly the displacement into the attuning tune.

[G360] And that is why this en-thinking is also never keen on proving and justifying. Seen from the vantage point of calculation and omniscient explanation, this en-thinking then looks like an arbitrary claim, like a point of view of an individual. If much is to be conceded to this thinking, then it may count as "poetry" – a concession that hardly hides a pity for the inability of this thinking to justify and enforce a universally valid accessibility.

But from where does the en-thinking of the truth of be-ing receive bindingness? From out of the ab-ground of the allotment unto the simple decisions. For bindingness here is never the same as enchainment to the order of importance of the phases of explanation but means liberating man unto persevering in his *other* ownmost, that is, unto Da-sein. Here, neither an attempt at a "rational" ground nor at a "rational" goal, nor at an explanation nor at a usefulness should distort the incisiveness of the knowing-awareness "of" be-ing. And nevertheless such attempts will always be made.

'Historically' and specifically as the crossing, the history of be-ing-historical thinking will present an entirely different phenomenon than the phenomenon of metaphysics. A fundamental failure marks the dominating beginning of metaphysics – the failure of grounding the *sheltering-unconcealment* as the truth of be-ing and the be-ing of truth – so that vis-à-vis this beginning, and without grasping its sway, metaphysics appears with its self-certainty as a progression towards higher "truth" and is filled with triumphs and exploitations. Futurally, the mastery of thinking lies in the reticence of the stillness, in freeing unto the simple, unto the unapparent "effect" that comes from far away and is only mediated. Rare, alone, in the stillness of exuberance, and out of a never-abandoned rigor, this thinking enters the historical word. The un-understood sign of an echo of the crossing is the obtrusive *end of philosophy* that is still simply denied by philosophical erudition, because precisely when this erudition as "ontology" seemingly receives once again a hint at the nearness to the guiding-question of metaphysics, this erudition will distance itself the furthest from every thoughtful knowing.

[G361] Be-ing-historical thinking can never respond to metaphysical objections or to objections that draw from the depth of the backwaters of metaphysics. And be-ing-historical thinking will never confront a thinking that is related to and attunedly approves [*zu-stimmen*] of be-ing-historical thinking with an objection, neither will be-ing-historical thinking offer its approval blindly; instead it will maintain more watchfully the purity of the aloneness of the guardianship that is entrusted to be-ing-historical thinking and will let the distress become more distressing and the questioning more hearable.

Here approval never comes from homonymity of views, but comes rather from the estrangement of a questioning that is held unto the ab-ground. Question and question recognize each other across the unbridge-able abyss wherein they are suspended – an abyss that is the clearing of the *same* abground and attests to an attunedness that is due to the attuning sound [*Stimme*] of stillness.

Here all the familiar claims to "intelligibility", "exchange of views", admiration and rejection that originate in erudition and public systems of writing and talking have become untenable.

99. The Be-ing-historical Question of Being

The be-ing-historical question of being is an inquiry into the truth of be-ing. This inquiry itself delivers the only possible response in the man-ner of inabidingness in the clearing of enownment.

But what becomes of "beings" in enowning?

If we no longer think beings from out of beingness how must beings be 'en-said'?

For the first time now – out of the clearing of be-ing – beings can no longer be explained with respect to what they "accomplish" for something and with respect to their origination, and equally less with respect to the provenance of what is their ownmost.

For the first time now the inquiry into beings from out of their being has a ground.

Formerly being was merely a refuge with whose help beings were put away in beingness.

[G362]   100. Metaphysics and the Question of Be-ing (Enowning)

The belonging together of the decision regarding the ownmost of man as *animal rationale*, person and subject, *and* the projecting-opening that represents the 'beings in the whole' in their beingness – *not* the projecting-opening that throws itself free – underlies all metaphysics. Yet, out of itself in its swaying as the originary onefold, this belonging together can neither be questioned, nor thought, nor said.

Nevertheless, what we see via such a mindfulness of metaphysics as its ground and its inner limit is the foremost reflection of *en-owning* – the reflection which is still fully bogged down in itself. What counts is to light up this *en-owning* via that projecting-opening that throws-itself-free from the subject's 'un-ownmost' unto Da-*sein*.

101. Projecting-opening and Projecting-opening

Among themselves the projecting-openings of beings unto beingness accord with each other in their history. Between these projecting-openings a dissociating exposition cannot ensue, but merely the exertion of an agreement vis-à-vis their seeming discord. This discord comes from the superficial view which holds that every representing projecting-opening sticks obstinately to what it erects and can no longer grasp what it erects in the light of the swayingness of the same sway (of beingness) of beings.

But how can the projecting-opening of the truth of be-ing that throws itself free still look like a representing projecting-opening and its entire history? Should not here a dissociating exposition take place that has overcome, as the negligible presumptuousness of calculating, all the 'urge of wanting to prove'? The necessity of a dissociating exposition does not come from the irreconcilability of standpoints, but rather from the distress to ground unto the abground of beingness the settlement as the swaying of be-ing. Such an exposition is the transformation of man as subject unto Da-sein as the site of inabiding the truth of be-ing.

[G363] However, projecting-opening the clearing of be-ing is en-thrown by be-ing itself. But man must find his way unto Da-sein wherein alone the resonance of that throw resonates and fosters the free-throw.

102. Forgottenness of Being

It seems as if 'forgottenness of being' is kept away from all metaphysics, because *it* (metaphysics) does indeed inquire into *the being* of beings. But metaphysics does not inquire into being and while inquiring into beings and *their beingness* metaphysics simply forgets being and its truth. The 'what' into which metaphysics inquires (beingness) pins metaphysics down to that lack of need which does not let an enquiry into being and its truth ensue.

Even 'nothingness' is not capable of thrusting metaphysics unto the truth of be-ing as what is primarily question-worthy since in metaphysics the 'nothing' is "explained" metaphysically in this or that way.

Thus, there lies in metaphysics a forgottenness that has forgotten itself.

But where or when this forgottenness is named, there or then already the truth of be-ing, the remembrance unto the clearing of be-ing, is enacted and experienced as distress.

103. The Jointure of Metaphysics

We will hardly succeed in differentiating being and beings, although this differentiation sustains all metaphysics as such and is inceptually a Greek differentiation.[a] Being looks like the paleness of beings – the paleness that we need for representing beings in general.[b] Taken in this manner, being [G364] is coordinated to beings and when pondered upon, being is also represented in the forms of representing beings: being is once again a being, but only a being that is thinned out.

However, if in this way this differentiation remains unclarified and ungrounded as something familiar and uninquired, then within the sphere of this differentiation, that is, within that which this differentiation designates as representable, being itself can never be experienced in its question-worthiness. Thus, be-ing shelters-conceals the possibility of its truth and its grounding, and lets beings loose into the mere generality of beingness. This sheltering-concealing is the refusal that comes from be-ing itself that sends away into forgottenness of being the empty beingness as refusal's 'un-swaying'. The unshaken predominance of that differentiation not only attests to the refusal of the truth of be-ing by be-ing itself but is itself the refusal of the truth of be-ing by be-ing itself. To the extent that it is experienced at all, *the differentiation as such and as a whole* reveals itself to an 'other' thinking as the swaying of be-ing itself.[c] In fact, this differentiation shows the countenance of a contrivance of representing, but in truth – and always subsequently – this differentiation reaches only so far as the decision on the concealing and unconcealing of be-ing itself by be-ing.

As a consequence of this refusal of its truth, be-ing does indeed restore the allotment to be-ing of man's ownmost, but in such a way that man has turned towards beings as such and is from the ground up dis-enowned by

---

[a] To what extent yes! To what extent no?

[b] Cf. *Contributions to Philosophy*, section 261. The Opinion about Be-ing.

[c] But in which shape? In the shape of *'un-swaying'*.

be-ing (the man who is grounded in metaphysics is the one who is let loose into disenownment). This established way of turning towards beings is capable of knowing being only as what belongs to beings as the highest and the most general, that is, as something of the kind of beings, but at the same time different from them.

The differentiation makes enownment inaccessible. And if something were ever to show itself from this enownment at all, it has to be a process that happens in the extant man – or even counts as an [G365] accomplishment of man in the sense of laying down "principles" and "conditions" that are brought about by subjectivity.

Thus when or where the *a priori* is determined subjectively-transcendentally, in one respect the differentiation does come more sharply into light, but nevertheless in such a way that the possibility of experiencing the swaying of be-ing in this differentiation is ultimately undermined.

In the same vein, the transcendental-idealistic interpretation of being as beingness (in the sense of categories) is what conditions in advance the lagging erudite overhaul of the categorial in systems that are supposed to have liberated themselves from the narrowness and one-sidedness of idealistic and other similar standpoints.

That is why metaphysics lacks the inner swaying power to think purely the differentiation out of which metaphysics replenishes its own sway, its own predominance and validity. If these were to happen it would have meant already that metaphysics breaks through its own sway and takes charge of itself.

The differentiation between being and beings determines thinking strictly only in that moment when, because of the inquiry into the truth of be-ing, metaphysics is already overcome and be-ing no longer faces the resistance of beingness and of beings.

In the moment when the fully knowingly aware enactment takes place, does not this differentiation become untenable? Obviously! Thereupon, this differentiation still serves merely as the surreptitious distraction of be-ing-historical thinking to the extent that be-ing-historical thinking attempts – out of, and through a grounding of this differentiation – to pass itself off as a mere continuation of metaphysical thinking.

But perhaps this interlude of the crossing is necessary in order to experience metaphysics as well as be-ing-historical thinking as the history of be-ing and to raise metaphysics to the level of an inceptual decision.

104. Φύσις and Metaphysics

Only in a rough outline[a] does φύσις names that which we come upon, when we speak of a rising prevailing. Rising is the *revealing* through which the sheltering-unconcealment of what is unconcealed specifically sways besides sheltering-concealing and sheltered-concealment and dissembling.[b]

The revealing in the specific sense mentioned above is undetermined in itself and in its swaying character as an occurrence. Indeed, this revealing offers itself only as sheltering-unconcealment and this immediately as the beingness of beings. This points out that the rising (revealing) lets beings as such rise unto what is sheltered-unconcealed whereby sheltering-unconcealment is the constancy of presencing wherein that comes to word which is called prevailing. This prevailing indicates that a being is drawn into *the sway of revealing*. Consequently this being itself is not only unconcealed, but is also determined in its ownmost by its belongingness to φύσις due to the overabundance of prevailing in φύσις. This belongingness to the revealing constancy of presencing is a '*re-ceiving*', that is, a 'per-ceiving taking-*in*' and a 'fore-having' of what is unconcealed as such. The 'receiving' is in itself simultaneously a gathering into the unity [*Einheit*], which does not at all mean indiscernibility [*Einerlei*] but rather the presencing of that which vis-à-vis itself apparently 'ab-sways' [*ab-west*].

Νοῦς and λόγος determine the belongingness of a being to revealing, a being that seen from the vantage point of φύσις is distinguished by being abundantly prevailed by φύσις. This being knows itself as man who forthwith immediately compares and determines himself exclusively from out of his difference to other beings instead of determining himself from out of his unique [G367] distinction, that is, from that belongingness. That is why "reason", (νοῦς, λόγος, *ratio*) becomes the mark of distinction vis-à-vis the mere animal.[c]

---

[a] If we think right away more comprehensively, then within φύσις we have to think the *sheltering-concealing positioning* (taking root) and the *receding* into constancy along with the rising as the self-spreading presencing. However, given the history of φύσις, we have to say that presencing thrusts οὐσία into preeminence and determines from out of itself the constancy (duration of ὑποκείμενον).

[b] How sheltering-concealment? Cf. the previous footnote.

[c] (What leads to such a determination of "man"?)

However, the φύσις itself – the revealing – lets the unconcealed, that is, beings, emerge, but φύσις *shelters-conceals* itself, which is a hint that revealing arises out of a sheltering-concealing and that the inceptual sway belongs to this sheltering-concealing.

From this we could perhaps gather why together with ἀλήθεια, φύσις itself never attains the brightness of the grounding swaying that is drawn from it and why somehow the uninquired and ungrasped aspects of its sway then degenerate into what becomes decisive determinations of being. The *enowning of revealing* shelters-conceals itself and this with-drawal belongs perhaps to every beginning because only in this way can the beginning retain the abundant prevailing. Until now, we do not have a field of knowing, of experiencing and of saying in order to interpret that enowning out of itself as enowning. Without having any knowing-awareness of the question-worthiness of this enowning of revealing, we defer immediately to explanations of beings in terms of their most general qualities and causes, and in the belief that one is able thus to obtain a knowing-awareness of the "physical", that is, of beings in the broadest sense, we submit to the interpretation of man as *animal rationale*.

The φύειν of φύσις – its 'that' and 'so' – cannot be explained. It cannot be *strictly* explained since in this context every explanation thinks inadequately and above all forgets that in this context what exclusively counts is the decision towards an appropriate relation to the beginning.

And what is this relation? Only those who begin, which means here, only those who prepare a beginning, comport themselves towards a beginning that has already been and whose swaying thus surpasses everything.

Such preparation is a remembering out of mindfulness.

Mindfulness as an inquiry into the dominating sway, respectively into the dominating 'un-sway' of truth, initially hits upon that which we call "metaphysics" because in metaphysics as the history of being itself [G368] a decision comes to an end on the truth of be-ing, respectively an undecidedness on this truth.

Meta-physics does seem simply to surpass all φύσις and to fall out of its sphere of mastery. However, *this surpassing* "beyond" the φύσει ὄντα takes the beings that are determined by φύσις above all as a leap-off and as an orientation. Thus, if to anything at all, the step beyond the φύσει ὄντα continues to refer to φύσις. And thereafter this surpassing goes towards nothing other than the ἀρχή of φύσει ὄντα. *Meta-physics searches for nothing other than φύσις.* And at the end metaphysics thinks φύσις exclusively as οὐσία in order to justify the φύσει ὄντα and to secure them by dwelling among the beings that are uncovered and explained 'in the whole'. Meta-physics unfolds and joins the sheltered-unconcealment of beings, and the joining (jointure) consists of the fact that what is present becomes specifically experienceable out of the presencing of "what is there from the first" as such (ἀρχή) and out of the presencing of the εἶδος as such; that is, what is present becomes specifically experienceable as what is constant and distant in itself and always properly differentiated – separated – from everything, and is placed in different places and so 'makes room' for "beings" within the sphere of being. Metaphysics *is* and brings about this 'making room' for beings in the sphere of being without experiencing the "space of this sphere" itself and mastering it in its sway.

Metaphysics is the jointure of revealing beings as such, that is, revealing what is sheltered-unconcealed whose sheltered-unconcealment determines itself as beingness in the sense of constancy of presencing – determines itself as beingness without any inquiry into, and knowing-awareness of, the 'time-space-character' of being and its truth.

If we say that metaphysics and only metaphysics confirms φύσις and ultimately transforms its predominance into the unrecognizableness of machination, in short if we say that metaphysics is the actual *"physics"* as the knowledge of φύσις in the sense of the being of beings and if we grasp φύσις as the counter-ground vis-à-vis the enduring τέχνη and its rebuilding into "technicity", then with φύσις we do not mean what was later called "nature" or even "the sensible", but mean rather the inceptual sense of rising [G369] prevailing that has nothing in common with the "nature" and the sensible just as little as it has anything in common with the "supernatural" and "spirit" and "super-sensible".

But as long as we leave φύσις to these downgrading assessments and obtain it only in abstraction as "nature" in opposition to "history" and to "spirit" and "god"; as long as we do not see that precisely *that which* is supposed to be grasped by these concepts owes its swaying origin solely to φύσις; so long do we think φύσις too supplementarily and superficially and *do not* think "metaphysics" as the jointure of the history of being. And as long as such opinion sets the measure, the overcoming of metaphysics will be subjected to the same assessment.

All these confirm *being's abandonment* of beings.

105. The "Shape" and the Φύσις

The "shape" is not an "optical" "phenomenon": metaphysically it indicates 'being-set-unto itself', it means arising into pure presencing. Therefore, it is not enough, indeed it is even strictly inadequate, to lead the Greek thinking of beings (εἶδος, ἰδέα) back to the "optical".

Rather, the "optical," *as* what is abstracted, *as* what comes to a halt, *as* what is encounterable by an added perceiving, has this distinction because it suits best the sway of φύσις.

The distinction of the countenance (ἰδεῖν, ἰδέα) as well as the formation of θεωρεῖν come later, although they are in accord with ἐόν. Without referring the perceiving and the gathering to the senses, νοεῖν and λόγος by contrast accomplish more cogently the perceiving and the gathering that make present.

The Greeks emphasize the "optical" because they think being as φύσις. However, as little as "senses as instruments" by themselves can posit anything about the sway of *being*, just as little does thinking being as φύσις come about because the Greeks are "visually oriented people".

[G370]   ## 106. Being as Φύσις

To think *being* in the sense of φύσις means something other than experiencing φύσις (as being) for we can do away with this "as being" because φύσις itself abundantly dominates "everything", that is 'beings in the whole' all the while as φύσις shows itself as the most-being.

It is only in be-ing-historical thinking that already looks ahead into the temporal-spatiality as the domain of projecting-opening metaphysics that φύσις becomes knowable in its sway 'as akin to be-ing' [*seynshaft*].

One can ascertain 'historically' – although pretty deficiently – that in Greek thinking the concept of φύσις had a decisive meaning. But that is never enough for enacting the *historical* mindfulness that shows that φύσις – ἀλήθεια – determined "thinking" into philosophy as "metaphysics". For even there, and above all there where φύσις is not named, it is still thought, especially it is thought there where φύσις has branched out – though not arbitrarily – into a multiplicity of meanings, each of which conceals rather than unveils a significant phase of "metaphysics" (cf. Aristotle, *Metaphysics* Δ 4).

In view of the manner of the swaying of being that is allotted to this thinking, and indeed in view of its en-ownedness by being itself, this thinking of being as φύσις requires already *the thinking of being itself*. By contrast, representing φύσις as beingness of beings unto beings thinks always already from beings and persists within the horizon of metaphysics. That thinking of being that 'thinks being as' . . . thinks from out of the history of being. That is why be-ing-historical thinking, as soon as it discusses metaphysics, remains ambiguous and doubly formed: in one respect be-ing-historical thinking thinks "more" than metaphysics (thinks differently and other than metaphysics), and in another respect, and for this reason, this thinking simply no longer thinks "metaphysically" in the sense of a deliberated metaphysics because, without even knowing a limit, be-ing-historical thinking can no longer shut itself within the horizon of the basic stance of metaphysics and limit itself to this horizon.

[G371] Historical mindfulness transforms history and must also know this transformation in order to retain thus its ownmost unblendedness.

107. How Φύσις Fosters What is Later Called "Metaphysics"

Φύσις as rising presencing lets beings as such "be". Out of its sway, φύσις shapes beings into what is constantly present and hence, given how the access to beings is experienced (through re-presenting producing), φύσις shapes them into 'what is extant', 'what lies-before', 'what is laid back unto itself' and is 'lain', – in short, ὑποκείμενον.

Φύσις as rising presencing bears itself unto its openness that is opened by φύσις and distinguished by φύσις. It thus renders beings *differentiable* among themselves – beings that are 'in this' or 'in that way', respectively, are 'there' and are 'then', and thereby are simply differentiable vis-à-vis being. Forthwith, *this differentiation* has the marks of being, that is, what comes before beings and is in this way common to all beings (κοινόν) – γένος as such – : is being*ness*.

The projecting-opening of beings upon beingness (as representing projecting-open) already claims the sheltering-unconcealment of being, claims the latter itself as revealing without knowing further the sway of this revealing.

This projecting-opening that belongs to being itself and owes itself unknowingly to being, makes up the basic jointure wherein beings as such are held, that is, wherein they "*are*".

This basic jointure is 'owned-over-to' representing, and such a representing – setting out from beings and knowing itself in view of beings – then experiences itself as the thinking of that which is not intended in the knowing of beings themselves, but which rather lies "beyond" beings, and yet thereby proves itself to be what comes before beings insofar as being, the presencing, is thought in view of its constancy. Being is always already what endures [*bestehend*] and is thus the constant *and* the most constant [G372] as such: in this way being is the foremost presencing. This thinking thinks τὰ μετὰ τὰ φυσικά, it "is" metaphysical, it "is" metaphysics.

Metaphysics is the jointure of the openness that is opened by φύσις for itself. In this jointure being itself has become a differentiable component and, as it were, it can be represented specifically along with beings, although it is differentiable from them.

Thereupon, "metaphysics" will be taken even exclusively as the representation of this jointure, as the enactment of the projecting-open, indeed as the presentation and statement of this representation, that is, as *theory* and *doctrine*.

Conversely, being then becomes an *object* of metaphysics vis-à-vis which beings appear to be "more being" in which case "being" will still, to some extent, prove to have the superior right as the "cause" and the condition that come before representing.

108. Metaphysics[*]

(Thought be-ing-historically), metaphysics is the jointure of revealing of beings unto their sheltered-unconcealed sway, which, when projected-open as beingness, is grasped in the sense of the constancy of presencing without the knowing-awareness of the time-character of this constancy of presencing.[a]

By bracing this jointure, beings *as* such can be represented whereby right away and without an express grounding beings are represented

---

[*] Cf. 97. The Be-ing-historical Thinking and the Question of Being.
[a] Constancy of presencing completes itself in the arrangement and enactment of the sway of power as machination. "Technicity" as the truth of beings in their beingness.

specifically in their 'being-what' and 'being-that',[b] [G373] and correspondingly projected-open unto γένος κοινότατον (later *ens commune*) and unto the first αἰτία (later *Deus creator*). Both make possible the study of ὄν ᾗ ὄν ἁπλῶς (οὐ κατὰ μέρος τι) and distinguish this study as πρώτη φιλοσοφία. Insofar as the ἀρχή of ὄν ᾗ ὄν ἁπλῶς could be called θεῖον (θεῖον is in this way interpretable as what always presences beforehand), the πρώτη φιλοσοφία in itself becomes ἐπιστήμη θεολογική. In itself this "theology" is what will later be called "ontology" and, on the ground of the Christian experiences of beings as *ens creatum*, complemented and explained by the *theologia rationalis*. For Aristotle, ἐπιστήμη θεολογική is the noblest of the "theoretical" forms of knowledge (such as ἐπιστήμη μαθηματική and φυσική), and, together with these, differentiates itself immediately from all ἐπιστήμη ποιητική and πρακτική. This determines in advance the basic thrusts of the history of Occidental metaphysics.

Aristotle's πρώτη φιλοσοφία should neither be grasped as "ontology" in the later sense nor be passed off as *theologia rationalis* in the sense of a specific discipline of *metaphysica specialis*. The πρώτη φιλοσοφία lies *before* this differentiation and is *in itself* θεολογική (ἐπιστήμη). What was later to become "ontological" is not yet set aside into the most general representations and "concepts", and what was later to become "theological" is not yet confined to the "divinity" of a creator god. Rather, the determinations of ὄν ᾗ ὄν according to its φύσις (cf. Aristotle's Met. Γ 1) and according to the first αἰτία, that is, the ἀρχή, *agree* in the specific Greek style with the one presencing of the 'foremost constant' that already beforehand bestows upon all the respective individuals and beings "the outward appearance" of a being and thus preserves itself also in its own completion because it is the "beginning" in the sense of the "first, from where comes" all presencing.[c]

(The question towards which some of the early interpretations of Aristotle still tended, namely, in which sense the πρώτη φιλοσοφία could immediately unite in itself both "ontology" and "theology" [G374] is, as a *question*, already *not* a Greek question. Nevertheless, mindfulness of the *"theological"* character of πρώτη φιλοσοφία remains a necessity. The onto-theology of the modern metaphysics in Kant, Schelling, Hegel and

---

[b] The origin of 'what' and 'that' from out of the differentiation of beings *as such* and 'beings *in the whole*'. This differentiation itself is *ungrounded*. 'What' and 'That' as difference in the presencing and constancy.

[c] πρῶτον, ὅθεν – rising.

Nietzsche becomes graspable and in its ground assailable only out of the πρώτη φιλοσοφία. The θεολογικὴ ἐπιστήμη is not "theological" in the Judeo-Christian sense, but *metaphysical*", that is, is determined in the *Greek* style of thinking.)

What is represented in the knowledge of ὄν ᾗ ὄν ἁπλῶς (not κατὰ μέρος) is χωριστόν (οὐ μετὰ τῆς ὕλης) and ἀκίνητον.

With the absencing of everything changeable, that is, everything that is referred to such and such outward appearance, χωριστόν means the pure presencing of outward appearance and *presencing* in this appearance as such.

The ἀκίνητον means that which is free of turning over (μεταβολή), that which is exempted from change; it means *pure constancy*.[d]

The constancy of presencing (as the sway of being) can still be expressed metaphysically as ἀεὶ ὄν[e], the *nunc stans*, the now that stays still and is constant (i.e., present = presence). Thus from out of the sway of the so-grasped beingness, "eternity" claims to be *a*, indeed becomes *the* basic measure of the metaphysical determination of beings. In unison with the guiding-projecting-opening unto the ἀρχή (i.e., the 'first' which presences forth prior to everything), that thinking arises that takes the direction of the 'un-conditioned' and thus the direction of the 'conditions of the possibility'. In this vein, the ultimately possible "eternal" can only be the "eternal return of the same".

Inceptually, the φύσις as being (especially as 'beings in the whole') is the most-being. With the completion of this beginning, *beings* (abandoned by being) become the most-being and, as it were, a substitute for being – provided that a substitute for the most transitory, for the last vapor of an evaporating reality, is still needed.

Both the beginning as well as the end of metaphysics, in different ways and because of different reasons, miss the differentiation between [G375] being and beings. But even in the course of the history of metaphysics where this differentiation becomes more clear it lacks any justification: it is indeed already *the* joining in the jointure of metaphysics that for the first time makes possible the metaphysically representable ἀρχαί, αἴτια, *principia*, grounds, causes, conditions and values and makes necessary the historical transformation of the basic stances of metaphysics.

---

[d] The casting as such, i.e., sheltered-unconcealment and beingness.
[e] But in the Greeks' style of thinking, the ἀεὶ as "that which always endures" has the character of presencing.

Although metaphysics inquires into being in a certain way in order thus to respond to the *question put by beings* as to what they are, metaphysics does not measure up to the thinking that strictly preserves being, and is thoroughly attuned to 'beings in the whole'.

Because by entrusting itself to beings metaphysics must renounce the knowing-awareness of be-ing, it can never by itself accomplish the grounding of Da-*sein*, that is, that which vouches for the en-ownment of the truth of be-ing unto beings. To this grounding belongs as the foremost contribution of man, magnanimity and forbearance, which equally decisively renounce "life's interests" and "eternal bliss" as measures for pursuing and judging beings.

As long as metaphysics holds power among beings and as long as this power has solidified itself in the off-shoots and imitations of metaphysics, that is, in the Christian and anti-Christian "world-views", be-ing is denied the dissemination into the 'nothing' of the 'free-play of the time-space' of a history – into the 'nothing' that arises out of be-ing and sways only from out of be-ing.

109. "What is Metaphysics?"[*]

The lecture *"Was ist Metaphysik?"* ['What is Metaphysics?'] which maintains itself in an explicitly limited, yet strictly modern, "perspective" insofar as it inquires from a modern basic form of relating to beings as such, that is, *sciences* [G376], goes already beyond metaphysics as the determination of beingness of beings. And yet, this lecture designates this 'going beyond' and the so-attained positioning of the inquiry simply as the actual metaphysics, so to speak as the *meta-metaphysics*.

This lecture preserves the historical tradition for a rigorous dissociating exposition, and without *specifically* naming Da-sein but with a view towards Da-sein this lecture simultaneously indicates something else, namely the question concerning the truth of be-ing. None of the things that is said in this regard, namely the "nothing", the "dread", the "logic", the 'preeminence of attunement', is *by itself* thematically significant as far as the content is concerned. What alone is singularly decisive is the *experience* of that which is *not* a being and cannot be a being and yet above all raises beings *as* beings unto the openness of its sway.

---

[1] Lecture of 1929 in *Wegmarken*, GA 9, pp. 103–22.

In this lecture two "propositions" of metaphysics are mentioned without unfolding them (be-ing-historically) in their ownmost question-worthiness:

1. *Being and 'nothing' are the same.*

   Following the guiding-thread of the projecting-open that represents beingness as objectness, here "nothing" is understood in the Hegelian, that is, metaphysical sense. In the same vein being is also understood as the most empty and the "most general", the κοινόν, the most extended framework of beingness. By contrast, this lecture thinks the *nihilating* 'nothing' as what arises from the swaying of be-ing as *refusal* (from enownment unto sheltering-concealing). *Negation* arises only from out of refusal.

2. 'Why are there beings at all and not rather 'nothing'?' (Cf. above G 267; see *Einführung in die Metaphysik*, the lecture-course of summer semester of 1935.*)

   a) When thought metaphysically, the inquiry here is into the *cause* through which beings are brought about [*beigestellt*] while 'nothing', as it were, is simultaneously eliminated and suppressed. Here, beings are grasped as [G377] representable and producible and 'nothing' as the negation of 'beings in the whole'.

   b) When inquired be-ing-historically, the question 'why are there beings at all and not rather 'nothing'?' means: on what ground do beings then obtain preeminence so that being just becomes a supplement; on what ground is the swaying of 'nothing' over-powered – 'nothing' understood in terms of its belongingness to be-ing as its ab-ground? (Response: because being's abandonment of beings has let beings loose unto the predominance of machination. And what is this? Cf. enowning).

Although not mastered in the least, the ambiguity of these propositions is intentionally articulated in connection with the ambiguity that the concept of metaphysics has within the crossing, that is, the ambiguity of the concept which as the title for the question of being inquires either only into the beingness of beings or into the truth of be-ing.

---

* See *Einführung in die Metaphysik*, lecture-course given in Freiburg in the summer semester 1935, GA 40, p. 3 ff.

(The Kant-book* is meant to show that *in a certain* way Kant is thrust into the sphere of the truth of be-ing, but shrinks back from it and does not know the question that belongs to the truth of be-ing and cannot know that question within the basic stance of metaphysics as such.

The interpretation of Kant's transcendental philosophy with a view to "schematism" and "the power of imagination" *exaggerates* deliberately in order to show that already *within* the history of metaphysics itself there is the necessity of a rigorous transformation of the question of metaphysics. That attempt is least interested in supplying the 'historical' Kant, "as he has been". Therefore, one can imperturbably go on to prove the inaccuracy of that attempt. But in this way one proves only one's inability to think-through rigorously the question of *being*.)

The lecture *"Was ist Metaphysik?"* and the book *Kant und das Problem der Metaphysik* not only originated at the same time, but also belong together as attempts at making discernible the meta-metaphysics from out of metaphysics and thus to clarify the question that *Sein und Zeit* raises for the first time.

[G378]   110. Aristotle, *Metaphysics* Δ 4 on Φύσις

In accord with the position that he occupies at the end of the first beginning, Aristotle grasps φύσις early on decisively as οὐσία τις, as *a kind* of beingness. This is to say that, in the meantime, being has consolidated itself (via ἰδέα) specifically as beingness, while conversely in truth, that is, according to the sway of being and not somehow only with respect to the course of knowledge, οὐσία φύσις τις determines φύσις for the representing projecting-open – indeed at the end by Aristotle – as ἐντελέχεια, that is, as a certain manner of sheltering-concealing prevailing that remains undifferentiated in relation to beings.

In [*Met.*] Δ 4, 1015 a 12 sq. Aristotle subordinates φύσις according to its swaying origin to οὐσία (to being), while still in the decisive unfolding of πρώτη φιλοσοφία in *Met.* Γ 1, 1003 a 26 sq. he says specifically that the ἀρχαί necessarily belong to a φύσις τις as such, which means that the basic determinations of beingness are those of the φύσις, and that οὐσία is subordinated to φύσις.

---

* See *Kant und das Problem der Metaphysik*, GA 3.

Here, in any case according to *the* perspective that inheres in φύσις, its basic sway still shines through: the presence that by itself presences forth ahead of everything – the presence that makes up all presencing as such. However, νοεῖν and λόγος understood as 'gathering taking-in' (i.e., making present) of the prevailing rising are now no longer the only measure for the relation to being and beings. Rather, the ποιούμενον of the ποίησις, the πρακτόν of the προαίρεσις, enter explicitly into the purview of the determination of being and correspondingly form the φύσει ὄντα indeed as *a* distinguished sphere of beings. But to the extent that being presences in its sway in all manner of ways, the representation of being as φύσις in the broadest sense is retained, although in a blurred way:

1. a) φύσις as γένσις – *arising* – taking place, coming forth (out of the root), erecting into the open *of plants*, of *that which grows* – (φύεσθαι) (the distinguished [G379] relation between *plants* and φύσις – blooming of the rose).

    b) the *'from where'* of this arising as *'from the first'* – *that which comes forth* and erects itself, that which *already constantly presences* "in the" *arising*.

    (b) the *'what'* and (a) the *'how'*. What doubling goes on here already?

2. The *'from where'* of the actual motion – of that which is constant *by itself*. (*Motion* as *the pesencing* of *the not yet of the already* as such; *presencing*).

    "Growing" (a) as *gaining* – *multiplying* (number "grows") through mere piecing together (ἁφή –); nothing else is needed here than the contact, that is, the joining of the one to the other. *That which is joined together* is *not the one and the same in itself* that in advance makes itself into things that belong together.

    "Growing" (b) as growing-together – as *over growing*. To be one *in holding together, in 'this manner,' and 'this much'*.

111. Φύσις and Metaphysics

In accordance with its historical sway, *meta-physics* – to which the word metaphysics itself with its strange origination still directly refers – is to be understood as a grasping of φύσις.

However, in accord with what is to be grasped (the constancy of presencing – the rising of what prevails), this grasping is a θεωρεῖν that takes being itself into view, that is, lets being presence as ἀρχή of beings whereby ἀρχή stands for that from where what is rising arises; and that is rising itself *as rising* (cf. the fragment of Anaximander!).

Yet, the 'rising' presencing is emerging into the enopened openness, it is in itself *un-concealing*, is unconcealment. That which all metaphysics tries to and must see is the "truth" – truth as the first and last name of being, yet truth as un-grounded because it is initially thought as *the* ἀρχή.

[G380]   112. Φύσις and Ἀλήθεια

The question concerning the truth in the inceptual sense of unconcealment is not at all raised in the beginning, because unconcealment is a basic naming of φύσις itself, the name for the being of beings.

After the inceptual interpretation of beingness had consolidated itself, for the first time the question of truth becomes a question concerning the nature of knowledge.

But before that, the fundamental interconnection between beingness (ἰδέα) and truth (ἀλήθεια) is thought through once again (cf. Plato's simile of the cave), but at the same time already in the transition to the transformation of ἀλήθεια into conformity and correctness. But be-ing-historically, truth should not be thought as a characteristic of "knowing". Rather, knowing itself and its relation to "truth" must be grasped as grounded in the sway of truth whereby inceptually (in the another beginning) truth raises itself into the sway of the clearing of be-ing.

113. Ἀλήθεια–Ἀτρέκεια

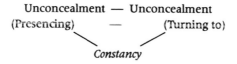

Unconcealment — Unconcealment
(Presencing)   —   (Turning to)
                    Constancy

Without hesitation we take the ἀτρεκές – the unconcealed – as that which simply lies in a 'direction' and thus leave the fundamental content unrecognized again.

The unconcealed is what is not distorted, is what is not twisted over, is what is not reversed and thus does not turn to the 'reverse side', but rather turns away from the 'reverse side': shows the right side.

[G381] Again, what is important here is the undisplaced, undistorted emerging in itself of what presences, that is, the emerging of what maintains itself fully in its ownmost, that is, in the presencing of its 'what' (the turning unto).

Via thinking back from here, the sway of the ψεῦδος is to be grasped.

Why are both [ἀλήθεια–ἀτρέκεια] inceptually ungroundable? The indication of ἀ-.

114. Metaphysics

Being: the rising – *the prevailing self-showing, presencing and unconcealing.*
The gatheredness (λόγος) unto the "one"; here, onefold is the unconcealing and self-sheltering-concealing presencing.[a]
The receivedness (νοεῖν) – presencing in the representedness.
Having-been-sighted (ἰδέα) sightableness.
That which maintains itself in the completion (τέλος) – *finishedness* (ἔργον, ἐντελέχεια, ἐνέργεια).
The most-being – as the first cause of all beings (*creator, actus purus*).[b]
The representedness (monas?) as what is thought in certainty (verum–certum).[c]
Objectness of the object (objectivity of the object).
The unconditioned objectness of the self-showing rationality.
Consolidating, securing the stock of what becomes and [G382] nothing else and thus the last smoke of an evaporating reality.[d]
The encompassing.

Metaphysics

Metaphysics is thought here in a strict sense. It is *never* understood as a doctrine or as a philosophical "discipline", or as a form of knowledge and

---

[a] Presencing from out of the rising unto retroceding: presence and constancy.
[b] Everything Greek is *blocked* by what is Roman; to what extent are we *prepared* by this?
[c] The metaphysics of modernity—*subjectum*.
[d] Cf. "Nietzsche-Essay" (Nietzsches Wort "Gott ist tot", *Holzwege*, GA 5, pp. 209–67).

the like. Rather, it is understood as the jointure of beings *as such* to 'beings in the whole' itself, that is, to what is enjoined through beingness and through what is uninquired in the truth of be-ing whose utmost is being's abandonment of beings.

Obviously, one has to speak peripherally so that "metaphysics" often enters the purview as a doctrine. However, such a "metaphysics" is a consequence of, and a deviation from, metaphysics as the jointure of beings out of their beingness. And this jointure arises out of the mastery of be-ing and the en-opening of this mastery on whose swaying ground is based all history as the enduring as well as the not enduring of the truth of be-ing.

"Metaphysics" as *the* Occidental-historical jointure of beings – wherein beings in the specific sense of the constancy of presencing as such enter in the ungrounded openness – ultimately peters out into what is known as "world-view". Reflecting its sway (being's abandonment), "metaphysics" is not master of its sway.

Metaphysics is the truth of 'beings as such in the whole' that holds back any grounding of the truth of be-ing out of be-ing – the whole that according to the unleashing of beings that is specific to such truth (openness as sheltering-unconcealment) gives beings preeminence over being.

[G383]   115. Metaphysics

Metaphysics commences with the Platonic differentiation between ὄντως ὄν and μὴ ὄν. But this commencing is only the consequence of the beginning of the Occidental thinking that en-thinks beings as φύσις–ἀλήθεια – without simultaneously being able to ground the truth of this projecting-open as such. (This inability is to be understood from out of the "greatness" of the inceptuality of thinking: ἀλήθεια and beingness itself are consolidated along with this inceptuality. And thereupon what remains as truth specifically for thinking becomes ὁμοίωσις and correctness.)

Metaphysics *begins* covertly with the beginning of Occidental thinking, and yet *commences* only with the first completion of this beginning in Plato and Aristotle. In *the* manner in which the pre-Platonic philosophy prepares the interpretation of beingness as ἰδέα as well as that differentiation, pre-Platonic philosophy is in a certain way pre-metaphysical. ("Metaphysics" thought be-ing-historically as the jointure of 'beings in the whole', and not as a "doctrine".)

Metaphysics begins through the rising of *being* as the rising prevailing. But in a certain way, being is here not differentiated (not *yet*) from beings; being as presencing is the most present (ὄντως) and thus the most-being and accordingly being is itself of the kind of beings, respectively beings are of the "kind" of being. The word kind here indicates "lineage", and provenance, whereby the sway of what beforehand and primarily presences already lies in the provenant.

The beginning and the commencement of metaphysics do not coincide, just as little as "completion" (the "end") and termination.

Metaphysics commences only where the differentiation between being as κοινόν (of beingness) and beings as ἕκαστον becomes the jointure of representation (becomes the manner in which, without further pondering, all comportment to beings as such submits and "enjoins" itself beforehand). Socrates – Plato put this *commencement* in place. Hegel concludes the history of metaphysics that commences in this manner [G384] by immediately transferring this *termination* into completion. For it lies in the sway of "absolute idea" that in a certain way it *retracts* the differentiation between "being" and beings. On the one hand, the differentiation is preserved because in metaphysics it is and could never be inquired into and grounded as such. On the other hand, the differentiation is effaced. In the epoch of the completion of metaphysics (when all possibilities of the ontological interpretation of beingness such as 'being', 'becoming', 'thought', 'ought', 'value', and 'appearing' fall together into the *one and only* "chaos", "that is life", and when these possibilities are confirmed in conformity with the chaos, and are rendered constant as the uninterruptable presence, that is, as 'the eternal return of the same'), and when along with the true world *even* the apparent one is abolished, then the differentiation is no longer fundamental as jointure. That which by virtue of the simple mastery of the awesomeness of φύσις was *not yet* needed to become differentiable in the beginning, is *no* longer differentiated in the completion. And Nietzsche's chaos can never count somehow as the regainment of φύσις, just as little as the completion of the beginning is the beginning itself, even though the completion indeed belongs to the beginning. But between Plato and Hegel the metaphysics and its history that specifically lead out into the jointure also determine for '*history*' the interpretation of the pre-Platonic and post-Hegelian philosophies. Metaphysics views itself and its history within the horizon of its jointure and as the transformation of it. By contrast, be-ing-historically the beginning is not a preform of what comes later, rather what comes latter is a declining formation of the beginning. That Nietzsche himself grasps his philosophy as the reversal of Platonism is justified historically only insofar as the horizon of metaphysics can guide the self-interpretation of philosophy. But this Nietzschean self-interpretation is not definitive because in the end the reversal compels Nietzsche to turn out of Platonism and thus out of the *commencement* of metaphysics. Hence Nietzsche can be understood only from out of the beginning of metaphysics as the completion of this beginning and that *not* because [G385] he had held the pre-Platonic philosophy in particularly high regard (after all, he took this philosophy in its *purely Platonic* interpretation: he saw in Heraclitus the "becoming", in Parmenides the "being".) It is not "Heraclitism" that brings Nietzsche into a historically foundational relation to the beginning, but that thinking according to which the *inquiry* into the *being* of beings disappears in the unlimited predominance of 'beings in the whole', understood as the "life" that renders itself constant and confirms itself, a life that is unassessable by any "value" but is only liveable. However, because in Nietzsche's thinking all basic positions of explicit metaphysics and its history come together in a transformed and blurred way, it is tempting simply calculatively to include his "metaphysics" in the hitherto instead of grasping that this metaphysics is an "end" because it entrenches the questionlessness of "being" – instead of grasping how this metaphysics accomplishes this entrenching. At any rate, this can only be grasped be-ing-historically out of an overcoming of "metaphysics" as such in the whole of its history.

116. "Ontology"–"Metaphysics"

Throughout the preceding endeavours the only task has been to unfold the *question of being*, indeed unfold it straightaway in the entirely different sense of inquiring into the *truth of be-ing*. In this way not only the "theme" and the "procedure" get transformed but also above all what is ownmost to man and the truth of beings themselves and thereby already the manner of saying and grounding.

But because the question of being is since long ago always *the* question of philosophy – since its first beginning – and because the question of being has since then become exclusively the inquiry into the beingness of beings, and because subsequently the Scholastics have characterized this question as "ontology"–"metaphysics", it was suggestive, nay even unavoidable to designate as "ontology" and "metaphysics" the *entirely other* question of being which does not push aside but grounds the first one all the more [G386] decisively.

However, by adopting the traditional title of the question of being for an inquiry into an entirely different kind of being, the unfolding of this inquiry through the employment of this title had obscured the very intention of this inquiry.

Thus in the lecture *"Was ist Metaphysik?"** the question of being is answered with reference to something that is indeed entirely different from *metaphysics* insofar as the latter is grasped strictly historically as that inquiry into the being of beings that can neither master the question of the truth of being nor be urged to raise this question. The lecture *"Was ist Metaphysik?"* calls "metaphysics" that which is never ever "metaphysics".

The projecting-opening en-grounding of *Da-sein* as the historical ground of the clearing of be-ing penetrates into a realm that did not "exist" up to now and can be enowned into a history only by be-ing itself insofar as *be-ing itself* enters its clearing. This "Da-sein" sways outside *the* jointure which as metaphysics has enjoined beingness of 'beings in the whole' and made it accessible to the hitherto Occidental history.

Therefore, it is impossible to speak of a "metaphysics of Da-sein" as is done in the Kant-book,** although it is indicated there that "metaphysics" (namely what is understood by this word in the above-mentioned lecture) grounds in Da-sein and belongs to Da-sein and only to it.

The same holds true of the titles "ontology" and "transcendence" in the treatise *Vom Wesen des Grundes*.***

By adopting the traditional leading titles, something entirely different is meant, so different that it simply overcomes what was formerly rightly designated with those titles. There, the overcoming [G387] of metaphysics – metaphysics understood in the foundational sense of that jointure – is still passed off as "metaphysics" but indeed "by word only" and never according to the "matter at hand" and the posture of questioning.

The title "ontology" is adopted as the title for the question of being, but the question of being in the sense of ontology is simply overcome. What "ontology" (the inquiry into being) means in *Sein und Zeit* is not determined by the title "ontology". Rather, this title has to consent to a different interpretation – one that actually runs ahead to meet this title,

---

* See *Wegmarken*, GA 9, pp. 103–22.
** *Kant und das Problem der Metaphysik*, GA 3, p. 218 ff.
*** See *Wegmarken*, GA 9, pp. 123–75.

one that steps entirely out of the range of meaning of this title. The name "fundamental ontology" is the expedient that indicates this.

This dubious procedure is initially unavoidable, specifically since what always counts is not to eliminate "metaphysics", that is, the inceptual question of being, but in and through metaphysics to allude to what is entirely different from metaphysics. When one does *not* follow *this* directive and instead brings along and uses as a measure all the rigidified metaphysical thinking, then everything becomes confusing specifically given the fact that this directive in truth has nothing to do with modification of disciplines, but with the en-ownment of man unto the truth of be-ing, an en-ownment that necessitates a particular kind of transformation.

117. Metaphysics

Metaphysics inquires into ὄν ἧ ὄν, *ens qua ens* (*ens qua tale*), beings as beings.

But at the same time this ἧ, this *qua*, this *as* is *uninquired*. What is named with these words is the direction of projecting-open, is what is open to projecting-open, simply the projecting-open as such. That something like this is and is claimed as ground and as what grounds, metaphysics explains by referring to νοῦς, *ratio*, and reason. To formularize this from the vantage point of metaphysical inquiry, one could say the following. The thinking in the crossing inquires into the swaying of the ἧ, *qua, as* in such a way that this swaying is recognized [G388] as belonging to *be-ing* itself whereby the truth of be-ing becomes what is interrogated. Nevertheless, this inquiry into the sway and ground and necessity of ἧ, *qua, as* is not a supplement and an *addendum* to the metaphysical inquiry, something like its epistemology. Rather, what is indicated here is the turning-point of the decisive transformation of the question of being, and along with this transformation, the destruction of all subjectivity and all determinations of man in the light of *animal rationale*.

All metaphysics thinks in the direction of 'causes', 'grounds' and "principles" that, differently modified, are exhausted in the four divisions that Aristotle established.

In modern thinking the *"ought"* as ground receives a particular pre-eminence and retrogressively twists the Platonic differentiation in such a way that corresponds to the position of man as subject.

The *causa finalis* lies at the background of this emergence of thinking in terms of value, so that – expressed or not – this thinking guides the *final purposiveness* of all reckoning of beings unto beingness.

Thus being is calculated into "causes" and "grounds" and these 'entry lines' of calculation themselves serve only the calculation and planning of beings and become more and more supplementary vis-à-vis beings.

Thus the swaying of be-ing into which no cause or ground is capable of reaching is thoroughly disguised.

118. ὂν ἦ ὄν

ὂν ἦ ὄν and indeed ὂν ἁπλῶς, that is, ὄν simply as ὄν in the whole (not κατὰ μέρος τι) (γένος περιγραψάμενον). The ἦ names *the view of* beings (unto beings themselves, *inasmuch as* beings are beings).

This 'view of' is one that does not 'view-*away*' from beings, but also not merely 'views' something περὶ ὃ πραγματεύεται τὰ ἕκαστα, but rather 'views' beings *as* beings (καθ᾽ αὑτό). Herein [G389] lies the question of beings in view of their pure presencing, that is, presencing already simply determines beingness.

And yet beyond this and in addition to it, there is only now the always determined manner of 'taking a view of' ὂν ἦ ὄν.

Beingness already bespeaks of presencing as such. And this must now be "*theoretically*" 'viewed' in such a way that its ἀρχή itself is experienced as such in the presencing of beingness itself.

Thus in general the 'view of' ἀρχή is the 'view' from 'whence' as that wherein constancy and presencing and consequently also αἴτιον actually come to pass.

The ἀίδιον belongs to the sway of ἀρχή and of αἴτια (αἴτιον) (see Aristotle, Met. E 1, 1026 a 17). But the 'preview' of ἀρχή is indeed already sustained and guided by the projecting-opening unto φύσις – what rises and presences and accordingly is *emerging* – that is, is in itself the presencing unto "*whence*".

Here is the origin of ἰδέα, *as well as* αἰτία in the sense of ontic *explanation*.

Hence, in Aristotle still the allusion in all manner of ways to φύσις τις (Met. Γ 1, E 1, K 7).

Here is the foundational retro-connectedness to the inceptual projecting-opening [but] already *after* going through Plato.

Φύσις – at one time and in general, is where ἀρχὴ ἐν αὑτῷ lies insofar as the ἀρχή is itself the rising unto presencing. Then and in particular φύσις is where ἀρχὴ τῆς κινήσεως means "nature" in its ontic sense. This is so only because φύσις is akin to be-ing. Cf. in Aristotle's *Metaphysic*, Γ 1 φύσις τις; but here also χωριστὸν καὶ ἀκίνητον (οὐ μετὰ τῆς ὕλης!!).

119. The Sway of θεωρία*

The sway of θεωρία is to be determined from out of ποίησις and πρᾶξις by grasping ahead into ἀρχή and ὄν *qua* οὐσία.

[G390] Θεωρία is such producing that lets beings presence in themselves, that is, from out of the ἀρχή that lies within them. What matters is 'putting in place' the constancy of presencing. Thereupon, πρᾶξις, ποίησις and θεωρία as well as the corresponding ἐπιστήμη are differentiated.

Although θεωρία is the supreme manner of relating to beings as such, it is grasped from out of *'putting in place'* and this is initially experienced as *producing* (making) and 'taking-a-*stance*' (dealing). However, θεωρία is *not* a kind of ποίησις and πρᾶξις.

ἐπιστήμη – *obtaining a stance in and as 'putting in place'*.

*

The Sway of Θεωρία
and
Θεολογικὴ Ἐπιστήμη

Θεωρεῖν —the τιμιώτατον ὄν as *θεολογικὴ ἐπιστήμη* unto τὸ θεῖον;
the χωριστόν – ἀκίνητον;
being itself – pure presencing (ἰδέα – ἄνευ ὕλης);
from out of itself – constant – *not* just from out of and in μεταβολή.
Even as πρώτη φιλοσοφία "being" is not taken ontologically in the conceptual modern sense; there is no distinction between *metaphysica generalis* and *specialis*. On the contrary, this distinction is fostered by the Christian way of thinking, whereas for the Greeks they are *one and the same*.

⸱ Cf. Aristotle, *Met.* Γ, E, K; *Eth. Nic.* Z.

[G391]   120. Metaphysics

Metaphysics: the interconnection between determination of ὄν ᾗ ὄν
(κοινόν) and θεολογικὴ ἐπιστήμη; *ens commune* – → 'being-what' [*Wassein*]
in the most general way – καθόλου; *summum ens* – → 'being-that' [*Daßsein*]
in 'what is from the first' – αἰτία. Each time ἀρχή.

Here the *Christian* severance is already at work in order to rescue
beforehand the person of the creator god! Therefore, ὄν ᾗ ὄν is purely
"conceptual", respectively is undetermined and then nevertheless
returned to god, the Τεχνίτης.

In other words, here [ὄν ᾗ ὄν] is "thought" according to dogma and faith
and not in the Greek style from out of the experience of beings as such.

*

Metaphysics

The *overshadowing* of being by beings as such is only possible when being is
already allocated into the foremost truth, that is, into rising – into φύσις.

Whence this *overshadowing* – the ungroundedness of the truth of being,
the not-being-able to know the truth in its sway as the truth of being?

The consequence of the *overshadowing*: being as the 'later addition'; the
most precise grasping of this '*additionality*' as "a priori". Here, *the impression
of 'what is reversed'*, namely the impression of '*what pre-cedes*'. But the
'pre-cededness' is not mastered, because its truth is not considered
question-worthy.

Thought be-ing-historically, 'pre-cededness' is an echo of the ab-
ground of the clearing that sways already beforehand and yet *at first*
remains unrepresentable because it cannot be re-presented at all.

In metaphysics, "being" always means '*beings* in the whole'. In metaphysics "being" is never said from out of the *truth of be-ing*.

[G392]   121. Metaphysics

Either metaphysics must take being as beingness *straightaway* as ἰδέα – the
most-being of beings which later proves to be the emptiest and the most
general that belong to beings – on account of which then *beings* are called
upon in order to cover up the vulnerability while the filling-up of the

'formal' with the 'content' [*die materiale*] rectifies the damage of abstraction, *or* metaphysics must take being as beingness *retro-related* to man as the subject which as the unconditioned is what conditions the objectness and constitutedness and this unconditionedness itself is the most-being (Hegel).

All metaphysical thinking then wavers back and forth between both possibilities and looks for ways out in order to avoid being becoming either a thing or a mere subjective contrivance. But basically, being remains always both, which is to say, that no sooner are beings locked in the constancy of presencing than they have the predominance and render questionless beingness as machination.

In all metaphysics, being is determined from out of the receiving of beings as such by reason and from out of the thinking that is understood in terms of reason. Historically and objectively this gives rise to the actual concept of metaphysics. Being is always grasped in the direction of beings, even where, on the basis of the un-conditionedness of thinking – as in Hegel's unconditioned thinking – seemingly an absolute detachedness from beings is obtained. Taking the shape of a renunciation, this "detachedness" nevertheless remains at the beck and call of beings in the constant necessity of renunciation, which renunciation coheres in the unconditionedness of thinking without, of course, being included and being includable into the "system" of this thinking. This is true, too, even where, reversing the course, all "being" is swallowed up into 'becoming', that is, into that which beings actually are, as *in* Nietzsche, that is, in a counter-play to the preceding Hegelian completion of metaphysics.

[G393]   122. How Metaphysics Thinks Being

Metaphysics must think being as beingness, it must take the presencing and its constancy itself as the most constant. In this vein the later objectification of being as the 'pre-ceded' is decided; being itself becomes the same as objectness.

All this means that being remains without clearing; turns into 'what is there first', into the utmost, into the 'encompassing', into the extant that in all manner of ways towers over everything, remains entirely without dimensions, is unlit, and set aside, or what says the same, turns into that which pervades everything as the most-present.

That is why being is also the unquestioned; there is nothing "about" being to be inquired into. That is why being is entangled in the emptiest concept; that is why being is still just a mere hollow word that as what is *effective* is cast off by and rubbed off beings. And the *effective* raves in the abandonment by being.

*

How Metaphysics Takes Beings

Metaphysics takes beings as the explainable out of 'what has pre-ceded' and thus as what is present and as such arises out of what is already present before what is present and as present is present *for* a receiving and *for* a renewed 'putting in place', for a manufacturing.

The ὄν as πρᾶγμα of the πρᾶξις; ἔκαστον of ποίησις – πρᾶξις – θεωρία – grasped from out of *'putting in place'*!

The *ens* as *ens creatum*.

The *res* as *objectum* of *repraesentatio*.

The *thing* of a conditionedness by the conditions of the unconditioned.

The *object* as presencing in representedness.

The *actual* in an effectiveness.

*

[G394] What becomes of beings and their beingness, when such a projecting-opening of 'what has pre-ceded' becomes null and void for receiving and explaining, because such a projecting-opening already and incessantly evades be-ing and its truth?

123. In-finitude and Eternity

In-finitude and eternity are the measure and the goals of metaphysics. And with these two the "finite" as what is extant and un-finished becomes important. However, the *be-ing-historical* emphasis on "finitude" signifies something different, which indeed will be said more appropriately outside this metaphysical opposition and its unity.

The emphasis on "finitude" was merely a preventive attempt that was articulated in the language of metaphysics in order to overcome the ἀεί in the sense of 'making presencing constant' – an overcoming not in favor of a "temporality" in the Christian sense and therefore also not intended as a superfluous rejection of the Christian "eternity".

'Making presencing constant' is *the* metaphysical concept of being. The 'leaping into' the "finitude" is grasping the truth of be-ing wherein the sway of be-ing lights up from out of its ground that is held unto ab-ground. The "being" that is solely known by metaphysics is, as the constancy of presencing, still in itself an ungrounded excerption [*Herausnahme*] of *one* foundational moment of being, that is, of 'rendering presentness' which is not even grasped in its swaying as "temporality". When with the first step of be-ing-historical thinking, be-ing is set in relation to "time", this does not mean that "being" is (1) *a* "being" and (2) this being is *a* "temporal" being in the sense of what is changeable (finite) and limited in its duration. But when the 'nothing' belongs to the sway of be-ing, this again does not mean that (1) being is "a being" and (2) that the latter is "nothing" in the sense of the frailness of a created being.

[G395] Rather, the sameness of be-ing with the 'nothing' confirms that be-ing can never be a "nihilated something" [*ein "nichtiges"*] *prior to* all beings, because be-ing is the ab-ground of the swaying of that in which *any* being as such grounds. However, the ab-ground is not a being that is "ab-solute", 'detached' and 'constant' by itself but the en-owning of the arrival. This ab-ground certainly should not be named "finitude" – a word that is metaphysically all too burdened – except when thinking and pondering free themselves beforehand from the familiar trajectories of representation and become a detached co-enacting of a question.

124. The Principle of Contradiction

What is thought in the principle of contradiction? An impossibility (ἀδύνατον).

On what is thought in this principle? On the beingness of beings.

Accordingly of what kind is the impossibility? Of the kind that belongs to being itself.

How does this impossibility bear itself to the sway of being? Is this impossibility a necessity and, if so, of what kind?

*

The traditionally disputed question is this: is the incapability of our thinking the consequence of the necessity of the being that is thought or is this necessity only a projection [*Projektion*] of our "subjective" incapability? Or, is this either–or itself insufficient and, if yes, to what extent?

To the extent that "thinking" as νοῦς provides the horizon for the truth of being, being is grasped as constant presence. And the principle of contradiction is valid for *this* "being". But for this very same reason, this principle is not "subjective" and is not just the expression of an "incapacity".

[G396] Had not then *Hegel* elevated, preserved and canceled the validity of this principle? No! He had only broadened this validity by correspondingly positioning beingness as absolute idea. In this way it is possible, indeed even necessary, to think everything that is to be thought and every "being" in several respects ("in itself", "for itself", "in *and* for itself"), which means to think what is contradictory as necessary.

With the help of this principle the transformation of the finite thought into in-finite thought is simply enacted. Hegel's metaphysics is the supreme confirmation *of* the principle of contradiction as the basic principle of metaphysics, that is, as the basic principle of the interpretation of beingness as constant presence and as objectness of representing.

125. The History of Metaphysics is the History of the History of Being

To grasp and experience the history of metaphysics as the history of the history of being what is needed is a disentanglement from that projecting-opening of the history of metaphysics that for the first time Hegel had enacted and that he alone was the first who could enact it because his thought had to bring metaphysics to completion.

Accordingly, Hegel sees the history of metaphysics and its beginning – both with respect to the three grounding stages and with respect to the dynamics whereby these stages merely become positable – with a view towards the completion of metaphysics.

Hegel's absolute thought posits what has to be its condition and its staging through immediate thought and mediation. Thus the ancient and the "Christian" philosophies as well as the modern philosophy from Descartes to Kant are decided. This projecting-opening of the history of metaphysics confirms the unique domination of the jointure "*being and thinking*". This projecting-opening not only confirms this unique domination but also consolidates it in '*historical*' "consciousness", and thereby decides about what should remain "historically" knowable of philosophy for its "further development".

[G397] 126. The Place of Aristotle in the History of Metaphysics

1. Aristotle as the completion of what was earlier still strange: φύσις grasped as ἐντελέχεια.
2. Aristotle as the commencement of what becomes subsequently conventional for a long time.

*

It is in be-ing-historical thinking that for the very first time the metaphysical basic positions can be historically experienced and thought through.

127. The Distinguished Metaphysical Basic Position of Leibniz

Seen *be-ing-historically*, the distinguished metaphysical basic position of Leibniz can be elucidated by focusing on *repraesentatio*.

The *repraesentatio* means the "subjective" representing that makes up the subject as *monas*. This 'striving'-representing "represents" that "subject" right away, lets that "subject" come to an open presencing (validity).

In Leibniz the representing is thought in the onefold of what is simultaneously modern and inceptually Greek.

And nevertheless not entirely: [*monas* is] the extant that has the character of the subject, and the *subjectum* that presences simultaneously *in its* subjectivity as well as *through* this subjectivity (whereby the openness of this presencing, of course, remains questionable, respectively it is already decided upon by the all-encompassing and unshaken Christian projecting-open, "*ens creatum–creator*").

And nevertheless the sway of the *monas*, the unity, must be grasped in the direction of gathering unto presencing and in the direction of the constancy of the same and thus from out of the twofold-radiating *repraesentatio*.

[G398] One cannot directly come across the *monas*, not even by the unconditioned gaze of the creator, since the swaying of *monas* is originary in the twofold sense of "*repraesentatio*".

Although Descartes does posit representedness and I-hood as the domain of projecting-opening of beingness and as the ground of projecting-opening of beingness, it is only Leibniz who, *with his own* originary appropriation of the metaphysical tradition (*substantia–monas*; *potentia* as *vis* and *possibilitas*; "energeia") enacts the actual modern beginning of metaphysics.

Only Leibniz secures the ground for Kant and for German Idealism and finally for Nietzsche. It is only through Leibniz that rationality obtains the unconditioned rank of becoming the jointure of 'beings in the whole' – the rank which is of the nature of subject – whereby the "mathematical" unfolds itself immediately "as the systematic character of" the system, and the full unfolding of representedness is secured as the domain of projecting-open and as the ground of projecting-open.

According to Leibniz (*Monadologie* § 30), beings as such (being) are experienceable through the "reflective acts" of the monad that is called "man". However, these acts are grounded in the knowledge of the "necessary truths" (*identitates*). And these? They are indeed the foundational knowing of being, such that only through this knowing is a "reflection" possible all the while as this "reflection" alone makes possible again a knowing of the *identitates*.

How are we to decide here? Is there a "circle" here, and if yes, did Leibniz recognize and simultaneously ground this circle as such in its necessity? Apparently not! For such would be possible only by inquiring into the *truth* of "being".

Raison – rationality – thought – are *self-knowing* and at one and the same time god's knowing and cognizing (*Monadologie* § 29).

Self-knowing is grounded in the knowing-awareness of identitates. Hence this knowing-awareness constitutes the ownmost of reason. Thereupon reason is the receiving of beingness in the sense of "identity" as *the constancy of presencing*.

[G399] Or does Leibniz mean that, on the basis of this knowing-awareness of the *verités necessaires*, we *find* the "primary" and the 'nearmost' being (and thus this being as such), that is, *us ourselves* and, therefore, we find "being" explicitly "in" us?

In that case then, we would be only saying that a being like man is what is *primarily* giveable *as such* and is given. In that case then, we would have only affirmed Descartes' basic position and simultaneously prepared the *transcendental* inquiry of Kant as a "subjective" inquiry which is referred to the objectivity of the object.

But in that case neither the unity of the human monad's ownmost with the knowing-awareness of the necessary truths is grounded, nor is the preeminence of this being in the hierarchy of the givenness of beings grounded, nor is the interconnection recognized of the guiding concept of *veritas* as *identitas* with the *certum* as the securing of a distinguished presence and constancy.

In that case, the Leibnizian metaphysics, too, remains ungrounded, and does not venture unto the ab-ground of the truth of be-ing.

128. Kant and Metaphysics

With Kant's "critical" demonstration of the impossibility of "speculative" metaphysics, for the first time "metaphysics" as the jointure of 'beings in the whole' is completely consolidated in accord with the inceptual and Platonic sense of beingness.

What follows, then, appears as the "metaphysics" of German Idealism which specifically brings together, in the unconditionedness of an absolute speculative knowledge and of an absolute actuality, both the jointure of 'beings in the whole' and the inceptual sense of beingness, and thereby hands over to the nineteenth century an unsurpassable richness of metaphysical perspectives. Moreover, it is not important whether these perspectives are taken up "idealistically" or "positivistically". Metaphysics as the jointure endures and in enduring it becomes increasingly unknowable in its predominance. The more conflicting and shallow the basic positionings [G400] towards "metaphysics" are, the more frantically the "world-views" assert themselves.

129. The Final Rise of Metaphysics

The final rise of metaphysics is the history of the unconditioned predominance of machination (cf. 8. "On Mindfulness", and *Überlegungen* XIII, especially 41 ff.'). Nietzsche's accomplishment consists in foundationally forging ahead into this final rise through thinking, even though Nietzsche's thinking is simply incapable of grasping itself as the completion of metaphysics.

___

' To appear in *Überlegungen* C, GA 96.

The overcoming of machination cannot be brought about immediately through some kind of destruction or even by "refuting" metaphysics. All immediate negation leads to nothing, especially since it cannot at all be decided whence the overcoming of machination should come and by whom it should be carried out.

The overcoming of machination can come about only mediately insofar as the other beginning of be-ing-historical inquiry leaves the completed metaphysics to its own devices. Such admittance of metaphysics calls for the specific resiliency of be-ing-historical thinking that must be sterner and more enduring than any "attack", because according to its ownmost, attack immediately dislodges itself into the bondage by what is attacked. Already the knowledge of the completion of metaphysics as the history of the unconditioned predominance of machination is only possible from out of the other beginning. Here the overcoming is foundationally a transformation of thinking – it is the crossing from the projecting-open that *represents* over to the pathway of that projecting-open *that throws itself free*.

[G401]   130. The End of Metaphysics

Is it an accident that in the epoch of the absolute forgottenness of being, "ontology" undergoes a renewal, even if this renewal is merely a scholastic-erudite and 'historical' renewal? This indeed creates the impression that "ontology" inquires into "being" and that the be-ing-historical question of being comes too late and cannot claim any inceptuality. Quite so! And yet, "ontology" in all manner of ways only disseminates the mere *semblance* of the be-ing-historical question of being and this semblance has its own historical mission. This semblance ensnares all those who lack every precondition for raising the be-ing-historical question of being – those who hold for 'being' that which is as removed from be-ing-historical inquiry as possible. Hence, "ontology" has the function of mistaking for metaphysics the question concerning the truth of be-ing – a mistaking that accords with the 'intractability' of this question. "Ontology" is thus a protection that metaphysics unintentionally brings to bear upon be-ing-historical thinking and thus safeguards it from getting deformed by the failure to grasp this thinking.

The predominance of "world-views" accomplishes the same thing but only in a diametrically opposed direction. The world-views are the calculating 'formations', respectively the calculating 'mis-formations' of metaphysics that are "actual", "close to life" and disseminated entirely in beings. As such 'formations' or 'mis-formations', world-views appeal to what is "actual" in relations, in occurrences, and circumstances; world-views appeal to that which in human attitudes is called "character" and the "instinct". World-views ward off all "ontology" as "mere" intellectual, empty reckoning with concepts and, nevertheless, like all "ontology", they give rise to the illusion that they supply an interpretation of beings and set measures. For world-views, what still remains questionable is confined to the more or less carefully and eruditely refurbished sacrosanct systems of teaching philosophy and faith. Therefore, if we consider "ontology" and "world-view" in terms of the consolidation of metaphysics which both pursue – if we consider the way both obfuscate the question of being as a be-ing-historical question – then "ontology" and "world-view" have a fundamental historical significance.

[G402]   131. Metaphysics and "World-view"

A "world-view" is an off-shoot of metaphysics and in fact becomes simply possible there, where metaphysics enters the state of its completion. "World-view" is a modern deformation of metaphysics, and the measure of "world-view" is publicness wherein everyone finds everything accessible and raises a claim on such accessibility. This is not contradicted by the fact that "world-views" are entirely "personal" and tailored to "individuals" who perceive themselves as the solitary 'everyone' that represents an image of the world, and represents the world as an image – "individuals" who provide themselves with a kind of self-orientation, (character), (e.g., Houston Stewart Chamberlain).

Fundamental to a "*world-view*" is:
1.   the preeminence of beings (the actual) (forgottenness of being);
2.   aiming at "goals" and "ideals" that should be realized;
3.   arranging the ways and means of such realization;
4.   all these in accord with a public common intelligibility that is willed in advance, which requires;
5.   accordingly, thinking '*historically*' but thinking without choosing, and thinking calculatively and that means thinking *unhistorically* through and through.

The world-view is the enactment of the confirmation of the predominance of an absolute lack of mindfulness in the epoch of the completed meaninglessness. (Regarding the fundamental concept of "world-view" and its interconnection with modern metaphysics, cf. the lecture of 1938, *"Die Begründung des neuzeitlichen Weltbildes durch die Metaphysik".*[*])

A "world-view" functions within the jointure of metaphysics. It knows "ideas" and fosters and pursues their realization [G403] in "existence". The ideas become "values" to a world-view, and the "existence" is required to take a stance and to evaluate ("existence" here understood as the extant man, the subject of "lived-experience").

As the occasion may simply demand, the "world-views" elaborate on the "concepts" and "propositions" of metaphysics without having a knowing-awareness of the origin and the limitations of these "concepts" and "propositions".

The "world-views" think "in a natural sort of way", they take their measures from "practical life" – whence their predilection for "biology".

132. "Mysticism"

All mysticism is the limit set by metaphysics itself either for itself or against itself.

"Mysticism" [is possible] only "within" metaphysics, that is, within the confines of the foundational domain of metaphysics. From here comes the predilection to let a "period" of "mysticism" precede the beginning of Occidental thinking – a period in which everything is already experienced that metaphysics subsequently brings into concept ("λόγος"). Properly observed, here one projects-open the mysticism from out of metaphysics. This corresponds to the historical-metaphysical function of neo-Platonism; this corresponds to medieval mysticism, to the mysticism during the unfolding of modern metaphysics and again during the age of Romanticism: Novalis, Baader, the ambiguity of Schelling's projecting-open and his negative and positive philosophy. But to the extent that metaphysics as such is overcome by the be-ing-historical inquiry into the truth of be-ing and thus the possibility of employing metaphysical concepts is barred, one seeks refuge in characterizing be-ing-historical

---

[*] Published under the title *"Die Zeit des Weltbildes"*, in *Holzwege*, GA 5, pp. 75–113.

thinking as "mystical". With this characterization one immediately and disparagingly identifies be-ing-historical thinking with what is unclear and obscure, with what revels in mere "attunements", that is, with a posture that can never be worthy of "rigorous" philosophy's attention, [G404] about which, however, one must be warned by the erudite supervision of the 'historical' philosophy-industry.

One fails to see that in this way one has already turned mysticism itself into a 'subspecies' and a 'degenerate variant' of metaphysics and so one fails to grasp the sway of either the one or the other.

"Mysticism" and calculation of beings from out of a machinationally thought being mutually foster each other. And in their accord mysticism and machination block the crossing from the metaphysical history of the first beginning into the other beginning. For crossing here is not the steadiness of a progression but rather the knowing-awareness of the suddenness of the rupture that occurs between the end and the beginning.

133. The Crossing

The crossing may be obtained only by a leap and upheld and grounded in the long run only by an en-leaping.

Here there is no escape into a missed but forward moving transition from one thing (the secured) to another thing (the established). Even the differentiation between the beginning and the end can no longer be grasped in terms of *opposition*, because this opposition too would have to acknowledge an agreement as a common ground.

Suddenly and incomparably, the end and the beginning soar unto each other, as each holds unto the ab-ground: the end as the interpretation of the swayingness of the sway (swayingness of beingness of beings) as *value*, and the beginning as the en-thinking of the truth of being as enowning.

For the 'historical' representation, crossing is always merely what is transitory and "episodic" that disappears vis-à-vis what is crossed over and vis-à-vis the whither of the crossing.

However, historically, that is, thought from out of the swaying of the truth of be-ing, what gathers in the crossing is the uniqueness of the history in the onefold of the rupture between the completion and the beginning. The 'historical' inconspicuousness of the crossing and the historical [G405] dignity of its unique sustaining power that leads into 'what has already been' and 'what is futural' and 'arriving' correspond to each other.

Hence the crossing is never a mediation, but the de-cision that can ground itself unto that for the sake of which the decision decides to be that which is to be grounded. Reckoned 'historically', crossing into the suddenness of the rupture of what cannot be mediated is a leap unto "the nothing". Historically, the nearness of be-ing nears itself in the crossing – nearness of be-ing unto which every being is already allotted and 'owned-over' before every being thinks itself and after every being forgets itself.

134. Towards Elucidation of the Be-ing-historical Concept of "Metaphysics"

The be-ing-historical interpretation:
1. of the differentiation between being (beingness) and beings;
2. of the differentiation between 'being-what' and 'being-that';
3. of the multiplicity of ἀρχαί;
4. of the differentiation between ὄντως ὄν and μὴ ὄν, (ἰδέα) εἶδος–ὕλη.

This interpretation shows that the thinking of being as beingness is not at all a beginning and so to speak does not arise from a "natural" represen-tation of beings in general, but originates from the swaying of be-ing that ever-first-inceptually as rising (φύσις) refused the grounding of its truth and along with it let ἀλήθεια become the presencing of what is constant (and thus let ἀλήθεια become the 'fore-form' of objectness). Of course, the consequence of this first beginning in its history is not the indifferent matter of mere opinion and of forming concepts about being. This history shows the predominance of machination in whose absolute empowering modernity completes itself and, unbeknown to itself and without intend-ing it, announces the other beginning.

[G406]   135. Steps

Judgement – validity – truth – being. (Dissertation*)

---

* See *Die Lehre vom Urteil im Psychologismus* (1913), in *Frühe Schriften*, GA 1, ed. F.-W. v. Herrmann, (Frankfurt am Main: 1978), pp. 59–188.

Doctrine of categories and meaning – being and language (Negation). (*Habilitationschrift***)

"Ontology" – the title that leads into the "question of being".

Fundamental-ontology. (*Sein und Zeit****)

Understanding of being as thrown projecting-open.

Being as beingness.

Beingness – constancy and presencing – time.

Transformation of being and, with and through it, the *"truth"* (*Wesen des Grundes*****).

Every step not only proceeds "further", but is also *different*.

Be-ing-historical enleaping into the *crossing*. The grounding of the historical uniqueness of the crossing.

** See *Die Kategorien- und Bedeutungslehre des Dun Scotus* (1915), in *Frühe Schriften*, GA 1, pp. 189–411.

*** *Sein und Zeit* (1927), GA 2.

**** *Vom Wesen des Grundes* (1929), in *Wegmarken*, GA 9, pp. 123–5.

APPENDIX

^[G409] A RETROSPECTIVE LOOK AT THE PATHWAY

(Addressed within the horizon of metaphysics and its overcoming) not yet from out of be-ing itself.

Written in 1937/38

Martin Heidegger

MY PATHWAY HITHERTO

Here my pathway hitherto is considered only as a means for a new mind-fulness, bearing in mind that the view and interpretation of the pathway always depends on the obtained level of mindfulness.

This pathway was never known to me in advance, it proved to be unstable, and entangled in setbacks and misleading trackways.

However, again and again the quest was driven into the *one* trajectory and forced to obtain more clarity. But at no stage is mindfulness privileged to know what actually transpires: what is experienced and attempted stands merely at the service of something entirely different that perhaps one day will become even "self-evident".

My Pathway Hitherto

My pathway hitherto is indicated in the following writings:

1.   The PhD dissertation *Die Lehre vom Urteil im Psychologismus*[1] of 1913. Here the question concerns *validity*, that is, concerns 'being-true of the true' and the truth – questions that are determined completely by the viewpoints prevalent at the time. Here, there is a penchant for *Lotze* that fails to gain clarity about itself. But the thrust is towards *the question concerning the truth of the true* as a foundational

---

[1] See *Frühe Schriften*, GA 1, ed. F.-W. von Herrmann (Frankfurt am Main: 1978), pp. 59–188.

question. The criteria are imprecise, especially given the fact that a total reliance on any direction or any system is rejected. Both in the choice of the question as well as in the manner of its treatment, the PhD dissertation originated without any assistance from "the actual teachers". (In this regard, see the reports on recent investigations in *logic* published in *Literarishe Rundschau* of the year 1912, edited by J. Sauer.[2])

2. The qualifying dissertation, *Die Kategorien- und Bedeutungslehre des Duns Scotus*[3] of 1916. The inquiry here into categories [G 412] is an attempt to gain a historical access to *ontology*, and simultaneously to the question concerning *language*. This inquiry too is a single-minded attempt, and contrasts with the hitherto interpretation of Scholastics which uses Neo-Scholasticism and so depends on it both as far as the far-reaching consequences of this interpretation and its exaction are concerned. On the whole this attempt failed, because it wanted to accomplish too much and did not adequately master the question itself. And nevertheless, there is at this stage already more behind the unmastered questions, namely the initial attempts at a dissociating exposition of German Idealism (Hegel). However, these attempts were not striving for a Neo-Hegelianism, but for honing the gaze on the triad 'Hegel – Middle Ages – Aristotle'.

3. The qualifying lecture, *Der Zeitbegriff in der Geschichtswissenschaft*[4] of 1915 as an inquiry into *time* and *history*. Behind this inquiry were questions concerning "eternity", actual beings, "negation", and the provenance of *'nothing'*. (See the conclusion of the qualifying dissertation on Duns Scotus.)

4. After these attempts, which were published only as the requisite academic communications and merely indicate some of the questions that urged themselves upon me without being differentiated, and mastered and which lacked an actual direction, there emerged a gradual clarity in *two directions*:

(a) the historical direction: a resolute reverting to the Greek philosophy via the figure of its first foundational termination, Aristotle.

---

[2] See *Frühe Schriften*, GA 1, pp. 17–43.
[3] See *Frühe Schriften*, GA 1, pp. 189–411.
[4] See *Frühe Schriften*, GA 1, pp. 413–33.

(b) the direction of a serious engagement with the methodology of Husserl's "phenomenology". From the outset I did not endorse the basic *philosophical* positions that in fact were adopted by this phenomenology, that is, Cartesianism and Neo-Kantianism. My own pathway led me to a mindfulness of history, to a dissociating exposition of Dilthey and the determination of "life" as basic actuality.

[G413] But "phenomenology" brought to my own work a confident manner of proceeding and questioning that became fruitful for my historical interpretations.

In the years 1920–23, all the up to then attempted inquiries that touched upon truth, categories, language, time and history came together in the plan for an "ontology of human Dasein". However, this ontology was not thought as a "regional" discussion of the inquiry into man, but as the laying of the foundation for the inquiry into *beings* as such – simultaneously as a dissociating exposition of the beginning of Occidental metaphysics with the Greeks.

5.   *Sein und Zeit*[5] of 1927. As an initial pathway, this attempt originated in the years 1922–26 for possibly rendering discernible – from the ground up and through an actual enactment – the question of being in a manner that fundamentally leads beyond all the hitherto inquiries and nevertheless simultaneously leads back to a dissociating exposition of the Greeks and the Occidental philosophy. (On this point, see the *Laufenden Anmerkungen zu Sein und Zeit*[6] of 1936.)

Operating in this attempt is at the same time the striving – through a new approach and with a renewed honing of the gaze – for rendering major inquiries within the history of metaphysics the master of this attempt.

However, in the first presentation of *Sein und Zeit*, the actual "systematic" section on "Time and Being" proved to be inadequate, while external circumstances (such as the enlargement of the volume of [Husserl's] Yearbook) fortunately hindered the publication of this section in which, considering its inadequacy, I had placed little confidence. This section was destroyed, but it was

---

[5] GA 2, ed. F.-W. v. Herrmann (Frankfurt am Main: 1977).
[6] To appear in *Zu eigenen Veröffentlichungen*, GA 82.

immediately approached [G414] anew in a more historical manner in the lecture-course of the summer semester 1927.[7]

Nevertheless, viewed from the standpoint of these retrospective observations, "Time and Being", that totally inadequate section would have been at the end quite important if it were to be printed. This publication would not have let the misinterpretation of *Sein und Zeit* as a mere "ontology" of man and the misconstrual of "fundamental ontology" go as far as these misinterpretations have gone and are going.

Precisely because vis-à-vis the entire metaphysics hitherto the inquiry of *Sein und Zeit* into the *meaning of being* (into a projecting-opening of the truth of being – not of beings –) is something entirely different, the inquiry in the withheld section on "Time and Being" could have shown nevertheless what *Sein und Zeit* accomplishes, although what this work strives for is often enough *said* in what is communicated. For the inadequacy of the withheld section on "Time and Being" was not because of an uncertainty concerning the direction of the inquiry and its domain, but because of an uncertainty that only concerned the appropriate elaboration.

And yet, who is now able to assess precisely what was, or what would have been "better"? The efforts of another decade show that the difficulties of mastering the question of the truth of be-ing are not of such a kind that pertain to the so-called "birth of a problem" and its isolated tackling. Rather: *because* the inquiry into being is grounded most intimately in the inquiry into Da-sein and vice versa, that is, because the intimacy of the relation between being and Da-sein continues to be basically the sustaining and prompting relation that immediately holds unto the abground, the inquiry into Da-sein must be made anew and begun more originarily, but at the same time in explicit relation to the truth of be-ing. Therefore, right away I had to subject anew *everything* that had to do with 'ground', [*Grund*] (cf. *Vom Wesen des Grundes*[8]) to the motions of questioning and thus simultaneously clarify and sharpen my entire position on [G415] the history of Occidental philosophy hitherto.

---

[7] *Die Grundprobleme der Phänomenologie*, lecture-course of summer semester 1927 held at the University of Marburg, GA 24, ed. F.-W. v. Herrmann (Frankfurt am Main: 1975).

[8] See *Wegmarken*, GA 9, ed. F.-W. v. Herrmann, (Frankfurt am Main: 1976), pp. 123–75.

Accordingly, once again there emerged the task of a comprehensive mindfulness of this history from its first beginning (Anaximander lecture of 1932[9] up to the Nietzsche-lectures of 1937).[10]

However, it became also clear to me for the first time what place this whole inquiry occupies within the crossing, given the onefold of this historical and fundamental mindfulness of the grounding-question. The difficulty grew as I had to show that this inquiry is a necessary one that actually arises out of the historical distress and as I had to remove the impression that this inquiry is a mere fortuitous erudite discussion of an isolated special question.

And who would not want to recognize that a confrontation with Christianity reticently accompanied my entire path hitherto, a confrontation that was not and is not a 'problem' that one 'takes up' to address but a preservation of, and *at the same time* a painful separation from, one's ownmost provenance: the parental home, homeland and youth. Only the one who was so rooted in such an actually lived Catholic world may be able to have an inkling of the necessities that like subterranean quakes have been at work in the pathway of my inquiry hitherto. Moreover, the Marburg period offered a profound experience of a Protestant Christianity – all of which as what had to be overcome from the ground up but not destroyed.

It is not proper to speak of these most inward confrontations since they do not revolve around issues that concern the dogma of Christianity and articles of faith, but rather only around the sole question: whether god is fleeing from us or not and whether we, as creating ones, still experience this flight genuinely.

[G416] And this has nothing to do with the simple "religious" background of philosophy, but with the one inquiry into the truth of being which alone decides on the "time" and the "place" that is historically preserved for us within the history of the Occident and its gods.

How many of those who distinguish themselves today as scholars in philosophy are according to their provenance still sustained and struck by the necessities of our Occidental history's most originary questions of decision? I know of no one! I know that these scholars get involved in

[9] See *Der Anfang der abendländischen Philosophie* (*Anaximander und Parmenides*), lecture-course of summer semester 1932 held at the University of Freiburg, GA 35.

[10] See *Nietzsches metaphysische Grundstellung im abendländischen Denken: Die ewige Wiederkehr des Gleichen*, lecture-course of summer semester 1937, GA 44, ed. Marion Heinz (Frankfurt am Main: 1986).

philosophy as a matter of education and "interest", and that by utilizing something that the political destiny of our people recently has thrown their way they subsequently invent a "basis" for themselves without even from there being struck by the necessity of actually raising the grounding question.

Whoever is not truly deeply rooted and is not immediately struck by questioning, how will he be able actually to experience the uprootedness? And how can the one who does not bear the experience of uprootedness be mindful from the ground up of a new grounding which is not a simple turning away from the old and a craving for the new, still less a feeble mediation and adjustment, but a creative transformation wherein everything inceptual grows up into the height of its summit?

But precisely because the most inward experiences and decisions remain foundational, these experiences must remain outside of the domain of publicness.

Perhaps the necessity of accomplishing *pure work* was never greater than it is today and as it will be in the future, since the distorting and destructive coercive force of proclaiming and gossiping, of admiring and of hubbub, of the mania for psychological analysis and psychological dissolution was never greater and more unrestrained and deliberate than today.

How much and how assuredly one succumbs to the delusion that when one is familiar with the "letters" and other 'expressions' as well as the "psychology" of the creator of the work one has grasped and appropriated the *work*?

[G417] Will we also succeed here in once again making a beginning by giving up curiosity and by becoming mature for the necessities of works? But *where* are the "works"? Granted that works could be created, can they simultaneously also create what belongs to their actual work-character, namely the 'time-space' wherein they themselves come to a halt? Will all of this not be blocked from the ground up by "psychology", by mass's way of being and by "propaganda"?

Certainly! And that is why there must be individuals who with their attempts accomplish the one thing, which although small enough when reckoned unto greatness, still lets the works *hint further into what is foundational and historically necessary* – hint further into the generation after the next upon which perhaps the destiny of the Occident as a whole will be decided.

THE WISH AND THE WILL

(On Preserving What is Attempted)

I.
What is On Hand:

1. The lecture-courses.
2. The lectures:
    The lecture on Hegel (Amsterdam).[1]
    On the sway of truth.[2]
    The contemporary situation of philosophy (lecture given in Konstanz).[3]
    On the origin of the work of art (lecture given in Freiburg).[4]
    On the origin of the work of art (lecture given in Frankfurt).[5]
3. Notes for the seminars, particularly those seminars held on:
    Kant's Transcendental Dialectic and his Critique of Practical Reason,[6]
    Hegel's Phenomenology of Spirit,[7]

---

[1] "Hegel und das Problem der Metaphysik (1930)", to appear in *Vorträge*, GA 80.

[2] "Vom Wesen der Wahrheit (1930)", to appear in *Vorträge*, GA 80.

[3] "Die gegenwärtige Lage und die künftige Aufgabe der deutschen Philosophie (30. November, 1934)", in *Reden und andere Zeugnisse eines Lebensweges, 1910–1976*, ed. Hermann Heidegger (Frankfurt am Main: 2000), GA 16.

[4] "Vom Ursprung des Kunstwerkes (1935)", to appear in *Vorträge*, GA 80.

[5] "Der Ursprung des Kunstwerkes (1936)", in *Holzwege*, ed. F.-W. v. Herrmann, (Frankfurt am Main: 1977), GA 5, pp. 1–74.

[6] *Seminare: Leibniz–Kant*, to appear in GA 84

[7] *Seminare: Hegel–Schelling*, to appear in GA 86.

Leibniz's Monadology,[8]
Kant's Critique of the Faculty of Aesthetic Judgement,[9]
Schiller's Letters concerning aesthetic education,[+]
the lecture-course on Nietzsche.[10]

4. The preparatory elaborations concerning the Work (including my criticism of *Sein und Zeit*).[11]

5. *Überlegungen und Winke*, Booklets II–IV–V.[12]

6. Lecture-course on Hölderlin[13] and preparatory work on "Empedocles".[14]

7. *From Enowning (Contributions to Philosophy)*[15] especially section 4.

II.
Regarding Each:
1. The Lecture-Courses

Concealed in another thinking is the groping in the lecture-courses mostly for the truth of be-ing and its grounding in Da-sein. The actual dynamics of thinking itself as the striving for the basic positioning of the other beginning lies behind the educational will to develop and strengthen the power of questioning, and the unrestrained mastery of the craft of philosophizing. This *other* inquiry into the truth of be-ing as differentiated from the inquiry into the sway of beings can be enacted only in a dissociating exposition of the history up to now and in a new opening up of this history. This dissociating exposition terminates in the lecture-courses on Nietzsche.

---

[8] *Seminare: Leibniz–Kant*, to appear in GA 84.

[9] *Seminare: Leibniz–Kant*, to appear in GA 84.

[+] {See editor's Epilogue, G 436.}

[10] *Seminare: Nietzsche, 1937–1944*, ed. Peter Ruckteschell (Frankfurt am Main: 2004), GA 87.

[11] *Eine Auseinandersetzung mit "Sein und Zeit"* (1935/36), to appear in *Zu eigenen Veröffentlichungen*, GA 82.

[12] See *Überlegungen A*, to appear in GA 94; *Winke* I and II, to appear in GA 101.

[13] *Hölderlins Hymnen "Germanien" und "Der Rhein"*, lecture-course of winter semester 1934/35 given in Freiburg, GA 39, ed. Susanne Ziegler (Frankfurt am Main: 1980).

[14] "Zu Hölderlins Empedokles-Bruchstücken", in *Zu Hölderlin – Griechenlandreisen*, ed. Curd Ochwad (Frankfurt am Main: 2000), GA 75.

[15] *Beiträge zur Philosophie (Vom Ereignis)*, ed F.-W. v. Herrmann (Frankfurt am Main: 1989), GA 65.

[G421] The lecture-courses always make up the foreground. From within the grounding-attunement they begin with a seemingly arbitrary stretch of the way and from there they provide glimpses unto the whole.

What always counts in the lecture-courses is the manner of proceeding – the sequence of steps – not a claim to final truths. The lecture-courses never wrap up in a completeness and in seemingly "finishing off" the works interpreted, but rather in the inner fullness of the hidden dynamics of questioning.

All the lecture-courses are *historical*, history-grounding, but never 'historical'.

Whoever *without hesitation* reads and hears the lecture-courses only as a 'historical' presentation of some work and whoever then compares and reckons up the interpretation [*Auffassung*] with the already existing views or exploits the interpretation in order to "correct" the existing views, *he has not grasped anything at all*.

All the lecture-courses belong to the sphere of that task which in the projecting-opening of "From Enowning" is called "*Playing Forth*". Perhaps at a later time some may succeed in experiencing from out of the grounding dynamics of reticence [*des Verschweigens*] that which is kept in silent reticence [*das Verchschwiegene*] and from there in setting the limits to what is explicitly said. On the other hand one may remain stuck in the 'historical' reckoning, and the 'knowing it inside out' – inescapable as it is – will find perhaps that all this is "superseded" by the "literature that has meanwhile appeared".

There are some *repetitions* within the individual lecture-courses and more so in their interrelation – repetitions that mutually support each other, and grasp *the same* from out of different thought-situations.

[In the lecture-courses] there are indeed "contradictions" and trans-formations of the earlier [interpretations,] without in each case these contradictions and transformations being specified.

With a more originary unfolding of the inquiry, most of the earlier lecture-courses – especially those related to Aristotle – are superseded and *set aside*.

The interpretation of [G422] *Sophistes*[16] and the lecture-course on

---

[16] *Platon: Sophistes*, lecture-course of winter semester 1924/25 delivered in Marburg, ed. Ingeborg Schüßler (Frankfurt am Main: 1992), GA 19.

Aristotle's *Rhetoric*[17] are still useful although they are already taken over in different ways by other lecture-courses.

What is more significant in the future than these groping attempts is grasping the philosophy of Aristotle out of the positioning of the guiding question ('What are beings?') and from within the crossing to the positioning of the grounding-question ('How does the truth of be-ing sway?') as the *first termination of the first beginning* of Occidental philosophy, that is, grasping Aristotle's philosophy in purely Greek terms, free and detached from all Christianization and Scholasticism, and all the old and new humanism.

In all the lecture-courses, the occasional remarks about contemporary circumstances are factually without relevance. A debate with the contemporary philosophical erudition is not intended anywhere. Occasional references are mostly responses to the queries from the audience.

Most important for understanding the unfolding of the question since *Sein und Zeit* are the lecture-courses from 1930/31 (*Hegels Phänomenologie des Geistes*)[18] to the lecture-courses on Nietzsche.[19] Because of the demands of the Rectorate, the lecture-course of the summer semester of 1933[20] is inadequate.

[G423]   The Lectures

These lectures, also, grew entirely out of the work's path and bear its thrust. In preparing the lectures certain issues are not fully evaluated, although they are important for the inquiry. Even if these lectures are published later on they do not come too late.

---

[17] *Grundbegriffe der aristotelischen Philosophie,* lecture-course of summer semester 1924 delivered in Marburg, ed. Mark Michalski (Frankfurt am Main: 2002), GA 18.

[18] *Hegels Phänomenologie des Geistes,* lecture-course of winter semester 1930/31 delivered in Freiburg, ed. Ingtraud Görland (Frankfurt am Main: 1980), GA 32.

[19] *Nietzsche: Der Wille zur Macht als Kunst,* lecture-course of winter semester 1936/37 delivered in Freiburg, ed. Bernd Heimbüchel (Frankfurt am Main: 1985), GA 43; *Nietzsches metaphysische Grundstellung im abendländischen Denken: Die ewige Wiederkehr des Gleichen,* lecture-course of summer semester 1937 delivered in Freiburg, ed. Marion Heinz (Frankfurt am Main: 1986), GA 44.

[20] *Die Grundfrage der Philosophie,* lecture-course of summer semester 1933 delivered in Freiburg. See *Sein und Wahrheit,* ed. Hartmut Tietjen (Frankfurt am main: 2001), GA 36/37.

3. The Notes for the Seminars

The actual path of the seminars cannot always be gleaned from these notes. Such insight is provided by the "minutes" of the seminars, which in each case are of different "value", and even when they report "verbatim" they do not reflect the issues as I have presented and thoroughly discussed them.

Of varying length and detail, the "notes" contain quite important additions, be it to the lecture-courses, be it to the actual elaboration on the *Work*. Important for example are the seminars on Plato's *Phaidros*,[21] on Hegel's *Phänomenologie des Geistes*[22] (here the 'minutes of the seminar' are particularly good), on Leibniz's *Monadologie*,[23] on Kant's *Kritik der Urteilskraft*[24] and on Schiller and the elucidation of the lecture-courses on Nietzsche (summer semester in 1937).[25]

[G424]   The Preparatory Elaborations Concerning the Work

(See also No. 7 below)

These "approaches" do not intend to "complete" *Sein und Zeit*. Rather, they hold fast more originarily on the entire inquiry and shift this inquiry into the proper perspective. Since the spring of 1932 the main thrusts of the plan are firmly established that obtains its first shaping in the projecting-opening called "From Enowning".[26] Everything advances unto this projecting-opening, and *Eine Auseinandersetzung mit "Sein und Zeit"*[27] also belongs to the domain of these deliberations. These preparatory elaborations are merely new approaches in order to find the basic position

---

[21] Platon, *Phaidros*, seminar of summer semester 1932, to appear in *Seminare: Platon–Aristoteles–Augustinus*, GA 83.

[22] Hegel, *Phänomenologie des Geistes*, seminar of summer semester 1935, to appear in *Seminare: Hegel–Schelling*, GA 86.

[23] Leibniz, *Monadologie*, seminar of winter semester 1935/36, to appear in *Seminare: Leibniz–Kant*, GA 84.

[24] Kant, *Kritik der aesthetischen Urteilskraft*, seminar of summer semester 1936, to appear in *Seminare: Leibniz–Kant*, GA 84.

[25] *Nietzsches metaphysische Grundstellung (Sein und Schein)*, seminar of summer semester 1937, in *Seminare: Nietzsche 1937–1944*, ed. Peter von Ruckteschell (Frankfurt am Main: 2004), GA 87.

[26] See *Contributions to Philosophy (From Enowning)* (1936–38).

[27] *Eine Auseinandersetzung mit "Sein und Zeit"* (1935–36), to appear in *Zu eigenen Veröffentlichungen*, GA 82.

for the inquiry into the truth of be-ing. The main domains of mindfulness may be brought under the following titles:

The Differentiation between Beings and Be-ing –	(origin and ground of the differentiation, which in the philosophy hitherto has always been considered in view of beings and therefrom in view of beingness, but now is seen strictly differently, that is, from out of the truth of be-ing).
The Da-sein –	as grounding the truth of be-ing.
The Truth	see the surveys given in the lecture-course of the winter semester 1937/38.[28]
The 'Time-Space'	as that unto which the originary temporality, that is, "Temporality" [*Temporalität*] advances and in turn is grounded in "enowning".
The Modalities –	to what extent modalities are basically inadequate for grasping the swaying of be-ing (cf. lecture-course of 1935/36[29]).
[G425] *The Attunement –*	as the attuning of man's originary own-most insofar as he – taking over Da-*sein* – becomes the preserver of the truth of be-ing. Here "attunement" falls *entirely outside* the hitherto psychological and anthropological considerations.
The Language –	belonging to attunement, language is grasped from out of the relation to the truth of be-ing. Grammar and logic hitherto are overcome here. See the lecture-course of the summer semester 1935.[30]

[28] *Grundfragen der Philosophie. Ausgewählte "Probleme" der "Logik"*, lecture-course of winter semester 1935/36 delivered in Freiburg, ed. F.-W. von. Herrmann (Frankfurt am Main: 1984), GA 45.

[29] *Die Frage nach dem Ding. Zu Kants Lehre von den transzendentalen Grundsätzen*, lecture-course of winter semester 1935/36 delivered in Freiburg, ed. Petra Jaeger (Frankfurt am Main: 1984), GA 41.

[30] *Einführung in die Metaphysik*, lecture-course of summer semester 1935 given in Freiburg, ed. Petra Jaeger (Frankfurt am Main: 1983), GA 40.

The Manner of Proceeding and the Ownmost of Questioning – considering the preceding remarks it is imperative that questioning is grasped as that *ur-action* of Da-sein by virtue of which Dasein places before itself the sphere of obfuscability [*Verklärbarkeit*] of beings from out of be-ing. *This questioning* should never be interpreted according to the usual understanding of questioning, that is, in terms of doubt and even negation.

Of great import for the comprehensive understanding of the preparatory elaborations, as an understanding of a more originary retrieval of *my* one and only question in *Sein und Zeit*, is my own *"Auseinandersetzung mit 'Sein und Zeit'"*.

Of course, the present public is too immature and too untutored for a proper reception of this "self-criticism". The "critics" hitherto of whom *not a single one* has grasped, let alone has thought more originarily the actual question – a grasping that is the prerequisite of every "criticism" – claim to possess *the* measure that belongs exclusively to that which is to be judged. Is it surprising that these "critics" will find that *they* were "right" after all when they refused their approval?

[G426]And others will easily be misled by the opinion that given the critical position of the author of *Sein und Zeit* towards this treatise, it does not pay to return to this work.

Only he who again and again can freely position himself vis-à-vis what is worked out, that is, he who again and again experiences the great moments of being affected by the self-sheltering-concealing of be-ing, that is, by be-ing's swaying, only he musters enough superiority for a critique, and the will as well, to discover and unfold the foundational steps precisely in these "[self-]criticisms" and their pathways.

5. 'Überlegungen und Winke'

What is recorded in these notebooks, especially in number II, IV and V, indicates in part also the grounding-attunements of questioning as well as the directives unto the uttermost horizon of the attempts at thinking. Apparently originated at certain moments, each of these notebooks bears the thrust of the unceasing striving for the one and only question.

6. The 1934/35 and 1935 Lecture-Course on Hölderlin and the Preparation for Interpreting "Empedocles"

After long deliberation, this lecture-course became the first attempt at interpreting Hölderlin's individual "works", such as his Hymns. What is attempted in this lecture-course nowhere accords in the least with the work of the poet, especially – and this is *imperative* – since in this lecture-course Hölderlin is not taken as a poet among others, not even as a poet who is supposedly more timely now, but rather as *the* poet of the other beginning of our futural history. Hence, this lecture-course is intimately connected to the task, already undertaken, of rendering into question the truth of being. In this vein, this lecture-course is not an excursion into a "philosophy of poetry as an art form" or into art in general.

[G427] The pedagogical intention operative in any of my lecture-courses, namely first to lead the student to the work (in this case to the poet's work) lies obviously always in the *foreground* of this lecture-course. But this does not at all touch upon the hidden intention that determines the choice of the "hymns" and the manner of handling them.

7. "From Enowning"

In its new approach this *Contributions to Philosophy* should render manifest the range of the question of being. A detailed unfolding here is not necessary because this all too easily narrows down the actual horizon and misses the thrust of questioning. But even here *that* form has not yet been attained, which, precisely at this point, I demand for a publication as a "work". For here the new style of thinking must announce itself – the reservedness in the truth of be-ing; the saying of silence in reticence, the maturing for the swayingness of the unblended.

*

The worst that could happen to these efforts would be the psychological-biographical analysis and explanation, that is, the counter-movement to what is precisely assigned to us, namely to place everything "psychic-emotional" – however intimately it has to be preserved and enacted – at the service of that aloneness which is demanded by the work that strikes one as strange.

Hence, if my *letters and the like* could be important at all, *no collection* of them should be published since such a collection only serves the curiosity and the comfort of those who want to evade the task of thinking "the matter of thinking".

What would happen if the pack of the curious once throws itself at the "posthumous works"! It cannot be expected from this commotion to grasp anything at all or to transform what is grasped into the futural. [G428] For the gang of the curious only longs for that which completes this gang's own already established calculation and confirms it in each case.

If deep down these "posthumous works" do not possess the power of 'letting-go-ahead' [*Vorlassen*] – do not posses the power of path-opening-grasping-ahead into an entirely other and quite drawn-out questioning – these "posthumous works" would not be worth being pondered upon.

The mere enlargement of what is already published is superfluous.

The least that may perhaps remain is *the dynamics of the raising of the only question*. And this may show that today the strongest and most consuming exertion of a modest power still cannot accomplish anything *against* the rigidness of beings *for* restoring be-ing as the sphere of the coming to pass of the arrival or the flight of the last god.

And yet – ahead of all "results," all propositions and all concepts there is the long pathway that perhaps occasionally succeeds in flashing the determining power of a great future.

The splendour of Da-sein rests upon the alternating, and overreaching struggle that consumes within and belongs to the self, shelters and conceals the most reticent and yet remains inexpressibly grateful for every little help.

EDITOR'S EPILOGUE

Divided in 28 parts and 135 sections, the manuscript *Besinnung* [*Mindfulness*] from Heidegger's literary remains appears here for the first time as volume 66 of his *Gesamtausgabe*. This manuscript was composed in the years 1938/39 following the just then completed *Beiträge zur Philosophie (Vom Ereignis)* [*Contributions to Philosophy (From Enowning)*]. It consists of 589 consecutively numbered handwritten pages in DIN A5 format – with only a few exceptions in smaller format. In addition to the numbering of these 589 pages there is the separate numbering of section 15 (pages 96 a–l with a further 11 pages) and the specific numbering of section 65 a (page 262 a–e). On the upper left-hand corner of every handwritten page, there is the number of the consecutive pagination, and in the upper right-hand corner, either in numerals or in letters of the alphabet, the numbering within the sections.

In the table of contents that is available only as a typescript, sections 15 and 65 a, which were mentioned at first, are subsequently crossed out. On a piece of paper that lies before the handwritten pages of section 15 Fritz Heidegger notes: "at the direction of the author not copied because inadequate". On the cover, this section is designated as "draft". Also before the handwritten pages of section 65 a there is a piece of paper with a note from Fritz Heidegger that reads "not copied, incomplete". However, since both of these sections not only deal with the material that is still to be worked out but also with fully formulated texts, they were included in the entire edited text. By contrast, the folder with the titles *"Das Sein als Apriori"* ["Being as *A Priori*"] and *"Ereignis"* ["Enowning"] were not included in the edition since they only contained pages of material still to be worked out. The same applied to some unnumbered sheets of paper with notes which were found here and there between the consecutively numbered handwritten pages.

[G430] At the disposal of the editor, besides the manuscript, was a typescript, which Heidegger's brother, Fritz Heidegger, had already prepared and finished typing right after the manuscript was completed in 1939. For on the folder that contains the typewritten table of contents and that in Heidegger's handwriting carries the title "Table of Contents" Heidegger notes: "Collated 1939". The consecutive numbering of the handwritten pages is inscribed on the upper right-hand corner of the typewritten pages. But since a typewritten page normally reproduces two or three handwritten pages, two or three consecutive numerals are found on the upper right-hand corner. The typescript itself has no pagination of its own.

Only the typewritten table of contents contains the Roman numerals I to XXVIII (with which the parts of the manuscript are numbered,) and the Arabic numerals 1 to 135 (with which the sections of the text are numbered). However, the 28 folders that belong to the manuscript and contain all its parts are distinguished by a small circle and an Arabic numeral that are placed on the upper left-hand corner. After preparing the typed copy of the table of contents, and consecutively counting the 135 sections with Arabic numerals, the Arabic numerals of the folders had to be replaced with Roman numerals. Thus *Mindfulness* shows the same formal division as *Contributions to Philosophy*: Higher ordered parts in Roman numerals and lower ordered sections in Arabic numerals.

The typescript that is prepared by Fritz Heidegger is for the most part an ingenious transfer of the handwritten text without any revision for a possible publication. This and many more typed copies that Fritz Heidegger prepared at the behest of his brother were not done with a view towards publication. Above all they were to provide Martin Heidegger with quicker and easier access to his manuscripts.

Heidegger [G431] had inserted by hand on a number of pages of the typescript minor changes in the text and inscribed shorter or even longer additions and notes on the left-hand wide margin of the page. Often these additional notes were also transferred into the pages of the manuscript. However, the thought and the language of the changes, of the additions and marginal notes reflect the same level of mindfulness as the main text and were written presumably at the time when Heidegger together with his brother compared the typescript with the manuscript.

In preparing the typewritten copy for publication, the editor transcribed all the parts of the manuscripts that were not yet transferred. With the help of the insertion marks used by Heidegger, the handwritten additions could be readily incorporated into the running text, while the marginal notes that could not be syntactically inserted were retained as footnotes.

The typescript prepared by Fritz Heidegger was repeatedly collated with the manuscript. A few inadvertent omissions and errors in readings which escaped even Martin Heidegger as he compared the typescript with the manuscript, were corrected and included in the text. Without indicating them in the edited text, a few obvious misspellings were corrected. By contrast, Heidegger's different or even peculiar way of spelling was retained. Abbreviations that Heidegger used in mentioning his own writings and manuscripts, and those he used in referring to the basic words of his own thinking or to those of other thinkers, as well as other unusual abbreviations, were written out. The divisions of paragraphs in the published text are those that Martin Heidegger indicated in the manuscript and Fritz Heidegger reproduced in the typescript. The punctuation was carefully examined and here and there completed. As a rule, by interspacing the words Fritz Heidegger reproduced in his type-script Heidegger's underlinings in the manuscript. The occasionally [G432] typed underlinings are additional corrections of the interspacing that Fritz Heidegger missed as he typed the manuscript. Since Martin Heidegger established italicization as the exclusive method of indicating emphasis in the volumes of the *Gesamtausgabe*, everything that is interspaced or underlined in the typescript appears in print uniformly in italics.

There are four types of footnotes in this volume. The footnotes that carry an asterisk indicate, as in *Contributions to Philosophy*, Heidegger's cross-references either within the manuscript or cross-references he later added to the typescript. These cross-references are either to pages or sections within *Mindfulness*, or to Heidegger's other writings or manu-scripts. However, there is a formal deviation from this arrangement in section 35 entitled "Question of Truth: A Directive". Considering the frequency of footnotes in this section the footnotes are numbered with Arabic numerals rather than indicated by asterisks. Both in the manuscript and in the typescript the cross-references are either placed under a title or added to the running text. In print the cross-references to the titles are reproduced only in footnotes, while the references in the text remain there in the form that Heidegger chose for them but, when needed, these references are completed in the footnotes. In those cases where the footnote begins by reproducing the original version of the cross-reference, abbreviations that are written out and the completed bibliographical information are placed in parentheses. The parentheses are left out when a footnote contains only the completed information that pertains to the cross-reference within the text.

Since the sequence of the volumes of the *Gesamtausgabe* and their numbering are now completed and published in the publisher's catalogue of March 1997, [G433] it was possible, for the first time, to specify the title and the number assigned to the volumes of the *Gesamtausgabe* in which all the manuscripts will appear to which Heidegger refers in *Mindfulness*. The reader finds the information about the editor and the year of publication of an already available volume of the *Gesamtausgabe* in the reference in which this volume is mentioned for the first time.

The Roman numerals that are found in *Überlegungen* – the work that Heidegger mentions both in *Mindfulness* and in *Contributions to Philosophy* – are the numbers given to the individual booklets. The Arabic numerals indicate the page numbers in each booklet. Booklets II–VI (booklet I is missing!) will appear in volume 94 of the *Gesamtausgabe* entitled *Überlegungen A*, booklets VII–XI in volume 95 entitled *Überlegungen B*, and booklets XII–XV in volume 96 entitled *Überlegungen C*.

The footnotes that are marked by a lower-case letter of the alphabet reproduce Heidegger's above-mentioned marginal notes to the typescript.

In the footnotes marked by Arabic numerals, the editor compiled the bibliographical information for the quotations that Heidegger introduced in the text from other authors.

Finally, the footnotes marked with a cross contain the remarks of the editor.

*

After Heidegger made the decision in September 1973 to publish the *Gesamtausgabe*, he began the preparations for the plan and the arrangement of this edition with the help of the present editor in the study of his retirement residence in *Fillibachstraße* in Freiburg. In the course of surveying and arranging the existing typescripts, he familiarized me for the first time with the treatises that he had assigned to the third division of the *Gesamtausgabe*. It was then that he told me that the treatises *Besinnung* of 1938/39, *Über den Anfang* of 1941, *Das Ereignis* of 1941/42 and *Die Stege des Anfangs* of 1944 [G434] are specifically and intimately interconnected with *Contributions to Philosophy* insofar as each of these treatises thinks through in a new approach the jointure which in its entirety is *Contributions to Philosophy*. *Die Überwindung der Metaphysik* of 1938/39 and also *Die Geschichte des Seyns* of 1939/40 are in thematic proximity to these five treatises.

Thus *Mindfulness* is the first of the above-mentioned four treatises that, following the *Contributions to Philosophy*, takes up the task of opening up, via questioning the whole domain of being-historical thinking. The being-historical thinking that understands itself as mindfulness enopens the clearing of be-ing as enowning wherein the countering of god and man crosses the strife of the earth and the world. The enownment of countering and strife happens as settlement. However, as the raising of the being-historical (other-inceptual) question of being, mindfulness gets enacted in a dissociating exposition of the metaphysical (first-ever-inceptual) question of being.

A page in Heidegger's handwriting that carries the title *"Zur Besinnung"* ["Regarding *Mindfulness"*] is inserted into the typescript. Under 1. Heidegger characterizes the table of contents of this work as a *Verzeichnis der Sprünge*, [a "Listing of Leaps".] Thereby he takes up a basic word of *Contributions to Philosophy*, "the leap", which in this work is also the title of the third "joining" of the "jointure in outline" and a designation of the being-historical thinking insofar as this thinking *leaps away* from the metaphysical question of being ("What is a being?") and *leaps unto* the being-historical question of being ("How does be-ing sway?") – the leap as the thinking-leaping unto the swaying of the truth of be-ing as enowning in such a way that this thinking experiences itself as enowned by be-ing and as belonging to enowning.

Heidegger notes under 2., entitled *"Vorbemerkung"* ["preliminary remark"]: *"no system, no doctrine, no aphorism, but rather a series of short and long leaps of inquiring into the preparedness for the enowning of be-ing. The 'repetitions' [are] necessary since each time the whole is to be said. Yet, still mostly a pursuing and a pondering, seldom is granted a saying of the saying [G435]. Without a mandate and without a calling."* Two things should be pointed out here: on the one hand, the renewed characterization of the thinking in the sections of *Mindfulness* as "leaps of inquiry into the preparedness for the enowning of be-ing", a characterization that would be incomprehensible without a familiarity with the *Contributions to Philosophy*. On the other hand, the warding off of the opinion that easily crops up, namely that the sections of *Mindfulness* should be characterized as aphorisms, and that the thinking in *Mindfulness* as well as in *Contributions to Philosophy* is aphoristic thinking.

The notes under *"Vorbemerkung"*, ["preliminary remark"] conclude with a second warding off: *"no 'poem' and not poetry – only an obligation of the thinking word in the moment of gathered mindfulness"*. Heidegger wants to say: neither the sections of *Mindfulness* nor the texts of its "Introduction" (part of which appeared privately already in 1941 under the title *Winke* [Hints] and republished in volume 13 of the *Gesamtausgabe*) are "poems" and "poetry", although given their typeface they appear that way.

Under 3. Heidegger notes *"to rework anew pp. 192/3, the foundational flight of man"*. This note has to do with section 54 of *Mindfulness* that consists altogether of three handwritten pages.

*

Published for the first time in this volume 66 is the text of an *appendix* from Heidegger's literary remains that is entitled *"Rückblick auf den Weg"* ["A Retrospective Look at the Pathway"] that was drafted in 1937/38. In its first part entitled *"Mein bisheriger Weg"*, ["My Pathway Hitherto"] Heidegger thinks over the path of his thinking from the Dissertation of 1913 to the *Contributions to Philosophy* of 1936–1938. In the second part *"Über die Bewahrung des Versuchten"* ["On Preserving What is Attempted"] he offers a survey of his unpublished manuscripts, divides them into seven divisions: [G436] lecture-courses, lectures, notes for the seminars, preparatory elaboration concerning the Work, notebooks, works on Hölderlin, on *From Enowning (Contributions to Philosophy)* and provides each one of these divisions with utmost instructive elucidations.

Both parts of the text are written down on papers in DIN A5 format and each of these parts has its own pagination from 1 to 12 and from 1 to 15. Both parts of the text were transcribed by the editor and provided with complementary footnotes that are arranged like the footnotes in *Mindfulness*, but instead of asterisks they are placed under Arabic numerals. Here too it was possible to indicate the volumes of the *Gesamtausgabe* and the number given to them where the manuscripts that Heidegger mentions in this text will appear.

However, under the "Notes for the Seminars" in "On Preserving What is Attempted" Heidegger mentions also notes on *"Schillers Briefen über die aesthetische Erziehung"* [Schiller's Letter on Aesthetic Education'] which, however, could not be found in his literary remains. Should these notes turn up one day, they will expand volume 84, *Seminare: Leibniz–Kant*, to include Schiller.

Near the end of this same text, and with a view towards the future publication of his literary remains, Heidegger rejects emphatically the inclusion of "collections of letters and the like". However, in the course of planning the publication of the *Gesamtausgabe* Heidegger made a different decision. The general contract drawn up between him and the publisher Vittorio Klostermann in 1974 assigns "*Briefe*" ["The Letters"] to the fourth division of the *Gesamtausgabe*. Hence, *Ausgewählte Briefe* will appear in volumes 92 and 93.

*

[G437] I thank Herr Dr Hermann Heidegger cordially for collating the parts of the manuscript that I had transcribed with the handwritten additions from the typescript as well as for his continued attentiveness to the editorial work.

I am grateful to my colleague, Frau Dr Paola-Ludovica Coriando, for the second round of collating and for the concluding examination and reading of the typed copy that I prepared for publication, that is, for a labor that was indispensable, and that she carried out with a reliable knowledge of the subject and diligent care. For her committed support I thank Frau Dr Coriando most cordially. Further, my cordial thanks are due her as well as Herr Dr Ivo De Gennaro for an extremely careful reading of the proofs while rethinking the material at hand.

F.-W. von Herrmann
Freiburg i. Br., June 1997